DISCARD

THE POWERS OF THE
U.S. CONGRESS

THE POWERS OF THE U.S. CONGRESS

Where Constitutional Authority Begins and Ends

Brien Hallett, Editor

 ABC-CLIO™

An Imprint of ABC-CLIO, LLC
Santa Barbara, California • Denver, Colorado

Library of Congress Cataloging-in-Publication Data

Names: Hallett, Brien, editor.
Title: The powers of the U.S. Congress : where constitutional authority begins and ends /
    Brien Hallett, editor.
Other titles: Powers of the United States Congress
Description: Santa Barbara, California : ABC-CLIO, 2016. | Includes bibliographical
    references and index.
Identifiers: LCCN 2016018038 (print) | LCCN 2016029398 (ebook) | ISBN 9781440843235
    (print : alk. paper) | ISBN 9781440843242 (ebook)
Subjects: LCSH: United States. Congress–Powers and duties. | Legislative bodies–United States. |
    Legislative power–United States. | Legislation–United States.
Classification: LCC KF4940 .P69 2016 (print) | LCC KF4940 (ebook) | DDC 328.73/074–dc23
LC record available at https://lccn.loc.gov/2016018038

ISBN: 978-1-4408-4323-5
EISBN: 978-1-4408-4324-2

20 19 18 17 16   1 2 3 4 5

This book is also available as an eBook.

ABC-CLIO
An Imprint of ABC-CLIO, LLC

ABC-CLIO, LLC
130 Cremona Drive, P.O. Box 1911
Santa Barbara, California 93116-1911
www.abc-clio.com

This book is printed on acid-free paper ∞

Manufactured in the United States of America

LiLi, Victoria, Kekoa

CONTENTS

PREFACE

The Powers of the U.S. Congress: Where Constitutional Authority Begins and Ends is the first in-depth, one-volume overview of the twenty-one enumerated congressional powers. These nineteen essays are written by knowledgeable scholars for students, the reading public, and scholars in allied fields. Each essay introduces a constitutional power and briefly retells the controversies that have surrounded it from its adoption in 1789 to the present and into the foreseeable future. The essays address the responsibilities of the Congress, whether the Congress has met or failed to meet these responsibilities over the past two centuries, and the outlook for the foreseeable future. Readers will also learn the meaning of obscure terms such as "to grant letters of marque and reprisal."

In this introduction, I would like to touch briefly on three points: First, the way in which the American colonists had a virtual monopoly on written constitutions during the seventeenth and eighteenth centuries. Second, the way in which the Articles of Confederation and Perpetual Union were so radically different from both the previous colonial charters and the new state Constitutions, not to mention the yet-to-be-drafted Constitution of the United States. And, third, the critical role the enumerated congressional powers played in transforming the old confederation into a new federation.

AN INNOVATION: WRITTEN CONSTITUTIONS

In the five thousand years of recorded history, written constitutions are a recent innovation. Written codes of law, such a Hammurabi's Code or Solon's laws of Athens, were, of course, common from the most ancient times. Other constitution-like documents, such as Oliver Cromwell's Instrument of Government, 1653, can also be found at various times in various places. These, however, are constitutions with a small "c."

Modern written constitutions with a capital "C," in contrast, first appeared in the English colonies of North America and the Caribbean. Indeed, the Fundamental Orders of Connecticut (1638) are said by many to be the very first. What made the Orders different were, first, that they were drafted by the inhabitants of the three villages of Windsor, Wethersfield, and Hartford to govern themselves, and not by a king or Lord Protector. Second, the Orders were not only the supreme constitutive law of Connecticut, but more importantly they dealt primarily with the structure of a representative government. The Orders created a governing structure consisting of a representative assembly, the General Court, a governor, and several magistrates. Once constituted, the General Court would then enact the specific laws that the governor and magistrates would administer or enforce. This, of course, was a significant departure from ancient practice. Hammurabi's and similar ancient codes had enacted specific laws, but did not explain or constitute the form of government. Subsequently, in 1662, the Fundamental Orders were promulgated as a royal charter that governed Connecticut until 1818.

Two factors may be said to account for the rise of written constitutions in the English colonies—one very practical, the other more theoretical. The practical factor was that the early seventeenth-century English colonies were commercial enterprises financed by private capital. The Spanish and Portuguese colonies were royal colonies ruled directly by the king and a colonial bureaucracy headquartered in Madrid or Lisbon. As a result, the wealth generated by these colonies went into the royal treasury. In contrast, the earliest English colonies were commercial enterprises. A Lord Proprietor or the directors of a joint stock company would obtain a royal charter that gave them the exclusive right to settle and profit from an expanse of territory. This commercial enterprise then organized and financed a colony. As a result, the Lord Proprietor or company directors both ruled the colony and received any wealth produced by it. Since direct rule from London was impractical for these private enterprises, a governor was sent out, with instructions to establish an advisory council and courts as needed. Over the course of the seventeenth century, the proprietary colonies and the joint stock companies were taken over by the king as crown colonies with royal charters that confirmed the indirect rule already established.

Central to the instructions of the Lords Proprietor and the joint stock companies was the now-familiar three-branch form of government: a London-appointed governor and judges and a locally elected legislature. This constitutional structure was later carried over to the royal charters. The first consequence of this was that the colonists had nearly two hundred years to experiment and figure out which powers should belong to the London-appointed governor, which should belong to the London-appointed judges, and which should belong to the legislative branch. Hence, by 1787, the three sets of powers were well defined and tested.

The second consequence was that, by the end of the eighteenth century and the Revolutionary War, the American colonists had been writing and living under these three-branch, small "c" constitutions for nearly two hundred years. With independence in 1776, it was only a short step for eleven of the colonies to rewrite their royal charters as state Constitutions with a capital "C." The two states that kept their royal charters unchanged were Connecticut (until 1818) and Rhode Island (until 1843). The transformation from "c" to "C" required only two small, but very significant, changes in the royal charters. The London-appointed governors had to be transformed into locally elected governors, and the London-appointed judges had to be transformed into locally appointed judges. No change was required for the legislatures, because they were already composed of elected representatives with well-established powers. The final step to national independence, then, was to draft and ratify a national Constitution—the Articles of Confederation and Perpetual Union in 1781 and, when that document did not work out as planned, the Constitution of the United States in 1789.

SOCIAL CONTRACT THEORY

Yet, if the commercial character of the English colonies was the practical factor, that same factor also played a critical theoretical role. This was the case because underpinning the English colonial enterprises was a larger sixteenth- and seventeenth-century commercial revolution in Europe. Indeed, establishing the English colonies themselves as private enterprises would not have been possible without the development of modern commercial contracts of all kinds—especially modern insurance contracts and modern joint stock company contracts. These contracts provided the essential financial and legal structure that made the English commercial colonies viable. Needless to say, as commercial contracts became more and more common, their political and philosophical implications became more and more obvious. Political philosophers such as Hugo Grotius (1583–1645), Thomas Hobbes (1588–1679), John Locke (1632–1704), Jean-Jacques Rousseau (1712–1778), and others, all saw the explanatory possibilities of the new commercial contracts.

Reinterpreted as a "social contract," the commercial contracts establishing a joint stock company easily provided an explanatory hypothesis about how the modern nation-state was formed and what accounted for its legitimacy. The hypothesis began by speculating that, before the founding of a political society, man had lived in a "state of nature." This "state of nature" was famously described by Thomas Hobbes as "the war of all against all," a time when no one was safe from an attack by another. To end "the war of all against all" and provide security, this sixteenth-century thought experiment proposed that men had gathered at some distant time in the past to sign a "social contract." Once signed, the "social contract" ended the "state of nature" and bound those who had signed in a political or civil society. More, the new political society not only ensured mutual security, but it simultaneously accounted for the legitimacy of that political society. Each of the original signatories had signed voluntarily for himself and his posterity.

Critically, the newly established English colonies were perfect examples of both the "state of nature" (as long as one ignored the well-established Native American societies) and a "social contract." Accordingly, the English colonists were easily imagined as individuals returning to a "state of nature" in the primeval forests of North America. Newly returned to this "state of nature," the individual colonists constructed a new and novel political society by agreeing freely to the proprietor's or the joint stock company's "social contract" for governing the colony.

The power of Social Contract Theory, needless to say, has indelibly shaped both American and world constitution writing. A subtle echo of this is found in the preamble of the 1789 Constitution of the United States:

> WE, the People of the United States, in order to form a more perfect union, establish justice, insure domestic tranquility, provide for the common defence, promote the general welfare, and secure the blessings of liberty to ourselves and our posterity, do ordain and establish this Constitution for the United States of America.

But the clearest expression is found in the preamble of John Adams' 1780 Constitution of the Commonwealth of Massachusetts. Notably, the Commonwealth's Constitution is still in force today, making it the oldest written constitution in the world. It was also the first constitution written by a constitutional convention, and not by a legislature. The preamble reads thus:

> The end of the institution, maintenance, and administration of government, is to secure the existence of the body politic, to protect it, and to furnish the individuals who compose it with the power of enjoying in safety and tranquillity their natural rights, and the blessings of life: and whenever these great objects are not obtained, the people have a right to alter the government, and to take measures necessary for their safety, prosperity and happiness.
>
> The body politic is formed by a voluntary association of individuals: it is a social compact, by which the whole people covenants with each citizen, and each citizen with the whole people, that all shall be governed by certain laws for the common good. It is the duty of the people, therefore, in framing a constitution of government, to provide for an equitable mode of making laws, as well as for an impartial interpretation, and a faithful execution of them; that every man may, at all times, find his security in them.
>
> We, therefore, the people of Massachusetts, acknowledging, with grateful hearts, the goodness of the great Legislator of the universe, in affording us, in the course of His providence, an opportunity, deliberately and peaceably, without fraud, violence or surprise, of entering into an original, explicit, and solemn compact with each other; and of forming a new constitution of civil government, for ourselves and posterity; and devoutly imploring His direction in so interesting a design, do agree upon, ordain and establish the following Declaration of Rights, and Frame of Government, as the Constitution of the Commonwealth of Massachusetts.

Notice how the interplay of Social Contract Theory and 160 years of colonial experimentation with a three-branch constitutional structure foreshadows the 1789 Constitution nine years later. In accordance with Social Contract Theory, the preamble explains that a "social compact" guarantees the legitimacy of a government whenever "The body politic is formed by a voluntary association of individuals." The preamble further explains that the purpose of government is to provide for the "safety, prosperity and

happiness" of the body politic. More specifically, though, 160 years colonial experience has also taught the people of Massachusetts "that every man may, at all times,
find his security in [a three-branch government that provides] for an equitable mode
of making laws, as well as for an impartial interpretation, and a faithful execution of
them." Therefore, to achieve all of this, "the People of Massachusetts" have entered
"into an original, explicit, and solemn compact with each other; and of forming a new
constitution of civil government, for ourselves and posterity."

In sum, both the thirteen state Constitutions as well as the 1789 Constitution of the
United States emerged out of the intersection of three elements: the European commercial revolution of the sixteenth and seventeenth centuries, Social Contract Theory
from the same period, and 180 years of colonial experimentation with a three-branch
constitutional structure. In light of this rich background, neither the three-branch structure nor the enumerated congressional powers of the 1789 Constitution come as any
surprise. What is surprising is the 1781 Articles of Confederation and Perpetual Union.

THE CONFEDERATION: A DETOUR

As a brief review of the Articles of Confederation and Perpetual Union in Appen-
dix A will show, the Articles reproduced the organization and structure of the Second
Continental Congress. It did not reproduce the three-branch organization and structure
of the state Constitutions, as one might expect. The principal reason for this, one might
speculate, is that the Articles were written by the Second Continental Congress during
the Revolutionary War period, between 1776 and 1781. During those years, the Second
Continental Congress was completely absorbed in managing the war and, hence, had
little time or energy to devote to drafting the Articles. Certainly, it had no time for the
lengthy and contentious debates that occurred in 1787 at the Philadelphia Convention;
nor for the even more contentious ratifying conventions in the thirteen states that followed the Philadelphia Convention. Those debates would have to await peace. During
the war, the path of least resistance was the better alternative. Since the state legislatures had already agreed to the organization and structure of the Second Continental
Congress in 1775, asking them to ratify basically the same organization and structure
represented just that path of least resistance.

Like the Second Continental Congress, the Confederal Congress was a single-
branch, coordinating body composed of thirteen state delegations. To fulfill the executive function, the Articles established a subcommittee, "'A Committee of the States',
[which is] to consist of one delegate from each State." This subcommittee looked after
things whenever the Confederal Congress was not in session. As for the judiciary, all
laws, national and state, were to be tried in state courts. The exception was that Art. IX,
§6 established an elaborate procedure for selecting a "commission" to resolve disputes
between two or more states.

For the Confederal Congress itself, the individual delegates were elected by each
state's legislature, as had been the case for the Second Continental Congress. Further,
the individual delegates were subject to immediate recall if the state legislature was
dissatisfied with one or another member of the delegation. And, finally, these multiple-
member state delegations voted by state, and not by individual delegate. This meant

that unanimity in the Confederal Congress required thirteen votes and that a delegation had to abstain whenever the vote within its multiple-member delegation did not produce a majority opinion. The Confederal Congress, like the Second Continental Congress, was, therefore, created by and answerable to the state legislatures. It was created as a national coordinating body. It was not created to produce an independent and purposeful national government.

THE FEDERATION: BACK ON TRACK

Being answerable to the states legislatures meant that the Confederal Congress could not be allowed to exercise four critical powers—two monetary and two military powers—that the state legislatures reserved for themselves. The possession of these four key powers, therefore, constituted the principal contribution of the United States Congress to breaking the dependence of the national government on the states and, hence, for the success of the new Federal Constitution. To appreciate this, compare the enumerated powers of the Confederal Congress with those of the United States Congress:

> *Enumerated congressional powers that are found in the Constitution, AND also in the Articles of Confederation and Perpetual Union*:
>
> Art. I, §8, cl. 2: To borrow money on the credit of the United States;
>
> Art. I, §8, cl. 3: To regulate commerce ~~with foreign nations, and among the several states, and~~ with the Indian tribes;
>
> Art. I, §8, cl. 4: To coin money, regulate the value thereof, and of foreign coin, and fix the standard of weights and measures;
>
> Art. I, §8, cl. 7: To establish post offices and post roads;
>
> Art. I, §8, cl. 10: To define and punish piracies and felonies committed on the high seas, and offences against the law of nations;
>
> Art. I, §8, cl. 11: To declare war, grant letters of marque and reprisal, and make rules concerning captures on land and water;
>
> Art. I, §8, cl. 12: (Implied) To raise and support armies, but no appropriation of money to that use shall be for a longer term than two years;
>
> Art. I, §8, cl. 13: To provide and maintain a navy;
>
> Art. I, §8, cl. 14: To make rules for the government and regulation of the land and naval forces;
>
> Art. I, §8, cl. 16: To provide for organizing, arming, and disciplining, the militia, and for governing such part of them as may be employed in the service of the United States, reserving to the States respectively, the appointment of the officers, and the authority of training the militia according to the discipline prescribed by Congress;
>
> *Enumerated congressional powers that are found in the Constitution, but NOT in the Articles of Confederation and Perpetual Union*:
>
> Art. I, §8, cl. 1: To lay and collect taxes, duties, imposts and excises, to pay the debts and provide for the common defence and general welfare of the United States; but all duties, imposts and excises shall be uniform throughout the United States;

Art. I, §8, cl. 3: To regulate commerce with foreign nations, and among the several states, ~~and with the Indian tribes~~;

Art. I, §8, cl. 4: To establish an uniform rule of naturalization, and uniform laws on the subject of bankruptcies throughout the United States;

Art. I, §8, cl. 6: To provide for the punishment of counterfeiting the securities and current coin of the United States;

Art. I, §8, cl. 8: To promote the progress of science and useful arts, by securing for limited times to authors and inventors the exclusive right to their respective writings and discoveries;

Art. I, §8, cl. 9: To constitute tribunals inferior to the supreme court;

Art. I, §8, cl. 12: (Explicitly) To raise and support armies, but no appropriation of money to that use shall be for a longer term than two years;

Art. I, §8, cl. 15: To provide for calling forth the militia to execute the laws of the union, suppress insurrections and repel invasions;

Art. I, §8, cl. 17: To exercise exclusive legislation in all cases whatsoever, over such district (not exceeding ten miles square) as may, by cession of particular States, and the acceptance of Congress, become the seat of the government of the United States, and to exercise like authority overall places purchased by the consent of the legislature of the state in which the same shall be, for the erection of forts, magazines, arsenals, dockyards, and other needful buildings;

A critical check on congressional power:

Art. I, §7, cl. 1: Every bill which shall have passed the house of representatives and the senate, shall, before it become a law, be presented to the president of the United States;

A critical check on both presidential and congressional power:

Art. II, §2, cl. 2: The President. . . shall have power, by and with the advice and consent of the senate, to make treaties, provided two-thirds of the senators present concur; and he shall nominate, and by and with the advice and consent of the senate, shall appoint ambassadors,. . . .

The two lists highlight the difference between a lose confederation of states and a purposeful national federation. In the first place, the single-branch structure of the Articles explains a part of the difference in the two lists. Without separate executive and judicial branches, no need existed in the Articles of Confederation for three of the eleven clauses. Two that check congressional power—Art. I, §7, cl. 1, the presentment clause, and Art. II, §2, cl. 2, the advise and consent clause—both require a separate chief executive before they make any sense. Likewise, the absence of a separate judicial branch made Art. I, §8, cl. 9, "To constitute tribunals inferior to the supreme court," entirely unnecessary in the Articles. The minute the three-branch system of checks and balances found in the state constitutions was adopted by the Federal Convention in Philadelphia, these clauses became instantly necessary. But they were not crucial in making the Federal government independent of the states.

In the second place, a further four of the enumerated congressional powers were neither controversial nor vitally different. The four less-than-vital section 8 clauses are the naturalization and bankruptcy clause, the counterfeiting clause, the patents and copyright clause, and the district and federal buildings clause. While certainly useful, the first three of these clauses are not what make the 1789 Constitution a *Federal* Constitution. As for the district and federal buildings clause, it is noteworthy only for its symbolic value. The new ten-square-mile capitol district symbolized geographically that the new federal government would be both separate from and independent of all of the states. But geographic symbolism is just that, symbolic, not vital.

That leaves four section 8 enumerated powers that were vitally transformative. These four clauses further subdivide into two groups: 1) two money clauses, taxing and commerce, and 2) two military clauses, to raise and support armies and to call forth the militia. Both groups make clear that the new federal government will be not only independent of the state legislatures but superior to them as well. The two money clauses are critical because they are a declaration of economic independence from state control by the national government. The commerce clause declares this independence by redefining the trade and commercial relationship among the states and between the states and the nation. No longer would the state legislatures be able to disrupt trade among the states with discriminatory laws. The commerce clause asserts clearly the superiority of national economic interests over local, state interests.

The taxing clause also asserts the financial superiority and the independence of the national over the local. No longer will the state legislatures be able to frustrate and choke the national government by not paying their "requisitions." Instead of making a request that "The taxes for paying that proportion [of each state's national assessment being] laid and levied by the authority and direction of the legislatures of the several States within the time agreed upon by the United States in Congress assembled," now the Congress would itself directly raise the taxes needed "to pay the debts and provide for the common defence and general welfare of the United States." The only restriction was that "all duties, imposts and excises shall be uniform throughout the United States." This last was hardly a restriction, but rather a rule of fairness. In sum, these two enumerated powers are vital in transforming the economics of a lose confederation into the economics of a purposeful federation.

This same fundamental transformation is also effected by the two military clauses. The difference is that the two money clauses declared the financial independence of the new federal government from the state legislatures, whereas the two military clauses ensured that the now–financially independent federal government would be able to defend itself. In addition, the adoption of the raise and support armies and the calling forth the militia clauses settled a two-hundred-year-old, raging controversy over the dangers of a standing army and the virtues of militias, a very much more controversial area than taxes and commerce at the time.

A STANDING ARMY: A DEADLY THREAT TO THE REPUBLIC?

Aversion to standing armies, bordering on a knee-jerk anathema, had characterized both British and colonial attitudes at least since the English Civil War (1642–1651), when Charles I led the Royal Army against Parliament. Closer to home, colonial experience with the king's standing army had been negative. Indeed, three of the twenty-seven grievances indicted in the Declaration of Independence concerned the "evils" of a standing army: "He has kept among us, in Times of Peace, Standing Armies, without the consent of our Legislatures"; "He has affected to render the Military independent of and superior to the Civil Power"; and "For quartering large Bodies of Armed Troops among us."

This deep-seated hostility to a standing army, however, had to come to terms with two harsh realities: The first was the proven military ineffectiveness of militia troops, as General George Washington had repeatedly warned the Second Continental Congress during the Revolutionary War. Indeed, had the Second Continental Congress not authorized a small Continental Army on June 14, 1775, the success of the Revolution would have been much less likely. The second reality was the disbanding of the Continental Army in November 1783, immediately after the Treaty of Paris ended the war in September 1783. This left the Confederal Congress totally dependent upon the state militias. This complete dependence meant that the Confederal Congress lacked even inadequate military resources when a crisis arose.

The depth of the problem can be seen in the convoluted and overly complex section of Art. IX of the Articles, which describes how a national military force was to be recruited. Notably, this procedure was taken directly from procedures used by the Second Continental Congress to recruit the Continental Army.

> The United States in Congress assembled shall have authority . . . to agree upon the number of land forces, and to make requisitions from each State for its quota, in proportion to the number of white inhabitants in such State; which requisition shall be binding, and thereupon the legislature of each State shall appoint the regimental officers, raise the men and cloath, arm and equip them in a solid-like manner, at the expense of the United States; and the officers and men so cloathed, armed and equipped shall march to the place appointed, and within the time agreed on by the United States in Congress assembled. But if the United States in Congress assembled shall, on consideration of circumstances judge proper that any State should not raise men, or should raise a smaller number of men than the quota thereof, such extra number shall be raised, officered, cloathed, armed and equipped in the same manner as the quota of each State, unless the legislature of such State shall judge that such extra number cannot be safely spread out in the same, in which case they shall raise, officer, cloath, arm and equip as many of such extra number as they judge can be safely spared. And the officers and men so cloathed, armed, and equipped, shall march to the place appointed, and within the time agreed on by the United States in Congress assembled.

The paralyzing effects of these two factors—military ineffectiveness and the dangers of relying entirely on state militias—were revealed during Shays' Rebellion (1786–1787). Shays' Rebellion was a widespread series of farmer-led protests throughout the nation. The farmers were protesting, sometimes forcefully, against high taxes and the forced sales of farms to pay off their debts. State militias were able to put down the more forceful protests, but many political leaders throughout the new nation were appalled that the Confederal Congress was entirely impotent to meet the crisis because it commanded no standing military force. The issue was serious. If the Confederal Congress was not able to meet relatively minor civil disturbances such as Shays' Rebellion, how was it to protect the nation from attacks by Indians on the frontier, not to mention an invasion by Great Britain or another European power?

Needless to say, Shays' Rebellion and the incapacity of the Confederal Congress to respond to the crisis was one of the major motivations for calling the Federal Convention in Philadelphia in 1787, in the first place. During the Federal Convention, empowering the new Federal government "To raise and support armies" and "To provide for calling forth the militia to execute the laws of the union, suppress insurrections and repel invasions" continued to be points of major controversy.

In the end, though, the military need for effectiveness and the national need for a standing crisis-response capacity won out, and both military clauses were included among the enumerated congressional powers. In so doing, these two clauses also redefined and transformed the military relationship between individual citizens, the states, and the national government. Under the Articles, the military relationship of individual citizens was with their state and its militia. With the new Federal Constitution, the military relationship of individual citizens was now directly to the national government, and only secondarily to their state and its militia. As a result, the military capacity of the national government was now independent of the state legislatures. Now the Congress of the United States could "call forth the militia" on its own authority, without consulting the state legislatures. Equally important, though, the government of the United States would have a standing army—once Congress organized one in 1792— to respond immediately to any crisis, such as Shays' Rebellion or a British invasion. In sum, these two military clauses, like the two money clauses, were fundamental to transforming the 1781 Articles Confederation and Perpetual Union into the 1789 Constitution of the United States.

CONCLUSION

The most obvious difference between the 1781 Articles of Confederation and Perpetual Union and the 1789 Constitution of the United States is the change from a single-branch structure without a system of checks and balances to a three-branch structure with a system of checks and balances. This obvious difference emphasizes how much of a radical departure the Articles were from 180 years of colonial constitution writing. Although the exigencies of the Revolutionary War explain the detour into a single-branch structure, the colonists had used their monopoly on written constitutions to perfect the three-branch structure during those same 180 years. Undergirded by the commercial revolution of sixteenth- and seventeenth-century Europe and inspired by "Social Contract Theory," the English colonialists off in the primeval forests of the New World had done the hard work of making theory practice.

Much less obvious, but much more vital, are the two monetary and two military clauses just discussed. The financial independence of the federal government from the state legislatures was made possible by the two money clauses. An effective defense of the new federal government from enemies foreign and domestic was made possible by the two military clauses. Without financial independence and military capacity, the Constitution of 1789 would have been no more viable than were the Articles of 1781. Indeed, one might go so far as to speculate that, if the Articles had included the two money and the two military clauses among the Confederal Congress's enumerated powers, the Articles of Confederation might possibly have created a Perpetual Union. There is, after all, no reason why a single branch government cannot work in practice. But without these four critical powers, the Confederal Congress was doomed from the beginning.

1 THE POWER TO TAX

Erik M. Jensen

Article I, section 8, clause 1
The Congress shall have Power To lay and collect Taxes, Duties, Imposts and
Excises, to pay the Debts and provide for the common Defence and general
Welfare of the United States; but all Duties, Imposts and Excises shall be uni-
form throughout the United States.

KEY TERMS

"To lay and collect Taxes, Duties, Imposts, and Excises" gives Congress the power to tax and was intended to correct one of the critical defects of the Articles of Confederation, under which the national government had no taxing power at all. Governments require revenue.

It was not the original understanding, nor is it the understanding today, that the four categories listed in the taxing clause (taxes, duties, imposts, and excises) are mutually exclusive. The long, duplicative list made it clear that Congress would have the power to enact almost any form of taxation—including forms that in the late eighteenth century were unknown—except insofar as the taxing power is constrained by other, specific limitations in the Constitution. The most important limitations, discussed later, are the uniformity rule, which applies to "duties, imposts, and excises," included at the end of the clause; the apportionment rule for direct taxes, set out twice, in Art. I, §2, and Art. I, §9, cl. 5; and the prohibition against imposing any "Tax or Duty" on "Articles exported from any State," provided for in Art. I, §9, cl. 5.

"Taxes," as used in the taxing clause, is an umbrella term, one that encompasses the three other listed categories, "duties, imposts, and excises"—referred to as **"indirect taxes"**—generally levies on articles of consumption. ("Indirect taxes" is not a constitutional term, although, given how much it was used in founding debates, it might as well have been.) But the term "taxes" also includes the "**direct taxes**" that must be apportioned among the states on the basis of population. Any proposed tax must therefore be classified under the constitutional structure as direct or indirect. Both are within Congress's power to enact, but direct taxes are subject to the apportionment rule, and indirect taxes must be uniform.

"**Imposts**" are duties on articles imported from other nations—what we now call tariffs. In general, duties and excises are levies imposed on articles when no importation is involved, such as the infamous whiskey taxes of the founding era.

But whether an indirect tax is a "**duty**," an "impost," or an "excise" generally does not matter for constitutional purposes. If a proposed levy fits within any one (or more) of the three categories, it is within Congress's power to impose, subject only to the uniformity requirement. So, is a whiskey tax a duty or an excise? The answer is yes. Either way the tax is authorized by the taxing clause, and either way it must be uniform in its application.

The term "**excise**" has also been used as a default category. A tax that is not a direct tax and that does fit easily into the categories of "duties" or "imposts" is often called an "excise"—a conclusory way of saying that the tax is indirect and therefore need not be apportioned. For example, the Supreme Court held that the corporate income tax imposed in 1909, before ratification of the Sixteenth Amendment, was a valid excise— a tax on the privilege of doing business in corporate form—even though no founder could possibly have been thinking about the characterization of such a tax. It was a tax and, for reasons to be discussed shortly, not a direct tax. It was therefore valid so long as it was imposed uniformly (as it was).

Taxes versus other nonpunitive, governmental charges is another definitional issue implicit in the language "taxes, duties, imposts, and excises." All refer to taxes of one sort or another, but not all governmental charges are taxes.

It has become common in political debates for tax skeptics to characterize any governmental charge as a tax: "if it walks like a duck and quacks like a duck, it's a duck," the saying goes. The implication is that all charges walk and quack in the same way.

But that conception would pull too much into the category of "taxes." The founding debates did not focus on this question, but it is understood today that a charge imposed by government for the provision of specific goods or services is not a tax. For example, an entry fee to a national park is not a tax—a specific benefit is received in exchange—even if the government uses the proceeds for purposes having nothing to do with parks. Nor is a charge imposed by the Government Printing Office for a publication a tax, or a charge for a souvenir at a gift shop on a federal installation. More generally, user fees—charges for particular services, such as port fees—are not taxes, at least insofar as the amount of the fee is tied to value received.

To be sure, Americans expect benefits from paying taxes—Justice Oliver Wendell Holmes, Jr., said he got "civilized society" for his payments—but, with taxes, there is no one-to-one correspondence between payment made and benefit received. Yes, as a taxpayer you will receive the protection of the military and FBI, the safety provided by the Food and Drug Administration, the convenience of the Interstate Highway System, and so on. But even if we could come up with some generally accepted way to value those benefits (what is the dollar value to a citizen of services provided by the U.S. Army?), the likelihood that the total would approximate what you paid in taxes is close to zero. With user fees, in contrast, there is a value-for-value exchange. You pay $1000 for the use of a port, and you get $1000 in value, more or less, in return. Such a charge is not a tax.

The boundary between a tax and a user fee can be fuzzy, but in most cases there will be little doubt about characterization. And the distinction between taxes and other governmental charges often does not matter anyway. So long as Congress has authority to impose a charge, however labeled, and so long as no limitation on the taxing power would come into play if the charge were characterized as a tax (user fees do not have to be uniform across the United States, for example), the label should be irrelevant. But if a charge authorized by Congress is for specific goods and services, the authority for imposing the charge cannot be the taxing clause. The authority would have to be found elsewhere in Art. I, §8.

Taxes versus penalties is another distinction of potential relevance. Indeed, this distinction was critical in the 2012 Supreme Court case, *National Federation of Independent Business v. Sebelius* (*NFIB*), which considered the constitutionality of the mandate to acquire health insurance contained in the Patient Protection and Affordable Care Act (popularly known as Obamacare) and the penalty imposed on persons who fail to do so.

In *NFIB*, the divided Court concluded that what Congress had called a "penalty" (although included in the Internal Revenue Code and enforced by the Internal Revenue Service) is really a tax authorized by the taxing clause. Had it been a penalty, a majority of the Court concluded that it would have been constitutionally problematic. (Congress has no power to command people to buy particular goods and services and to penalize them for failing to do so.) Penalties are imposed for behavior that Congress does not want people to engage in at all or for failing to behave in a prescribed way.

With most taxes, in contrast—except for capitations, which are imposed simply on existence—people can do cost-benefit analyses to determine whether to act in a particular way. They can decide to engage in the congressionally favored, but not mandated, behavior (acquire health insurance), and thus avoid the tax, or not to acquire the insurance and pay the associated tax. In addition, no opprobrium attaches to those who make a choice that leads to tax liability. The Court concluded that Congress, with the individual mandate "penalty," did not intend to create "outlaws" (a term Chief Justice John Roberts used in his controlling opinion). If a person decides not to acquire insurance and instead to pay the "penalty"—recharacterized as a tax—so be it. (Whether the Court was right about Congress's supposed indifference to taxpayers' insurance choices is another matter.) If the amount of the "penalty" had been larger compared to the cost of insurance—so that the arrangement would have looked more like a real command, enforced by punishment, rather than a choice—the result might have been different.

Taxation versus regulation is a subset of a larger issue of the taxes-versus-penalties issue that was important historically: whether Congress can use its taxing power to regulate activities when straightforward regulation would be outside the powers enumerated in Art. I, §8. If, for example, Congress does not believe it has authority to regulate or altogether to forbid a particular activity, can it get the same result by imposing a burdensome tax? If Congress increases the cost, the activity will be discouraged; if Congress increases the cost sufficiently, the activity will effectively be outlawed.

This question engaged the Supreme Court repeatedly in the late nineteenth and early twentieth centuries, before the commerce clause was interpreted expansively. For example, when Congress tried to regulate child labor, the Supreme Court in 1918, in *Hammer v. Dagenhart*, held that Congress had no authority to do so. Shortly thereafter, Congress imposed a "tax" of ten percent on the net profits of businesses "knowingly" employing children. The goal was clearly to make the use of child labor uneconomical. In the *Child Labor Tax Case*, decided in 1922, Chief Justice William Howard Taft wrote that the usual deference to Congress in tax matters did not apply when, "on the very face of its provisions," the levy was a penalty, not a tax. Congress's use of the term "knowingly" was the giveaway. (And the Court seemed irritated that Congress had so quickly tried to circumvent the earlier decision.)

The narrow holding of the *Child Labor Tax Case* is no longer relevant because the Court overruled *Hammer v. Dagenhart*, making it clear that Congress may regulate child labor directly. In any event, in nearly all other cases in which the Court has looked at the tax-versus-regulation issue, it has upheld Congress's use of the taxing power to get results that, under the constitutional understanding then in effect, would otherwise not have been permissible. As long as some revenue would be generated, and assuming Congress used the right language in imposing the "tax," the Court would not second-guess Congress.

For example, in *Sonzinsky v. United States*, a New Deal–era case, the Court considered a license tax imposed on dealers in firearms. The National Firearms Act defined "firearms" in such a way that it picked up weapons like sawed-off shotguns; the obvious purpose was to establish federal control over the disfavored weapons. Sonzinsky argued that the levy was not a true tax, and Congress had no power to regulate the firearms. But the Court concluded that

> a tax is not any the less a tax because it has a regulatory effect, . . . and it has long been established that an Act of Congress which on its face purports to be an exercise of the taxing power is not any the less so because the tax is burdensome or tends to restrict or suppress the thing taxed.

The levy "purport[ed] to be an exercise of the taxing power," it produced "some revenue," and that was good enough. The Court refused "to ascribe to Congress an attempt, under the guise of taxation, to exercise another power denied by the Federal Constitution."

There is much to be said for deference to Congress, and the tax-versus-regulation issue has largely disappeared anyway. As the conception of what Congress can do under other enumerated powers increased in the early twentieth century, the need diminished for Congress to look for alternative sources of power.

But as the discussion above of *NFIB v. Sebelius* illustrates, the tax-versus-regulation issue has not disappeared. It was interesting that, although the Court in

NFIB deferred to Congress in upholding the individual mandate penalty as an exercise of the taxing power, it relabeled what Congress had called a "penalty." Had Congress taken the politically unpopular route and referred to the penalty as a tax, the case for deference would have been strengthened.

"**Direct taxes**" is a term not used in the taxing clause, but it is impossible to understand the structure of the clause without understanding **the direct-tax apportionment rule**, which is set out in two places in the Constitution. Direct taxes must be apportioned among the states on the basis of population, just as population must be used to determine a state's representation in the House of Representatives:

> Representatives and direct Taxes shall be apportioned among the several States which may be included within this Union, according to their respective Numbers, which shall be determined by adding to the whole Number of free Persons, including those bound to Service for a Term of Years, and excluding Indians not taxed, three fifths of all other Persons.

That provision, in Art. I, §2, has been modified only by the Fourteenth Amendment's elimination of the distinction between "free Persons" and "all other Persons"; the effective elimination of the category of "Indians not taxed" by legislation; and by ratification of the Sixteenth Amendment, which provides that "taxes on incomes" need not be apportioned.

For a direct tax, a state with, say, one-twentieth of the national population must bear one-twentieth of the aggregate liability for the tax, regardless of how the tax base is spread across the country. When apportionment would be required, the rule makes imposition of a tax almost impossible, except in the unlikely event that each state's percentage of the tax base approximates its percentage of the national population.

Suppose an income tax must be apportioned (which, to be clear, is not the case with the Sixteenth Amendment in force), and suppose two states have the same population but very different income levels. If the apportionment rule applied, the aggregate income tax liability collected from the two states would have to be the same. To satisfy the rule, the tax rates in the poorer state would have to be higher than those in the richer state, or some other awkward mechanism would have to be used to make the numbers come out right.

Imposing higher rates on those in the poorer state would be absurd, and critics of apportionment—those who think it should have been discarded long ago—have emphasized what they see as the rule's absurdity. Why enforce a rule that can lead to ridiculous results? But the rule is not so absurd if it is understood as a disincentive for Congress to impose a direct tax that would have sectional effects—where the taxed items are distributed across the country in a way different from population. Congress should be unwilling to enact a nonsensical tax.

The two examples of direct taxes included in almost all founding discussions were real-estate taxes and capitations. The latter is specifically mentioned in Art. I, §9, cl. 4 ("No Capitation, *or other direct*, Tax shall be laid, unless in Proportion to the Census or Enumeration herein before directed to be taken"), and is generally understood to mean a lump-sum head tax. Taxes on land were also universally understood as direct.

In *Pollock v. Farmers' Loan & Trust Co.*, the *Income Tax Cases* (the plural is appropriate because two sets of opinions arose from the dispute), the Supreme Court in 1895 extended that conception to include a tax on *income* from all property, including personal property as well as real estate. The Sixteenth Amendment, ratified in 1913, exempted "taxes on incomes" from apportionment, but capitations and taxes on property that are not income taxes still seem to require apportionment.

One enduring issue is whether any other taxes, particularly those unknown to the founders (and which therefore could not have been mentioned in founding debates), might have to apportioned. However, Chief Justice Roberts's opinion in *NFIB* seemed to accept the proposition that capitations and property taxes were—and are—the only direct taxes still subject to apportionment.

"To pay the Debts and provide for the common Defence and general Welfare of the United States" is an issue about the taxing power that goes far beyond the boundaries of this chapter but that is worthy of note. The issue is whether the reference to the "common Defence and general Welfare of the United States" increases the scope of the taxing power or whether it simply states the obvious—that the taxing power must be exercised for a legitimate governmental purpose. Might a charge that otherwise does not fit easily within the requirements of the taxing power nevertheless be valid if the charge is enacted to promote the general welfare? Suffice it to say that, given the expansion of congressional power in the twentieth century, this issue will arise only in unusual circumstances.

"Uniform throughout the United States": The uniformity clause in Art. I, §8, cl. 1 by its terms applies only to "Duties, Imposts, and Excises"—indirect taxes. Other taxes, the direct taxes subject to the apportionment rule, are not subject to the uniformity rule.

To satisfy the uniformity rule, as it has been interpreted by the Supreme Court, indirect taxes must be geographically uniform, on a state-by-state basis. A duty, impost, or excise must apply in the same way in Montana as it does in South Carolina: it must be imposed on the same items and at the same rates.

At one level, uniformity of that sort seems to be a matter of fairness, not a serious limitation on congressional power. And it is a technical rule easy to satisfy: Congress must ensure that a gasoline excise tax, for example, applies at the same rate per gallon (or liter), or at the same percentage of sales price, in each of the 50 states. But that is not a meaningless requirement. Suppose Congress would like to use the gasoline excise to lessen consumption where air pollution is a problem. Higher rates on gasoline in California than in North Dakota might make conceptual sense, but, because of the uniformity rule, Congress could not vary the tax rate in that way.

A tax must either be direct, and subject to the apportionment rule, or indirect, and limited by the uniformity rule. The rules are mutually exclusive. Indeed, if you think about this for a moment, you can see that the two rules cannot apply to the same levy. An apportioned tax could not be geographically uniform except in the unlikely event that the tax base is distributed state by state in the same proportion as population.

The export clause, in Art. I, §9, cl. 4, provides that "no Tax or duty shall be laid on Articles exported from any State." The possible application of that limitation on the taxing power is going to be an issue only in limited circumstances, but the clause was critical to acceptance of the Constitution. (The southern states, which were dependent on exportation, were worried that the national government could use taxes on exports to cripple their economies.) But the clause is not of only historical interest. Twice in the late twentieth century the Supreme Court struck down the application of taxes, such as the Harbor Maintenance Tax, on the ground that they violated the export clause. The clause is chock-full of interpretive issues, such as what a "tax or duty" is (the distinction with user fees has been important in this context) and, perhaps most intellectually intriguing, when (or if) an article enters the stream of commerce that leads to exportation and thereafter cannot be taxed.

HISTORY AND DEVELOPMENT

One important goal—some would say it was the *most* important goal—in creating the Constitution was to establish a national taxing power, something that had not existed under the Articles of Confederation. (Roger Brown has argued that "[t]he experience with the breakdown of taxation . . . drove the constitutional Revolution in 1787.") Under the Articles, the national government, such as it was, could not even impose duties on imports, much less impose a tax on the wealth or income of citizens. The national government had to rely on sending requisitions to the states for revenue, and the states were often not forthcoming.

The requisitions process interposed the state governments, which were supposed to raise revenue and pass some of it on, between the citizenry and the national government. With no national revenue officers, citizens were protected against abuse by a faraway government. But they were overly protected, and the national government was starved for funds. The difficulties were bad enough on an everyday basis; they were compounded during times of emergency, like wartime.

The power to tax is, in short, foundational, and there were founders who wanted a nearly unlimited taxing power. For example, in *Federalist* No. 23, Alexander Hamilton argued that several powers, including taxation, were necessary for an "energetic government": they "ought to exist without limitation, *because it is impossible to foresee or to define the extent and variety of national exigencies, and the correspondent extent and variety of the means which may be necessary to satisfy them.*" And in *Federalist* No. 30, Hamilton insisted that the taxing power should be limited only by the "resources of the community":

Money is, with propriety, considered as the vital principle of the body politic; as that which sustains its life and motion and enables it to perform its most essential functions. A complete power, therefore, to procure a regular and adequate supply of revenue, as far as the resources of the community will permit, may be regarded as an indispensable ingredient in every constitution.

In *Federalist* No. 30, Hamilton asked, "What remedy can there be for this situation, but in a change of the system which has produced it—in a change in the fallacious and delusive system of quotas and requisitions?" At the Virginia ratification convention on June 7, 1788, Virginia Governor Edmund Randolph agreed, "Money is the nerve—the life and soul of a government. . . . Ought [the general government] to depend for the means of its preservation on other bodies [that is, the states]?"

By its terms, the taxing clause seems to permit Congress to "lay and collect" taxes on *anything*, and some have characterized the Constitution as a pro-tax document. That is true, up to a point, but, while the Constitution grants Congress a broad power to tax, the power is not unlimited.

Few, if any, founders were indifferent to the potential for overreaching by the national government. But with what were called "indirect taxes"—duties, imposts, and excises, which are generally imposed on articles of consumption, and the burden of which would be passed on to the ultimate consumer—the danger is minimal. A citizen can decide whether to be subject to an indirect tax by deciding whether to buy the taxed item. And the government has no incentive to try to exact confiscatory indirect taxes because, as Hamilton noted in *Federalist* No. 21, if the government raises the taxes too high, consumption of the taxed items will decline, efforts to evade the tax will increase, and revenue will actually decline. As a result, the uniformity rule—applying indirect taxes state-by-state in a consistent way—was thought to be enough protection against governmental abuse.

But *direct* taxes were fundamentally different, lacking the built-in protections of indirect taxes. Direct taxes are more difficult to avoid, and, unless the Constitution limited their use, the potential for abuse remained. In a sense, any tax can be avoided, of course. Commit suicide and you will not be subject to a capitation, a tax imposed on existence. Do not own property, and you will not be obligated to pay a property tax (not directly, at least). But the efforts to avoid a direct tax go far beyond what is involved in deciding whether to purchase a taxed good. With direct taxes, the long arm of the national government would reach individuals directly—and maybe dangerously.

Many founders were also worried about the potentially damaging effects of national taxes, particularly direct ones, on state governments. Anti-federalists feared that, if the national government brought in too much revenue, little would be left for the states, and the states' existence could be endangered. Debating the merits of a constitutional amendment that would have continued requisitions as the primary revenue source of the national government, Elbridge Gerry referred in 1789 to the possible "annihilation of the State Governments."

The idea of taxes being imposed by the national government directly on Americans was so different from what had gone before that resistance could be expected. Hamilton wrote in *Federalist* No. 12, "It is evident from the state of the country, from the habits of the people, from the experience we have had on the point itself that it is impracticable to raise any very considerable sums by direct taxation." While essential to meet the extraordinary revenue needs of wartime—imposing direct taxes had to be possible—direct taxation could not be counted on to meet the expenses of everyday operations.

And, it was often emphasized, direct taxation would not ordinarily be necessary. Ratification debates, including commentary in *The Federalist*, are full of reassurances that the bulk of government revenue would be raised through indirect taxes. At the Virginia ratifying convention on June 16, 1788, for example, James Madison stressed that national defense requires the availability of extraordinary taxing powers, but

> [w]hen . . . direct taxes are not necessary, they will not be recurred to. It can be of little advantage to those in power to raise money in a manner oppressive to the people. . . . Direct taxes will only be recurred to for great purposes. . . . [I]t is necessary to establish funds for extraordinary exigencies, and to give this power to the general government; for the utter inutility of previous requisitions on the states is too well known.

Most founders accepted the idea that the national government had to have power to impose taxes other than indirect taxes, but even staunch nationalists like Hamilton recognized that limits had to be imposed. (He might not have thought limits were a good idea, as some of his comments quoted earlier suggest, but he knew the Constitution could not be sold to the people without protections.) He argued in *Federalist* No. 21 that "[i]n a branch of taxation where no limits to the discretion of the government are to be found in the nature of the thing [as was true with indirect taxes], the establishment of a fixed rule, not incompatible with the end, may be attended with fewer inconveniences than to leave that discretion altogether at large."

Apportionment for direct taxes was that "fixed rule": "An actual census or enumeration of the people must furnish the rule," Hamilton wrote in *Federalist* No. 36, "a circumstance which effectually shuts the door to partiality or oppression. The abuse of this power of taxation seems to have been provided against with guarded circumspection." Apportionment makes direct taxes much more difficult to implement than they otherwise would be, and that was, he thought (or said he thought), a good thing.

Apportionment also seemed to make the imposition of direct taxes fairer. In trying to reassure his fellow Virginians about the Constitution, on June 12, 1788, Edmund Pendleton emphasized the practical effect of apportionment: "We have hitherto paid more than our share of taxes for the support of the government. . . . But by this system we are to pay our equal, ratable share only."

The apportionment rule that applies to direct taxation is the same as that used for determining representation in the House of Representatives. It is not an overstatement to suggest that coupling representation and direct taxation made the Constitution possible.

At the Constitutional Convention, there was initially sentiment for using wealth as a measure for apportioning representation, but that changed. It became apparent that population might be a reasonable surrogate for wealth, and, even more important, population was much easier to determine, given the mandated decennial census.

If population was to be the measure for representation, how should slaves be counted? Contrary to the popular understanding today, it was the *southern* states that wanted slaves counted fully, not as three-fifths of a person. In contrast, northerners said that counting slaves would give the southern states representation based on property.

The convention nearly deadlocked on this issue. On July 12, Gouverneur Morris of Pennsylvania introduced a motion to add to a clause tying representation to both wealth and population a "proviso that taxation shall be in proportion to Representation." Madison described the proposal's "object [as] lessen[ing] the eagerness on one side, & the opposition on the other, to the share of Representation claimed by the [Southern] States on account of the Negroes."

After a number of objections had been raised to the proposal, including concern that it could lead to the revival of requisitions, Morris answered that he

> supposed [the objections] would be removed by restraining the rule to *direct* taxation. With regard to indirect taxes on *exports* & imports & on consumption, the rule would be inapplicable. Notwithstanding what had been said to the contrary he was persuaded that the imports & consumption were pretty nearly equal throughout the Union.

The Morris motion received immediate support from both northern and southern delegates.

Linking taxation and representation would limit the risk that one section of the country could cripple another through taxation, and, reassuring to the southern delegates, it would prevent a future Congress from trying to destroy slavery through taxation. Slaves were to be counted as less than whites for purposes of representation, bad for the South, but were also to be counted as less than whites for measuring a state's apportioned tax liability, a benefit to the South.

The linkage worked because it was a real compromise. Madison discussed the point in *Federalist* No. 54:

> As the accuracy of the census to be obtained by the Congress will necessarily depend . . . on the disposition, if not on the co-operation of the States, it is of great importance that the States should feel as little bias as possible to swell or to reduce the amount of their numbers. . . . By extending the rule to both [representation and direct taxation], the States will have opposite interests which will control and balance each other and produce the requisite impartiality.

What is a direct tax? One of the most quoted passages from Madison's notes on the Constitutional Convention describes the silence following a question from Rufus King of Massachusetts on August 20, late in the deliberations: "Mr King asked what was the precise meaning of *direct* taxation? No one answered."

That passage is used to support the proposition that no one knew then, and therefore no one can know now, what a direct tax is. Without other guidance, it is said, we must rely on what the Supreme Court said about direct taxation in 1796, in the great case of *Hylton v. United States*. And what the Court said was that apportionment applies to very little.

Hylton has attained special status because Alexander Hamilton, former secretary of the treasury, argued the case for the government; the case was decided only seven years after the Constitution's ratification; and the four participating justices were all founders. James Wilson, William Paterson, and Samuel Chase had been delegates to the Constitutional Convention, and James Iredell had been a delegate to the North Carolina ratifying convention.

At issue in *Hylton* was a tax on carriages "kept by or for any person, for his or her own use, or to be let out to hire, or for the conveying of passengers." The tax was enacted in 1794, at Hamilton's urging, as a major revenue measure. It was challenged by a group of Virginians on the ground that it was a direct tax that had not been apportioned. The Court disagreed.

Hylton is understood to stand for two propositions. The first is that, if apportionment would be difficult because the tax base is concentrated in a few states, apportionment should not have to be done. That is a peculiar way to interpret a *limitation* on congressional power, but that is what the Court said. The second, in Justice Chase's words, is that the direct taxes "contemplated by the Constitution, are only *two,* to wit, a *capitation,* or *poll* tax, *simply,* without regard to *property, profession,* or any *other circumstance; and a tax on LAND.*" This was dictum—unnecessary to resolving the dispute—and it was in tension with the first proposition: Why is a tax on real estate easy to apportion? Furthermore, it suggested that apportionment, a constitutional limitation on governmental power, could not possibly apply to forms of taxation that had not been developed at the time. Why should a constitution be interpreted in that way?

Neither proposition is self-evidently correct, but that limited view of direct taxes prevailed for a century—and it continues to have effect today. For example, in 1881, in *Springer v. United States*, the Court upheld a Civil War tax, which fell primarily on earned income, against a challenge that it was an unapportioned direct tax: "*[D]irect taxes,* within the meaning of the Constitution, are only capitation taxes, as expressed in that instrument, and taxes on real estate. . . ." The Court characterized the income tax as "within the category of an excise or duty."

The Civil War income tax had been allowed to expire in 1872, but there was substantial pressure to revive the tax. For most of the nation's history, the government had relied for revenue on taxes on consumption, like tariffs, and those indirect taxes were thought to be unfair, to hit the poor disproportionately hard. The wealthy, it was thought (by those other than the wealthy), were not paying their fair share. The debates on reinstating an income tax in the late nineteenth century contain vitriolic language of a sort that make modern political debates seem namby-pamby.

In 1894, the "revolutionaries" won, temporarily: Congress enacted a new income tax, one that reached only the wealthy—it applied only to incomes above $4000, affecting about one percent of the population—and with a rate that, by modern standards, was strikingly low (two percent). But in the *Income Tax Cases*, decided the next year, a divided Court struck the tax down. It was a direct tax that had not been apportioned.

The opinions in the *Income Tax Cases* are full of overblown rhetoric, but the majority's conclusion was tied, in a not irrational way, to *Hylton*: If a tax on real property is direct, a tax on the income from that property is direct as well. (Lord Coke had written, "[W]hat is the land, but the profits thereof?") The Court said, "[W]e are unable to conclude that the enforced subtraction from the yield of all the owner's real or personal property . . . is so different from a tax upon the property itself, that it is not a direct, but an indirect tax, in the meaning of the Constitution." And because reaching income from property was so central to the 1894 income tax, directed as it was at the wealthy, the entire tax had to fall.

A push for a new, unapportioned income tax started almost immediately after the *Income Tax Cases* had been decided, with many suggesting that no constitutional amendment was necessary because the Supreme Court had been so clearly wrong. (Many think that today.) But the risk of enacting a new income tax without amending the Constitution was great. The Court might not change its mind in evaluating a reinstituted tax, particularly since many justices would have been irritated by a clear challenge to the Court's authority. Whether or not a constitutional amendment should have been legally necessary, it was politically necessary if there was going to be a new income tax.

What an amendment should include was itself a subject of controversy. Although some argued that the direct-tax clauses should be jettisoned, so that apportionment would never again be an issue, Nebraska Senator Norris Brown—the sponsor of the resolution that ultimately became the amendment—rejected such a sweeping step. His proposed language provided only that a "tax on incomes" would not require apportionment. Brown presumably wanted a narrow change to increase the prospects for ratification.

Even so, ratification was not a given. There is evidence that Rhode Island Senator Nelson Aldrich, chair of the Senate Finance Committee, nominally supported the amendment only because he thought the ratification process would slow down the move to a new income tax and he assumed ratification would fail. If that is what Aldrich thought, however, he was wrong. The resolution was submitted to the states in 1909, and the requisite number of states had ratified the amendment by early 1913. Congress enacted the first modern income tax later that year.

What the Sixteenth Amendment did is often misunderstood. An income tax had always been permissible under the language of the taxing clause. (After all, the clause gives Congress the power to lay and collect "taxes," and the income tax is a tax.) But the Supreme Court had held in the *Income Tax Cases* that an income tax was a direct tax that had to be apportioned. An apportioned income tax would have been a travesty, and the amendment provides that "[t]he Congress shall have power to lay and collect taxes on incomes, from whatever source derived, *without apportionment among the several States, and without regard to any census or enumeration.*" Whether or not the Supreme Court got it right in the *Income Tax Cases*, the amendment made the modern, *unapportioned* income tax unquestionably constitutional.

The amendment did not eliminate all interpretive issues, of course. The amendment applies only to "taxes on incomes," and a number of Supreme Court cases in the twentieth century considered whether a tax, or a part of a tax, was on income. If not on income, a direct tax is not exempted from apportionment by the amendment. For example, in 1920, in *Eisner v. Macomber*, the Court concluded that a stock dividend— one that did not change a shareholder's proportionate interest in the earnings or assets of a corporation—was not income under the amendment and that Congress's attempt to include the value of such a dividend in the base of an unapportioned income tax was therefore invalid. The stock dividend was the equivalent, the Court said, of unrealized appreciation—a simple increase in the value of property—and a tax on unrealized appreciation is one on wealth, not income.

Although most commentators today think that *Macomber* was wrongly decided— that Congress can define "income" as it wishes—the case has not been overruled. In fact, Chief Justice Roberts cited it favorably in 2012, suggesting that whether an economic benefit is income or not, as a matter of constitutional law, is not a dead issue.

Other Limitations (or Possible Limitations) on the Taxing Power:

A few other constitutional provisions that might be seen as limitations on the taxing power are worth mentioning, although none of them is likely to seriously constrain that power.

Importation of slaves. The Constitution contains a specific limitation on the taxing power that, for obvious reasons, long ago ceased to have any practical consequences. In Art. I, §9, cl. 1, Congress was forbidden to limit or prohibit the importation of slaves (a word not used in the Constitution) prior to 1808, but it could impose a "Tax or duty" on each importation, not to exceed ten dollars per person.

The due process clauses. Professors (you know those people!) can conjure hypothetical taxes that would violate due process and equal protection requirements of the Fourteenth and Fifth Amendments. A tax imposed only on black Americans, for example, would clearly be impermissible. But one hopes that the constitutional merits of such a ridiculous tax would not have to be resolved judicially. Any proposal like that should expire quickly in Congress, long before the courts have to get involved.

The takings clause. Tax skeptics have occasionally argued that certain taxes are governmental takings of private property for public use; if so, the Fifth Amendment would require that the government provide "just compensation." But the Takings Clause seems to be an imperfect way to analyze taxes paid in cash. The Takings Clause should, at least as a general matter, be reserved for situations when the property taken by government is something other than cash—as, for example, under the power of eminent domain. If the government were to impose an arguably confiscatory levy, the constitutional question should not be whether a taking has occurred, but whether the levy is really a "tax" authorized by the Taxing Clause.

The origination clause. This clause, in Art. I, §7, cl. 1, requires that bills "for raising revenue . . . originate in the House of Representatives," with the Senate having the power only to "propose or concur with Amendments as on other bills." The clause was intended to ensure that the legislative body closer to the people would have the first crack at drafting tax legislation.

The clause has had little practical effect. Legislation in which raising revenue plays a substantial role almost always winds up bearing a House number before enactment, as if it had originated there. If the relevant language in fact came from the Senate, the Senate will usually have "amended" the House legislation and substituted its own handiwork. A "House" bill, that is, may wind up containing little or no language written in the House.

This is a subterfuge, to be sure, but it is common practice. And it may not be harmful, except in the sense that Congress ought to be following procedures set out in the Constitution. Wherever it originates, no revenue legislation can become law without the approval of both House and Senate. If the House waives its prerogatives and signs off on language that was drafted in the Senate—or in the executive branch or the faculty lounge at Harvard Law School, for that matter—ought anyone else to care?

FUTURE IMPLICATIONS

With the Sixteenth Amendment making an unapportioned income tax unquestionably constitutional, the big issues concerning the taxing power have largely gone away. The individual income tax has become so ensconced, and so important a source of government revenue, that it is hard to imagine that it will be displaced. Almost everyone complains about the income tax, but there exists a grudging acknowledgement of its need, as well as support for how it is generally applied—higher-income people pay more in income taxes even if the rates are not graduated, in contrast to taxes on consumption, which have disproportionately negative effects, at least in general, on lower-income people.

The details of the income tax will inevitably change—indeed, simplification would be welcomed by almost everyone—but proposed fixes to the income tax are unlikely to raise serious constitutional issues. Yes, there may be questions in unusual cases as to whether a tax really reaches "income." To the extent it does not, the Sixteenth Amendment would not apply. But the likelihood of success in challenging the constitutionality of a section of the income tax is small. Courts typically give substantial deference to Congress's use of its taxing power. The Supreme Court in 2012, in *NFIB v. Sebelius*, seems to have endorsed the idea that the category of direct taxes subject to apportionment includes only capitation taxes (understood to mean lump-sum head taxes) and taxes on property that are not income taxes. And courts give scope to Congress to define income.

The periodic grass roots movements to tear the tax system up by the roots and start over are unlikely to succeed, and that is probably a good thing. We have a good sense of what the consequences of an income tax are, even if we do not like them. Moving to an entirely new tax system would increase uncertainty, and people—and financial markets—generally do not like uncertainty.

With governmental deficits at high levels, however, there will inevitably be pressure for additional revenue. One of the commonly proposed fixes is enactment of a value added tax (VAT), a consumption tax of the sort used in many European countries that works, albeit in a less visible way, like the sales taxes imposed by most American states. Such proposals might be politically controversial, but it is unlikely that there will be serious issues about Congress's constitutional power to enact such an indirect tax so long as it meets the uniformity rule.

Some conservative commentators have urged that a VAT or other form of consumption tax replace the income tax, in part as a simplification measure. It is more likely, however, that a VAT would be enacted as an additional tax, as is the case in most western European countries, and, if that were to happen, the VAT would complicate the American tax system, not simplify it. Even if a VAT were enacted to replace the income tax, there would be no guarantee that the income tax would not make a return in years ahead.

Although some tax resisters urge the repeal of the Sixteenth Amendment, doing so would require another constitutional amendment, and it is hard to imagine that a proposal of that sort would survive the ratification process. In addition, those who urge repeal may be wrong in their assumptions about the effect of repeal. Many, perhaps most, commentators think the *Income Tax Cases* were wrongly decided. If that is so—and who knows how the modern Supreme Court would rule if required to reconsider those cases—the Sixteenth Amendment was unnecessary to begin with, and its repeal would change nothing.

Some academics and an occasional political candidate have recommended enactment of a national tax on wealth, measured not by income generated by wealth but by its value—what is called an *ad valorem* tax. Such a tax has obvious administrative difficulties: valuing property is not easy, except for property that is publicly traded, such as shares of stock in corporations that are traded on public exchanges.

And a wealth tax would have legal issues as well. Congress has the power under the taxing clause to impose such a tax, but it would probably be treated as a direct tax subject to apportionment (and not exempted from the requirement by the Sixteenth Amendment if the tax is not measured by income). The founding debates are clear that a tax on real property (land, buildings, and fixtures) was considered a direct tax—indeed, Congress apportioned several land taxes between 1798 and 1861—and real property was the measure of wealth at that time. In the *Income Tax Cases*, the Supreme Court extended that understanding to *personal* property—basically all property that is not real property. Thus, a tax on any property is a direct tax that would have to be apportioned, unless it is measured by income. Chief Justice Roberts's 2012 opinion in *NFIB* seems to have blessed that analysis.

An apportioned wealth tax would be absurd. The rates would have to be higher in poorer states than in richer ones, a political non-starter. Esoteric arguments have been advanced in support of the idea that a tax on wealth is effectively a tax on income, and that apportionment would therefore not be required because of the Sixteenth Amendment. But those arguments are not automatically winning ones. If, without the benefit of a constitutional amendment, Congress were to enact an unapportioned wealth tax, the risks are not trivial that the Supreme Court would strike the tax down. Congress is unlikely to enact far-reaching changes in the tax system if there is any serious doubt about constitutionality.

FURTHER READING

Brown, Roger H. 1993. *Redeeming the Republic: Federalists, Taxation, and the Origins of the Constitution*. Baltimore, MD: The Johns Hopkins University Press.

Brownlee, W. Elliot. 1996. *Federal Taxation in America: A Short History*. New York: Cambridge University Press.

Graetz, Michael J. 1997. *The Decline (and Fall?) of the Income Tax*. New York: Norton.

Jensen, Erik M. 2005. *The Taxing Power*. Westport, CT: Praeger.

Johnson, Calvin H. 2005. *Righteous Anger at the Wicked States: The Meaning of the Founders' Constitution*. New York: Cambridge University Press.

2 THE POWER TO BORROW MONEY

Jacob Holt

Article I, section 8, clause 2
To borrow money on the credit of the United States

KEY TERMS

Bills of credit were issued during the Revolutionary War as legal tender, but during the war they had no intrinsic value and carried no interest. (But see Chapter 6, Key Terms.)

Certificates of indebtedness are short-term, interest-bearing securities with a maturity date of a year or less.

Federal debt includes **public debt**, which is debt not held by the national government but by the "public"; **monetized debt**, which is debt held by the Federal Reserve Bank; and **federal government account debt**, which is debt owned by the government itself, by one of its many agencies.

Treasury bills are short-term securities yielding no interest but sold at a discount rate, that have a maturity date of a year or less.

Treasury notes are medium-term interest-bearing securities that have a maturity date of two to five years.

Treasury bonds are long-term interest-bearing securities that have a maturity date of at least ten years.

A sinking fund is a fund that sets aside revenue over a long period of time to repay long-term debt.

HISTORY AND DEVELOPMENT

The power to borrow money was originally given to the national government under Article IX of the Articles of Confederation. It was vital for the national government to possess this power when the Articles of Confederation were adopted, because the United States needed to borrow large sums of money to finance the Revolutionary War. Although the power to borrow money existed under the Articles of Confederation, like most powers granted to the Congress under the Articles of Confederation, it was difficult for Congress to use this power. The Articles of Confederation required any borrowing to be approved by nine of the thirteen states. While this supermajority requirement was not problematic during the war, it would prove to be problematic afterward.

During the war, the government borrowed large sums of money, mostly from the government of France and Dutch bankers. By January 1, 1783, the public debt of the United States would stand at $43,000,000. However, its main source of financing was bills of credit. These bills of credit were backed only by a declaration of legal tender (so they had no intrinsic value) and carried no interest. They began to serve as a form of paper money during the Revolutionary War. The government relied on them for several reasons. First, the national government lacked taxing power, so it could not raise revenue on its own. Second, state governments found tax collection difficult while the war was ongoing, so they could not provide the financial resources needed to finance the war. Finally, it was difficult for the United States to obtain foreign loans because loans to the fledging nation were considered a risky investment. If the United States lost the revolution, whoever loaned them money would lose their entire investment. By the end of the war, the national and state governments had issued over $400,000,000 worth of bills of credit.

At the Constitutional Convention on August 6, 1787, the Committee of Detail presented the first draft of the powers granted to Congress. The Committee proposed that Congress be given the power to "borrow money, and emit bills on the credit of the United States." The phrase "and emit bills" would be the most debated part of this proposed power. Opponents of this phrase feared it would explicitly give Congress the power to issue paper money (currency that cannot be redeemed for anything of intrinsic value, but is simply a government sanctioned form of exchange). Supporters of the phrase claimed there might arise situations in which the government would need to use bills of credit.

Late on August 17, 1787, the Constitutional Convention took up the borrowing clause, the last clause to be discussed that day. Gouverneur Morris of Pennsylvania began by moving to strike out the phrase "and emit bills." Morris claimed such bills would be unnecessary if the government had credit, since it could obtain financing through other means, and useless (for those who received them) if the government lacked credit. Morris's motion was seconded by Pierce Butler of South Carolina.

The debate over Morris's motion began with James Madison of Virginia asking whether it would be preferable simply not to allow these bills to be used as currency. Madison noted that there might be instances where it would be best for the government to use bills of credit. Morris warned that "The monied interest will oppose the plan of government, if paper emissions be not prohibited."

John F. Mercer of Maryland challenged Gouverneur Morris's claim that allowing bills of credit would alienate the wealthy class. Mercer claimed the wealthy would support the proposed Constitution. Striking the phrase would simply upset supporters of paper money, whose support would be needed to ratify the Constitution. Nathaniel Gorham of New York stated he was for striking out the phrase without inserting any prohibition to the use of bills of credit. Gorham feared that including the phrase allowing bills of credit would lead to their use. While Gorham's argument implied not specifically granting Congress the power to emit bills of credit, it did not prohibit their use.

George Mason of Virginia argued that Congress could not issue bills of credit unless it was explicitly stated in the Constitution. Therefore, Mason argued, the phrase should remain in the Constitution. Although Mason opposed paper money, he was unwilling to bar the legislature from issuing it. Mason pointed out that the country could not have fought the Revolutionary War if it could not have issued bills of credit. Oliver Ellsworth of Connecticut and James Wilson of Pennsylvania argued in favor of striking the phrase because they wanted to remove the possibility of the government issuing paper money. John Langdon of New Hampshire stated that he would rather reject the whole document than retain the power of the government to issue bills of credit.

After the debate on Morris's amendment, the convention voted 9–2 to remove the phrase "and emit bills" from the proposed clause. The convention then voted to approve the borrowing clause and adjourned for the day.

The borrowing clause, as written in the Constitution, contains two important parts. First, it allows the government to borrow money. Second, it requires the Congress to maintain public credit. The borrowing clause as written places no limits on Congress's borrowing power. It does not limit what debt instruments may be used, does not state how the government should finance its debt, makes no mention of repudiating debt, and does not state how credit should be obtained. Consequently, one of the major debates early in the Washington administration would be how to handle the nation's debt.

The Washington Administration and Debt

Under its new constitution, the United States faced several issues regarding its debt and its borrowing power. Article VI of the Constitution states that the new government would be responsible for any debts incurred under the Articles of Confederation. At the same time, many states had large amounts of debt left over from the Revolutionary War. Some felt the national government should assume responsibility for this debt. By 1790 the combined debt held by the national and state governments was approximately $54,000,000, and a plan was needed to finance this debt and create public credit. To deal with the nation's debt and finances, Congress created the Treasury Department in September of 1789. On September 21, 1789, Congress requested that Treasury Secretary Alexander Hamilton submit a plan to deal with the country's debts and establish public credit. On January 9, 1790, Hamilton submitted a written plan to the Congress to deal with the debt and establish public credit.

Hamilton's plan contained several important elements. First, he wanted the federal government to assume the states' debts. Hamilton believed that assumption of states' debts was necessary because it would give creditors a financial interest in the success of the new American government. Also, like many of his contemporaries, he felt the debts incurred by the states to finance the Revolutionary War were part of a shared project, and so the entire nation should work to pay off these debts. Further, he believed the national government would be better able than the states to efficiently finance this debt.

The second major point of Hamilton's plan was to pay the debt at its face value. The value of the debt issued by the national government and by the states had declined dramatically by 1790. Paying the debt at its depreciated value would have saved the government a large sum of money, but Hamilton believed that only paying the debt at its depreciated value would harm the credit of the United States. In his written address, Hamilton argued the government needed to honor its obligations so as to instill confidence in investors and improve the public credit.

Finally, Hamilton believed the United States should follow the example of Great Britain and fund the debt. Rather than pay the debt down as quickly as possible, Hamilton wanted to make regular interest payments on the debt.

To accomplish this, Hamilton wanted to issue new bonds to pay off the old debts. This would increase the interest cost on the debt, but Hamilton believed that issuing new bonds would increase the amount of investment capital available and fuel economic growth. Although Hamilton did not want to pay the debt down quickly, his plan did create a sinking fund (a fund that sets aside revenue over a long period of time to repay long-term debt) whose revenue was derived from the sale of western lands to slowly pay down the debt. Under Hamilton's plan, the government would have the option of paying off up to two percent of the principle of its debt every year. Although Hamilton may not have desired to actually pay the debt off, he wanted at least to create the illusion the United States planned to pay off its debts. This may have been for political reasons (to get the necessary backing in Congress) and also to please investors in government debt.

Hamilton's plan, however, aroused strong opposition in Congress and from other political leaders in the United States. Many opposed the assumption of states' debt, because the states had differing levels of debt. The states had borrowed different amounts of money, and some states had begun to pay down their debt. Representatives from low-debt states felt they would be paying higher taxes to finance other states' debts if the national government assumed the states' debts. Others feared that assumption of states' debts would strengthen the national government and lead it to overpower the states. There was also opposition to funding the debt. Some critics, including Thomas Jefferson and James Madison, felt that a large funded debt would become a financial burden for the country. There were also complaints that a large funded debt placed an unfair financial burden on future generations.

Probably the greatest opposition was against Hamilton's plan to pay the bonds at face value. As the value of government bonds declined, many speculators had bought them at discounted rates, hoping to profit when the government paid off the debt. Many southern and western representatives wanted to provide some compensation for the original bondholders. They argued that the government's failure to honor contracts had led to speculation in government debt. Paying the bonds at face value would benefit speculators who had taken advantage of the original bondholders. James Madison of Virginia proposed a bill that would provide compensation for the original bondholders and not honor the bonds at face value. Supporters of Hamilton's plan argued that failing to honor the original bonds would harm the nation's credit and it would be almost impossible to determine the identity of the original bondholders. They also asserted that honoring the existing bonds was the best way to prevent speculation in the future.

Congress ultimately voted down Madison's proposal to compensate the original bondholders, but this debate showed the regional divisions over Hamilton's plan. While northern representatives mostly favored Hamilton's plan, southern and western representatives often opposed it.

Despite the objections to Hamilton's specific plan, many understood the need for good public credit. Also, many believed that a prolonged debate over Hamilton's plan would make the new government look weak. Eventually, Thomas Jefferson helped broker a compromise between James Madison and Alexander Hamilton. The compromise plan paid the debt at face value and provided no compensation to the original bondholders. It funded the debt and created Hamilton's sinking fund to gradually pay down the debt. Finally, it assumed states' debts, but this was changed to make it more favorable to low-debt states. This would not be the last debate over the national government assuming states' debts, nor over the government's needs to honor its debts. Both of these issues would be debated again in the 1800s.

From the Panic of 1837 to the Civil War

Following 1790 but prior to the Civil War, the biggest dispute involving Congress's borrowing power dealt with the national government assuming state debts following the Panic of 1837. By 1840, many states had borrowed large amounts of money for internal improvement projects or to invest in private banks. When the panic hit, many states were unable to pay their debts, and several states defaulted or repudiated their debts. This scarred investors, and all states soon found it difficult to borrow money. Some thought the national government should assume state debts to remedy this problem. Opponents claimed that assuming state debts would set a bad precedent of the national government providing aid to fiscally irresponsible states. They also asserted that the Constitution did not grant the national government the power to assume state debts. Although the national government had assumed state debts in 1790, the argument against it would carry the day in 1840. Whether the Constitution allows Congress to assume responsibility for state debts is an issue that has been debated several times since and one the United States is still debating today.

As originally written, the borrowing clause places no limits on Congress's power to borrow money. It does not state how Congress can borrow money, it does not put limits on its ability to borrow money, and it does not prevent Congress from repudiating government debt. After the Civil War, however, the 14th Amendment would place new restrictions on the government's borrowing power. Section 4 of the 14th Amendment says

> The validity of the public debt of the United States, authorized by law, including debts incurred for payment of pensions and bounties for service in suppressing insurrection or rebellion, shall not be questioned. But neither the

United States nor any state shall assume or pay any debt or obligation incurred in aid of resurrection or rebellion against the United States, or any claim for the loss or emancipation of any slave, but all such debts, obligations, and claims shall be held illegal and void.

Section 4 contains three important parts. First, it clearly states that lawful United States debt cannot be questioned. This implies that Congress may not repudiate U.S. debt. Second, it forbids the federal and state governments from assuming any debts "incurred in aid of resurrection or rebellion." This language was initially focused on repudiating Confederate debt. During the Civil War, many foreign creditors had bought Confederate debt, and there were some people calling for these debts to be honored. However, the language of the 14th Amendment covers more than Confederate debt. It actually places a limit on what debt the Congress may authorize, although this limit on Congress's borrowing power only applies to a very specific situation.

The last part of section 4 of the 14th Amendment prevents the United States or the states from providing compensation for emancipated slaves. This language had two main purposes. First, it aimed to prevent the federal courts from declaring emancipation (especially for slaves freed before the ratification of the 13th Amendment) violated the taking clause of the Fifth Amendment. Second, during the Civil War there had been proposals (including ones from President Lincoln) to compensate slave owners who emancipated their slaves. This clause was thus crafted to eliminate the possibility that a future Congress might approve some form of compensation for former slave owners.

When originally proposed in the Senate, what would become section 4 of the 14th Amendment only stated that neither the United States nor state governments would pay any debt owed in aid of an insurrection or rebellion and that neither the United States nor the states would provide compensation for freed slaves. Senator Jacob Howard, the floor manager for the 14th Amendment, argued that the inclusion of a section repudiating Confederate debt and compensation for slavery was necessary to prevent these two issues from disrupting American politics. Many investors wanted the debts incurred by the Confederacy honored, and many former slave owners wanted compensation for the loss of their slaves. Howard argued that unless the 14th Amendment barred Confederate debt assumption and compensation for former slave owners, these would be issues constantly discussed in the next several decades.

Senator Ben Wade felt the proposed amendment did not go far enough. While he agreed that Confederate debt must be repudiated and compensation to former slave owners barred, he also believed United States debt must be guaranteed. Wade feared a scenario in which Confederate sympathizers might seek to deny compensation to former Union soldiers and their widows. Wade also felt that denying Congress the power to repudiate government debt would help the government's credit and make investors feel safer about investing in United States debt. Although there would be some legislative maneuvering over the language of the proposed amendment (some in the Senate only wanted to guarantee debts incurred for suppressing insurrection or rebellion), the final language would come close to fulfilling Wade's proposal. Thus, the first limits on Congress's borrowing power were placed in the Constitution. In future years, the main focus of debates concerning section 4 of the 14th Amendment dealt with the first part, stating that the lawful debt of the United States must be honored. While this appears to deny Congress the ability to repudiate government debt, what happens if congressional action, or inaction, prevents the government from meeting its debt obligations? This became important in the twentieth and twenty-first centuries, when Congress began to put statutory limits on the government's ability to borrow money.

The Federal Debt Ceiling

Until 1917 Congress had no statutory limit on federal debt. Congress had approved specific borrowing, such as loans to build the Panama Canal. It had passed laws allowing the Treasury to use certain debt instruments: certificates of indebtness, treasury bills, treasury notes, and treasury bonds, to fulfill government obligations. In some cases it gave the Treasury limited discretion over what instruments to use. However, the Treasury was required to seek congressional approval for any debt issuance. In 1917, Congress passed the Second Liberty Bond Act to finance the United States' entry into World War I. This act allowed the Treasury to issue long-term Liberty Bonds, which helped hold down the interest costs of financing the war. The Second Liberty Bond Act also allowed the Treasury to issue these bonds without a specific congressional approval, but it set a statutory limit on federal debt. However, this limit only applied to certificates of indebtedness and bonds. Later, Congress would places limits on other categories of debt. In 1939, Congress eliminated the separate categories of debt and instead began using an aggregate debt limit. From 1939 to 2015, Congress raised the debt ceiling ninety times.

The debt limit applies to almost all federal debt. This includes both public debt (debt not held by the national government), monetized debt (debt held by the Federal Reserve), and federal government account debt (debt owned by the government). As of August 1, 2015, the total national debt stands at approximately $18,150,000,000,000— of which approximately $13,135,000,000,000 is held by the public. Budget deficits increase the public debt, while budget surpluses decrease public debt. Monetized debts are bonds bought by the Federal Reserve to put more money into the economy. Therefore, the amount of monetized debt is not affected by budget surpluses or deficits. The amount of debt held in public accounts is not affected by budget deficits or surpluses. Rather, the amount of debt in public accounts is affected by the net financial flows into the accounts holding the debt. Examples of this type of accounts include the Social Security Trust Fund, Medicare Trust Fund, and Transportation Trust fund.

There is some debate about whether the debt limit is constitutional, since the 14th Amendment explicitly requires the United States to fulfill its debt obligations. If the United States reached the debt ceiling, in theory it could no longer borrow money to pay its current debt obligations and would therefore default on its debt. The federal courts have not ruled on this issue because the United States has never officially hit the debt ceiling (as discussed below, the U.S. Treasury has in the past used certain measures to avoid doing so); thus, no moot case involving the debt ceiling has yet appeared before the federal courts.

Regardless of the debt limit's constitutionality, one important question is whether there is a benefit to the United States in having a debt limit. Most countries do not have statutory limits on governmental debt. Proponents of the debt limit argue it allows Congress to assert its constitutional power to control spending. Proponents also claim the debt limit helps reduce budget deficits. When the government needs to borrow more money to cover deficits, Congress and the president must take a visible action to allow increased governmental borrowing, so proponents of the debt ceiling feel this will lead both Congress and the president to limit borrowing. Proponents of the debt limit also argue it serves as a congressional check on executive authority.

However, there are some costs to having a debt limit. When the government is near the debt limit, the options available to the Treasury to manage the government's finances become limited. Compounding this problem, government revenue and spending vary by month. Even if there is no annual deficit, the government may need to borrow money in certain months to meet its obligations. If the government is near the debt limit, the Treasury may be forced to use certain debt options that have greater long-term cost, in order to stay within the debt limit. Again, this can happen even if there is no annual increase in government borrowing. The debt limit can also lead to uncertainty in Treasury operations, which can increase future borrowing cost. In some cases, the government will need to take extreme measures, such as not investing government account surplus revenue immediately into federal debt as required by law (federal law requires trust fund account surpluses to be invested in federal government securities), to avoid hitting the debt limit. These types of measures can raise borrowing cost because they make government debt seem like a riskier investment. Finally, increases in the debt limit are not necessarily a sign that Congress is being fiscally irresponsible. The amount of governmental debt can increase even when government accounts are running surpluses, because federal law requires these funds to be invested in federal government securities. This happened from 1998 to 2001. The national government ran large budget surpluses and the public debt declined $448,000,000,000, while the amount of total debt increased by over $403,000,000,000, mostly due to surplus revenue from the Social Security Trust Fund.

It should again be stated that most of these problems exist when the government is near the debt ceiling. If the debt limit is raised well enough in advance, many of these problems no longer exist. Unfortunately, Congress does not have a good record when it comes to raising the debt ceiling in a timely fashion. In fact, Congress has on occasion threatened to withhold debt ceiling increases, treating it as leverage to limit government borrowing and spending or to advance other policy goals. This has caused some problems for the United States.

In the years during and immediately after World War I, the debt limit was set far above the amount of federal debt, but this would prove to be the exception to how Congress would handle the debt limit. In 1919, Congress authorized a debt limit of $43,000,000,000 when national debt sat at approximately $25,500,000,000. In 1939, the debt limit was set at $45,000,000,000 when the federal debt was approximately $40,400,000,000. Congress would raise the debt ceiling every year from 1941 to 1945, to help finance World War II. There would not be another increase in the debt limit until 1954.

The first fight to increase the debt limit after World War II would in many ways set the stage for future fights over increasing the debt limit. In 1953, President Eisenhower requested that Congress increase the debt limit. Eisenhower, a Republican, faced a

Congress controlled by his own party. The House quickly passed the increase, but there was a partisan divide in support for the measure. Republicans overwhelmingly voted for the measure, 169 for versus 33 against, while almost two-thirds of Democrats voted against the measure. The Senate finance committee refused to act, and no bill to raise the debt limit was voted on in the Senate in 1953. To avoid hitting the debt limit, the Eisenhower administration used some extreme measures, such as selling gold reserves. When Congress did increase the debt limit in 1954, it was less than the amount requested by President Eisenhower.

Eisenhower's effort to raise the debt limit revealed several truths about debt limit increases. First, the president must deliver votes from his own party to pass debt limit increases, especially when his party controls Congress. In future fights to raise the debt ceiling, Eisenhower would face a Democratic Congress, and a majority of members of both parties would support these increases. When the Democrats did not control Congress, they heavily opposed increasing the debt limit. When Democrats controlled the White House under Kennedy and Johnson, Republicans would overwhelmingly oppose debt limit increases while Democrats overwhelmingly voted in favor of them. In the years since the Johnson administration, the president's party has needed to provide the votes to pass debt limit increases when they control Congress. When the out-party is the minority party in Congress, they often vote almost unanimously against increases in the debt limit. When the out-party controls Congress, they often require the president to deliver votes from his party, but the out-party is more supportive of increases in the debt limit.

Second, Congress is not always timely in raising the debt limit, and the Treasury often needs to use extraordinary measures to avoid a default on government debt. This would occur many times in the future. Third, Congress often will not approve debt increases as large as the president desires. Finally, Congress often sees debt limit fights as a way to control government spending. The increase passed in 1954 was officially temporary. Congress hoped this would force the president to eventually balance the budget and pay down the debt. This pattern repeated itself in the 1950s through the 1970s. Most debt limit increases were officially temporary, but in reality the amount of government debt was unlikely to decrease. It was not until 1983 that Congress eliminated the distinction between temporary and permanent debt limit increases.

Fights over raising the debt limit in the 1970s changed how both Congress and the president used debt limit increases. Starting in 1970, Congress attempted to place amendments on debt ceiling bills that were unrelated to the debt limit or government borrowing. Although Congress had amended debt limit bills in the past, often to lower the amount of a debt limit increase, using debt limit bills to achieve other policy goals was a new strategy. In 1970, amendments were proposed on a bill to increase the debt ceiling to cut the military budget, prevent congressional pay raises, and place a cap on federal expenditures. President Nixon also tried to attach other policy provisions onto debt limit increases. In 1972, Nixon tried attaching a spending ceiling and an increase in presidential impoundment power onto a debt limit increase. Although the practice of placing non-germane amendments on debt limit increases has continued, most of these amendments have been unsuccessful. These amendments often fail because the debt limit is viewed as an essential piece of legislation, so many members of Congress fear doing anything that would prevent its passage.

The 1970s also saw the adoption of two major changes that affected Congress's borrowing power. In 1974, Congress passed the Budget and Impoundment Reform Act. Although this act mostly changed the budget process and made no change to Congress's borrowing authority, the changes in budget process affected Congress's use of its borrowing authority. The Budget and Impoundment Reform Act required the Congress to pass a budget resolution, a non-binding joint resolution, which set spending and revenue goals. The Budget and Impoundment Reform Act requires this resolution to "specify the amount by which statutory limit on the public debt is to be changed and to direct the committees having jurisdiction to recommend such change." The hope was that this would force Congress to approve increases in the debt limit before approving deficit spending. This would not come to pass, as the accumulation of debt actually accelerated in the 1980s.

Another major change occurred in 1979, when the House adopted the Gephardt Rule. The Gephardt Rule stated that when the House adopted a budget resolution that increased the national debt, the House must automatically pass a similar increase in the debt limit. The goal was to stop the House from taking separate votes to raise the debt limit. Although this rule did not eliminate separate votes on debt limit increases (the Senate would have to approve the budget resolution and agree to the increase in the debt limit), it did reduce the number of separate votes on the debt limit.

When Republicans took control of the House of Representatives in 1995, they repealed the Gephardt Rule—the main reason being that they thought debt limit increases could be used to negotiate policy concessions from President Clinton, a Democrat. During debate over the budget in 1995, Speaker Gingrich refused to raise the debt ceiling unless President Clinton agreed to certain budget cuts. As the impasse between the Clinton White House and Congress deepened, the Treasury Department was forced to use extraordinary measures to prevent a default on U.S. debt. This same dynamic—a Republican-controlled Congress seeking to extract policy concessions from a Democratic president by refusing to raise the debt ceiling—also took place in 2011 and 2013. This causes a problem because it makes some members of Congress question deadlines for raising the debt limit. In all three cases, the Treasury Department was able to delay defaulting on U.S. debt for several months after it had reached the debt limit. This has made some members of Congress question the necessity of acting on the debt limit, but failure to act in a timely manner is costly. The 1995 debt limit showdown raised the borrowing cost for three- and six-month treasury bills, although cost returned to normal after the crisis passed. The 2011 debt limit fight led to the first downgrade of United States debt. A downgrade of U.S. debt could lead to higher borrowing cost in the future. One of the biggest problems facing Congress in the future is how to avoid delaying needed increases in the debt limit.

FUTURE IMPLICATIONS

In the future one of the major issues involving Congress's borrowing power is whether the national government should help state and local governments with their debts. In 2016, Puerto Rico's accumulated debts forced it to begin repudiating some of these debts and to seek authority for bankruptcy from the Congress. More generally, state and local governments have huge debt obligations, and the Great Recession of 2008 hurt state and local tax revenues. In recent years, several local governments have gone into bankruptcy due to their debt problems. Although no state has defaulted on its debt since the Great Depression (federal law prohibits states from declaring bankruptcy), many states are financially distressed. If any state were to default, it likely would negatively affect the ability of all states to borrow money. This would likely set off a domino effect, causing other states to default because they cannot borrow new funds. Also, states would be forced to reduce expenditures for capital projects if the bond markets become frozen due to another state defaulting, which would negatively impact the national economy. The national government could contain this problem if it was willing to bail out financially distressed states, but some members of Congress fear bailing out states because they think it will set a dangerous precedent. As Puerto Rico's bankruptcy exemplifies, many state and local governments face a similar prospect of bankruptcy. This is an issue that will likely be brought up again in the near future.

Probably the biggest issue surrounding Congress's borrowing power that the United States faces is what would happen if the United States hits the debt ceiling and Congress refuses to authorize further borrowing. If this occurs, the United States would default on its debts. Many economists believe this would have a severe negative impact on the American economy. A default would almost assuredly increase borrowing cost for the United States. Although the United States has never official defaulted, in 1979 computer malfunctions lead to some treasury payments being delayed. This led to a permanent increase of six-tenths of a percent in interest, which cost the government almost $12,000,000,000.

Some members of Congress have proposed that Congress should eliminate the debt limit to prevent this from occurring, but that seems unlikely, at least in the near future. If congressional inaction on the debt limit forces a default, it will likely lead to conflict between the Congress and the president. During the 2013 fight over raising the debt limit, former president Bill Clinton suggested the president could invoke section 4 of the 14th Amendment and order the Treasury Department to ignore the debt limit and continue borrowing money. While the constitutionality of the debt limit is questionable, it is doubtful Congress would willingly accept a president violating its will in such a fashion. Going forward, though, many observers assert that Congress needs to take greater care to make sure that fights over the debt ceiling do not harm the country.

FURTHER READING

Austin, D. Andrew. 2010. *Debt Limit: History and Recent Increases*. Collingdale, PA: Diane Publishing.

Buchanan, Neil H., and Michael C. Dorf. 2012. "How to Choose the Least Unconstitutional Option: Lessons for the President (and Others) from the Debt Ceiling Standoff." *Columbia Law Review* 112: 1175-1243.

Hamilton, Alexander. 1790. *Report of the Secretary of the Treasury to the House of Representatives, relative to a provision for the support of the public credit of the United States*. New York: Francis Childs and John Swaine.

Krishnakumar, Anita S. 2005. "In Defense of the Debt Limit Statute." *Harvard Journal on Legislation* 42: 135.

Ostro, Zachary K. 2014. "In the Debt We Trust: The Unconstitutionality of Defaulting on American Financial Obligations, and the Political Implications of Their Perpetual Validity." *Harvard Journal on Legislation* 51: 241.

Robinson, Marshall A. 1959. *The National Debt Ceiling: An Experiment in Fiscal Policy*. Washington DC: Brookings Institution.

3 THE POWER TO REGULATE COMMERCE

Brien Hallett

Article I, section 8, clause 3
To regulate commerce with foreign nations, and among the several states, and
with the Indian tribes.

KEY TERMS

Concurrent powers are powers shared by both the federal and the state governments in a federal system. Both levels of government may exercise these powers over the same territory, people, or subject matter at the same time. The distinction is with "states' rights"—powers reserved to the states under the Tenth Amendment—and "exclusive federal powers," powers reserved to the federal government that can be exercised by the states only with permission of the federal government.

Dictum (singular)/**dicta** (plural) are "things that are said." In a judicial context, **obiter dictum** are "things that are said *in passing*" by a judge in an opinion. The judge finds the information or opinions expressed "in passing" to be indirectly persuasive, but not directly relevant either to the case or to his decision. Consequently, what is said "in passing" should not serve as a precedent.

The **"dormant" commerce clause** (or "negative" commerce clause) is a self-executing power that prohibits states from improperly discriminating against interstate commerce, without congressional permission. Even when the Congress has not enacted a positive law, the "dormant" congressional power to regulate commerce "among the several states" is still plenary and renders null any such state law.

Intrastate refers to any matter that occurs exclusively within the boundary of a state, any occurrence that does not cross the territorial or jurisdictional limits of a state.

Interstate refers to any matter that involves two or more states, any occurrence that does cross the territorial or jurisdictional limits of a state.

Police powers are the traditional powers of the "city" to protect the health, safety, welfare, and morals of its citizens. Examples would include zoning and land use regulations; the licensing of professionals; fire and building codes; motor vehicle, bicycle, and parking rules; racial and other discrimination; gambling and other criminal laws; liquor laws; nuisance ordinances, schooling, sanitation, and the like.

Under the Constitution, the "police powers" of the states are guaranteed by the Tenth Amendment: "The powers not delegated to the United States by the Constitution, nor prohibited by it to the States, are reserved to the States respectively, or to the people." Any state law enacted as an exercise of the state's "police powers" that does not protect the health, safety, welfare, and morals will be found unconstitutional.

HISTORY AND DEVELOPMENT

The treatment of trade and commerce in the Articles of Confederation and Perpetual Union was starkly different than in the Constitution of the United States. During and after the Revolution, all agreed that a flourishing trade and commerce among the states, with foreign nations, and with the Indian tribes, was vital for economic prosperity. All agreed as well that developing a national market was essential for ensuring this prosperity. To develop a national market required uniform regulations across the nation, of duties, impositions, and other restrictions. If individual states were able to impose local duties, impositions, and restrictions, the market would soon fragment and prosperity would diminish as trade and commerce were strangled.

The Federal Convention resolved this dilemma succinctly and forcefully by granting to the Congress the plenary power "To regulate commerce with foreign nations, and among the several states, and with the Indian tribes." The Federal Convention further backed up this plenary power with two additional provisions: Art. I, §9, cl. 5, the export taxation clause, "No Tax or Duty shall be laid on Articles exported from any State"; and Art. I, §10, cl. 2, the import-export clause:

> No State shall, without the Consent of the Congress, lay any Imposts or Duties on Imports or Exports, except what may be absolutely necessary for executing its inspection Laws: and the net Produce of all Duties and Imposts, laid by any State on Imports or Exports, shall be for the Use of the Treasury of the United States; and all such Laws shall be subject to the Revision and Controul of the Congress.

Taken together, little doubt remained which level of government would regulate commerce.

In stark contrast, the Articles had waffled. For example, Article IV announced the desirability of free trade in a national market, but hoped to achieve this beneficial goal without uniform rules and regulations. The "free citizens" of other states would be "entitled" to enter and leave each state with their goods and would be subject to the same regulations as native "free citizens," but each state would make its own regulations:

> The better to secure and perpetuate mutual friendship and intercourse among the people of the different States in this Union, the free inhabitants of each of

these States, paupers, vagabonds, and fugitives from justice excepted, shall be entitled to all privileges and immunities of free citizens in the several States; and the people of each State shall free ingress and regress to and from any other State, and shall enjoy therein all the privileges of trade and commerce, subject to the same duties, impositions, and restrictions as the inhabitants thereof respectively, provided that such restrictions shall not extend so far as to prevent the removal of property imported into any State, to any other State, of which the owner is an inhabitant; provided also that no imposition, duties or restriction shall be laid by any State, on the property of the United States, or either of them.

However well-intentioned this hope might have been, it could only lead to a fragmentation of the national market. More, this fragmentation was reinforced in Article IX:

The United States in Congress assembled, shall have the sole and exclusive right and power of . . . entering into treaties and alliances, provided that no treaty of commerce shall be made whereby the legislative power of the respective States shall be restrained from imposing such imposts and duties on foreigners, as their own people are subjected to, or from prohibiting the exportation or importation of any species of goods or commodities whatsoever . . . [and of] regulating the trade and managing all affairs with the Indians, not members of any of the States, provided that the legislative right of any State within its own limits be not infringed or violated.

In effect, the Confederal Congress was not given any power to regulate interstate commerce and only limited power to regulate foreign trade indirectly through its treaty powers. It could "regulate" trade with the Indian tribes, but only in the unorganized lands west of the Appalachian Mountains, far outside the reach of the thirteen state legislatures. As one might expect, the national market soon fragmented, and economic recovery from the Revolutionary War was hindered as a result.

Overcoming these negative economic impacts became one of the primary factors that motivated the delegates who met in Philadelphia between Friday, May 25, and Monday, September 17, 1787. For example, writing to James Madison as early as November 30, 1785, George Washington argued that

The proposition [for the regulation of a national commercial system] in my opinion is so self evident that I confess I am at a loss to discover wherein lies the weight of the objection to the measure. We are either a united people, or we are not. If the former, let us, in all matters of a general concern act as a nation, which have national objects to promote, and a national character to support. If we are not, let us no longer act a farce by pretending it to be.

With this in mind, Edmund Randolph introduced the Virginia Plan at the Federal Convention on Tuesday, May 29, 1787, the first day of substantive debate. Among the provisions of the Plan, Randolph suggested that "there were many advantages, which the U.S. might acquire, which were not attainable under the confederation—such as a productive impost [i.e., taxes]—counteraction of the commercial regulations of other nations—pushing of commerce ad libitum [at pleasure]—&c &c."

Two weeks later, on Friday, June 15, 1787, William Paterson introduced the New Jersey Plan in response to the Virginia Plan. The second resolution of this plan proposed to empower Congress "to pass Acts for the regulation of trade & Commerce as well with foreign nations as with each other." "As with each other" was, of course, the critical power missing from the Articles of Confederation. With little controversy, this provision became "To regulate commerce with foreign nations, and among the several states" on Monday, August 6, 1787, when the Committee on Detail &c. reported out its initial draft the Constitution. Then, on Wednesday, September 12, 1787, the Committee on Style reported out the final text, which added "and with the Indian tribes." A final debate ensued on the entire draft, which was amended in a number of other places. The amended draft was approved unanimously on Saturday, September 15, 1787.

As amended, the commerce clause gives the Congress a plenary, but not unlimited, power "To regulate commerce." Some undefined limits exist. These limits are to be found in the specification that this plenary congressional power extends only to regulating "commerce with foreign nations, and among the several states, and with the Indian tribes." Hence, the story of the commerce clause since 1787 is an oxymoronic one. It is the story of clarifying the limits of this plenary power.

In searching for these limits, the Supreme Court has seldom disagreed with the Congress in regards to regulating commerce with foreign nations and with the Indian tribes. In these two areas, congressional power is truly plenary. The battleground, instead, has been interstate commerce. In this area, the Court's struggle has been one of defining a domain of "exclusively internal commerce," a domain into which the plenary power of the Congress may not intrude. This struggle has gone through four phases according to Laurence Tribe: from 1824 until 1887, from 1887 until 1937, from 1937 until 1995, and since 1995.

A Substantial Economic Effect, 1824–1887

The story begins, as with so many other constitutional stories, with *obiter dictum* written by Chief Justice John Marshall, in this case, in *Gibbons v. Ogden* (1824). Of equal importance, however, is Justice William Johnson's very significant concurring opinion. In 1808, Robert Fulton and Robert Livingston received a monopoly from the State of New York to sail steamboats on all navigable waters in the state. In 1815, Aaron Ogden purchased from Livingston the right to sail between certain points in New Jersey and New York City. Thomas Gibbons subsequently obtained a license under the Federal Coasting Act of 1793 to establish a competing service between Elizabethtown, New Jersey, and New York City. Ogden brought suit against Gibbons in the New York courts for violation of his monopoly rights. The New York courts granted a permanent injunction against Gibbons in 1820. On appeal to the Supreme Court, Ogden's lawyers argued that many states had passed similar laws that "affected" interstate commerce and that this was permissible because the states held "concurrent" powers with the Congress in matters of commerce. Hence, the New York law overrode Gibbons's federal license. Gibbons's lawyer, Daniel Webster, argued, no, that the regulation of commerce was an exclusive, plenary congressional power under the commerce clause. Hence, the Federal Coasting Act of 1793 trumped the New York monopoly.

In Marshall's opinion, the case was decided for Gibbons on the narrow grounds of the supremacy clause (Art. VI, §2). The New York monopoly conflicted with the Federal Coasting Act of 1793; federal laws are "supreme"; therefore, the state statute fell. He preceded this narrow decision, however, with an extensive discussion of the commerce clause, "in passing." First, he adopted an expansive definition of "commerce": "Commerce, undoubtedly, is traffic, but it is something more: it is intercourse. It describes the commercial intercourse between nations, and parts of nations, in all its branches, and is regulated by prescribing rules for carrying on that intercourse." Next, he compared foreign to interstate commerce: "But, in regulating commerce with foreign nations, the power of Congress does not stop at the jurisdictional lines of the several States. It would be a very useless power if it could not pass those lines." In the same manner, "Commerce among the States cannot stop at the external boundary line of each State, but may be introduced into the interior."

Once he had expanded the definition to "intercourse" and "introduced" commerce "into the interior" of the states, Marshall had enunciated what Laurence Tribe calls an empirical principle of "substantial economic effect." When a state law exceeds its general police powers and, instead, produces a "substantial economic effect" on commerce, it violates the commerce clause and must be struck down. This empirical principle of "substantial economic effect" governed Court rulings on the commerce clause over the next sixty years. Further, during this same period, Congress passed very few laws regulating commerce. Hence, during this sixty-year period, the cases brought before the Supreme Court dealt with the constitutionality of state laws, as in *Gibbons v. Ogden*, and not with constitutionality of congressional enactments. The constitutionality of congressional enactments would only come after 1887 with the enactment of the Interstate Commerce Commission, which regulated the railroads, and the Sherman Antitrust Act of 1890.

However, Marshall's *obiter dictum* did not stop there. He also asked, "What is this power? It is the power to regulate, that is, to prescribe the rule by which commerce is to be governed. This power, like all others vested in Congress, is complete in itself, may be exercised to its utmost extent, and acknowledges no limitations other than are prescribed [elsewhere] in the Constitution":

> Comprehensive as the word "among" is, it may very properly be restricted to that commerce which concerns more States than one . . . the enumeration of the particular classes of commerce [foreign, interstate, with the Indian tribes] to which the power was to be extended would not have been made had the intention been to extend the power to every description [of commerce]. The enumeration presupposes something not enumerated, and that something, if we regard the language or the subject of the sentence, must be the exclusively internal commerce of a State. . . . The completely internal commerce of a State, then, may be considered as reserved for the State itself.

The states do not have a "concurrent" power in matters of foreign or interstate commerce and commerce with the Indian tribes, as Gibbons's attorneys had argued. But they do regulate purely intrastate commerce, commerce that occurs entirely within the "interior" of a state. And this is in addition to their normal police, taxing, and other powers that "affect" commerce "indirectly." Marshall enunciated the principle, but Justice Johnson's concurring opinion spoke more directly to the issue.

In his concurring opinion, Justice Johnson introduced what came to be called the "dormant" commerce clause. Even when the Congress has not passed a law specifically regulating some aspect of interstate commerce, any state law that does so is still unconstitutional. In other words, the commerce clause is reinforced by the supremacy clause but is not dependent on it. The nullification of a state law, according to Johnson, does not require the existence of a conflicting federal law, as was the case in *Gibbons v. Ogden*. This is so because the mere existence of the state law is an encroachment upon the plenary commerce clause power of the Congress, which is effective even when it is inactive or "dormant."

In Justice Johnson's words, "By common consent, those [state] laws [concerning commerce] dropped lifeless from their statute books [after the ratification of the Constitution] for want of the sustaining power that had been relinquished [by the states] to Congress." Accordingly, "I cannot overcome the conviction that, if the licensing act [i.e., the Federal Coasting Act of 1793] was repealed tomorrow, the rights of the appellant [Gibbons] to a reversal of the decision complained of would be as strong as it is under this license." Johnson's *obiter dictum* set the stage for the next sixty years of commerce clause litigation.

Formality, 1887–1937

With the Industrial Revolution and rapid urbanization after the Civil War, the nation's economy changed rapidly. The largely local, agrarian economy of antebellum America was transformed into an increasingly national, industrial economy. In particular, mining and manufacturing exploded as a larger and larger share of the economy, while agriculture developed on an industrial scale to feed the rapidly growing cities. A truly national economy, naturally, needed national regulations, which the Congress slowly proceeded to legislate. This new congressional legislation collided, however, with three realities: First, steamships and railroads moved across state borders. Second, the newly important mines, factories, and farms did not move across state borders. They appeared to be entirely local, entirely intrastate endeavors. Third, national regulations inevitably meant the demise of local, state regulations. This demise upended the "federal" character of the Constitution, as previously understood.

With regard to the first reality, national regulation of transportation was fully constitutional. In 1886, the Supreme Court ruled in *Wabash, St. Louis & Pacific Railway Company v. Illinois* that state regulations of interstate railroads were unconstitutional under the commerce clause. Although local responses to local needs were very desirable, the Court reasoned, whenever the local response became too disruptive of the national uniformity required for national prosperity, local regulations must fall to federal regulation of interstate commerce. This ruling led the next year to the Interstate Commerce Act of 1887, the first federal law to regulate a private industry. The

Interstate Commerce Act was soon followed the Sherman Antitrust Act of 1890, a second act to regulate private businesses.

In essence, *Wabash* concluded that a national transportation network could not operate successfully if several different states imposed several different regulations on it. If any doubt existed on this point, the principle was confirmed most forcefully in the *Shreveport Rate Case* (1914). As Chief Justice Charles Evans Hughes wrote,

> Wherever the interstate and intrastate transactions of carriers are so related that the government of the one involves the control of the other, it is Congress, and not the State, that is entitled to prescribe the final and dominant rule, for otherwise Congress would be denied the exercise of its constitutional authority [under the commerce clause] and the State, and not the Nation, would be supreme within the national field.

But, if Marshall's "substantial economic effect" test continued to decide cases where commerce could be defined narrowly as "traffic," what about the new mining, manufacturing, and agricultural industries that did not move? Should they not be decided with a different test that preserved a modicum of power to the state legislatures?

To settle this question, the second and third realities came into play. Marshall had noted that, "The enumeration [of congressional powers] presupposes something not enumerated, and that something, if we regard the language or the subject of the sentence [of the commerce clause], must be the exclusively internal commerce of a State." In search of this "exclusively internal commerce," the Supreme Court, after the Civil War, seized upon a "formal classification." That is, it made a formal distinction between interstate transportation industries that obviously crossed state lines and intrastate mining, manufacturing, and agricultural industries that did not. As the Court ruled in *Kidd v. Pearson* (1888):

> If it be held that the term ["commerce"] includes the regulation of all such manufactures as are intended to be the subject of commercial transactions in the future, it is impossible to deny that it would also include all productive industries that contemplate the same thing. The result would be that Congress would be invested, to the exclusion of the states, with the power to regulate not only manufacture, but also agriculture, horticulture, stock-raising, domestic fisheries, mining—in short, every branch of human industry . . . The power being vested in Congress and denied to the states, it would follow as an inevitable result that the duty would devolve on Congress to regulate all of these delicate, multiform, and vital interests—interests which in their nature are, and must be, local in all the details of their successful management.

Thus, by reverting to a narrow definition of commerce as "traffic," the Court could hope to carve out a "formal" domain of "exclusively internal commerce." Armed with this formal classification, the Court's attention turned from invalidating state laws under the "dormant" commerce clause to invalidating congressional laws that did not meet the "movement" requirement of commerce as "traffic."

The first federal law overturned by the Supreme Court on the grounds that it exceeded the congressional powers under the commerce clause was *United States v. DeWitt* (1870). The Internal Revenue Act of 1867 had outlawed the sale of naphtha and illuminating oils inflammable at less than 110°F for obvious safety reasons. This regulation, the Court decided, could have "no constitutional operation" within the "territorial" limits of any state because the regulation was in fact a police regulation for the purpose of health, safety, and welfare. It was not a regulation of commerce "among the several states." In other words, the act trampled upon the internal trade of the states and simultaneously diminished the police powers of those same states. By these same facts, however, the regulation was constitutional in the Western territories of the United States and in the District of Columbia, where all state legislation was excluded, "territorially."

United States v. DeWitt was a harbinger because the heart of the decision was the fact that the regulation violated the police powers of the states. The Court's frontal assault on the congressional commerce powers had to await *United States v. E. C. Knight* (1895). In an 8–1 decision, the Supreme Court found that the purchase of stock in four Philadelphia sugar refineries by the American Sugar Refining Company did not violate the Sherman Antitrust Act because "Commerce succeeds to manufacture, and is not a part of it. The power to regulate commerce is the power to prescribe the rule by which commerce shall be governed, and is a power independent of the power to suppress monopoly." The suppression of monopolies, of course, was the purpose of the Sherman Antitrust Act. But, since the creation of the monopoly bore "no direct relation to commerce between the states or with foreign nations," only an "indirect relation," therefore:

> It is vital that the independence of the commercial power and of the police power, and the delimitation between them, however sometimes perplexing, should always be recognized and observed, for while the one furnishes the strongest bond of union, the other is essential to the preservation of the autonomy of the states as required by our dual form of government, and acknowledged evils, however grave and urgent they may appear to be, had better be borne, than the risk be run, in the effort to suppress them, of more serious consequences by resort to expedients of even doubtful constitutionality.

Monopolies may be bad, but weakening "the autonomy of the states as required by our dual form of government" was worse, in the Court's opinion.

Still, the need to tame and regulate the Industrial Revolution could not be ignored, especially after the Great Depression commenced in 1929. This said, one must keep the adoption of a "formal classification" in perspective. In particular, the Supreme Court's restrictive commerce decisions between 1887 and October 1937 were part and parcel of a more general reaction to rapid industrialization and a desire to preserve some local, state prerogatives. A signal example of this in tax law was the Court's 1895 decision in *Pollock v. Farmers Loan Trust Co.* declaring the 1894 federal income tax unconstitutional. An income tax, a divided Court ruled 5–4, was a "direct tax" that was not "apportioned" among the states on the basis of population in accordance with Art.

I, §2 and Art. I, §9, cl. 5 (See Chapter 1). The constitutionality of the federal income tax was not assured until 1913 and the ratification of the Sixteenth Amendment.

Further, this restrictive period also overlaps with the so-called "Lochner era." *Lochner v. New York* (1905) abrogated many state and federal laws regulating working conditions on Fourteenth Amendment "due process" grounds. In *Lochner*, the Supreme Court held that New York could not legislate that "no employee shall be . . . permitted to work in a biscuit, bread, or cake bakery or confectionery establishment more than sixty hours in any one week." Such a rule interfered "with the right of contract between the employer and employees," because "the general right to make a contract in relation to his business is part of the liberty of the individual protected by the Fourteenth Amendment of the Federal Constitution" (See Chapter 19). The Court's reading of the "substantive right" to enter into contracts into the Fourteenth Amendment's protection of "procedural rights" was overturned in 1937 by *West Coast Hotel Co. v. Parrish*, at the same time as the Court reversed its restrictive commerce clause decisions.

And, finally, in the end, the Court invalidated only eight congressional laws between 1887 and 1937, and none successfully thereafter, until 1995. The last of these overturnings occurred in 1935, when the Court abrogated Title I of the National Industrial Recovery Act of 1933 (NIRA)—one of President Franklin Roosevelt's first pieces of "New Deal" legislation after his election in 1932. The act had two titles, both of which aimed to stimulate the economy and reduce unemployment. Title II funded a large program of public works and established the Public Works Administration to oversee the program. Title II was not constitutionally controversial; Title I was. To encourage recovery, Title I regulated the price and transportation of certain petroleum products, guaranteed union rights, regulated working standards, and authorized the writing of industrial codes to regulate industries, as opposed to labor. *Schechter Poultry Corp. v. United States* (1935) became the case with which the Court found Title I of the NIRA unconstitutional.

The Schechter Poultry Corp. bought live poultry from commissioners in New York City and Philadelphia and sold the slaughtered poultry to kosher retail stores in Brooklyn. Although most of the live poultry had come from outside New York State, Schechter's slaughtering and delivery business was entirely local. During 1934, Schechter was charged with selling "unfit chickens," among several other violations of the Live Poultry Code. This industrial code was one of many that had been written under Title I of the NIRA.

In reversing the conviction of Schechter Poultry Corp., Chief Justice Charles Evans Hughes, writing for the majority, could find very little in Title I that was constitutional. Many of the terms used in Title I, such as "fair competition," were unconstitutionally vague. Worse, Title I was an entirely unacceptable delegation to the president of the unshared legislative power of the Congress. The industrial codes would be, in effect, laws that the Congress had not written. In addition, the ambiguous "fair labor" provisions of Title I violated the commerce clause:

> [Concerning,] . . . the provisions of the Code as to the hours and wages of those employed in defendants' slaughterhouse markets. It is plain that these requirements are imposed in order to govern the details of defendants' management

of their local business. The persons employed in slaughtering and selling in local trade are not employed in interstate commerce. Their hours and wages have no direct relation to interstate commerce."

But, finally, the entire title was deeply destructive of the federal system itself because Schechter's business never entered the "*'current'* or *'flow'* of interstate commerce." "So far as the poultry here in question is concerned, the flow in interstate commerce had ceased. The poultry had come to a permanent rest within the State." Consequently:

> Although the validity of the [Industrial] codes (apart from the question of delegation) rests upon the commerce clause of the Constitution, . . . If the commerce clause were construed to reach all enterprise and transactions which could be said to have an indirect effect upon interstate commerce, the federal authority would embrace practically all the activities of the people, and the authority of the State over its domestic concerns would exist only by sufferance of the federal government . . . the distinction between direct and indirect effects of intrastate transactions upon interstate commerce must be recognized as a fundamental one, essential to the maintenance of our constitutional system. Otherwise, as we have said, there would be virtually no limit to the federal power, and, for all practical purposes, we should have a completely centralized government.

If anyone had any further doubts of the Court's opinion of President Roosevelt's New Deal, Chief Justice Hughes concluded that "Extraordinary conditions [of the Great Depression] may call for extraordinary remedies. But the argument necessarily stops short of an attempt to justify action which lies outside the sphere of constitutional authority. Extraordinary conditions do not create or enlarge constitutional power."

A Substantial Economic Effect, 1937–1995

In the same year that Chief Justice Charles Evans Hughes found Title I of the NIRA unconstitutional, Congress passed the National Labor Relations Act of 1935, better known as the Wagner Act. Going much further than the labor provisions of Title I of the NIRA, the Wagner Act ensured the right of private-sector workers to form unions and bargain collectively. It also established National Labor Relations Board (NLRB) to conduct elections among workers to determine whether they wanted to form a union or not and to enforce the provisions of the act on employers. The Wagner Act did not cover railroad workers, who were covered under the Railway Labor Act of 1926. Nor did it cover public employees and several other categories of workers.

The employees at Jones & Laughlin Steel attempted to organize under the Wagner Act against the wishes of the company. To show its displeasure, the company fired ten employees for their organizing activities. When the NLRB ordered the company to stop interfering with the organizing effort and to reinstate the ten employees, Jones & Laughlin sued on the grounds that, under the commerce clause, the Wagner Act was as unconstitutional as Title I of the NIRA.

National Labor Relations Board v. Jones & Laughlin Steel Corporation came before the Court in 1937. Between 1935 and 1937, the "extraordinary" severity of the Great Depression and the "extraordinary" public opinion in favor of the New Deal had become more and more apparent. In what many saw as a complete reversal, Chief Justice Charles Evans Hughes upheld the Wagner Act, saying that "Although activities may be intrastate in character when separately considered, if they have such a close and substantial relation to interstate commerce that their control is essential or appropriate to protect that commerce from burdens and obstructions, Congress cannot be denied the power to exercise that control."

With this, the fifty-year era of defining commerce as "traffic" and the use of a "formal classification" of commerce was over. No longer would transportation be classified as interstate commerce and mining, manufacturing, and agriculture as intrastate commerce. The Court would no longer seek to preserve a domain of "exclusively internal commerce" within which state legislative powers could regulate intrastate commerce. The Supreme Court had returned to Marshall's "substantial economic effect" standard. Not only would the Court uphold all subsequent New Deal legislation, but it soon expanded its standards to include what Laurence Tribe calls a "protective principle" and a "cumulative effect" standard (Tribe 2000). The Court now extended the reach of the commerce clause not just to single acts of intrastate commerce, but to internal acts that "cumulatively" or "in the aggregate" affect interstate commerce, such as strikes in the auto industry. The only requirement now is that the Congress finds a "rational basis" for the law. Likewise, the Court ruled that Title II of the Civil Rights Act of 1964, banning discrimination "on the grounds of race, color, religion, of national origins," was a permitted use of the commerce clause. It did so in *Heart of Atlanta Motel v. United States* (1964). Ensuring that all persons traveling across state boundaries could find suitable public accommodations, the Court ruled, was indeed a "rational basis" for outlawing discrimination and segregation in motels and restaurants under the commerce clause.

The New Federalism, 1995–2005

Still, it must be said, as Chief Justice Marshall put it, that "The enumeration [of congressional powers] presupposes something not enumerated," and that, in the words of Chief Justice Charles Evans Hughes, unless the "something not enumerated" can be defined, "there would be virtually no limit to the federal power, and, for all practical purposes, we should have a completely centralized government." Had the New Deal's use of the commerce clause swept away all of these "Federalism" concerns? In the minds of many, most certainly, yes—but not in the minds of others, including Supreme Court Justice William Rehnquist.

William Rehnquist was nominated as an Associate Justice by President Richard Nixon in 1971 and elevated to Chief Justice by President Ronald Reagan in 1986. He subsequently served as Chief Justice until his death in 2005. His "New Federalism" concerns with the commerce clause were first voiced in 1976 in *National League of Cities v. Usery*—which, however, was overturned in 1985 in *Garcia v. San Antonio Metropolitan Transit Authority*. Ignoring this setback, he finally succeeded in establishing his "New Federalism" concerns with the commerce clause in *United States v. Lopez* (1995), after Presidents Ronald Reagan and George H. W. Bush had appointed several like-minded justices to the Supreme Court.

In general, *National League of Cities* asked whether the federal government could set labor standards for *all* state and local government employees. In particular, *National League of Cities* called into question the constitutionality of several of the 1974 amendments to the Wagner Act—i.e., the Fair Labor Standards Act of 1938. The constitutionality of the original act was not in question. This key piece of New Deal legislation had been upheld in *United States v. Darby Lumber Co.* (1941). In 1938, the act had established national labor standards for private-sector "industrial" workers: a forty-hour work week, "time and a half" for overtime. It had also banned child labor and set a national minimum wage of $0.25, or $4.19 in 2015 dollars. Like Title I of the NIRA, the original Fair Labor Standards Act did not cover several categories of workers, most notably public employees at the state and local levels. In 1961, an amendment to the act extended its provisions to several new groups, including school employees and health care workers, many of whom work for state and local agencies. At the same time, the minimum wage was raised to $1.25, or $9.65 in 2015 dollars. The wage hike became effective in 1963. In 1966, five years before Rehnquist's 1971 nomination to the Court, coverage was expanded again to include many, but not all, state and local government workers. The minimum wage was also raised, effective in 1968, to $1.60—or $10.86 in 2015 dollars. Then, in 1974, three years after Rehnquist's 1971 nomination to the Court, the minimum wage was again raised, effective in 1976, to $2.30, or $9.55 in 2015 dollars. Critically though, this amendment also extended the new minimum wage and hours to all the other state and local employees who had not previously been covered. In effect, *all* the power of state and local legislators to determine the wages and hours of *all* their employees had been taken away.

In *National League of Cities v. Usery* (1976), Associate Justice Rehnquist argued for the 5–4 majority that the ever-expanding scope of the commerce clause had now come into conflict with a set of "traditional activities" of state and local governments—setting wages and working conditions for their employees—and, hence, bumped up against the restraints of the Tenth Amendment, "The powers not delegated to the United States by the Constitution, nor prohibited by it to the States, are reserved to the States respectively, or to the people":

> the dispositive factor is that Congress has attempted to exercise its Commerce Clause authority to prescribe minimum wages and maximum hours to be paid by the States in their capacities as sovereign governments. In so doing, Congress has sought to wield its power in a fashion that would impair the States' "ability to function effectively in a federal system." This exercise of congressional authority does not comport with the federal system of government embodied in the Constitution. We hold that, insofar as the challenged amendments operate to directly displace the States' freedom to structure integral operations in areas of traditional governmental functions, they are not within the authority granted Congress by Art. I, § 8, cl. 3.

Significantly, Justice Harry Blackmun concurred with the opinion because Rehnquist had adopted "a balancing approach, and does not outlaw federal power in [other] areas such as environmental protection." Subsequently, however, in *Garcia v. San Antonio Metropolitan Transit Authority* (1985), Blackmun changed his mind and concluded that Rehnquist's approach did in fact not "balance" the "traditional aspects of state sovereignty" with the need for the regulation of a national economy. With Blackmun's change of heart, the expansive powers of the commerce clause since the New Deal appeared to be as strong as ever. Until *United States v. Alfonso D. Lopez, Jr.* (1995), that is.

The Gun-Free School Zone Act of 1990 outlawed the unauthorized carrying of a gun within a thousand feet of a school. On March 10, 1992, Alfonso Lopez, Jr., a 12th-grade student at Edison High School in San Antonio, Texas, was arrested for possessing an unloaded .38 caliber revolver in school. After his conviction, he appealed on the basis that the Gun-Free School Zone Act was an unconstitutional exercise of the commerce clause. With the retirement of Justice Blackmun in 1994 and the arrival of several conservative justices, Chief Justice Rehnquist was able to secure a majority decision in *Lopez* holding, that, indeed, the Gun-Free School Zone Act was an unconstitutional exercise of the commerce clause. What the law actually did, according to the Court's decision, was to create a criminal offense. On the one hand, enacting criminal laws is more properly seen as an exercise of the states' traditional police powers. On the other hand, guns carried to a school had an insufficient nexus with interstate commerce. The gun may well have travelled in interstate commerce, but neither Lopez nor the school had done so. To qualify as interstate commerce, Rehnquist summarized, involved either 1) movement through the channels of interstate commerce, or 2) instrumentalities of or the persons and things in interstate commerce, or 3) activities substantially affected by or related to interstate commerce. A high school senior carrying a gun to school simply did not meet any of the three tests, especially the third. Hence:

> To uphold the Government's contentions here, we would have to pile inference upon inference in a manner that would bid fair to convert congressional authority under the Commerce Clause to a general police power of the sort retained by the States. Admittedly, some of our prior cases have taken long steps down that road, giving great deference to congressional action. The broad language in these opinions has suggested the possibility of additional expansion, but we decline here to proceed [*sic*] any further. To do so would require us to conclude that the Constitution's enumeration of powers does not presuppose something not enumerated, and that there never will be a distinction between what is truly national and what is truly local. This we are unwilling to do.

Unlike *National League of Cities*, *Lopez* has not yet been overturned. Indeed, it was affirmed in *United States v. Morrison* (2000), which overturned certain provisions of the Violence Against Women Act of 1994.

Still, *Lopez* did not so much limit congressional power under the commerce clause as require clearer, less hasty drafting of its laws. Subsequent to the decision, Attorney

General Janet Reno noted that virtually all guns enter interstate commerce at some point. If, she suggested, the act were amended to reflect this fact, it would meet the Rehnquist Court's tests. This was done in 1996. Since then, the amended Gun-Free School Zone Act has been upheld by a number of lower courts and none of the convictions overturned.

FUTURE IMPLICATIONS

After William Rehnquist's death in 2005, John Roberts was appointed Chief Justice by President George W. Bush. Roberts had served as a law clerk for Rehnquist during the 1980s when Rehnquist was still a young associate justice. Roberts was generally in sympathy with Rehnquist's judicial philosophy, especially on his "New Federalism" concerns. In 2011, the constitutionality of President Barack Obama's Patient Protection and Affordable Care Act of 2010 (also known as Obamacare) came before his Court. The most controversial part of the act was the "individual mandate," which required individuals to either purchase health insurance or pay a "penalty" for not doing so. Congress had justified this provision under its commerce clause powers. Congress had, however, ignored the lesson of *Lopez*, that clear and careful drafting was required whenever it invoked the commerce clause. Chief Justice Roberts, writing for the majority, concluded that the mandate was unconstitutional under the commerce clause, but that the "penalty" was constitutional under the congressional taxing power, Art. §8, cl. 1.

Thus, the future of the commerce clause will be as oxymoronic as its past. Ever since the Civil War and the advent of the Industrial Revolution and urbanization, Congress has struggled to build and regulate a national market by using the plenary of the commerce clause. In response, the Court has periodically struggled to define the limits of this unlimited, plenary power, to find the "something not enumerated" in the commerce clause that will define a domain of exclusively intrastate commerce. The struggle has not yet ended.

FURTHER READING

Abel, Albert S. 1941. The Commerce Clause in the Constitutional Convention and in Contemporary Comment. *Minnesota Law Review* 25: 432.

Newton, Nell Jessup. 1984. Federal Power Over Indians: Its Sources, Scope, and Limitations. *University of Pennsylvania Law Review* 132: 195.

Philips, Michael J. 2001. *The Lochner Court, Myth and Reality: Substantive Due Process from the 1890s to the 1930s*. Westport, CT: Praeger, Greenwood.

Prakash, Saikrishna. 2003. Our Three Commerce Clauses and the Presumption of Intrasentence Uniformity. *Arkansas Law Review* 55: 1149.

Regan, Donald. 1986. The Supreme Court and State Protectionism: Making Sense of the Dormant Commerce Clause. *Michigan Law Review* 84: 1091.

Tribe, Laurence H. 1978. 2000. *American Constitutional Law*. Mineola, NY: The Foundation Press.

4 THE POWER TO REGULATE IMMIGRATION

Joanna Mosser

Article I, section 8, clause 4
To establish an uniform rule of naturalization . . .

KEY TERMS

Alien: A foreigner living in a country either legally or illegally.
Immigration: The act of moving to another country to live permanently.
Naturalization: The legal process by which immigrants become citizens

One of the most distinguishing features of the U.S. Constitution is its remarkable brevity and the simple, elegant logic of its outline of a general theory and practice of republican government. The document is striking, relative to the sprawling federal governmental apparatus it has nurtured and sustained today, for what it does *not* say—what is missing, implied, self-consciously and strategically omitted or ambiguous, and what can be found or understood only in, and through, many "clues and hints" that emerge throughout. The Constitution is, in short, remarkable for the *capacity* of its silences.

This is especially the case in the Constitution's provisions for immigration and naturalization, two governmental functions that are constitutive of modern understandings of territorial state sovereignty but appear little—and immigration not at all—in the text of the Constitution. Today, the United States regulates entry into the country and access to citizenship through a range of bureaucratic offices located in the Department of Homeland Security, including U.S. Customs and Border Protection (CBP), U.S. Citizenship and Immigration Services (CIS), and U.S. Immigration and Customs Enforcement (ICE). The Constitution does not prescribe or proscribe this bureaucratic order, nor does the subject that motivates the bureaucracy's work—immigration—appear by term in the text. Instead, the Constitution merely, and succinctly, grants to the U.S. Congress the prerogative and duty to "establish an uniform rule of Naturalization."

From the capacious silence and brevity of this single clause comes, first, the statutory apparatus that regulates entry into, and exit from, the United States and access to formal citizenship and, second, the range of federal enforcement agencies charged with administering it. The silences of the text, too, structure the terrain upon which contemporary immigration debates proceed. Indeed, what is missing provides cause, justification, and force for what is notably *present* in modern American immigration politicking: ongoing, and seemingly intractable, conflict between states and the federal government and, within the federal government, between Congress and the president, over the distribution of the authority to regulate entry into and presence within the country. The Constitution's capacious silences, in turn, have been informed by prevailing economic, social, and political demands that shape constructions of the meaning of the text.

HISTORY AND DEVELOPMENT

Naturalization and the Founding

The naturalization function of the state functioned centrally in the Founders' thinking about the Constitution—so centrally, in fact, that it played only a marginal role at the convention, and in the subsequent ratification debate. The topic did not elicit much discussion at the Constitutional Convention, because it was widely understood that the federal government should determine the boundaries of access to citizenship. Among the grievances listed in the Declaration of Independence, for example, is the British colonial state's interference with the American colonies' decisions about "Laws for the Naturalization of Foreigners." The Articles of Confederation, too, were a significant liability during the Revolutionary War and were a foundation for free-riding, failed governance and a hobbled central government. They also fostered competitive, self-protective relationships among the states and allowed each state to establish its own rules for admitting newcomers to citizenship.

The Constitution, then, in demanding that Congress establish a "uniform rule of naturalization," implied what was widely acknowledged and, in Alexander Hamilton's *Federalist* No. 32, expressly stated: individual state powers to separately and variably "prescribe a distinct rule" of naturalization would, by semantic and logical necessity, make a "uniform" rule impossible. James Madison, in *Federalist* No. 42, further remarked that allowing each state to establish rules of access to citizenship would produce "confusion" and "nourish unceasing animosities" among the states, as one person's access to, and enjoyment of, the rights of citizenship in a state might not be recognized in another. The Constitution proffered a largely agreed-upon solution to this dilemma: lodge the state's naturalization authority exclusively in a central government.

Immigration, as such, received even less attention during the Ratification debate between the Federalists and Anti-Federalists. Indeed, the title of this chapter—Congress's "power to regulate immigration"—is something of a misnomer. The U.S.

Constitution does not reference "immigration," except obliquely: the citizenship requirement attached to elected offices (Art. I, §2 and §3; Art. II, §1) and fears that the authority of Congress to regulate interstate commerce would be used to undermine southern commercial interests by restricting the importation and migration of slaves. In conversation, these two issues converged. During the August 9 convention debate, Gouverneur Morris, convention delegate from Pennsylvania, expressed a desire to require fourteen, rather than four, years of citizenship for Senators. Oliver Ellsworth, delegate from Connecticut, worried that such a lengthy time horizon would, in effect, "discourag[e] meritorious aliens from emigrating to this country." Other delegates lamented the "illiberal" intent and implications of the restriction. Charles Pinckney, from South Carolina, nonetheless echoed Gouverneur Morris's concerns, noting that the Senate held significant foreign policy responsibilities and that its members must be free from the tether of "foreign attachments" that only time and distance, presumably, could remedy. Immigration, however, was only obliquely present in the exchange.

Immigration emerged similarly obliquely in the context of conversation about Congress's power to regulate commerce among the states. Several subcommittees were engaged to address southern fears that Congress's commerce authority would be invoked to introduce regulations or prohibitions on the slave trade. A first proposal, produced by the Committee of Detail, chaired by South Carolina's John Rutledge, forbade Congress to end or tax the slave trade. The proposal was deemed, by several delegates, too extreme, inconsistent with the Constitution's interest in guarding the promise of republican self-governance, and problematic in its grant of permanent legitimacy—in Gouverneur Morris's words—to "a nefarious institution." John Rutledge of South Carolina, nonetheless, indicated that "interest must be the governing principle" of the proceedings, that his state's economy depended upon slavery, and that a refusal to limit Congress's commerce power would call into question "whether the Southern States shall or not be parties of the Union."

The success of the emerging constitutional plan pivoted around a compromise that would affirm congressional prerogative to regulate interstate commerce *and* also allay fears sufficient to broker a stable compromise. A successful compromise would, in turn, secure the Constitution's approval. This compromise took the form of a collective agreement to delay talk of, and possible congressional action upon, the slave trade until 1808:

> The Migration or Importation of such Persons any of the States now existing shall think proper to admit, shall not be prohibited by the Congress prior to the Year one thousand eight hundred and eight, but a Tax or duty may be imposed on such Importation, not exceeding ten dollars for each Person. (Art. I, §9.)

The provision is remarkable for its pre-emptive constraint on congressional prerogative and reduction of moral demands to political calculations. It is remarkable, too, for its oblique and passing reference to migration—but those subject to the involuntary, forced migration and importation of their bodies, the document would not, ultimately, affirm as full, rights-bearing political and legal persons.

Naturalization and Immigration in the Early Republic: Inclusive Immigration

Immigration, then, did not factor prominently during the Convention or Ratification debate. Indeed, during the early years of the new American republic, immigration and naturalization proceeded on largely parallel, non-converging courses. They were treated as functionally separate questions—the first, immigration, dealing with the regulation of entry into the territory of the United States, and the second, naturalization, involving the conferral of formal citizen status upon a foreign newcomer. This is remarkable, first, for the way these terms, today, are otherwise used in rhetorical tandem. In the early years of the republic, however, immigration and naturalization were governed by largely separate legal apparatuses and by different political logics—and neither invited nor produced particular controversy. Congress, too, did not claim the immigration function of the federal government until 1875—nearly a century into the nation's existence. Until that time, Congress claimed its textual prerogative to regulate naturalization and impose restrictions on access to citizenship but did little to legally codify, articulate, and enforce a clear sense of the national territorial border.

The federal government's new role governing naturalization did, nonetheless, reflect a departure from historical practice, in which the individual states established separate criteria for admission of aliens to citizenship and arrived at different determinations about what rights "citizen" status implied. The Constitution was intended to resolve the inconvenience of this inconsistency. Lodging exclusive jurisdiction over admission to citizenship to the central government, then, represented a departure from practice under the Articles, but one widely affirmed as necessary.

The first Congresses, accordingly, produced a patchwork of naturalization statutes in the first 25 years of the republic. The first, in 1790, set the residency requirement for naturalization at two years, while a second, in 1795, upped the residency requirement to five years and imposed a requirement that petitioners declare their intention to seek citizenship three years before naturalizing. A third statute, in 1798, one prong of the Alien and Sedition Acts, raised the residency requirement for naturalization from five to fourteen years and, in an early immigration-related move, conferred upon the president the ability, in times of emergency, war, or invasion, to exclude or remove "alien enemy" males from the United States. Each statute also restricted access to citizenship to "free white persons." The 1802 Naturalization Act repealed the 1798 statute, which was alleged to have been motivated by political partisan interests, among the Federalists, in reducing the Democratic-Republican party's foothold among immigrant newcomers; the 1802 act reduced the residency requirement for naturalization to five years. This act also established the basic terrain of federal rules that govern access to citizenship today: that applicants for citizenship be of sound moral character, express allegiance to the Constitution, and formally declare their intent to naturalize, in the presence of witnesses. Together, too, these statutes gave rise to early state-building efforts at the state and local levels; officials had to record and track a newcomer's arrival to provide the records necessary to establish residency vis-à-vis federal naturalization requirements.

Importantly, the range of early statutory efforts that implicated newcomer entry, settlement, and mobility—the 1798 Alien and Sedition Acts, the 1790 and 1795

Naturalization Acts, and the 1819 Steerage Act—anticipated the federal government's future role in regulating territorial entry and exit but were not, properly, "immigration" statutes. The border, as such, had not yet been articulated—institutionalized, that is, through a collection of statutes and a bureaucratic apparatus charged with policing, excluding, and expelling statutorily "illegal" or "unlawful" bodies that violate prohibitions on territorial entry. The notion of immigrant illegality, as such, had not yet been invented.

In fact, early statutes regulated persons for the statist threats and opportunities they presented to a slowly consolidating federal state—not for the fact of the body's legality or illegality. The four prongs of the 1798 Alien and Sedition Acts, for example, were defensive moves motivated by a range of converging partisan/electoral and statist interests. The Alien Friends and Enemies Acts, as referenced above, raised the residency requirement for naturalization (from five to fourteen years) to blunt the effects of new immigrants' sympathies with Democratic-Republican interests. It is important, nonetheless, to position each act in the broader—statist—context in which they emerged. The Federalist Party, certainly, sought to entrench its partisan interests, which meant tracking and regulating the mobility of "foreigners." The Alien and Sedition Acts, nonetheless, register a far more bi- and cross-partisan fear of suppressing opposition, dissent, and organized conspiracy in the context of a new government seeking to consolidate its perceived authority and legitimacy. Congress, in the 1790s, was fresh from the experience of Shays' Rebellion and the Whiskey Rebellion and a legacy of difficulty, under the Articles of Confederation, in marshaling a credible national militia to suppress insurrection. In short, there is reason to suspect that xenophobic motivations and partisan electoral interests combined with cross-partisan structural-institutional demands to incentivize early congressional interest in state-building activities. Congress faced the imperative of building a state apparatus capable of suppressing rebellion and insurrection, whatever the (citizen, non-citizen) source, and manufacturing the perceived necessity of deference to the new federal government.

The 1790 and 1795 Naturalization Acts, similarly, regulated access to citizenship, not territorial entry, exit, and presence. They did so, moreover, under a statist interest in manufacturing an American *people*—a public committed to the habits of republican self-governance. The Constitution affirms the possibility of an "imagined" American "we," but unity had to be self-consciously constructed in the wake of the colonial period and governance under the Articles of Confederation, both of which fostered allegiance to state and locality. The residency requirements imposed by the Naturalization Acts were designed to socialize newcomers to the demands and habits of self-governance. Territorial presence was understood as necessary to this process, and, for much of the nation's first century, political elites were guided by a structuring logic of inclusive immigration and territorial settlement directed to the principles of republican citizenship. State criminal, public charge, and vagrancy laws that regulated the behavioral effects of migration across state borders applied to all bodies, not merely alien non-citizen ones. The 1819 Steerage Act, finally, was an early effort by the fledgling U.S. state to co-opt, codify, and manage bodies; the act introduced a scheme for import duties and imposed reporting requirements that enabled the tracking of newcomers. The idea and practice of an articulable border, of aliens "lawfully" and "unlawfully" present, had not yet been constructed, nor were "aliens" a target of the state or federal government by reason of their foreignness. Indeed, persons, not aliens, were the primary subjects of these early laws—and the laws themselves, not properly understood as immigration statutes.

The Convergence of Naturalization and Immigration

A series of actions in the 1870s and 1880s, nonetheless, defined the contours of access to U.S. citizenship and, for the first time in the republic's history, imposed a set of immigration exclusions designed to regulate entry into the territory of the United States. In short, the period 1875–1882 saw the first convergence of the naturalization and immigration functions of government—and the first time Congress claimed, indirectly, that its constitutional prerogative to regulate access to citizenship implied a like prerogative to regulate alien entry into the United States. In 1875, Congress passed the Page Act, which prohibited criminals and prostitutes from entry into the United States. It also allowed inspection officials at ports of entry to inspect vessels suspected of carrying other such "obnoxious" or "disturbing" persons. Importantly, too, the Page Act responded to growing concerns that, in the wake of the late-1840s gold rush in California and work on the first transcontinental railroad in the 1850s and '60s, a market in involuntary labor among Chinese and Japanese workers was depressing local labor markets. The act, accordingly, required that all Chinese and Japanese newcomers to the United States come by "free and voluntary consent."

Nonetheless, the law did not contain a deportation provision—something that, today, we regard as central to border enforcement. The Page Act anticipated the Chinese Exclusion Act of 1882, which suspended the immigration of Chinese laborers to the United States for ten years, pushed for the deportation of Chinese illegally in the country, and barred Chinese from naturalization, under the justification that the presence of Chinese laborers was "endanger[ing] the good order of certain localities." The act nonetheless allowed "curious" Chinese, including teachers, merchants, and students, to continue to come to the United States.

The Chinese Exclusion Act necessitated, in turn, the emergence of a fledgling federal immigration bureaucracy, to enforce the terms of the statute. In the Immigration Act of 1891, Congress created the Bureau of Immigration and charged it with implementing a broader range of immigration restrictions, which included prohibitions on prostitutes and criminals (from 1875) and persons likely to become public charges, persons who presented public health concerns, polygamists, and newcomers who received payment of passage (into the United States) from others. A subsequent act, in 1893, also charged Bureau of Immigration officials with collecting information about immigrant newcomers: occupation, marital status, literacy, amount of money in possession, and data about mental and physical health. Acts in 1903 and 1906, finally, expanded the grounds of inadmissibility to anarchists, made knowledge of the English language a requirement for naturalization, and allowed immigration officials to deport immigrant aliens who became "public charges" within two years of entry into the United States. The Bureau of Immigration, in turn, trained and staffed inspection officers at select ports of entry to the United States to determine newcomer eligibility vis-à-vis an increasingly expansive set of legal exclusions and established procedural protocols—including forms and fee schedules—to lend regularity to the enforcement of immigration and naturalization provisions. The Naturalization Act of 1906, in turn, recognizing the now twin and converging forces of immigration and naturalization, changed the "Bureau of Immigration" into the "Bureau of Immigration and Naturalization." When the Department of Commerce and Labor was divided into two executive departments in 1913, the naturalization and immigration functions of government were divided into two separate offices and both housed in the Department of Labor.

Naturalization and Immigration in the Twentieth Century: Inventing a "National Border" and the "Foreigner"

These bureaucratic machinations are worthy of note because they are revelatory of the dominant forces that structured Congress's first-century effort to articulate and institutionalize the immigration and naturalization functions of government. Congress, under its constitutional prerogative and duty to "establish a uniform rule of naturalization," was quick to articulate a loose patchwork of regulations, including residency requirements, to govern access to citizenship. It was, nonetheless, remarkably slow to claim jurisdiction over territorial entry into and presence in the United States—and did so for the first time only in an 1875 statute that restricted the immigration of criminals and prostitutes and prohibited the entry of Chinese and Japanese laborers under conditions other than free and voluntary consent. Moreover, only with the Immigration Act of 1891 did Congress begin to articulate a comprehensive class of restrictions governing the admissibility of alien newcomers and create an executive agency, the Bureau of Immigration, charged with implementing the border.

In this sense, it took nearly a century for Congress to articulate—in a legally codified and administratively enforceable way—the territorial U.S. border. When it did so, it effected a wholesale change in the nation's approach to immigration. Until 1875, the regulation of migration to the United States had been the province of state and local governments, which exercised relatively exclusive jurisdiction under their traditional policing powers to regulate threats to public health, safety, and morals. It was widely understood, until this point, that the effects of immigration were local and within the jurisdiction of individual states to regulate. And, indeed, states used these traditional policing powers quite aggressively, passing a range of laws—criminal statutes, public charge provisions, vagrancy laws—meant to regulate the migration of bodies across state borders. The late nineteenth century disrupted states' conventional discretion and saw the gradual, then punctuated, *re*-imagination and re-*construction* of an articulable and enforceable *national* territorial border—and of immigration regulation as the proper, even exclusive, jurisdiction of the federal government. The contemporary idea and practice of an articulable border, and of aliens lawfully and unlawfully present, was still, until 1875, an unarticulated *possibility*.

Indeed, the notion of the suspect alien "foreigner"—as much as a national territorial border that invites notions of legality and illegality—had to be invented. For much of the nation's early history, an inclusive immigration policy—internal borders defined by states' interpretations of their traditional policing powers but an external territorial border that remained very much porous—was constitutive of foreign policy. An open border was required to further the young republic's interest in growing a labor force committed to the principles of republican self-governance—and from whom the state could extract forms of allegiance, including taxes, votes, and bodies for the militia. Legal scholar Matthew Lindsay (Lindsay 2013, 750), for example, identifies compelling historical evidence to suggest that political elites in the early republic had capacious faith in "the assimilative power of republican cultural and institutions" and that this faith, in turn, invited a rather "liberal" early approach to immigration and naturalization. From Jefferson's musings on America as "a predominantly agrarian republic of small, independent producer-citizens" (753) to de Crèvecoeur's romantic vision of an immigrant's "metamorphosis" under republican influence, the founding generation embraced, according to Lindsay, profound "confidence in the regenerative power of republican political culture," an equally "deep faith in human moral nature," and, in turn, confidence that the pairing would take root and convert the potentially dangerous heterogeneity of immigration into a uniformity of immigrants "reeducated in the principles and spirit of republicanism" (Lindsay 2013, 753, 757).

Political elites' confidence in the "regenerative" powers of republicanism, however, began to crack in the mid-nineteenth century and crumbled, decisively, at the turn of the twentieth. The mechanism, accordingly to Lindsay, was a growing perception that immigrant poverty, urbanization, and social and geo-spatial isolation in urban centers had taken root and effectively displaced the republican vision of independence, spatial diffusion, and social and cultural assimilation. This perception, paired with a Eugenics movement that enjoyed increasing traction among social and political elites, compromised the perceived "digestive capacity" of American institutions to "transform Europe's outcasts into patriotic republicans." Advocates of the 1924 Immigration Act, in step with a growing Eugenics movement and anti-immigrant sentiment among the public, argued that the United States should "shut the door and breed up a pure, unadulterated American citizenship" and "engage in a serious struggle to maintain our historic republican institutions through barring the entrance of those who are unfit to share the duties and responsibilities of our well-founded government."

It was this historical moment, in turn, that gave birth to the immigrant's foreignness as a legally constitutive status. That is, state and federal law, until the turn of the twentieth century, had treated alien newcomers on the basis of their personhood; aliens were subject to an array of state and local laws—governing vagrancy, criminality, and dependency—that regulated their performance of habits of republican self-governance. Their non-citizen status was not, however, the dispositive force that rendered them subject to these laws; indeed, foreignness did not necessarily spell differential legal treatment. It was only when economic strain increased and a growing sense took hold among political elites and the citizen public that immigrant labor was depressing local wages and disrupting local labor markets, that enduring Nativist sentiment emerged, the notion of the "unassimilable" immigrant took root, and the immigrant's status as foreigner became the operative principle by which states, and then the federal government, would govern them.

The immigrant's perceived foreignness factored centrally in twentieth-century immigration policy. In 1918, for example, Congress delegated extraordinary powers to the president to remove aliens whose presence was contrary to public safety during times of emergency or war. It also, for the first time, imposed passport requirements on entry and exit. In 1921, Congress passed its first quota-based immigration law, limiting the number of aliens of any nationality entering the country to three percent of the foreign-born persons of that nationality who lived in the country in 1910. The 1924 Johnson-Reed Immigration Act reached even more aggressively, imposing a quota system that limited entry based upon the number of persons of that nationality present in the United States in 1890—well before, that is, a wave of immigration from Southern and Eastern Europe. In this way, the law defined the security interests of the state in terms of racial and ethnic homogeneity. The law also, importantly, conferred immigration authority upon the State Department, which was charged with vetting applications for immigration visas in U.S. consular offices abroad; advanced legal definitions of the categories "immigrant," "quota immigrant," "non-quota immigrant," "non-immigrant," and "nationality"; and authorized the secretary of the Department of Labor to deport all persons illegally in the United States. All such efforts to legally codify, define, and co-opt—in this case, to construct a legally codified definition of the "immigrant" and build a bureaucratic apparatus to enforce it—was part and parcel of the American state's late consolidation in the early twentieth century.

Importantly, then, Congress's approach to the non-citizen alien, "foreigner," and "legal" or "illegal" immigrant always has tracked the state's purposes for that person. By the 1940s, Congress asserted its immigration authority in the rhetoric and demands of national security—and the immigrant, in turn, was constructed as a presumptive security threat. The 1940 Alien Registration Act required registration and fingerprinting of all non-citizens over age 14, and a 1941 act gave the president power, during national emergency or war, to prevent departure from or entry into the United States. In 1950, Congress also passed the Internal Security Act, which enhanced immigration screening, made present or former membership in the Communist Party grounds for exclusion, eliminated the Attorney General's authority to make discretionary decisions to admit otherwise inadmissible persons, and conferred upon the attorney general the prerogative to oversee (and effectively enforce) an immigrant alien's deportation order. In 1940, finally, in the wake of the Brownlow presidential reorganization plan, the Immigration and Naturalization Service was moved from the Department of Labor to the Department of Justice, signaling—in tangible institutional form—the decided shift in the federal government's construction of immigration and the immigrant to law enforcement.

At each historical moment, the immigrant body has been constructed in ways that mirror the prevailing political, social, and economic issues of the day—and Congress's response to the political-electoral risks and opportunities these issues presented. In the early years of the republic, a porous border, paired with state and local statutes that enforced republican norms of personal responsibility and self-governance, was central to U.S. foreign policy interests—and meant a largely "hands-off" federal approach to immigration and varying lengths of residency requirements for newcomers. In the wake of the 1870s labor market crisis in California, immigration and immigrants were re-conceived as articles of commerce, and Congress—with help from the Supreme Court—passed laws that prevented the immigration of Chinese laborers. In the twentieth century, immigration was re-invented as a matter of enforcement, investigation, deportation, and security. Wartime statutes—in 1918, 1940, 1941, and 1950—conferred significant emergency- and crisis-based removal powers upon the president. The 1921 and 1924 immigration acts defined the demands of security—of the now cultural commitments of republicanism—relative to racial homogeneity. The 1952 Immigration and Naturalization Act—the law under which U.S. immigration practice still proceeds—abolished the race-based quota system of the 1921 and 1924 Acts but introduced an elaborate approach to entry based upon skills, agricultural labor, and family reunification, which tracked the political needs of the day. It also defined and expanded the investigative powers of the Border Patrol. The 1986 Immigration Reform and Control Act, similarly, increased enforcement at the southern U.S. border. A 1990 Immigration Act increased the cap on overall numbers of visas issued and, echoing the demise of the Cold War and the fall of the Berlin Wall, lifted the historical ban on admitting individuals with ideological commitments to Communism. The 1996 Personal Responsibility and Work Opportunity Reconciliation Act, similarly, introduced time limits and work conditions on the receipt of welfare and imposed special restrictions on legal immigrant access to cash assistance. It also barred undocumented/illegal immigrants from most federal, state, and local social benefits. A parallel act, the 1996 Illegal Immigration Reform and Immigrant Responsibility Act, stepped up border enforcement, increased already existing federal penalties on those who facilitated undocumented entry, introduced accelerated removal procedures, and expanded the reach of deportation by broadening the list of criminal violations deemed deportable.

What this broad summary tracks, overall, is the constitutive force of immigration and naturalization. Both, historically, have functioned as an important tool of state: in the early republic, as a tool of a new, growing, and consolidating state, and today, as a tool of a still-consolidating state seeking to confirm its perceived legitimacy relative to the pressing social, political, and economic issues of the day. At each historical moment, though, immigration and the immigrant have been defined relative to the Congress's need for, and interest in, both. In the first century of the new republic, the legitimacy and state-building interests of the new Congress meant a hands-off approach to territorial entry and settlement—and, instead, a range of state and local vagrancy, public charge, and criminal statutes that enforced the demands of republican self-governance. Converging cultural, political, and economic demands at the turn of the twentieth century, however, produced incentives to formally—legally—define and enforce the border. In the first two decades of the twentieth century, incentives to define and enforce the border led to parallel efforts to construct the category (and practice) of the "illegal" immigrant. Since the post-war 1940s, in turn, elected officials—in Congress and the White House—have tracked and reinforced the social, cultural, and political currency of the "dangerous" illegal immigrant and used the immigrant body to engage in an expansive project of border enforcement to political gain. The Constitution, certainly, neither prescribed nor proscribed this statutory and bureaucratic history. The *capacity* of the document's silences has, nonetheless, provided incentive for a politically enterprising and electorally risk averse Congress. Congress self-consciously claimed immigration (and the immigrant) by the pull of perceived political, social, and economic need.

FUTURE IMPLICATIONS

The capacious silences of the Constitution, in turn, continue to structure the contemporary politics of immigration in Congress. The Constitution grants to the U.S. Congress the duty and prerogative to establish a "uniform rule of Naturalization." The first Congress, accordingly, passed a series of statutes that imposed residency and race-based requirements on access to citizenship. Subsequent Naturalization Acts imposed additional criteria—moral character, public expression of allegiance, knowledge of English—that govern access to citizenship today. Congress, nonetheless, was much slower to self-consciously claim the prerogative to control entry and exit through the territorial border. When it claimed jurisdiction over immigration, Congress bumped up against states' historical discretion to address (what was understood to be) migration's "local" effects. Indeed, it had to claim, justify, and institutionalize its prerogative to regulate territorial entry, exit, and mobility.

The politics of jurisdiction, in turn, is a dominant feature of the modern political landscape of immigration in the United States—and is fueled, in part, by equivocal constitutional directives. Congress, as previously discussed, had to claim, justify, and institutionalize its exclusive prerogative to regulate immigration—a governmental function that, up to the late nineteenth century, had been squarely the province of state and local governments. It did so in the context of its capacity to regulate commerce with foreign nations. Immigration, that is, was imagined as "the business of bringing foreigners," and the immigrant was constructed as an article of commerce. Both—the process of territorial migration and the body of the foreigner—became, in that legal breath, the province of Congress. The 1891 Immigration Act, accordingly, created a Bureau of Immigration and housed it in the *Treasury* Department, and populated a growing list of immigration exclusions with qualities that suggested the immigrant's likelihood of becoming a public charge. The Supreme Court, similarly, in the 1889 case *Chae Chan Ping v. United States*, affirmed Congress's foreign commerce-based justification for regulating the immigration of Chinese laborers and, in turn, also claimed immigration as an "instrument of self-defense."

The Supreme Court's decision in *Chae Chan Ping*, then, also positioned Congress centrally in asserting the federal government's foreign affairs prerogatives. An inclusive immigration policy—no articulable border, paired with local efforts to socialize newcomers to the habits of independence and self-governance—had previously been constitutive of foreign policy and was necessary to grow the labor force of the United States. At the turn of the twentieth century, though, the courts began to justify restrictive immigration policies, relative both to foreign policy priorities—which were increasingly defined by deterrence, protection, border closure, and defense—and to the inherent powers of sovereignty, a government's right to articulate, define, and defend itself. It is in this latter context that the body of the immigrant became presumptively threatening.

Until recently, the federal government has asserted relatively unchallenged exclusive jurisdiction over immigration. However, the terrain of immigration politics changed decisively starting in the 1980s, when a call to reduce the size of government, shrink budgets, privatize governmental functions, and re-imagine government along private-sector lines put pressure on state and local governments. An economic recession in the 1990s led to a resurgence of nativist, anti-immigrant sentiment and put undocumented immigrant claims on public social services, in particular, under fire. In 1994 Californians passed Proposition 187, also called the "Save Our State" initiative, to prohibit the state's estimated 1.3 million undocumented immigrants from using public social benefits like health care and cash assistance. The proposition also enlisted local service providers, including teachers, in immigration enforcement, calling upon them to verify students' immigration status.

The California law was an early example of a later wave of state-level efforts to preempt congressional claims to plenary/exclusive jurisdiction over immigration. In 2010, Arizona passed the Support Our Law Enforcement and Safe Neighborhoods Act, also known as Arizona S.B. 1070, which authorized state and local law enforcement personnel, in the course of a legal traffic stop, to verify the immigration status of individuals suspected of being in the country illegally. The U.S. Department of Justice filed an injunction before the law took effect, claiming that the statute was "unconstitutional" and was "usurping" a federal prerogative, and that "The Constitution and the federal immigration laws do not permit the development of a patchwork of state and local immigration policies throughout the country." Arizona governor Jan Brewer countered that the federal government had "failed" to fulfill its constitutional duty of protecting the border and that Arizona, accordingly, had a right to "protect" itself against undocumented immigration. Federal district court Judge Susan Bolton, in granting the Justice Department's request for a temporary injunction, argued that the law enforcement and verification provisions of the statute improperly interfered with, and made unconstitutional demands upon, "federal law enforcement priorities" and, thus, were preempted under federal law. The Ninth Circuit Court of Appeals affirmed the injunction, arguing that the Arizona law interfered with federal immigration authority. Between 2010 and 2012, thirteen additional states introduced legislation that mirrored Arizona's statute.

The Constitution itself does not anticipate—or provide rules to navigate—this intergovernmental conflict over immigration. Indeed, the courts did not discover and articulate Congress's preemptive immigration powers until the 1870s, in the context of congressional statutes that restricted the immigration of Chinese laborers and asserted Congress's authority to address foreign commerce. In the intervening years, the courts have constructed an elaborate body of preemption law to settle the question of state action in immigration matters. In its decision in *Arizona, et al. v. United States*, the U.S. Supreme Court invalidated three provisions of the Arizona law on the basis of preemption. These provisions of the statute, the Court argued, present an "obstacle" to federal law. The most controversial, fourth, prong of the statute—the provision that required Arizona law enforcement officials to conduct an immigration status check— nonetheless survived the Court's preemption scrutiny. The majority reasoned that the federal government had not demonstrated that the requirement "has . . . consequences that are adverse to federal law and its objectives." The Court, nonetheless, affirmed the federal government's "broad, undoubted power over immigration and alien status" and its (related) constitutional prerogative to "control and conduct foreign relations," thus guaranteeing continued conflict over state and federal immigration authority—and a moving boundary line that is negotiated in politics.

Constitutional silence also fuels separation-of-powers conflict at the federal level. Indeed, the courts have repeatedly affirmed the federal government's prerogative—under the logic of foreign relations, commerce, and the inherent demands of sovereignty—to regulate immigration. Less clear, however, is how that prerogative should be distributed between the legislative and executive branches. Indeed, the conflict between the president and Congress has been the defining feature of U.S. immigration politicking since 2001, when Congress first tried, unsuccessfully, to pass a version of the Development, Relief, and Education for Alien Minors, or DREAM, Act, which confers protection from deportation and a pathway to legal citizenship upon a limited class of undocumented childhood arrivals. The DREAM Act was re-introduced, each time unsuccessfully, in the 108th, 109th, 110th, 111th, and 112th Congresses.

In the absence of congressional action, President Obama has asserted executive discretion to selectively enforce and administer Congress's immigration laws. In 2010, the U.S. ICE issued a bureaucratic memo that announced the agency's intention to prioritize particular enforcement activities. It followed, in 2011, with a memo that claimed the use of prosecutorial discretion in detection, detention, and removal for public safety and national security purposes. In June 2012, President Obama announced a new Department of Homeland Security policy for deferred removal action vis-à-vis undocumented childhood arrivals. The action created a new category of administrative person—the Deferred Action Childhood Arrival (DACA) recipient—and conferred a two-year window of freedom from deportation upon a limited class of undocumented childhood arrivals who met age, residency, education, and moral character requirements. The status did not confer a pathway to citizenship, and it remains a contingent administrative category that can be revoked by future presidents. Arguing that Congress had abdicated its responsibility to respond to the problem of undocumented immigration, Obama claimed the prerogative to "focus our immigration enforcement resources in the right places"—not, presumably, upon the class of undocumented childhood arrivals designated by DACA, who have "been raised as Americans" and "understand themselves to be part of this country." In this way, President Obama concedes Congress's power to affirm and codify the undocumented immigrant's legal status but affirms the executive's administrative discretion to decide when, whether, how, and against whom the law governing undocumented territorial presence will be invoked.

In November 2014, President Obama announced his administration's intention to extend similar deportation protections under DAPA, or Deferred Action for Parents of Americans and Lawful Permanent Residents. Supporters of the action argue that the president is merely exercising "humdrum" prosecutorial discretion—that is, deciding, as with DACA, to focus the federal government's limited resources on the most pressing immigration enforcement priorities. Critics, in contrast, argue that the president is engaging in a systematic "end-run" around Congress that is "contrary to" congressional action and makes a constitutional grab at policymaking, rather than merely selective policy implementation. Congress has not, in the course or wake of these actions, mustered sufficient collective strength to counter the president's discretionary immigration claims.

The Constitution, too, provides little help in negotiating this debate. The contours of contemporary immigration politicking—as much as the history of Congress's slow claim to, and articulation of, its immigration authority—track the silences and ambiguities of our constitutional inheritance. The Constitution commands only one thing: that Congress "establish an uniform rule of naturalization." Much, historically, has had to be claimed and invented in the context of this capacious silence: the idea and practice of the territorial border, the "immigrant," the notion of "illegal" or unlawful territorial presence, and an administrative-bureaucratic order capable of enforcing regulations on entry and exit. Much, too, awaits definition and resolution: the states' authority to regulate immigration matters that occur within, and across, their borders, and the division of the federal government's immigration authority between the political—legislative and executive—branches. The only certainty is that the demands of the document will be identified, negotiated, and applied in politics, relative to the terrain of political risk and opportunity it fuels, and to which it defers.

FURTHER READING

Anderson, Benedict. 1998. *Imagined Communities: Reflections on the Origin and Spread of Nationalism*. London: Verso.

Lindsay, Matthew J. 2003. "Immigration, Sovereignty, and the Constitution of Foreignness," *Connecticut Law Review*, 45: 3, 730.

Neuman, Gerald L. 1996. *Strangers to the Constitution: Immigrants, Borders, and Fundamental Law*. New Jersey: Princeton University Press.

Ngai, Mae. 2014. *Impossible Subjects: Illegal Aliens and the Making of Modern America*. New Jersey: Princeton University Press.

Smith, Rogers. 1999. *Civic Ideals: Conflicting Visions of Citizenship in U.S. History*. New Haven, CT: Yale University Press.

Tribe, Laurence H. 2013. *The Invisible Constitution*. New York: Oxford University Press.

5   THE POWER TO REGULATE BANKRUPTCIES

Judith K. Fitzgerald and Nancy Marcus

Article 1, section 8, clause 4
To establish . . . uniform Laws on the subject of Bankruptcies throughout the United States.

KEY TERMS

Arrangement is an agreement between a debtor and that person's creditors about the debt or repayment.

"The code" or "the bankruptcy code" is shorthand used to refer to the *The Bankruptcy Reform Act of 1978* (Pub. L. 95–598, 92 Stat. 2549, November 6, 1978), which generally became effective on October 1, 1979.

Composition is an agreement between a debtor and his or her creditors, in which creditors agree to accept an immediate dividend less than the whole amount of their claims, to be distributed pro rata, in discharge and satisfaction of the whole. To be successful, a composition requires the consent of all creditors.

Discharge is the extinction of the debtor's *in personam* obligation to repay the debt. A discharge in bankruptcy does not affect a creditor's right to proceed against its collateral, *in rem*.

Exemptions are privileges allowed through state or federal law to a judgment debtor by which a certain amount or class of property may be retained by the debtor, free of the creditor's ability to levy, attach, or execute against that property in satisfaction of the debt.

Nondischargeable debt is debt that does not to come within the privilege of extinction of a debtor's *in personam* obligation to repay. To determine whether a debt is nondischargeable, reference must be made to the applicable provisions of the bankruptcy code, which typically requires a judicial proceeding to be commenced for the purpose of making that determination.

Summary jurisdiction and plenary jurisdiction are terms of art used to describe the scope of jurisdiction that could be exercised by referees in bankruptcy. A referee had authority to hear only matters within his summary jurisdiction if a timely objection to jurisdiction was made. Plenary jurisdiction was reserved to non-bankruptcy court. Battles over the nature of jurisdiction asserted were time-consuming and often resulted in denial of effective relief to the parties, primarily on technical grounds. The bankruptcy code attempted to remove those disputes by broadening the authority of the bankruptcy courts to hear all matters related to the debtor's property and claims against the debtor and against property of the debtor's estate.

HISTORY AND DEVELOPMENT

Bankruptcy may best be regarded as a remedy for the financial and business woes that plague individuals, businesses, and municipalities. With roughly a million people, companies, and municipalities filing bankruptcy each year, exposure to the reach of the bankruptcy laws is widespread. Despite current awareness, however, the historical origins of bankruptcy, as practiced in the United States since the most recent wholesale revision to the law in 1978, are less well known. A brief overview of the background of our current law will help illustrate current views on the subject of congressional power in this area.

The framers of the Constitution were landowners and businessmen or farmers residing in the various colonies prior to the formation of these United States. The framers were aware of the enormous problems encountered by each government's efforts to deal with insolvency, particularly as those efforts affected nonresident creditors and commerce across geographical lines. There was no provision for dealing with bankruptcies in the Articles of Confederation. The absence of a uniform provision, and the concern regarding inconsistent laws that impacted the growing commerce among the colonies, led to the idea that bankruptcy should be addressed as a matter of federal legislation.

As former Englishmen, perhaps it was natural for the framers to look to the English model for guidance. At the time of the Constitutional Convention, the 1732 Statute of George II was the English bankruptcy law in effect. It provided a harsh remedy for uncooperative debtors who acted in a fraudulent manner: death. However, it also recognized that the honest but unfortunate debtor needed relief from debts he could not pay and an allowance to begin afresh. Debtors were permitted to exempt—that is, protect from creditor collection action—a modest amount of property. The Statute was limited in its application; only creditors of traders could place their debtor into bankruptcy. Voluntary declarations of bankruptcy were not permitted.

Despite their understanding of the need for a system that would smooth out the discrepancies among the colonial and confederation governments and the availability of the English model, the subject of bankruptcy received little attention and apparently little debate from the framers during the Constitutional Convention of 1787. There is similarly little discussion of bankruptcy in *Federalist* No. 42, although James Madison described the purpose of the Bankruptcy Clause this way:

The power of establishing uniform laws of bankruptcy is so intimately connected with the regulation of commerce, and will prevent so many frauds
where the parties or their property may lie or be removed into different states
that the expediency of it seems not likely to be drawn into question.

James Madison's prediction proved not to be 100 percent accurate. Although Congress's power to make uniform laws on the subject of bankruptcies was incorporated
into the Constitution, no federal law was enacted until 1800, eleven years after the
Constitution was ratified.

Nineteenth-Century Acts, 1800–1898

The 1800 act was purely a creditors' remedy, in that no voluntary bankruptcy
could be invoked by debtors. To qualify for bankruptcy, a debtor had to be a merchant.
Fraud was punishable by imprisonment but not by death. A discharge of certain unpaid
debts was permitted if the requisite number of creditors holding the required value of
claims agreed. Minimal exemptions and an allowance from the estate were permitted. Although some prominent citizens, including Robert Morris, former treasurer of
the United States, received discharges under this act, public pressure against the act
swelled, and it was repealed in 1803.

One short-lived bankruptcy law was followed by another. This flux is best illustrated by simply listing the laws: The Bankruptcy Act of 1800 was *repealed by* act of
Dec. 19, 1803, and was in effect from 1800 to 1803. The Bankruptcy Act of 1841 was
repealed by act of Mar. 3, 1843, and was in effect from 1841 to 1843. The Bankruptcy
Act of 1867 was *repealed by* act of June 7, 1878, and was in effect from 1867 to 1878.

In all, there were only three periods from 1800 until 1878—for a total of sixteen
years—where Federal bankruptcy laws were extant. Naturally, the absence of federal
legislation created the same problems in addressing insolvency among the states that
existed prior to the Constitution. As interstate commerce increased and the young
nation faced periodic economic crises from, among other causes, crop failures and
overextensions of credit that led to bank failures and runs on banks, the need for consistency in bankruptcy policy became ever more evident. With no long-term federal
law in place, states attempted to deal with the lack of federal law by enacting their own
insolvency legislation, with intermittent decisions by the United States Supreme Court
lending some focus to congressional authority over bankruptcies. The primary concern
of the early cases was whether a state could constitutionally discharge preexisting debt
held by its citizens. In 1819 and again in 1827, the Supreme Court ruled against state
authority over discharge regarding preexisting debt. Nonetheless, various state laws
served as models for ensuing federal legislation, which was often hard fought and the
subject of significant compromise.

By 1841, facing the aftermath of a severe economic depression (the Panic of 1837),
an inability to gain relief of debt through discharge, and a growing distaste for impris-
oning debtors, lawmakers increasingly debated whether any legislation that provided
for voluntary bankruptcy would be constitutional. Orators of national fame weighed
in, with John Calhoun declaring his opposition to a federal law and Daniel Webster

and Joseph Story advocating it. Supporters eventually prevailed. The Bankruptcy Act of 1841, allegedly modeled after a similar insolvency law in Massachusetts enacted in 1838, was simple and short. This law permitted both involuntary and voluntary bank-ruptcies and did not exclude those who were not merchants from its scope. Permitting voluntary invocation of bankruptcy was a true innovation of Congress, which passed the law despite debates on whether it had the authority to pass such a law under its bankruptcy power. That issue was never addressed by the Supreme Court.

One of the features of the 1841 act—the inability of a debtor to claim state exemp-tions, was later revoked in favor of a process declaring that each state might determine whether its debtors could claim state or federal exemptions, or limit them only to the state exemptions—all in the name of "uniformity." The discharge was now made a federal privilege, subject to certain exceptions and to the right of creditors to dissent by majority in both number and value of claims. Grounds for denial of discharge included the making of preferential transfers. This act was repealed early in 1843, after barely one year in operation.

The inability of states to grant discharges and the Panic of 1857 led to the enact-ment of the Bankruptcy Act of 1867. This law expanded concepts in a fashion that still exists. The statute extended to corporations the ability to invoke bankruptcy. Debtors now had the opportunity to elect state exemptions rather than the less favorable federal scheme, and use of state exemptions laws in bankruptcy continues today. For the first time, debtors were permitted to propose a repayment percentage to creditors (essen-tially, a composition), which, if accepted by a majority in number and 75 percent in value, was binding on all creditors named in the proposal. In exchange, debtors could receive a discharge and retain their property.

One additional provision of the 1867 act is noteworthy: a precursor to the current judicial process was adopted, in that federal district courts had original jurisdiction over bankruptcies with the assistance of court-appointed registers. The later appoint-ment of referees and bankruptcy judges succeeds from the registers. This act, too, suf-fered from widespread criticism and was repealed in 1878.

The twenty years after 1878 were a period of railroad expansion. It was also a period of illiquidity that caused insolvencies affecting interstate transportation and other economic concerns. Yet there was no federal bankruptcy law. States again tried to fill the gap, but the inherent interstate nature of operating railroads proved the inefficacy of state relief. A process was implemented, using federal court-appointed receivers to run the railroads while selling assets to pay creditors. One of the concepts adopted to pro-tect creditors can still be found in current-day bankruptcy laws—that is, use of an upset price (now more commonly known as a "stalking horse" bidder) to set an adequate sales price and permitting a sale as a going concern rather than a fire sale at liquidation prices.

Finally in 1898, following the Civil War and the Panics of 1884 and 1893, perma-nent federal bankruptcy legislation took effect. This act remained in place, although amended many times, until the 1978 act (generally referred to as "the bankruptcy code" to distinguish it from the long-running 1898 act, and abbreviated herein as "the code") passed. Once again, getting the 1898 act passed was subject to strong opposi-tion in Congress. This time, members of Congress argued for and against the use of involuntary bankruptcy as a tool for debt collection. Once again, Massachusetts set the pathway for enactment, with Judge Lowell of Massachusetts serving as a drafter of many revisions that foreshadowed current law. His vision did not gain enough support, however, and the Torrey Bill, named for its drafter, a lawyer from St. Louis, was eventually revised and enacted. The 1898 act provided more favorable treatment to debtors than had the prior creditor-friendly laws. The discharge was broadened, and the forever-troublesome exemption question was answered in this bill by authorizing only state exemptions to be claimed. Challenges to the constitutionality of this provision as violating the Uniformity Clause failed when the Supreme Court so decided in *Hanover Nat'l Bank v. Moyses*, 186 U.S. 181 (1902).

Once again, the federal district courts assumed jurisdiction as courts of bankruptcy and were aided by referees, to whom most of the administrative and judicial work devolved. Many efforts to repeal this act failed, but amendments were often passed, although none that adversely impacted the primary scope of the act. Of major concern to creditors was the breadth of the discharge, but the ensuing Great Depression (1929–1940) resulted in even more favorable debtor amendments and opportunities for reorganization rather than liquidation. Challenges to congressional efforts to expand bankruptcy to railroads, agricultural concerns, and municipalities all eventually lost. Although issues were brought to the Supreme Court and the justices sometimes determined that a particular action was unconstitutional, Congress passed new laws that met with Supreme Court approval. One major renovation to the act came in the form of the Chandler Act, which passed after years of debate, in 1938. Substantial changes were made to the 1898 act, which was itself reorganized into Chapters that dealt with particularities—for example, Chapter X dealt with corporate reorganizations, Chapter XII to real property arrangements, Chapter XII to wage earner plans.

From then until the code was enacted in 1978, numerous amendments changed the act. In 1973, the law was amended to do away with referees and install bankruptcy judges instead. Problems with jurisdiction were rampant under this act. The distinction between summary and plenary jurisdiction and which court—state (which retained concurrent jurisdiction over many of the issues that arise in bankruptcy) or federal (which had original, but not exclusive, jurisdiction over most matters)—should hear an action led to confusion and litigation. Retracing roots, both voluntary and involuntary actions were permitted for individuals, but corporations were not provided the option of voluntary filing. Trustees were appointed to administer assets and liquidate them for the benefit of creditors and were given fairly broad powers to avoid and recover preferential and fraudulent transfers. Compositions were again permitted as an alternative to liquidation if the requisite majority in number and value of creditors consented. Perhaps the most significant change came in 1973 when, pursuant to authority conveyed on the Supreme Court by the 1898 act to make rules in bankruptcy, rules of bankruptcy procedure came to be and were given precedence over provisions of the act that contradicted the rules. (Note that today, rules cannot supersede a statute.)

Issues with the 1978 Code

By 1970, the need for major revisions to the law enabled the creation of a commission to study the issue and report to Congress. This report, presented in 1973, led to the enactment of the Bankruptcy Reform Act of 1978 ("the code"), which was the first bankruptcy law not enacted in response to a panic. The code took effect on October 1, 1979, and is still in effect today, although it has been the subject of numerous amendments since its initial passage, the most pronounced of which occurred in 2005.

The major revisions in 2005 involving congressional authority include the so-called "means test" and a restriction on certain types of advice (that is, to not incur debt in contemplation of bankruptcy) a lawyer may give a client preparing to file bankruptcy, coupled with a requirement to advertise as a "debt relief agency." The means test, set out in 11 USC. § 707(b)(2), applies to individuals whose debts are primarily consumer debts. It requires a determination of an individual debtor's "current monthly income," a term defined in Section 101(10A), through an aggregation of standards used by the Internal Revenue Service and other governmental bodies for purposes unrelated to bankruptcy. For example, the IRS uses its standards to determine the extent of repayment plans that debtors can afford through offers in compromise. The means test is applied in bankruptcy to determine whether an individual debtor's choice of Chapter 7 passes muster or is abusive. If abusive, the case must be dismissed, or the debtor can convert and attempt a reorganization plan, usually in Chapter 13, for periods of time related to the outcome of the means test. As has happened from time to time, this statute made it significantly more difficult for individual debtors to obtain relief in bankruptcy, but the issue of congressional authority to so legislate seems not to be of serious concern.

Issues regarding the "debt relief agency" advertising requirements and restrictions as applied to attorneys, however, created a flurry of cases, one of which percolated to the Supreme Court. The case began with a First Amendment challenge to code provisions that imposed certain requirements and prohibitions on debt relief agencies. The challenge was brought by bankruptcy attorneys, law firms, and two bankruptcy clients. Specifically, the plaintiffs contended that 11 USC § 526(a)(4), prohibiting debt relief agencies from advising clients "to incur more debt in contemplation" of filing bankruptcy, and Section 528(a)(4), (b)(2), requiring that debt relief agency advertisements contain language identical or substantially similar to: "We are a debt relief agency. We help people file for bankruptcy relief under the bankruptcy code," were First Amendment violations. The plaintiffs also argued that the debt relief agency provisions should not apply to bankruptcy attorneys.

In a ruling rejecting the government's motion to dismiss, the United States District Court for the District of Minnesota ruled in favor of the plaintiffs on each of their arguments. On appeal, the Court of Appeals for the Eighth Circuit affirmed in part and reversed in part, agreeing that the speech restriction of Section 526 was unconstitutional but concluding that the disclosure requirements of Section 528 were constitutional and that bankruptcy attorneys and law firms were included within the statutory definition of "debt relief agency."

On certiorari, the Supreme Court unanimously upheld the constitutionality of all the challenged provisions of the act, and ruled that bankruptcy attorneys and law firms were subject to its debt relief agency restrictions and requirements. In part of the majority opinion with which all but one justice concurred, Justice Sotomayor wrote:

Because § 528's requirements that Milavetz identify itself as a debt relief agency and include certain information about its bankruptcy-assistance and related services are "reasonably related to the [Government's] interest in preventing deception of consumers," we uphold those provisions as applied to Milavetz.

Regarding the Section 526 restriction on advising clients to incur debt prior to bankruptcy, the Supreme Court unanimously interpreted the section narrowly, as applying to prohibit such advice "only when the impetus of the advice to incur more debt is the expectation of filing for bankruptcy and obtaining the attendant relief." The Court consequently rejected the plaintiffs' vagueness arguments, having accorded a narrow interpretation of the statute under which it would survive constitutional scrutiny.

Article I versus Article III Judges

A number of curiosities developed in the code even before the 2005 amendments. One dealt with the ever-politically rife issue of exemptions. In this formulation of the law, states now had the right to "opt out" of the federal exemption scheme by choosing to deny their citizens the right to select the federal exemptions and limit them only to their own state's exemptions. The vast majority of states have opted out. The code initially adopted a basic balance between the interests of debtors and their creditors, a balance which has been largely eroded in favor of special interest groups of creditors with each amendment. Nonetheless, there appears to be no appetite to re-examine the question of whether a statute that enables debtors in different geographic locations to obtain significantly different benefits from filing bankruptcy is sustainable under the Uniformity Clause, Art. I, § 8, cl. 1.

Another issue that found its way to the Supreme Court concerned the dispute over congressional authority to provide expansive jurisdiction to Article I judges—i.e., those to whom Congress assigns adjudication powers over some issues, rather than saving all jurisdictional authority for Article III courts. As a consequence of the jurisdictional disputes that plagued the former Bankruptcy Act, Congress sought to use the code to expand the jurisdiction of the bankruptcy judges so that all of the issues that arise in a bankruptcy case could be consolidated for adjudication in one forum. The debate over the status of bankruptcy judges was fierce, spearheaded in part by then-Chief Justice Burger, who lobbied forcefully against Article III status, and eventually concluded by appointing them as Article I judges, rather than as Article III judges.

Despite its decision not to provide Article III status to bankruptcy judges, the Senate gave bankruptcy judges expansive jurisdiction over all matters arising in, under, or related to bankruptcy cases as adjuncts of the district court, without the protections of Article III. That enactment forced frequent and costly litigation regarding issues created by virtue of the fact that only Article III judges have life tenure and protection from diminution in salary, as well as the fact that the lines between Article I and Article III court authority were shifting significantly between the Supreme Court's 1855 *Murray's Lessee v. Hoboken Land and Improvement Co.* decision—in which the Court ruled that Article I courts may hear "public rights" disputes, leaving "private rights" disputes to Article III courts—and later decisions that blurred the lines between public and private rights. Following that case, in *Cromwell v. Benson*, the Court further explained that "private rights" are those involving the liability of one individual to another, but in some cases, a non-Article III adjudicatory body (in that case, an employees' compensation commission) may nonetheless decide private rights cases as long as there was review by an Article III court. Since those two seminal cases identifying the framework for allocating respective Article I and Article III court authority, bankruptcy court cases have become front and center in the redefinition of the "public vs. private rights" parameters in the allocation of Article I and Article III court jurisdiction.

In *Northern Pipeline Construction Company v. Marathon Pipe Line Company*, the constitutional limitations of Article I bankruptcy courts' authority to decide rights that might traditionally be deemed "private rights," but are nonetheless part of "core" bankruptcy matters, came into question. In that case, a plurality of the Court determined that Section 1471 of the code, which granted bankruptcy courts "jurisdiction over 'all civil proceedings arising under title 11 [bankruptcy] [of the United States Code] or arising in or related to cases under title 11,'" was unconstitutional as violating Article III. As the plurality explained:

> The Federal Judiciary was therefore designed by the Framers to stand independent of the Executive and Legislature—to maintain the checks and balances of the constitutional structure, and also to guarantee that the process of adjudication itself remained impartial. Hamilton explained the importance of an independent Judiciary: "Periodical appointments, however regulated, or by whomsoever made, would, in some way or other, be fatal to [the courts'] necessary independence. If the power of making them was committed either to the Executive or legislature, there would be danger of an improper complaisance to the branch which possessed it; if to both, there would be an unwillingness to hazard the displeasure of either; if to the people, or to persons chosen by them for the special purpose, there would be too great a disposition to consult popularity, to justify a reliance that nothing would be consulted but the Constitution and the laws." The *Federalist* No. 78, p. 489 (H. Lodge ed. 1888). The Court has only recently reaffirmed the significance of this feature of the Framers' design: "A Judiciary free from control by the Executive and Legislature is essential if there is a right to have claims decided by judges who are free from potential domination by other branches of government."

In sum, our Constitution unambiguously enunciates a fundamental principle—that the "judicial Power of the United States" must be reposed in an independent Judiciary. It commands that the independence of the Judiciary be jealously guarded, and it provides clear institutional protections for that independence.

The Court further explained that "[p]rivate-rights disputes . . . lie at the core of the historically recognized judicial power" under Article III, and could not, therefore, be subject to the jurisdiction of non-Article III Courts, rejecting the appellants' argument "that Congress' constitutional authority to establish 'uniform Laws on the subject of Bankruptcies throughout the United States,' Art. I, § 8, cl. 4, carries with it an inherent power to establish legislative courts capable of adjudicating 'bankruptcy-related controversies.'"

Elaborating upon the constitutional separation of powers issue, the Court explained:

The constitutional system of checks and balances is designed to guard against "encroachment or aggrandizement" by Congress at the expense of the other branches of government. *Buckley v. Valeo*, 424 U. S., at 122. But when Congress creates a statutory right, it clearly has the discretion, in defining that right, to create presumptions, or assign burdens of proof, or prescribe remedies; it may also provide that persons seeking to vindicate that right must do so before particularized tribunals created to perform the specialized adjudicative tasks related to that right. Such provisions do, in a sense, affect the exercise of judicial power, but they are also incidental to Congress' power to define the right that it has created. No comparable justification exists, however, when the right being adjudicated is not of congressional creation. In such a situation, substantial inroads into functions that have traditionally been performed by the Judiciary cannot be characterized merely as incidental extensions of Congress' power to define rights that it has created. Rather, such inroads suggest unwarranted encroachments upon the judicial power of the United States, which our Constitution reserves for Art. III courts.

We hold that the Bankruptcy Act of 1978 carries the possibility of such an unwarranted encroachment. Many of the rights subject to adjudication by the Act's bankruptcy courts . . . are not of Congress' creation. Indeed, the cases before us, which center upon appellant Northern's claim for damages for breach of contract and misrepresentation, involve a right created by state law, a right independent of and antecedent to the reorganization petition that conferred jurisdiction upon the Bankruptcy Court. Accordingly, Congress' authority to control the manner in which that right is adjudicated, through assignment of historically judicial functions to a non-Art. III "adjunct," plainly must be deemed at a minimum.

Chief Justice Burger, Justice White, and Justice Powell dissented. Chief Justice Burger's dissent emphasized that the plurality holding of the Court was narrow in scope, limited to the holding "that a 'traditional' state common-law action, not made subject to a federal rule of decision, and related only peripherally to an adjudication of bankruptcy under federal law, must, absent the consent of the litigants, be heard by an 'Art. III court' if it is to be heard by any court or agency of the United States." Justice White's dissent, joined by Burger and Powell, took issues with the plurality's analysis and conclusions for a number of reasons. The dissent chastised the plurality for exaggerating the separation of powers tension while not recognizing the historic role of bankruptcy courts in handling issues that, particularly because they are tied to state law issues, would generally not be Article III court issues to begin with:

[T]he majority's proposal seems to turn the separation-of-powers doctrine, upon which the majority relies, on its head: Since state-law claims would ordinarily not be heard by Art. III judges—i.e., they would be heard by state judges—one would think that there is little danger of a diminution of, or intrusion upon, the power of Art. III courts, when such claims are assigned to a non-Art. III court. The plurality misses this obvious point because it concentrates on explaining how it is that federally created rights can ever be adjudicated in Art. I courts—a far more difficult problem under the separation-of-powers doctrine. The plurality fumbles when it assumes that the rationale it develops to deal with the latter problem must also govern the former problem. In fact, the two are simply unrelated and the majority never really explains the separation-of-powers problem that would be created by assigning state law questions to legislative courts or to adjuncts of Art. III courts.

The ruling by the *Northern Pipeline* plurality placed the bankruptcy system in disarray due to the confusion created as to what authority the bankruptcy courts could exercise and when a final order could be issued. Despite the thirty-five-year history of the code, the confusion has not been fully clarified. For a time, it was not clear that bankruptcy judges could act at all, and district courts utilized creative techniques to keep the system functioning. One technique was to appoint the bankruptcy judges as federal magistrates and assign all of the bankruptcy cases to them. Congress tried to resolve the structural problem by amending the code in 1984 to redefine bankruptcy courts' jurisdiction. Congress designated bankruptcy courts as units of the district courts and provided that bankruptcy judges could hear cases only by reference from the district courts. Every district court has a procedure in place that automatically refers bankruptcy petitions to the bankruptcy courts. But the reference can be revoked at any time. Orders of the bankruptcy court can be final orders subject to appeal to the district court or bankruptcy appellate panel ("BAP") if one exists in the jurisdiction, only when the issue involves a "core" bankruptcy matter. For "non-core" matters, the bankruptcy judge must enter an order in the nature of a recommendation to the district court, which the district judge hears de novo. Appeals then follow to the appropriate federal court of appeals.

The concept of "core" versus "non-core" is not one capable of easy application. The non-exclusive sixteen illustrations of what constitute "core" proceedings are found in 28 USC § 157(b)(2) and include such diverse topics as matters affecting the administration of the estate, orders to turn over property of the estate, proceedings to determine, avoid, or recover preferences, confirmations of plans, and counterclaims by the estate against persons filing claims against the estate. Until the Supreme Court decided *Stern v. Marshall*, the prevailing thought was that when Congress designated a matter as "core," the bankruptcy court could enter a final order. However, *Stern* cast that formula into question.

The Supreme Court's *Stern* decision arose out of a bankruptcy court award to Vickie Lynn Marshall (aka Anna Nicole Smith) of over $425 million in damages on a counterclaim regarding her inheritance from her deceased husband J. Howard Marshall II ("a man believed to have been one of the richest people in Texas") that was filed in response to a defamation claim against her stepson brought in bankruptcy court. The Supreme Court in *Stern* determined that although in 28 USC § 157(b)(2) provides the authority to adjudicate a core issue regarding a counterclaim by entering a final order, there is no constitutional authority for the bankruptcy court to treat all state law counterclaim as "core" proceedings, which, the Court explained, "raises serious constitutional concerns." In particular, the Court elaborated, the bankruptcy court's determination of a state law-based counterclaim that was not "core" to the proceeding would violate Article III of the Constitution. Citing the previous *Murray's Lessee* and *Northern Pipeline* cases, the Court declared,

> Article III could neither serve its purpose in the system of checks and balances nor preserve the integrity of judicial decisionmaking if the other branches of the Federal Government could confer the Government's "judicial Power" on entities outside Article III. That is why we have long recognized that, in general, Congress may not "withdraw from judicial cognizance any matter which, from its nature, is the subject of a suit at the common law, or in equity, or admiralty."

In its analysis, the Court again relied on a distinction between adjudication of public versus private rights, offering that what "makes a right 'public' rather than private is that the right is integrally related to a particular government action," as opposed to a right that "'depend[s] on or replace[s] a right to compensation under state law.'" The Court consequently reversed the large damage award to Anna Nicole Smith, ruling, "The 'experts' [at] resolving common law counterclaims such as [hers] are the Article III courts, and it is with those courts that her claim must stay."

As a result of the uncertainty *Stern* imposed on the bankruptcy process regarding its treatment of state law claims or counterclaims, particularly those that had previously been considered "core" issues, the decision once again placed the bankruptcy system in an upheaval that exists to this day—though calmed somewhat by the Court's recent decision in *Wellness International Network, Ltd. v. Sharif*. Although the Supreme Court stated that its holding in *Stern* was narrow, those below the Supreme Court level generally reject that view. Rather, after *Stern*, anything and everything that could be considered to have had its origins in a state law dispute (fraudulent conveyances are the prime example) faced potential legal challenges as to whether the bankruptcy judge assigned the matter could issue a final decision. Some courts went so far as to determine that some types of nondischargeability actions, and even the discharge itself, although "core," could not be the subject of final orders by the bankruptcy court. For several years, the fallout from *Stern* predominated bankruptcy litigation.

In *Wellness*, the Court clarified that its previous *Stern* decision had been narrow in scope, as with previous decisions in which the Court "found a violation of a litigant's right to an Article III decisionmaker," all of which, the Court explained, "involved an objecting defendant forced to litigate involuntarily before a non-Article III court." While limiting and distinguishing *Stern*, the *Wellness* Court held "that Article III is not violated when the parties knowingly and voluntarily consent to adjudication to a bankruptcy judge." Thus, to the extent that there is party consent, *Wellness* resolved the problem with Article I courts entering final decisions regarding "*Stern* claims," that is, those designated for final adjudication in the bankruptcy court as a statutory matter but prohibited as a constitutional matter. The decision did not, however, address ongoing constitutional tensions underlying the delegation of authority to bankruptcy courts without extending to them the protections of Article III tribunals.

With the *Wellness* decision, Congress has apparently prevailed in its formulation of the bankruptcy power now that the Court has ruled that parties with private rights claims voluntarily ignore a structural constitutional defect by consent. Furthermore, with the Court having affirmed the authority of bankruptcy courts to address "core" issues, and to enter final orders when the parties give consent, consistent with both the express power of Congress to regulate bankruptcies and the Article III powers of the judicial branch, perhaps all may be well for the foreseeable future, the separation of powers constitutional tensions on this front laid to rest.

FURTHER READING

Balleisen, Edward J. 2001. *Navigating Failure: Bankruptcy and Commercial Society in Antebellum America*. Chapel Hill, SC: University of North Carolina Press.

Brubaker, Ralph. 2000. On the Nature of Federal Bankruptcy Jurisdiction: A General Statutory and Constitutional Theory. *William and Mary Law Review* 41: 3, 743.

Countryman, Vern. 1985. Scrambling to Define Bankruptcy Jurisdiction. *Harvard Journal on Legislation* 22: 1, 1–45.

History of the Federal Judiciary, Bankruptcy http://www.fjc.gov/history/home.nsf/page/jurisdiction_bankruptcy.html. Accessed August 18, 2015.

Klee, Kenneth N., and Whitman L. Holt. 2015. *Bankruptcy and the Supreme Court: 1801–2014*. St. Paul, MN: West Academic Publishing.

Mann, Bruce H. 2002. *Republic of Debtors: Bankruptcy in the Age of American Independence*. Cambridge, MA: Harvard University Press.

Mussman, William E., and Stefan A. Riesenfeld. 1948. Jurisdiction in Bankruptcy. *Law and Contemporary Problems* 13, 88–113.

Report of the National Bankruptcy Review Commission, October 20, 1997. http://govinfo.library.unt.edu/nbrc/reporttitlepg.html Accessed August 18, 2015.

Skeel, David A., Jr. 2001. *Debt's Dominion: A History of Bankruptcy Law in America*. Princeton, NJ: Princeton University Press.

Warren, Charles. 1935. *Bankruptcy in United States History*. Cambridge, MA: Harvard University Press.

6 THE POWERS TO REGULATE MONEY, WEIGHTS, AND MEASURES AND TO PUNISH COUNTERFEITING

David R. Smith and Robert Jefferson Dillard

Article I, section 8, clause 5
To coin Money, regulate the Value thereof, and of foreign Coin, and fix the Standard of Weights and Measures;

Article I, section 8, clause 6
To provide for the Punishment of counterfeiting the Securities and current Coin of the United States;

KEY TERMS

The power to "**fix the Standard of Weights and Measures**" did not spur much debate among the framers. James Madison in *Federalist* No. 42 speaks to the general consensus of the Framers of the Constitution on the matter: "The regulation of weights and measures is transferred from the Articles of Confederation, and is founded on like considerations with the preceding power of regulating coin." Like coinage, the standardization of weights and measures had been traditionally accepted as part of the Crown's prerogative powers under the English system.

The standardization of weights and measures is not a power that has been exercised frequently by the U.S. Congress. It was through policy pursued by the Department of the Treasury rather than Congress that traditional English measures such as yards, pounds, and gallons became the standard units of measures. In 1866, Congress did finally authorize the use of the metric system, which a number of prominent political leaders had been advocating for a while, but did *not* mandate its use. The Metric Conversion Act of 1975 called for a plan of increased use of the metric system, as it represents the international standard. The 1975 law further encouraged the adoption of the metric system as a national standard, but did not supply an enforcing mechanism. Consequently, the metric system still struggles for adoption.

Bills of credit are non-interest-bearing paper money based on the good credit of a government and traditionally redeemable for gold or silver coins. (But see Chapter 2, Key Terms.)

Fiat money is a more general term for paper currency based on decree or faith in government, rather than actual redemption value for gold or silver.

Legal tender constitutes any authorized medium of exchange for economic transactions between private individuals and between governments and private individuals. Paper currency became fully acceptable as legal tender only after a series of U.S. Supreme Court decisions known as the Legal Tender Cases in the second half of the 1800s, as discussed below. Paper currency was printed to fund of the American Civil War. But, after the war, multiple court decisions were necessary before paper currency was finally accepted as legal tender.

The power **"to coin Money"** is an ambiguous phrase for the contemporary scholar due to the dual use of the word "coin" as both a noun and a verb. Whether or not the word "coin" refers strictly to currency composed of a metal alloy or to the congressional right to produce a medium of exchange composed of *any* material would become a subject of debate long after the writing of the U.S. Constitution. Late in the nineteenth century, the controversy turned on "free silver" versus the "gold standard," as discussed below.

The power **"to regulate the Value thereof, and of foreign Coin"** was in keeping with the general push for achieving national uniformity in money. With regard to "foreign coin," James Madison again observed in *Federalist* No. 42, "It must be seen at once, that the proposed uniformity in the value of the current coin, might be destroyed by subjecting that of the foreign coin to the different regulations of the different states." However, the Coinage Act of 1792 (also called the Mint Act) did not immediately produce the needed currency and instantly replace the foreign coins then in circulation. Rather, the undertaking of both production and circulation took a number of years. It was during this interval that the Congress authorized foreign coin of various national origins as legal tender. Through a second act passed in February of 1793, Congress regulated the value of foreign coins of both gold and silver quality and their specific weights in order to satisfy a pressing national demand for a circulating currency. While the 1793 act also specified an optimistic timeline whereby foreign coin would be removed from circulation and replaced by American-produced currency, foreign coin remained legal tender until 1857.

The American utilization of the dollar rather than the English pound as the standard unit of currency can be traced to the prevalence of Spanish dollars throughout the colonies prior to the ratification of the Constitution and to the passage of the Coinage

Act of 1792. The Coinage Act takes its inspiration from the work and advocacy of Alexander Hamilton, who pushed for the establishment of a mint and regulation of alloys utilized in coinage in a report issued the year before.

HISTORY AND DEVELOPMENT

Among the least controversial clauses in the Constitution are the two enumerated powers discussed in this chapter, Art. I, §8, cl. 5 and Art. I, §8, cl. 6. Equally uncontroversial is the closely related Art. I, §10, cl. 1, which is not an enumerated power. Rather, it is a prohibition on what the states can do. Article I, §10, cl. 1, reads in full:

> No state shall enter into any treaty, alliance, or confederation; grant letters of marque and reprisal; coin money; emit bills of credit; make any thing but gold and silver coin a tender in payment of debts; pass any bill of attainder, ex post facto law, or law impairing the obligation of contracts, or grant any title of nobility.

Ultimately removing from the states the power to coin money and reserving such power exclusively for Congress ensures uniformity and, ideally, reduces the propagation of counterfeit coin. The state record for producing currency, including paper money, under the Articles of Confederation was mixed. Rhode Island, in particular, had caused financial turmoil by issuing an excessive amount of paper currency without backing. But depreciation and inflation had been experienced by a number of other states. Granting Congress the sole authority to coin money would also prevent what James Madison foresaw in *Federalist* No. 44 as additional practical concerns: "a right of coinage in the particular states could have no other effect than to multiply expensive mints and diversify the forms and weights of the circulating pieces."

Counterfeiting

As one of the true enumerated power of the Congress, Article I, §8, cl. 6, providing for the punishment of counterfeiting, was approved unanimously with little debate. Delegates remembered the wartime counterfeiting of colonial currency carried out by the British. They were also worried that "[b]ills of exchange . . . might be forged in one State and carried into another" or that the counterfeiting of "foreign paper" might cause trouble with other countries. In addition, James Madison argued in *Federalist* No. 42 for placing this power on the hands of Congress because, "The punishment of counterfeiting the public securities, as well as of the current coin, is submitted of course to that authority, which is to secure the value of both."

While Madison is no doubt correct, Art. I, §8, cl. 6 is also peculiarly redundant. In the first place, the Art. I, §8, cl. 5 power "to coin Money, regulate the Value thereof" already presupposes the power to punish counterfeiting. In the second place, Art. I, §8, cl. 18, the "necessary and proper" clause, also empowers Congress to punish counterfeiting in order to make Art. I, §8, cl. 5 effective. (Art. I, §8, cl. 18: "To make all laws which shall be necessary and proper for carrying into execution the foregoing powers, and all other powers vested by this constitution in the government of the United States, or in any department or officer thereof.") The Founding Fathers obviously thought counterfeiting was an important problem that required multiple responses.

However, with *Fox v. Ohio* (1847), the Supreme Court made Art. I, §8, cl. 6 superfluous. Punishing "the *counterfeiting* of the Securities and current Coin," the Court held, was the sole responsibility of the federal government. But punishing the "fraud" committed on the citizens of the states by those who "passed" or "uttered" counterfeit money was not unconstitutional. Fraud was a serious crime, and the states needed to protect their citizens from all forms of fraud. In effect, both the federal government and the states have concurrent power to punish counterfeiting.

The Colonial Experience with Coinage

The origins of the congressional power to regulate coinage can also be found in the very deficiencies of the Articles of Confederation—and prior to that, in the colonial experience. The practice of coining money, dating back to the Iron Age, has always served the triple purposes of facilitating trade, centralizing governmental authority, and promoting national unity. The modern English tradition of coinage began during the reign of King James I (1566–1625). This routine element of normal English life, however, did not initially exist in the colonies. As might be expected, the lack of coin available for exchange was a product of an economic structure that characterized the colony-to-mother country relationship. As a primarily agricultural society, the colonies in their earliest days relied on the English for manufactured goods. Because importation was essential to colonial life, the colonists soon found themselves without any form of currency, having used almost all of it on the purchase of imports as a matter of necessity. The available gold and silver coins, usually in the form of Spanish dollars, were usually quickly used to pay debts back in the mother country, thus leaving a dearth of usable specie throughout the colonies.

Generally speaking, rather than address what was a pressing need for issues of currency in the colonies, the crown preferred that the colonists continue using various foreign specie for the conduct of day-to-day commerce. One exception to this was a temporary mint that began operating in Massachusetts in 1652. This mint operated beyond English control but was a practical solution to the unavailability of usable currency, until it closed in 1682. Outside of this, the colonists had to rely on the more traditional practice of bartering commodities. While these commodities lacked any status as legal tender, the commodities carried an intrinsic value, which made them a de facto currency. Popularly traded items among the early settlers included grain, pelts, and wool. The native practice of utilizing wampum (consisting of shells, stones, or beads) as a form of currency also proved popular with English settlers.

Almost constant war between England and France during the late 1600s inevitably reached the colonies. By 1690, in order to deal with escalating war debts and to pay its soldiers, the colonial government of Massachusetts issued the first authorized paper currency in the western world. In time, each of the colonies resorted to issuing some form of paper currency in order to facilitate trade. The bulk of these colonial issues of bills of credit were fiat money, or currency based on decree or faith in government, rather than actual redemption value for gold or silver. The underlying logic was that these bills would eventually be taken out of circulation through taxes, but, due to overprinting and mismanagement, the money supply was often irresponsibly increased, resulting in rapid depreciation and inflation, the twin evils of paper money.

As the value of the colonially issued bills of credit plummeted, English merchants suddenly found themselves on the losing end when conducting business with colonists. They began pleading to the English government for relief. In response, the British Parliament began regulating the colonial use of paper money. The first of these measures, the Currency Act of 1751, restricted the emission of bills of credit within the New England colonies only. The subsequent Currency Act of 1764 extended the prohibition of bills of credit as legal tender throughout the remaining colonies in hopes of stemming the tide of inflation. The resulting inflammation of tensions between the colonists and the British government came about as a result of a rapid deflation, driving another wedge between the colonies and the British authorities.

By the time of the Second Continental Congress in May of 1775, the vulnerable colonial position vis-à-vis the British government with regard to currency had become painfully obvious. Lacking any legitimacy as a government or recognized sovereignty as a nation, the financial prospects for carrying out a war effort against the mighty British without foreign credit seemed dim. The idea of taxation at a national level was out of the question since the future prospect of unified nationhood itself remained dubious. In this environment, the Continental Congress was left with no choice but to issue a Continental Currency in hopes that the colonial governments would in turn be able to raise funds for redemption through taxation. With few guarantees of long-term sustainability, the first congressional issuance of bills of credit, to the amount of two million Spanish-milled dollars, in May of 1775 was followed by subsequent issues amounting to $240 million by 1780. In June and August of 1775, Massachusetts and Rhode Island respectively declared congressional bills of credit legal as tender, with criminal consequences for refusal to accept such bills as payment for debts. At the suggestion of the Continental Congress in 1777, most of the colonial governments followed suit by creating laws demanding the acceptance of the bills as a matter of patriotism and national security.

As the American Revolutionary War was itself a clash over the right of taxation, the difficulties experienced by the Second Continental Congress in financing the war effort should come as no surprise. The popular consensus among the colonists at the time was that taxation should be administered at the local level, in keeping with the spirit of the revolution, wherein centralized government authority was abhorred and smaller independent communities were celebrated. Thus, in one of the great paradoxes of the American Revolution, economic progress during the revolution was strong and the people generally prospered, while the Second Continental Congress struggled at every front to maintain the war effort due to a lack of national administrative authority. The actions of the states themselves did little to help this situation, as compliance with national authority remained inconsistent on most fronts, particularly with regard to financial needs.

With the ratification in 1781 of the Articles of Confederation, Congress was granted concurrent power to control coinage and sole power to regulate value in Article IX: "The United States in Congress assembled shall also have the sole and exclusive right and power of regulating the alloy and value of coin struck by their own authority, or by that of the respective States—fixing the standards of weights and measures throughout the United States." However, the Congress under the Articles of Confederation did not actually coin any money, while a number of the states did. It is perhaps indicative of the continued revolutionary spirit, which had motivated the colonies up to this point that the power to declare bills a legal tender remained a matter of commonly accepted state sovereignty. While a number of states were able to effectively manage the power of emitting bills, extreme examples of depreciation and inflation were seen in some states, such as Rhode Island. The deficiencies inherent in such a piecemeal system would have surely hampered future commerce throughout the United States, prompting James Madison to address the issue in *Federalist* No. 44:

> Had every State a right to regulate the value of its coin, there might be as many different currencies as States, and thus the intercourse among them would be impeded; retrospective alterations in its value might be made, and thus the citizens of other States be injured, and animosities be kindled among the States themselves. The subjects of foreign powers might suffer from the same cause, and hence the Union be discredited and embroiled by the indiscretion of a single member. No one of these mischiefs is less incident to a power in the States to emit paper money, than to coin gold or silver. The power to make anything but gold and silver a tender in payment of debts, is withdrawn from the States, on the same principle with that of issuing a paper currency.

The Nineteenth Century

The power to coin money bestowed on Congress through Art. I, §8, cl. 5 was intentionally vague. The Coinage Act of April 1792 (also called the Mint Act) would set in motion the process whereby the newfound United States could properly carry out the mandate of the coinage clause. Throughout the nineteenth century until the establishment of the Federal Reserve System in 1913, the main struggle was over "bimetallism." Would both gold and silver constitute legal tender, or gold alone? After the Civil War, a second controversy swirled around the constitutionality of the government issuing paper money as legal tender. And, finally, with the establishment of the Federal Reserve System, the power of the Congress to regulate the value of money was gradually overtaken by the development of the modern financial system and larger international market forces. The first two struggles would soon be resolved and fade away. The last—the power of international market forces—would only grow stronger down to the present.

On the advice of Alexander Hamilton, the Coinage Act of 1792 established the Mint of the United States, a bimetal monetary system, and fixed the value of a dollar at 24.75 grains of gold or 371.25 grains of silver—that is, 15 to 1. While the Congress could certainly fix the value of gold and silver, the market actually "regulated the value thereof." During the Napoleonic Wars, an increase in the price of gold made it profitable to melt down gold coins to sell as bullion, which meant that gold coins soon disappeared. With the Coinage Act of 1834, the ratio was change to 16 to 1, and the problem of overpriced gold faded away. Shortly after 1848, however, the California and Australian gold rushes decreased the price of gold and made it profitable to melt down silver coins to sell as bullion, which meant that silver coins soon disappeared. The laws of supply and demand were a constant threat to a policy of bimetallism.

Silver prices remained high until the discovery in 1859 of the Comstock Lode in Nevada. This discovery brought the price of silver down, after some delay, in 1876. At the same time, Europe was moving from bimetallism to a gold standard after the Napoleonic Wars. The Bank [of England] Charter Act of 1844 put Great Britain on the gold standard. Other European countries soon followed. With international trade and commerce moving to the gold standard and the influence of the Comstock Lode not yet fully felt, the Coinage Act of 1834 appeared out of date and in need of revision. This led to the Coinage Act of 1873, which ended the unlimited minting of silver dollars and effectively put the United States on the international gold standard. With this, a thirty-year battle between advocates of the "sound money" gold standard and the populist cry for "free silver" began.

When the price of silver dropped in 1876, silver miners were upset to learn that the U.S. Mint would no longer mint their silver. They were upset because they could no longer bring silver bullion worth fifty to seventy cents in the market to the Mint and receive newly minted silver dollars in return. More importantly, a series of financial panics (i.e., depressions) between 1873 and 1893 led many Americans to oppose the "sound money" gold standard and advocate for "free silver." Since silver was more plentiful, a return to bimetallism would significantly increase the supply of money, counteract the deflationary effects of the gold standard, and restore economic health. The advocates of "free silver" began calling the Coinage Act of 1873 the "Crime of '73." In response, Congress passed the Bland-Allison Act of 1878, over the veto of President Rutherford B. Hayes. The act called for the Mint to purchase between $2 to $4 million of silver bullion per month at the market price, for coinage as silver dollars. This purchase at the market price meant that the difference between the market price of silver and a newly minted dollar would accrue to the government and not to the miners. The Sherman Silver Purchase Act of 1890 doubled the monthly purchase of silver.

However, in the wake of the Panic of 1893, President Grover Cleveland demanded the repeal of the Sherman Act. The struggle for bimetallism and "free silver" only grew more heated as the negative effects of the Panic of 1893 continued. William Jennings Bryant's famous "Cross of Gold" speech at the 1896 Democratic National Convention in Chicago marked the high point of the fight for "free silver." The battle, however, was decided in favor of the gold standard with the passage the Gold Standard Act of 1900. This aligned the United States with European countries. Silver dollars continued to be minted and circulated, but they could now be redeemed for gold, if the holder so desired. The United States stayed on the gold standard until President Richard Nixon abandoned it in 1971, as is discussed below in connection with the Federal Reserve System.

The Civil War and "Greenbacks"

Meanwhile, in order to finance the Civil War, the Federal government was forced to issue fiat money for the first time. This paper money came to be called "greenbacks" because of the color of the back of the bill. The Legal Tender Act of 1862 promised that redemption of the "greenbacks" in gold was only "delayed." It also authorized "greenbacks" as payment for both public and, for the first time, private debt. For the War of 1812 and the Panic of 1837, various sorts of interest-bearing notes had been issued and authorized for the payment of taxes and other public debts, but not for private debt. In *Veazie Bank v. Fenno* (1869), the Supreme Court held that the necessary and proper clause (Art. I, §8, cl. 18) covered the issuing of bills of credit to fund both the war and other government expenses. *Veazie*, however, was not the last word on the issue.

After the war, the "delay" in redeeming "greenbacks" in gold became a question. The question was settled in a dramatic series of cases, the Legal Tender Cases. In the nineteenth century, many private contracts were written specifying payment in gold. Since "greenbacks" could not be immediately redeemed in gold, would payment in "greenbacks" not violate many private contracts that specified payment in gold? In *Hepburn v. Griswold* (1870), the Court held by 4 to 3 that the Legal Tender Act retroactively altered contract terms and, hence, violated Art. I, §10, cl. 1, the obligation of contract clause. On the same day that *Hepburn* was decided, President Ulysses Grant nominated two new justices to fill vacancies on the Supreme Court. These two, William Strong and Joseph Bradley, were confirmed. The very next year, the expanded Court overturned *Hepburn* in *Knox v. Lee* (1871), noting that, during a war, extraordinary measures are often required. Then, in *Juilliard v. Greenman* (1884), the Court extended *Knox* to peacetime. Since then, the use of paper (fiat) money as legal tender for all debts, both public and private, is accepted law, despite the aversion of the drafters of the Constitution to "bills of credit."

A Central Bank?

As important as the Legal Tender Cases and the adoption of the gold standard were, neither resolved the recurrent problem of financial panics. Indeed, as the "free silver" advocates pointed out, adopting the "sound money," but deflationary, gold standard only made the panics worse. To better manage their economies, several European countries had developed a central bank system. The Bank of England was the primary model. After the severe Panic of 1907, the need for a central bank in the United States was recognized, again. Without a central bank, to manage the economy—and, hence, the value of "coins"—one financial panic after another was predictable. To be sure, eastern financial and mercantile interests had long recognized the need for a central bank. However, southern and western agricultural interests were strongly opposed until the twentieth century and the establishment of the Federal Reserve System in 1913.

After the adoption of the Articles of Confederation and Perpetual Union on March 1, 1781, one of the first acts of the Confederal Congress was to charter the Bank of North America on May 26, 1781. The Bank was a private business, but the government owned 63.3 percent of its shares. The Bank was essentially an experiment, although it did facilitate the financing of the final two years of the Revolutionary War. With the end of the war in 1783, Robert Morris, Superintendent of Finances, sold the government shares, took back the government deposits, and ended the Bank's congressional charter. The Bank was then chartered under Pennsylvania law and flourished as the county's first commercial bank.

After the adoption of the Constitution of the United States in 1789, Alexander Hamilton championed the establishment of the First Bank of the United States (1791–1811). The First Bank was bitterly opposed by Thomas Jefferson, James Madison, the Jeffersonian Democrats, and other agricultural interests. But Hamilton and the Federalists prevailed—until 1811. When the Bank's charter was up for renewal in 1811, James Madison was president and the Jeffersonian Democrats controlled Congress. Their opposition to the First Bank had not diminished. The vote on legislation to renew the First Bank's charter produced a tie in the Senate, which Vice-President George Clinton broke by voting against renewal. However, the War of 1812 commenced the very next year. Without a bank to facilitate the financing of the war, the Treasury struggled. In addition, the war crippled the economy, especially foreign trade. Congressman John C. Calhoun and others soon realized that the solution to both problems was to charter a new bank. President Madison reluctantly agreed. The Second Bank of the United States received a twenty-year charter, 1816–1836.

In anticipation of the 1836 end of its charter, a bill to renew the charter of the Second Bank was introduced in 1832. It passed, but President Andrew Jackson, an ardent opponent of the Second Bank, vetoed the bill. The veto was taken up by Henry Clay, presidential candidate for the National Republican Party, and made the central issue of the 1832 presidential campaign. Jackson won reelection with 55 percent of the popular vote. Continuing his "War on the Bank," Jackson withdrew all government funds from the bank in 1833. In 1836, the Bank turned itself into a private corporation, but did not survive as the Bank of North America had. It was liquidated in 1841.

President Jackson has not been the only ardent opponent of the Second Bank. Two important attempts were made to find the Second Bank unconstitutional. In the first, Maryland passed a law taxing bank notes issued by the Second Bank. James McCulloch, cashier of the Baltimore branch, refused to pay the tax. In *McCulloch v. Maryland* (1819), Chief Justice John Marshall held, first, that the necessary and proper clause empowers the Congress to charter a bank, even though chartering banks is not one of the enumerated powers in the Constitution. This was one of the first, and most important, decisions expanding the power of Congress to legislate beyond a very strict interpretation of its enumerated powers. Second, Marshall held that Maryland had no power to tax an entity created by Congress under the necessary and proper clause. The federal law that created the entity is superior to state law under the supremacy clause, Art. VI, cl. 2. Again, this was a fundamentally important judicial decision.

In the second attempt, the issue was how to define the Art. I, §10, cl. 1 that prohibited states to "coin money; emit bills of credit; [and] make any thing but gold and silver coin a tender in payment of debts." The Bank of the Commonwealth of Kentucky was a state-chartered bank that was also wholly owned by the state of Kentucky. Could such a bank issue bank notes without violating the section 10 prohibition? In *Briscoe v. Bank of Kentucky* (1837), Chief Justice Roger Taney ruled that the Bank of Kentucky could issue such notes because the notes had not been issued directly by the state and because the notes were backed by the bank's own credit, and not the credit of the state.

Together the two decisions established the framework within which both banking and the economy would be managed for the remainder of the nineteenth century. Both a central bank and state banks were constitutional, and both could issue paper money.

But animosity against the establishment of a central bank was such that state chartered banks would provide most banking services and issuing paper money. On this decentralized, largely uncoordinated basis, the United States built its financial system. The system, however, was characterized by a regular series of financial panics that produced great suffering and economic dislocation. Finally, though, the Panic of 1907 drove home the need for a more rational system. This realization led to the Federal Reserve Act of 1913.

The Federal Reserve Act of 1913

The Federal Reserve Act created twelve regional reserve banks that are owned by the member banks in each region. The Federal Reserve is governed by a Board of Governors appointed by the president and confirmed by the Senate to fourteen-year terms. Although it is a federal agency, it is independent in that it makes its own decisions without seeking approval from either the president or Congress. Its monetary policy objectives, as revised in 1977, are to "maintain long run growth of the monetary and credit aggregates commensurate with the economy's long run potential to increase production, so as to promote effectively the goals of maximum employment, stable prices, and moderate long-term interest rates." The Federal Reserve System is generally thought to have mishandled the Great Depression of the 1930s, making it much worse. But it is generally thought to have responded to the 2008 financial crisis in a much more successful manner by moderating the negative impacts.

In effect, the establishment of Federal Reserve System was the first step in acknowledging that the Congress could no longer "regulate the Value" of "coin." What had always been true was increasingly obvious. In a modern financial system, the international market sets the value of money, and a central bank is needed to actively intervene and regulate the market to the extent this is possible. But, if the international market is the ultimate regulator, how is it to be regulated?

The answer to this question was given in July 1944, during the concluding months of World War II. Wishing to avoid the economic turmoil that had followed World War I, including the Great Depression, delegates from forty-four Allied nations met in Bretton Woods, New Hampshire, to formulate a plan for post-war economic cooperation. The plan called for three new international institutions: the International Bank of Reconstruction and Development (IBRD), which became part of the World Bank, the International Monetary Fund (IMF), and the International Trade Organization. The Senate quickly ratified the agreements for IBRD and the IMF, but failed to ratify the agreement to establish the International Trade Organization. Not until 1995 was this third organization, now called the World Trade Organization (WTO), established.

At its core, the new international system allowed countries to regulate unusual capital flows, but also established fixed exchange rates among the countries of the world to encourage foreign trade among them. These rates were based on a gold standard that valued one ounce of gold at US$35. In support of the Bretton Woods System, the United States Congress promised to convert dollars into gold at US$35 to an ounce whenever such payment was requested.

From 1945 until the end of the 1960s, the Bretton Woods Agreement worked well. All the different currencies of the world were pegged to the dollar at the fixed rate of $35 per ounce of gold. The values of different currencies moved up or down, but the value of the dollar did not change. This stabilized the international monetary system and fostered post–World War II economic development. During the 1960s, though, changes in the international economic system, the costs of President Lyndon Johnson's "Great Society" programs, and the escalating cost of the War in Vietnam, all led to inflation and a deteriorating economic situation in the United States. In response, President Richard Nixon took the United States off the gold standard on August 15, 1971, by ending the convertibility of dollars into gold. Since then, the dollar and most other currencies have floated. The international foreign exchange market now determines the value of dollar and every other currency—not the Congress or anyone else.

FUTURE IMPLICATIONS

With the coming of the Bretton Woods Institutions after World War II, the ability of the Congress to "regulate the Value" of money essentially disappeared, but it vanished altogether when President Nixon took the United States off the gold standard definitively and for good. The demands of an interdependent world economy, which had always been the main driving force "regulating the value" of money, were now literally overwhelming. Thus, in the future, the states will continue to be prohibited to "coin money; emit bills of credit; make any thing but gold and silver coin a tender in payment of debts," in accordance with Article I, §10, cl. 1. Likewise, the Congress will continue to exercise its power under Art. I, §8, cl. 6 to "punish counterfeiting," and, under Art. I, §8, cl. 5, to "fix the Standard of Weights and Measures." The Congress will also continue to "coin Money" under Art. I, §8, cl. 5, that is to actually mint or print dollars. The Congress, however, has lost for evermore its Art. I, §8, cl. 5 power to "regulate the Value" of "coin." This power is now in the hands of yet-to-be-negotiated international agreements.

FURTHER READING

Currie, David P. 1999. Weights & Measures. *Green Bag* 2d. 261–266.

Judson, Lewis V. 1976. *Weights and Measures Standards of the United States.* Washington, D.C.: National Bureau of Standards.

Natelson, Robert G. 2008. Paper Money and the Original Understanding of the Coinage Clause. *Harvard Journal of Law and Public Policy.* 31:3. 1017–1081.

Timberlake, Richard. 1991. *Gold, Greenbacks, and the Constitution.* Berryville, VA: George Edward Durrell Foundation.

Wilson, Thomas. 1992. *The Power "to Coin" Money: The Exercise of Monetary Powers by the Congress.* Armonk, NY: M. E. Sharpe.

7 THE POWER TO ESTABLISH POST OFFICES AND POST ROADS

Richard B. Kielbowicz

Article I, section 8, clause 7
To establish Post Offices and post Roads

KEY TERMS

Parcel Post: In 1913, the post office was authorized to deliver small packages of up to four pounds. Before then, it delivered only letters.

Postal Savings Bank: Between 1910 and 1966, local post offices provided convenient savings account services for small savers, especially in rural areas.

Rural Free Delivery (RFD): Between 1902 and 1916, Congress mandated that mail be delivered to the doorstep of rural households. Previously, these households had to drive into town and pick up their mail at the post office.

HISTORY AND DEVELOPMENT

In arguing for the adoption of the Constitution, James Madison downplayed the potential—and potential controversy—associated with the postal clause: "The power of establishing post roads must, in every view, be a harmless power, and may, perhaps, by judicious management, become productive of great public conveniency," he wrote in *Federalist* No. 42. Within a few decades, however, the postal clause became one of the most valuable sources of authority for those who envisioned an activist federal government. Indeed, throughout most of American history, the post office operated the largest institution, public or private, in the nation, thereby projecting the federal government's presence into communities far from Washington, D.C. Not surprisingly, then, the seemingly innocuous constitutional language eventually triggered wide-ranging debates about the limits of congressional authority and the role of the federal government in people's daily lives.

From the adoption of the Constitution until 1971, Congress controlled—or could control, if it cared to—virtually all facets of the nation's postal operations. As a practical matter, the Post Office Department gained considerable administrative discretion by the late 1800s. But the latitude accorded the post office often depended on the politics of the moment—the urgency of other matters preoccupying lawmakers' time, partisan configurations in Congress, presidential–congressional relations, and the activities of postal patrons and competitors. In 1971, Congress relinquished much of its control over postal affairs by converting the Post Office Department into an independent government corporation, the U.S. Postal Service (USPS). Despite loosening its grip over mail operations, Congress continues to prescribe the broad terms governing today's postal system.

The Colonial American Post Office

The colonial American post office naturally inherited some of the features and underlying principles of the British system. The British post office had long been a government monopoly. Although domestic security furnished the original rationale—controlling the flow of information sustained the monarch's authority—the basis for the monopoly shifted as the government opened the service to merchants and other customers. The British jurist William Blackstone, whose legal treatise influenced legal thinking in the colonies and the early United States, saw the maintenance of a government postal monopoly as an economic necessity. Competing services, he explained, would skim off the profitable routes and drain revenue needed to sustain the government mails.

Britain attempted to regularize its North American postal operations in 1692 with the appointment of a postmaster general for the colonies. For decades, however, service remained underdeveloped, erratic, and unprofitable for the crown. When Benjamin Franklin became one of two deputy postmasters general for the colonies in 1753, the indefatigable printer expanded the network and improved services, finally earning the revenue long sought by British authorities. Franklin's dismissal as postmaster general in 1774, and the mounting tensions between colonists and British authorities, degraded postal operations. Newspaper publisher William Goddard launched his short-lived Constitutional Post in 1774 to give colonists, especially those sympathetic to the revolutionary cause, a communication network free from British control. A year later, the Continental Congress authorized the new nation's first official postal system and appointed Benjamin Franklin as the postmaster general, though he served only until becoming minister to France.

The United States' first national charter, the Articles of Confederation (1781), gave Congress "the sole and exclusive right [of] . . . establishing and regulating post-offices from one state to another." This language suggests that congressional purview did not extend to intrastate communication and made no reference to post roads. When the exigencies of war permitted, Congress revised and codified postal regulations. The

Ordinance of October 18, 1782, which guided the post office for ten years, articulated a rationale for governmental postal services that emphasized the importance of communicating intelligence for the safety and commercial development of the nation. The Ordinance also protected the sanctity of the mails, perhaps a reaction to the British practice of monitoring communications, but it retained language about maintaining a government postal monopoly except on the frontier where settlements were permitted to arrange private posts if the public mails did not reach their towns.

The debates over the Constitution provide limited insight into contemporaries' understanding of Congress's postal power. Scattered references to the postal clause leading to ratification suggest that some viewed the post office as a revenue-raising agency for the federal government. Conferring power to establish post offices occasioned little debate, but the additional authority to establish post roads, which some feared intruded on the prerogatives of states, passed by a narrow margin. Benjamin Franklin proposed going further—allowing the government to dig canals—a motion that failed to attract much support. Franklin's idea, however, anticipated one of the major postal controversies of the nineteenth century: did the authority to establish post roads entail the power to build a transportation network that carried the mails?

Establishing a Postal Network

While the meaning of "the power to establish post offices" occasioned little confusion, the meaning of establishing post roads prompted debates in the young republic. In practice, Congress quickly built out the nation's postal network, usually with little regard for cost, and often working in partnership with the private sector. In fact, the boundaries between public and private, federal and state, often triggered debates about the reach of the postal clause. Did *establish* confer the power to simply designate existing roads as post routes or, much more expansively, authorize Congress to build roads? Could the federal government build post roads without the consent of the affected states? Furthermore, post offices and post roads needed transports to actually move the mail throughout the nation. Did the postal clause empower the post office to operate its own system of transports, or should this function be left to private carriers? And did the postal clause give the government a monopoly over the carriage of mail matter, with authority to ban private services?

The post office initially operated as a unit of the Treasury, with the postmaster general designating routes largely guided by revenue expectations. But the imperative to provide universal service, connecting all communities of any consequence to the network, quickly trumped the expectation that postal operations should be extended only where revenues would cover costs. With the Post Office Act of 1792, Congress began directing the postmaster general to contract for mail delivery on routes that lawmakers themselves specified in excruciatingly detailed postal acts.

Frontier communities began flooding Congress with petitions asking for mail service. The House Committee on the Post Office and Post Roads, with members from most states, proved particularly responsive; serious petitions were rarely if ever ignored, assuring the rapid expansion of postal operations to newly settled areas. In the early 1800s, the postal network grew several times faster than the population. Congress sporadically worried about unproductive routes, especially with chronic deficits after the War of 1812. Postal laws required the postmaster general to report unproductive routes to Congress and sometimes gave the department leeway to discontinue revenue-losing services, but the laws still protected essential services. Even as postal deficits mounted in the mid-1800s with the rapid extension of service into the West, Congress reaffirmed its commitment to continue enlarging mail service. An 1851 law that reduced postage also barred the Post Office Department from closing offices or discontinuing service on a post route because of declining revenues. Direct congressional control over postal operations, and lawmakers' responsiveness to constituents meant that for decades Congress did not seriously entertain a return to the 1790s' policy of a break-even postal service. Congress regularly appropriated money from the Treasury to cover the post office's deficits.

By the close of the nineteenth century, Congress had created a postal network that connected all towns, with daily delivery to many residents' doorsteps. The most noticeable gap in true universal postal service was the relatively poor access to the network for people living in the countryside. Members of Congress representing rural constituencies increasingly pointed to the inequities in a system that provided daily free delivery to city households while requiring country residents—half of all Americans—to travel to town, often many miles, to retrieve their mail. The inauguration of Rural Free Delivery (RFD) narrowed the gap between urban and rural service. Congress put RFD on a permanent footing in 1902, and in 1916 mandated that mail delivery reach the nation's entire rural population, a policy retained in the statute establishing the modern postal establishment. In authorizing this last component of a national postal network, Congress launched "the least heralded and in some ways the most important communications revolution in American history," according to historian Daniel J. Boorstin. "Now for the first time it was normal for every person in the United States to be accessible by cheap public communications . . . From every farmer's doorstep there now ran a highway to the world."

Congress found a number of ancillary purposes for the nationwide infrastructure it established under the postal clause. Thousands of post offices routinely sold savings bonds, reported aliens' addresses, stored flags used at veterans' funerals, sold migratory bird stamps, located relatives of deceased servicemembers, displayed recruiting material and FBI wanted posters, assisted the Federal Housing Administration in conducting surveys of housing conditions, and distributed income tax forms in lobbies. Local post offices, in short, dispensed information to residents about a range of federal programs.

Government Posts and the Transportation Network

Prominent lawmakers of the early republic argued that the postal clause did empower the federal government to engage in road building or repair to move the mails. Exponents of this view believed that the word *establish* necessarily entailed creating the infrastructure. Furthermore, they pointed out that the omission of this enumerated power in the Articles of Confederation meant that its inclusion in the Constitution supported an expansive reading. Other lawmakers seemed more ambivalent.

Thomas Jefferson recognized the potential value of federal involvement in internal improvements, but suggested this might require an express grant of power through a constitutional amendment.

Despite calls for the federal government to finance new post roads, Congress proceeded cautiously, expecting state and local governments to arrange for construction and repair. Although the Cumberland or National Road, begun in 1811, was a noteworthy exception to this rule, Congress generally understood its authority to mean that it could designate existing roads as postal routes. Even the power to designate, though, stimulated local and state governments to upgrade their transportation infrastructure. On a smaller scale, communities seeking RFD service often had to improve country lanes. Indeed, RFD became a powerful stimulus for paving country roads.

Congress used contracts to transport mail as a proxy for a more direct federal transportation policy; these contracts helped develop and shape the nation's stagecoach lines, steamships, railroads, and airlines. Even before the Constitution, Congress closely supervised the modes used to move the mails because they affected the quality of postal service and stimulated improvements in the young nation's transportation system. Initially, post riders employed by the post office carried mail from town to town. The first noteworthy improvement in mail transport, the use of stagecoaches, was authorized by the Continental Congress. After the adoption of the Constitution, Congress renewed the postmaster general's authority to contract with private stagecoach firms, though post riders and sulkies continued to provide much of the transportation. Congress set the basic terms under which the postmaster general purchased transportation services.

With the inducement provided by mail contracts, stagecoach companies expanded their operations into new areas, building a transportation network for the growing nation. Rather than competing with private transports, except on rare occasions, the Post Office became one of their biggest customers and boosters. One of the rare occasions in which the post office directly entered the transportation business came at the close of the 1700s. When private stagecoach transportation failed to provide satisfactory service on key lines, the post office experimented with operating its own transports—both schooners along the coast and stagecoaches on key segments of the main North–South post road. Although the schooner service lasted only sixteen months, the post office continued to operate segments of the nation's stagecoach network until 1818. By then, the lines were no longer profitable, the postmaster general was devoting too much time to managing the service, and private contractors were complaining about government competition.

Steamboats represented a major innovation in transport technology before railroads. In 1813 Congress authorized the use of steamboat lines where they would provide service comparable, in regularity and cost, to land transports. In 1823, Congress declared waterways on which steamboats traveled to be post roads, curtailing the growing practice of steamboat crews and passengers carrying letters outside the mails, and depriving the post office of revenue. Although steamboats had a relatively modest impact on domestic mail transportation, ocean-going steamship lines proved significant in international mail exchanges. Moreover, Congress used contracts to carry mail across the Atlantic and Pacific oceans as a stimulus to the American maritime industry.

Railroads provided the bulk of inter-city mail transportation from the mid-1800s to the mid-1900s. The attributes of railroad transport—fast, regular, and able to accommodate bulky shipments—perfectly suited the Post Office Department's needs. Touting these advantages, railroad promoters sought aid from Congress, beginning as early as 1819, to help launch the first rail lines. Congress declined to act at first. Nonetheless, mail contractors continued to incorporate railroads into their operations. In 1838, Congress declared every rail line a post route and authorized the postmaster general to contract for mail transport at a 25 percent premium over carriage by stage. For decades thereafter, mail contracts gave Congress leverage over the railroad industry and often prompted disputes about appropriate levels of compensation.

Contracts to carry the mail played an even more important role in shaping the fledgling airline industry and producing public benefits beyond simply transporting letters. Early barnstorming operations—small, poorly capitalized airlines flying unsafe craft over short routes on irregular schedules—did not suit the needs of the Post Office Department or most passengers. Dangling mail contracts as incentives, Congress and the department encouraged private firms to provide regular service using larger, safer equipment (the post office paid a premium to those whose craft could carry passengers) over long distances. In the long run, visionary lawmakers believed, an airline industry earning most of its revenue from passengers would be in a better position to carry mail than one largely dependent on government contracts.

Protecting the Government's Postal Monopoly

From the earliest days of the Constitution, Congress interpreted the postal clause as limiting private mails that competed with the public posts. The long and often contentious history of relations between the public posts and private carriers frequently erupted into disputes about the legitimacy and scope of the government's monopoly over the mails. Although Congress relaxed some restrictions on private delivery services in the Postal Reorganization Act of 1970, this issue remains a flashpoint in postal policy.

Early statutory language about the postal monopoly hints at the reason behind the ban on private carriers. The 1792 law, the first overhaul under the Constitution, prohibited the transportation of letters "on any established post-road, or any packet [i.e., boat], or other vessel or boat, or any conveyance whatsoever, whereby the revenue of the general post-office may be injured." Five years later, Congress extended the monopoly to bar private carriers from using any roads parallel to a post road. These early laws suggest that the monopoly was intended to protect the government's ability to raise revenues that could be remitted to the Treasury. Indeed, the post office earned a surplus every year until 1808 and for many years after, until 1820.

The advent of railroads, with their easy and rapid transportation of letters between cities, marks the dividing point in congressional attention to the postal monopoly. From the Articles of Confederation until the early 1840s, Congress reflexively reenacted laws establishing a basic postal monopoly. When railroads enabled private express companies to provide cheap inter-city mail delivery, Congress focused on the nature of the government's monopoly and articulated a rationale for it. Without ever using terms now associated with modern communication networks—*universal service, natural monopoly, cream-skimming, network effects,* and *cross-subsidy*—lawmakers engaged in an analysis that implicitly linked these concepts. An 1845 act closed loopholes in laws that had allowed the private expresses to thrive. The floor debate revealed widespread agreement that the post office had a duty to provide service to all citizens (universal service); that private competitors would impair fulfillment of that mission by serving only areas where profitable to do so (the government's natural monopoly versus private-sector cream-skimming); and that areas of high-volume, low-cost service appropriately subsidized areas of low-volume, high-cost operations (cross-subsidies) because of the value to everyone on the network of adding new users (network effects). The Supreme Court has upheld the postal monopoly's constitutionality, recognizing its importance in protecting the department's revenues from private-sector firm cream-skimming—serving high-value, low-cost areas and leaving the money-losing segments to the government.

The 1845 law laid the foundation for the modern private express statutes. Derived from the postal clause, this cluster of federal laws prevents private couriers from carrying letter-type mail (historically the post office's chief source of revenue) on any post road, essentially all land and water routes. The law also bars access to household and business mailboxes unless postage has been paid, another barrier to private delivery. Not surprisingly, these restrictions have aroused the ire of those who view them as unnecessary limitations on private enterprise. In response, Congress has selectively relaxed the private express statutes, most notably by allowing private couriers to deliver high-value letter mail, for which a premium fee has been paid, mainly express mail.

The Postal Clause and the Press

Like a computer without software, a postal infrastructure without content accomplishes little. Relying on the postal clause, Congress decided what information and materials could be carried by post—content that activated the potential of the physical network. Although all types of mail presented vexing questions at one time or another, the meaning of the postal clause regularly came into play in connection with public information—newspapers, magazines, books, and advertisements—in the mail. Since the adoption of the Constitution, Congress has emphasized the postal system's role in circulating information that sustained the civic life of the nation. The postal clause thus provided the basis for an affirmative communication policy that balanced the First Amendment's negative admonition that Congress shall not abridge freedom of the press.

In the first overhaul of postal policy after the adoption of the Constitution, Congress committed the federal government to underwrite the circulation of news, especially intelligence about public affairs. A 1792 postal law fixed exceptionally low postage on newspapers—a maximum of 1.5 cents for circulation anywhere in the country. In contrast, a three-sheet letter sent beyond 450 miles paid 75 cents. The same law also allowed editors to exchange their papers postage-free. This enabled editors to obtain nonlocal news by copying stories from out-of-town publications, the principal means of newsgathering before wire services emerged at mid-century. Together, these two provisions allowed newspaper editors to gather news from anywhere at no cost and then disseminate it to readers at low rates, a policy that Congress hoped would bind the geographically and socially diverse United States at a time of fragile nationalism. During the next two hundred years, Congress extended the most-favored postal status to other types of *public* information circulating in the mails. In the mid-1800s, lawmakers granted magazines the same postal status as newspapers. And in the twentieth century, Congress created favored rate categories for books, library materials, and mail circulated for the benefit of nonprofit organizations.

Conferring these postal benefits also positioned Congress to impose conditions and regulate the media in ways that raised questions about the relation of the postal clause to the First Amendment. Congress developed mail classifications that distinguished between periodicals that carried some advertising and advertising publications that carried some editorial content—a distinction involving major differences in postage. To administer its mail classification scheme, Congress allowed postal officials to scrutinize the advertising and subscription practices of publications. Such federal intrusion into the operations of the press would normally violate the First Amendment, but courts recognized that Congress was simply imposing conditions on publications that took advantage of a government benefit—cheap postage. Most strikingly, Congress passed the Newspaper Publicity Act (1912), which made use of the second-class rate conditional on the disclosure of a publication's ownership, on the clear separation of news and advertising content, and on the truthful statement of circulation. The Supreme Court rejected a First Amendment challenge to these rules, and they still apply today.

Congress relied on the postal clause to censor the mails. The issue first arose in connection with antislavery literature circulated by abolition societies in the 1830s. Southern states, which prohibited the dissemination of messages challenging slavery, urged the post office to ban such mail, and Congress debated the constitutionality of postal censorship without reaching a decision. Southern postmasters and mobs took matters into their own hands, destroying such mail from the North, with the acquiescence of post office headquarters. Congress did expressly authorize postal censorship at times of perceived danger to national security in the twentieth century. During World War I, potentially seditious material was declared non-mailable, and foreign-language periodicals were required to file translations of articles touching on the war effort. Platoons of translators worked under the auspices of the Post Office Department to monitor the contents of the numerous foreign-language publications in the United States. Congress also enlisted the post office in 1962 to detain communist propaganda, until the Supreme Court three years later held that the statute violated addressees' First Amendment rights.

Congress also wielded the postal clause as an instrument of federal police power to protect the public welfare. Most notably, the Post Office Department became the federal government's biggest censor of obscene and indecent materials. Congress first outlawed obscene material in the mail in 1865 and then broadened its scope with the Comstock Act in 1873. In the ensuing decades, postal officials prosecuted all manner of material, including pamphlets about birth control and irreverent reflections on religion, until the Supreme Court imposed First Amendment limits on postal censorship in *Hannegan v. Esquire* (1946). At various times federal law banned the mailing of foreign divorce information, liquor and lottery advertising, materials that violated copyright law, illegally obtained defense intelligence, and more. Mail fraud statutes, in addition, gave the post office far-reaching police powers. The federal government, through the reach of the post office, established jurisdiction over a wide range of illegal activities even when use of the mails did not constitute a central part of the scheme.

Stretching the Meaning of "Postal"

While the Constitution's commerce clause empowered Congress to regulate many private-sector activities, it did not authorize the federal government to directly compete with businesses. Enthusiasts for government enterprise instead looked to the postal clause. After all, it provided the basis for establishing federal offices throughout the country, and Congress often appeared eager to graft non-postal functions onto this ready-made network. Citing the postal clause, Populists and Progressives (1880–1920) spoke of postal savings, a postal express (i.e., parcel post), and a postal telecommunication network all in the same breath—and attained the first two objectives by 1912. This marked the heyday of efforts to expand the domain of postal enterprise. Later innovations occurred *within* the boundaries of postal enterprise drawn before the First World War.

Postal Savings Banks

As early as 1861, a patron of the Pittsburgh post office urged the local postmaster to establish a bank where citizens could safely deposit money without fear of losing their savings. The idea continued to receive sporadic attention, prompting the postmaster general in 1874 to urge that "the time has come when a resolute effort should be made to determine how far the Post Office Department can properly go in its efforts to accommodate the public, without trespassing unwarrantably upon the sphere of private enterprise." By the 1880s, Populists saw a savings system as a logical extension of the Post Office Department's mandate. Postal banks, they asserted, would encourage thrift among immigrants, the working class, and rural inhabitants, while promoting economic stability by bringing unused money into the economy to stimulate business and by slowing the flow of U.S. dollars to other countries. These government banks would also protect vulnerable people against "swindlers, unsafe deposits and unwise investments, and at the same time increase the investors' loyalty to the government by giving them a stake in a stable economy." And, proponents claimed, all this could be accomplished with the existing postal network.

The 1907 financial panic, which forced the closure of many banks, provided the impetus for the enactment of the 1910 postal savings law. The American Bankers Association and other businesses charged that a government banking system managed by the post office exceeded the authority of the postal clause and intruded into the private sector. To smooth the way for passage, Congress gathered data about the success of postal savings banks in countries around the world. Although the American Bankers Association committed one million dollars to block the legislation, it finally conceded that the creation of postal savings banks was inevitable and certainly preferable to legislative action to guarantee bank deposits, another remedy proposed in the wake of the 1907 panic.

In January 1911, post offices began offering saving accounts to the public. Postal savings proved especially attractive during the Depression, when many private banks cut depositors' interest rates or failed altogether. The system peaked shortly after World War II, and then started a steady decline as private banks raised interests and offered protection against the loss of funds. By the 1960s, Congress and postal administrators concurred that postal savings banks had outlived their original usefulness. In 1966, Congress voted to discontinue the banks, though offering banking functions under the auspices of the postal service is an idea still occasionally raised today.

Parcel Post

In many respects, authorizing parcel post represented Congress's most far-reaching use of the postal clause. Though perhaps hard to appreciate today, parcel post was one of the most contentious public policy issues in turn-of-the-century America, provoking cries that Congress had exceeded its powers by putting the federal government in direct competition with well-established private firms. Parcel post legislation stopped short of appropriating private firms, but proponents and opponents both acknowledged that it redefined the accepted domain of postal activity.

Before the inauguration of parcel post on January 1, 1913, the post office refused to carry any parcel weighing more than four pounds. Heavier items came by private delivery firms, mainly express companies that operated as subsidiaries of railroads. Investigations by the Interstate Commerce Commission and muckraking journalists revealed that express companies double-charged and overcharged, refused to tell customers about free delivery areas beyond rail depots, sent shipments by circuitous routes to inflate costs, discriminated among customers, and more. Proponents also pointed out that adding parcel post to the suite of other mail services made good business sense, because it capitalized on the department's underutilized nationwide infrastructure. The success of Rural Free Delivery heightened demand for parcel post among rural Americans, many of whom lived outside express companies' service areas. RFD routes radiating from small towns provided an infrastructure, and the advertising-filled periodicals reaching farmers' lanes stimulated the demand for mail-order merchandise, but before 1913 the post office could not deliver the fruits of all this communication—parcels.

Congress resisted repeated calls to hold hearings on parcel post until 1910. Critics blamed congressional obstructionism on the railroad lobby's influence over such lawmakers as House Speaker Joseph Cannon and key senators. The 1910 elections reconstituted Congress along lines more amenable to parcel post, and by 1912 all major parties and their presidential candidate endorsed parcel post; socialists subsumed it among more radical proposals. Accordingly, at least twenty parcel post bills introduced in the House of Representatives were referred to the post office committee. As the debate crested, Congress considered four options: (1) leave the parcel delivery business entirely to the private sector; (2) subject private carriers to stricter regulation by the Interstate Commerce Commission; (3) empower the post office to compete with the private sector; or (4) establish an outright public monopoly of package delivery under the Post Office Department. Congress ultimately chose the third option, concluding that public–private competition in the package delivery business would maximize service and benefits for society while minimizing rates.

Postal Telegraph and Telephone

Except for the United States, virtually every nation regarded the telegraph and telephone as natural extensions of the state's mail monopoly and operated them under a postal ministry. The Constitution's postal clause put the oldest information-transmitting institution in government hands, and many considered the telegraph to be the functional equivalent of the mails. Why, then, did the Post Office Department fail to secure its most far-reaching expansion of service—into telecommunication?

Most people associated with the first American telegraph line, built with federal funds, viewed it as a natural extension of the federal government's postal power. The Secretary of the Treasury's 1837 call for proposals to establish a telegraph system assumed that it properly belonged with the post office. When Samuel F. B. Morse submitted his plan, he similarly compared a telegraph network to the mail system. Built with federal funds, Morse's Washington-to-Baltimore telegraph operated under the supervision of the Treasury until Congress shifted control to the post office. Although the postmaster general recommended that Congress retain and extend the network of wired communication, lawmakers declined, and the line was sold to private interests in 1847. The decision to remove telegraphy from the post office stemmed mostly from circumstances of the moment rather than concerns about the constitutionality of a postal telegraph. An 1845 report from the House Ways and Means Committee had concluded that the postal clause furnished sufficient authority.

After two decades of wildcat development, the telegraph industry exhibited a pronounced tendency toward monopoly. In 1866, the year that Western Union absorbed its two major rivals, Congress passed a law with the potential to restructure the telegraph industry. On one hand, the law gave telegraph companies land-grant privileges similar to those enjoyed by railroads. On the other hand, the legislation provided that the government could purchase, after 1871, any company that accepted these privileges. The purchase price would be set by a five-person committee jointly selected by the government and industry. This law gave the government two options for "postalizing" (a nineteenth-century term) the telegraph: the government could take over all telegraph companies to operate as a monopoly, or it could acquire one firm and operate it in competition with Western Union.

The 1866 law heartened advocates of post office innovation. The nationalization of the British telegraph in 1869 invigorated the American campaign for a postal telegraph. Accordingly, at least one hundred bills to create a postal telegraph (later including the telephone) were introduced in Congress before 1900, and congressional committees reported—many favorably, usually noting Western Union's abuses. Similar legislation was continually debated between 1900 and 1920. Proponents of postal telecommunication popularized the view of telegraphy and telephony as natural monopolies. Furthermore, telecommunication had become a strategic input for other sectors of the economy—finance, commerce, transportation, and more. Left in private hands, some feared that a monopolistic telegraph company could use its power to restrict competition in industries dependent on the information it transmitted.

The campaign for postal involvement in telecommunications also received support from the U.S. Supreme Court. An 1877 decision, *Pensacola Telegraph Co. v. Western Union Telegraph Co.*, construed the postal clause elastically. In this case, Florida law blocked Western Union from competing with a company chartered within the state. The Supreme Court upheld Western Union's challenge to such state regulation; it considered both the Constitution's postal and commerce clauses in reaching its decision. "Post-offices and post-roads are established to facilitate the transmission of intelligence," the Court wrote.

> The powers thus granted are not confined to the instrumentalities of commerce, or the postal service known or in use when the Constitution was adopted, but they keep pace with the progress of the country, and adapt themselves to new developments of time and circumstances. They extend from the horse with its rider to the stage-coach, from the sailing-vessel to the steamboat, from the coach and the steamboat to the railroad, and from the railroad to the telegraph, as these new agencies are successively brought into use to meet the demands of increasing population and wealth.

The court, however, declined in this case to decide whether the post office could monopolize the nation's telegraphy or simply compete with private companies.

With passage of postal savings (1910) and parcel post (1912), it seemed to many—including the new telecommunication giant, AT&T—but a short step to a postal telegraph and telephone. Informed commentators proclaimed passage of such legislation a near certainty. But AT&T responded with a broad and sophisticated campaign against any further expansion of postal enterprise. Legislation authorizing the post office to offer telecommunication services languished in Congress, until the outbreak of World War I gave the Post Office Department an opportunity to prove its administrative capability. In December 1917, Congress put the Post Office Department in charge of the nation's wire communications as a wartime measure. The postmaster general hoped that this was the first step in permanently converting the Post Office Department into a Department of Communication. A number of problems, however, plagued the nation's telephone system while under post office control, and Congress returned the wires to private hands after one year because the experience had been so bad. The campaign for postal involvement in telecommunication was dead, until the advent of the Internet resurrected some possibilities.

FUTURE IMPLICATIONS

Ever-mounting postal deficits, widely publicized breakdowns in mail delivery, and concerns about its own partisan meddling in postal affairs prompted Congress in 1970 to pass the Postal Reorganization Act. Under this law, Congress relinquished direct control over postal affairs by converting the Post Office Department into a government corporation, the U.S. Postal Service. A Postal Service board of governors exercised ultimate management authority and selected the postmaster general, removing the position from the president's cabinet. A new independent regulatory body, the Postal Rate Commission, reviewed the board's requests for rate hikes. The lobbying that had characterized congressional ratemaking was now forbidden by law. The Postal Reorganization Act stipulated that rates reflect the costs of delivering each type of mail, though it retained some consideration for the social and cultural value of periodicals and materials sent by nonprofit organizations. Challenges to the commission's decision could be appealed the courts, unlike congressionally set rates. Despite this transformation, Congress continued to exercise its authority in politically sensitive postal matters, especially those affecting businesses and rural constituents.

When the U.S. Postal Service repeatedly attempted to close rural post offices and then experimented with electronic mail, Congress reined in the nominally independent agency. Postal Service analyses in the 1970s and 1980s revealed that small-town offices served relatively few patrons for a disproportionate cost. Plans to consolidate these offices, however, ran afoul of members of Congress in the affected districts, who emphasized the intangible value of a post office in the social life of rural communities. Similarly, the Postal Service's pioneering e-mail service, launched in the late 1970s, aroused opposition from businesses and regulatory agencies. Significantly, too, members of Congress raised concerns about the government mail service expanding into telecommunication, a field long occupied by private firms. Hemmed in by a number of restrictions, the Postal Service abandoned its electronic mail service in 1985. In one sense, little had changed with the conversion of the Post Office Department into the Postal Service: Congress mandated that the government mails operate in a businesslike fashion, but do so while providing some money-losing, socially beneficial services and while avoiding innovation that put it in competition with private-sector businesses.

In 2001, the Government Accountability Office placed the USPS on a list of federal agencies likely to fail, because it had been losing vital revenue to electronic communication, neglecting to innovate in dynamic markets, and managing its resources inefficiently. Similar pressures have forced postal systems around the world to overhaul their operations; some countries have fully privatized this once-core government function, while others are moving rapidly in that direction. To better position the Postal Service to survive in this modern communication environment, Congress passed the 2006 Postal Accountability and Enhancement Act. The law allows the Postal Service to compete vigorously in some sectors as long as it does not cross-subsidize those services with revenue from its monopoly over letter mail or its market-dominant offerings. The law streamlined the ratemaking process, and converted the Postal Rate Commission into the Postal Regulatory Commission with enhanced powers.

With the 2006 law, Congress has charted a course for the near future of the Postal Service. Congress has clearly signaled that the USPS should not expand into electronic communication, but allows—even encourages—partnerships with private carriers, which relish access to the Postal Service's last-mile delivery. That is, private firms transport material—usually packages—between cities, but rely on the Postal Service for the last step in delivery to the nation's households and businesses, which its carriers visit six days a week. The Postal Service has even begun delivering parcels on

Sundays for online retailer Amazon. Such partnerships, however, are nothing new: since the advent of parcel post, even before, the postal system has worked closely with the nation's merchandisers and publishers.

Community activists have recently pressed Congress to revive the Progressive Era's more visionary interpretation of the postal clause. Champions of small-town post offices have urged lawmakers to view postal facilities as community centers, especially where state and federal agencies need a physical presence. Registering voters, providing Medicare and Medicaid assistance, delivering prescriptions drugs, and serving as Homeland Security information centers are a few possible functions for such expanded-purpose post offices. Other groups have suggested reinstituting the early twentieth-century farm-to-table service in which the post office connected small farms outside cities with urban households seeking regular deliveries of high-quality, local produce. Similarly, reformers concerned about the sizable numbers of Americans lacking basic banking services have been calling for the resurrection of the postal banking system.

FURTHER READING

Fowler, Dorothy G. 1977. *Unmailable: Congress and the Post Office*. Athens, GA: University of Georgia Press.

Fuller, Wayne E. 1972. *The American Mail: Enlarger of the Common Life*. Chicago: University of Chicago Press.

John, Richard R. 1995. *Spreading the News: The American Postal System from Franklin to Morse*. Cambridge, MA: Harvard University Press.

Kelly, Clyde. 1932. *United States Postal Policy*. New York: D. Appleton and Co.

Kielbowicz, Richard B. 1989. *News in the Mail: The Press, Post Office, and Public Information, 1700–1960s*. Westport, CT: Greenwood Press.

Kielbowicz, Richard B. 2000. *Postal Enterprise: Post Office Innovations with Congressional Constraints: 1789–1970*. Report prepared for the Postal Rate Commission. Accessed Aug. 31, 2015 at http://www.prc.gov/sites/default/files/papers/enterprise.pdf

Lawson, Linda. 1993. *Truth in Publishing: Federal Regulation of the Press's Business Practices, 1880-1920*. Carbondale, IL: Southern Illinois University Press.

Rogers, Lindsay. 1916. *The Postal Power of Congress: A Study in Constitutional Expansion*. Baltimore: Johns Hopkins Press.

8 THE POWER TO REGULATE PATENTS AND COPYRIGHT

Colin D. Moore

Article I, section 8, clause 8
To promote the progress of science and useful arts, by securing for limited
times to authors and inventors the exclusive right to their respective writings
and discoveries.

KEY TERMS

The Constitution's **intellectual property (IP) clause** grants Congress the power to provide authors and inventors with an exclusive right to intangible property through two
legal mechanisms: patents and copyrights. Both forms of protection are, in essence,
state-sanctioned monopolies that may only exist for a defined period of time, and both
patents and copyrights offer the creator some exclusive rights over her artistic expres-
sions or discoveries.

Patents protect an inventor's application of an idea as long as that idea is novel and
nonobvious.
Copyrights secure an author's expression of an idea—as a written work, musical
recording, or other form of creative media—but not the idea itself.

This difference in common law practice between the "application of an idea" and
the "expression of an idea" also leads to a principal distinction between copyrights and
patents. The inventor must acquire the original patent, even if it is later sold. This is not
true of copyrights, which may be acquired by any person or corporation.

The specificity of the intellectual property clause might seem surprising, given that
most powers enshrined in the Constitution are fairly broad and open to interpretation,

but the relative clarity of the IP clause demonstrates just how important the Framers considered this power to be. Indeed, their decision to grant Congress the power to protect intellectual property was a response to the failures of the Articles of Confederation, which contained no national-level protections for intellectual property. By giving Congress these powers, the Framers hoped to foster a friendly environment for the creation and dissemination of new inventions and creative works.

This chapter begins with a discussion of the language that forms this distinctive clause. The second section turns to the history of intellectual property by looking at the development of copyright and patent regulations. In the third section, we will consider the long-term effects of American copyright and patent law, and the role of these institutions in democratizing invention in the United States. The chapter concludes with a short discussion of some contemporary challenges in American intellectual property policy, such as piracy, "patent trolling," and Congress's recent decision to extend the length of copyright protections.

THE LANGUAGE OF THE INTELLECTUAL PROPERTY CLAUSE

"To promote the progress of science and useful arts."

The intellectual property clause is the only place in the Constitution where a specific reason is given for granting an enumerated power. The Framers were clear that Congress's powers to grant short-term monopolies on intellectual property were provided to increase human knowledge and to improve the efficiency of helpful trades. In this way, the phrase seems to restrict Congress's powers and to provide a simultaneous justification for them. Most legal historians agree that this was done intentionally. As Akhil Reed Amar argues, "Patent and copyrights could not be given merely to reward political allies, but only 'to promote the Progress of Science and the useful Arts'" (112). In short, the clause justifying this particular enumerated power also restricts how Congress can exercise it.

"[B]y securing for limited times to authors and inventors the exclusive right to their respective writings and discoveries."

The second half of the IP clause gives Congress the right to grant short-term monopolies, but only to "authors" or "inventors." In this way, the clause is a significant grant of power, but one with some important limitations. First, such exclusive monopolies can only be extended to those who qualify as authors or inventors. This restriction was intended to prevent the creation of the corrupt English monopoly system, whereby exclusive patents were granted for everyday items such as salt, as a way to raise revenue for the Crown. A second limitation comes from the demand that such monopolies can only be given "for limited times." Congress is thus forbidden from granting patents or copyrights in perpetuity, although, as we will see, the appropriate length of such monopolies has long been a matter of contention.

A third potential restriction arises from the words "writings" and "discoveries." Does "writings" limit copyright protection to books and other written materials, or can Congress grant protections for musical works and film? Over the years, Congress and the Supreme Court have largely responded in the affirmative, and legislation and case law have extended copyright protections to new forms of media unknown in the eighteenth century. A more significant restriction comes with the inclusion of "discoveries," which seems to imply that a patent may only be extended to a genuinely new and original invention. What is a discovery? Is it simply a new product, or must it make a genuine contribution to science to be worthy of a grant of this exclusive property right? In practice, Congress and the Court have concluded that patents may be granted for incremental improvements in technology. In other words, patents do not need to be major scientific advancements, but they must be genuine innovations. They cannot be granted for knowledge that is already in the public domain or for improvements that would be obvious to people familiar with the field.

HISTORY AND DEVELOPMENT

Both patents and copyrights are economic rights. They can be classified with other enumerated powers, such as the power to established post offices, that were designed to enhance communication and intellectual life in the future United States. Although eighteenth-century America was hardly a center of learning or innovation, the care with which these powers were designed clearly indicates that the Framers anticipated that their new nation would become a leader in all of these fields. Indeed, the necessity of having uniform patent and copyright laws was considered so important that the Framers made sure to grant Congress explicit authority to do this, because it was not clear that such a power could be read into the other enumerated powers.

Despite the importance they attached to the protection of intellectual property, the clause's origins remain somewhat mysterious. Compared to the other enumerated powers, intellectual property generated almost no debate during the Constitutional Convention, and relatively little was written about it before ratification. In fact, in the journal he kept to record the proceedings of the convention, James Madison made barely a passing reference to this clause. In his recording of the proceedings from August 18, 1787—one of the few places where intellectual property is mentioned—he listed several topics that were discussed by the delegates:

To secure to literary authors their copy rights for a limited time

To encourage, by proper premiums and provisions, the advancement of useful knowledge and discoveries

To grant patents for useful inventions

Less than a month later, these inchoate ideas were joined to form the language that would eventually be inserted into the Constitution. Although the decision to combine these separate powers into one clause might have generated some discussion, Madison provided no background on this development, merely noting that the delegates "agreed" to the changes. The notion that the law should protect creative expression and invention may seem commonplace today, but even the term "intellectual property" was not in wide use until after the Civil War—and this makes the Framers' silence all the more surprising.

The clearest justification that we have for this decision comes from Madison's brief discussion of intellectual property in *Federalist* No. 43—but it, too, provides precious little insight. After writing that "the utility of this power will scarcely be questioned," Madison quickly concludes that "the public good fully coincides in both cases with the claims of individuals. The States cannot separately make effectual provisions for either of the cases, and most of them have anticipated the decision of this point, by laws passed at the instance of Congress." In this way, Madison suggests two rationales for the inclusion of this power in the Constitution. The first is a familiar one: that the protection of intellectual property must be made at the federal level to avoid chaos and to provide robust legal security for inventions and creative works. The second is more complex: that providing an individual incentive for authorship and invention will lead to a public benefit through an increase in creative and scientific production. In short, individuals will benefit economically through their exclusive ownership of their books or inventions, and the public good will be served through the increase in economic and cultural output.

Why, then, were intellectual property protections important enough to be enumerated in the Constitution, but not central enough to generate considerable commentary or debate? The answer may simply be that there was almost no opposition to this clause. Most of the delegates to the convention had experience in developing patent and copyright laws in their respective states. As one historian of intellectual property wrote, "the chief contributions made by the colonial and state patent and copyright institutions were, first, to prepare the intellectual ground for the Federal power which rendered them obsolete, and, second, to provide a fund of experience and legal precedent upon which Constitution-makers and Federal legislators could draw selectively" (Bugbee 158). Perhaps the leader in this regard was Charles Pinckney of South Carolina, whose state had developed the first detailed patent policy in 1784. Furthermore, the notion that the government should support the sciences and education was relatively common in colonial America. The Massachusetts Constitution of 1780, for example, included support for learning and invention as a principal goal: "it shall be the duty of legislatures and magistrates, in all future periods of this commonwealth, to cherish the interests of literature and the sciences . . . [and] to encourage private societies and public institutions, rewards and immunities, for the promotion of agriculture, arts, sciences, commerce, trades, manufactures, and a natural history of the country." The intellectual property clause, then, simply applied this commonplace belief in the role of government to foster learning and creation to the specific area of patents and copyrights.

This is not to suggest that everyone was pleased with the intellectual property clause. No less an authority than Thomas Jefferson had serious reservations about granting Congress the power to create legal monopolies, which he initially considered a threat to liberty. Jefferson's concerns were well founded, given the abuse of the patent and copyright systems under English common law, where they were widely seen as a way for the Crown to raise money or as a give-away to favored printers. To counter these reasonable objections, Madison provided a vigorous defense of this new power in a letter to Thomas Jefferson of October 17, 1788. Madison, it seems, agreed in principle that monopolies were odious, but he believed that the costs were greatly outweighed by potential benefits to American industry and creativity:

With regard to monopolies they are justly classed among the greatest nuisances in Government. But is it clear that as encouragements to literary works and ingenious discoveries, they are not too valuable to be wholly renounced? . . . Is there not also infinitely less danger of this abuse in our Governments, than in most others? Monopolies are sacrifices of the many to the few. Where the power is in the few it is natural for them to sacrifice the many to their own partialities and corruptions. Where the power, as with us, is in the many not in the few, the danger can not be very great that the few will be thus favored. It is much more to be dreaded that the few will be unnecessarily sacrificed to the many.

Along with the benefits to industry, Madison made it clear that the danger of granting monopolies was less severe when such decisions were in the hands of an elected legislature. Although he does not mention it in this letter to Jefferson, he took the added precaution of tying the hands of future Congresses by restricting such grants of monopoly to those that would "promote the progress of science and useful arts." In other words, unlike the much-hated patents granted by the Crown, Congress could only grant patents for a limited period and for inventions that furthered American science and industry. Finally, it is clear that the experience of many of the Framers in drafting their own state copyright and patent policies led them to conclude that a federal policy was necessary. In a 1787 essay, Madison mentioned his concerns about "the want of uniformity in the laws concerning naturalization and literary property."

In sum, the protection of intellectual property was generally seen as a necessary power by policymakers in the early Republic, most of whom supported Congress's power to create uniform intellectual property policies. As Justice Joseph Story concluded in his famous commentaries on the Constitution, the IP clause was crucial and relatively uncontroversial:

In short, the only boon, which could be offered to inventors to disclose the secrets of their discoveries, would be the exclusive right and profit of them, as a monopoly for a limited period. And authors would have little inducement to prepare elaborate works for the public, if their publication was to be at a large expense, and, as soon as they were published, there would be an unlimited right of depredation and piracy of their copyright. The states could not separately make effectual provision for either of the cases; and most of them, at the time of the adoption of the constitution, had anticipated the propriety of such a grant of power, by passing laws on the subject at the instance of the continental congress. (403)

The next sections will review copyrights and patents in more detail, and examine how later Congresses and the Supreme Court have administered these particular property rights. Although they are part of the same enumerated power, patents and copyright began a separate legal and administrative trajectory when separate statutes created them each in 1790.

Copyright

The origins of copyright can be found in early English printing regulations. For much of the sixteenth and seventeenth centuries, royal monopolies were granted to favored printers of the Crown that gave them exclusive rights for the printing of certain classes of works. But such grants were given to the printer, not to the author. It was not until the 1709 Statute of Anne that authors were given the right to own their works for fourteen years, with an option to renew the right for another fourteen years if the author was living. This act, which is often seen as the first law to establish a formal copyright, allowed authors to obtain copyrights, but it also established an important precedent in intellectual property that such rights should not be perpetual. Since a copyright is the expression of an idea—usually in a written work—the right was not attached to the idea, but rather to its expression.

More important for the purposes of the Constitution's IP clause, however, was the Statute of Anne's ostensible purpose, as defined by its longer title: "An Act for the Encouragement of Learning, by Vesting the Copies of Printed Books in the Authors or Purchasers of such Copies, during the Times therein mentioned." It was this notion of copyright as a way to encourage learning through the protection of authors' creative works that seems to have influenced the development of the Constitution's IP clause and the state copyright laws that preceded it. In this way, copyright was thought of along with other ideas, such as the possible establishment of a national university, as a way to promote learning. The protection of an author's rights over her publications was, for the Framers, clearly a secondary purpose.

The tension between the idea of copyright as the natural right of an author or a statutory right granted by the government was revealed in the Copyright Act of 1790—the first time Congress exercised this enumerated power. In this case, Congress revealed that it regarded copyright as a privilege granted to authors by the government and not as a defense of a natural right of authors in their published works. This idea was reinforced several decades later in *Wheaton v. Peters* (1834), the first Supreme Court ruling on a copyright case, which reaffirmed that copyright was a government grant of monopoly and not a natural right. In this case, the Court agreed that an author may have property rights to a manuscript, but held that the limited monopoly provided by copyright existed merely through statute.

A similar theory governs American copyright law to this day. Copyright protections exist to provide incentives to an author to produce creative works and to encourage learning. Yet the fact that copyright is a statutory right and not a natural right allows Congress to restrict the length of time a copyright may be granted. Congress has largely retained this understanding of copyright, even as it tinkered with the length and scope of the law, such as an 1831 revision that granted copyright protections to written music.

The most notable—and notorious—decision made in the 1790 act was to limit copyright protection to Americans. As Section 5 of the original act made clear, foreigners and foreign works would receive no protection under American copyright law: "nothing in this act shall be construed to extend to prohibit the importation or vending, Reprinting or publishing within the United States, of any map, chart, book or books, written, printed, or published by any person not a citizen of the United States, in foreign parts or places without the jurisdiction of the United States." While

European nations joined treaties and recognized foreign copyrights, the United States freely allowed its printers to publish pirated copies of European works—a practice that continued for a century—until the United States adopted the International Copyright Act of 1891, which finally allowed foreign artists, authors, and musicians to obtain copyright protection in the United States.

During the twentieth century, the nature of copyright was not changed, but several bills were passed—most notably the Copyright Act of 1976—to adjust to new technologies and to make U.S. copyright law conform to international standards. The 1976 act provided copyright protection for the life of the author plus 50 years, and granted a total of 75 years of protection for works done for hire. In 1998, additional protections were added under the Copyright Term Extension Act, which extended copyright protections to the life of the author plus 70 years, and provided protection for works for hire for 120 years after creation or 95 years after publication, whichever was the shorter time period.

Patents

The Patent Act of 1790 reflected the extensive experience and the importance assigned to the cultivation of new inventions in the United States. It should come as no surprise that the protection of intellectual property through patents faced little opposition in the first Congress. In his 1790 State of the Union Address, George Washington himself provided forceful support for any polices that would encourage the development of science and innovation in the United States:

> The advancement of agriculture, commerce, and manufactures, by all proper means, will not, I trust, need recommendation; but I cannot forbear intimating to you the expediency of giving effectual encouragement, as well to the introduction of new and useful invention from abroad, as to the exertions of skill and genius in producing them at home . . . Knowledge is in every country the surest basis of public happiness.

This vigorous support was echoed in Alexander Hamilton's Report on Manufacturers of December 1791, where he debated the best ways to encourage American invention and entrepreneurship. Although he supported using federal funds to sponsor prizes and even to fund a federal bonus for invention, he concluded that the market itself would be the best judge of an invention's value. "It is probable," Hamilton wrote, "that the placing of the dispensation of those rewards under some proper discretionary direction, where they may be accompanied by *collateral expedients*, will serve to give them the surest efficacy. It seems impracticable to apportion, by general rules, specific compensations for discoveries of unknown and disproportionate utility." The market, in other words, would provide rewards to inventors when patents protected their inventions.

Perhaps the most surprising decision made in the 1790 act was Congress's decision to forbid patents of importation. Such patents would have granted protection for foreign technologies imported to the United States. Although this was a well-known practice at the time in England, the early Congress—and Hamilton in particular—concluded that they were prohibited by the intellectual property clause, because imported technologies were not genuinely new discoveries. This, it hardly needs to be pointed out, was far different from the same Congress's decision to refuse foreign authors American copyright protection.

Despite his early opposition to patent protection, Thomas Jefferson quickly became impressed by the effect this new law seemed to have on spurring ingenuity in the United States. As he wrote just three months after the 1790 act was adopted, "An act of Congress authorizing the issuing of patents for new discoveries has given a spring to invention beyond my conception . . . Many of them indeed are trifling, but there are some of great consequence which have been proved by practice, and others which if they stand the same proof will produce great effect." And, by 1813, although still suspicious of these monopolies, Jefferson concluded in a letter of August 13 that patents were a necessary evil:

> Inventions then cannot, in nature, be a subject of property. Society may give an exclusive right to the profits arising from them, as an encouragement to men to pursue ideas which may produce utility, but this may or may not be done, according to the will and convenience of the society, without claim or complaint from anybody . . . Considering the exclusive right to invention as given not of natural right, but for the benefit of society, I know well the difficulty of drawing a line between the things which are worth to the public the embarrassment of an exclusive patent, and those which are not.

Minor modifications to the law were made in the nineteenth century. Although non-Americans were excluded from holding patents for a period in the early 1800s, American patent law remained relatively stable. The most significant change to patent law in the twentieth century came in 1952, when Congress added "non-obviousness" as a requirement to receive patent protection. This required that an improvement could not be obvious "at the time the invention was made to a person having ordinary skill in the art to which said subject matter pertains" (35 USC 103). This stipulation was later clarified in the landmark decision of *Graham v. John Deere Co.* (1966), which justified the non-obviousness requirement on the Framers' views that patents were a way to promote discovery, and should not be justified merely based on an inventor's moral right to his innovations.

Today, patents may only be granted for "any new and useful process, machine, manufacture, or composition of matter, or any new and useful improvement thereof" (35 USC 101). Along with these requirements, discoveries cannot be naturally occurring in nature or a scientific principle, and they must also be both novel and nonobvious. The adoption of the America Invents Act (P. L. 112-29) in 2011 did not change the requirements for patentable items, but it did change patent registration from a "first to invent" system to a "first to file" system.

Long-Term Effects of the IP Clause

Congress's early support for intellectual property protection ushered in an era of tremendous innovation and creativity in the United States. In many ways, the success of American industrialization was due to the relatively free and inexpensive access that average tinkerers and artisans were given to the patent system. In England, the fees for filing patents were so high that they generally prevented working citizens from receiving protection for their discoveries; indeed, the fee to file a patent could be over £100, which in 1860 was about four times the per capita income. Moreover, patents were rarely given to incremental improvements in existing technologies. In contrast, the far less expensive and more permissive American system led to tremendous growth in innovation.

This difference in the patent policies of England and the United States had long-term effects. Although England was the leading industrial nation in the world at the beginning of the nineteenth century, the United States quickly began to overtake it as a center of innovation. Merely thirteen years after the first patent act was adopted, the United States issued more patents than England—a remarkable development for a largely agrarian nation. By 1869, Washington was issuing almost seven times the number of patents as London. As economic historian B. Zorina Khan argues, "The U.S. patent system was soon acknowledged to be the most advanced in the world, and other countries drew causal connections between American achievements and its protection of inventive activity through patent property rights" (Khan 2005, 13).

The U.S. patent system was not only successful in generating a large number of patents; it also encouraged Americans from all walks of life to become amateur inventors. This was especially true in the nineteenth century, which saw an explosion of inventive activity in the United States. The number of patents created, however, is less impressive than the diversity of inventors in the United States. As the number of per capita patents increased, the patents' owners increasingly represented more rural areas and a more diverse set of occupations.

Madison and Hamilton's opinion that patents should serve the market, combined with Jefferson's fear of monopolies, helped to structure a patent system that provided monopoly protection for long enough to spur innovation, but was democratic enough to open up patent protection to working-class inventors. Along with the low fees required to patent inventions in the United States, the patent award was (until 2011) given to the first inventor, not to the first person to file, which often helped poorer inventors who needed more time to raise funds for an application. Finally, the fact that the patent office itself was financed through patent application fees left it relatively free of political influence—a remarkable achievement in nineteenth-century America. All of these developments contributed to the success of American innovations. This democratization of invention also led to a significant number of women and African Americans applying for and holding patents. Unlike many other aspects of American life, the patent system—at least on paper—gave all Americans an equal right to apply for patent protection.

Although the patent protection provided to anyone who wished to file in the United States was strong and open, copyright protection was far weaker. Until 1891, works by foreigners were refused copyright protection and could be freely reprinted in the United States. This policy infuriated European—and especially English—authors, but most member of Congress saw little gain in offering protection to the works of foreign writers, a policy they thought would hurt learning in the United States in an era when much of the literature and research was still produced in Europe.

FUTURE IMPLICATIONS

Threatened by piracy, perpetual copyright, and patent trolls, the triumph of early American intellectual property policy has not been matched in recent years. A series of unfortunate developments has moved American intellectual property away from the Framers' original intentions. This change in attitude, along with many new technological innovations and practices, may be weakening the very IP institutions that led to so many artistic and scientific innovations in the United States.

The first contemporary challenge for American IP policy is piracy. How much protection should copyright holders expect from the federal government? Despite the fact that the United States was among the world's leading producers of pirated books and music for a century, the nation has led the way in lobbying for vigorous enforcement of copyright laws and the establishment of international copyright regimes. The No Electronic Theft Act (1997) made non-commercial file-sharing a criminal offense, while the 1998 Digital Millennium Copyright Act expanded prosecution efforts for digital copyright infringement. These increasingly severe copyright restrictions are designed to protect American rights holders who have lost considerable money to piracy in recent years. The Business Software Alliance, for example, estimates the loss to American business at nearly $64 billion, while the Recording Industry Association of America claims that digital music piracy has cost over 70,000 U.S. jobs.

Although Congress's aggressive response to piracy may seem reasonable, it is less clear that it reflects the spirit of the Constitution's IP clause. The Framers never considered copyright to be a natural right of an author; after all, the original copyright laws did not even offer protections for non-citizens. Rather, it was merely a statutory monopoly granted for a short period, to encourage learning and scientific advancement. Furthermore, such stringent copyright enforcement pits Congress against the balance of public opinion in the United States and the world.

Despite the claims from the publishing and recording industries that citizens support such laws, the evidence indicates that most consumers have a clear understanding of file-sharing and digital piracy, but *do not* support more aggressive enforcement regimes. One recent study, for example, demonstrates that anti-piracy campaigns have done little to change consumer opinion, particularly among the 70 percent of young Americans who report that they have downloaded electronic media for free. In point of fact, nearly 40 percent of these respondents do not support penalties of *any kind* for downloading and sharing media. Moreover, these same young Americans pay careful attention to the development of copyright legislation. In January of 2012, when Congress was debating contentious anti-piracy legislation, the Pew Research Center's weekly measure of news interest found that 23 percent of Americans under 29 reported that they were carefully following these bills.

Such enforcement regimes are wildly out of step with public opinion. They also privilege the copyright holders' rights to retain exclusive control over their intellectual property over the rights of individual users to make use of such learning. The current regime that favors a copyright owner's total control over her creative works seems to trample on the rights of individuals to freely express their own ideas.

The second challenge in contemporary American IP policy is a related one: How long should copyright protection last? In 1998, the Sonny Bono Copyright Term Extension Act increased copyright protections to the life of the author plus 70 years, which moved the United States much closer to the creation of a perpetual copyright. Proponents of such extensions have argued that the Constitution merely specifies that such protections are for limited times. In their view, Congress could provide copyright protections for hundreds or even thousands of years!

Unfortunately for critics of such legislation, the Supreme Court upheld these copyright term extensions in *Eldred v. Ashcroft* (2003), and concluded that the Constitution granted Congress complete discretion to set the term of copyright as long as such protection was not provided forever. This view, however, does not reflect the original purpose of a power that was intended to promote science and creative expression. As an amicus brief presented by several intellectual property law scholars argued in opposition to copyright extension,

> Authors and inventors build on the work of their predecessors. The public domain is the reservoir for the raw material that authors and inventors use to create new writings and discoveries. The enrichment of the public domain is not a by-product of the "limited times" restriction but its purpose—it is the means that the Framers chose to ensure that our copyright and patent system would promote the progress of Science and useful Arts. (*Eldred v. Ashcroft*, Amicus Brief)

The third challenge to America's current intellectual property structure comes from so-called "patent trolls." These "trolls" are people or organizations who purchase patents, often from failed companies, and then engage in aggressive legal actions to intimidate users who, they claim, are stealing their protected inventions or discoveries. These firms hope to receive large legal settlements through their intimidation tactics—and they have been remarkably successful. Most companies prefer to settle out of court than to engage in expensive and protracted legal battles. These practices are particularly troubling because the companies that engage in them are not responsible for any innovation at all; indeed, they rarely make use of the patents they do hold. Instead, they use patent laws to stifle innovation and discovery, and thereby pervert the founding spirit of the patent system. As we know, the Framers saw patent protections as a statutory monopoly granted in the service of innovation, not because inventors had an inherent right of property in their discoveries. Fortunately, President Obama has recently taken action to curb many of these practices by issuing a series of executive orders asking the Patent and Trademark Office to approve more narrowly tailored patents. These new policies, many observers hope, will help to limit the legal rights of the "trolls."

Despite these recent developments, the Constitution's intellectual property clause is, in many ways, responsible for creating the robust creative and entrepreneurial environment in the United States. Since 1790, when Congress first passed legislation using this enumerated power, copyrights guaranteed that authors would receive compensation for their creative works, while patent laws provided secure protection for the ideas of all Americans. Although the Framers were suspicious of monopolies in all forms, they concluded that patents and copyrights were necessary to provide just rewards to authors and innovators in a way that would lead to increased learning and innovation in the United States. The remarkable success of American science and creative expression over the past two centuries has proven them right.

FURTHER READING

Amar, Akhil Reed. 1998. *The Bill of Rights: Creation and Reconstruction*. New Haven, CT: Yale University Press.

Bugbee, Bruce W. 1967. *Genesis of American Patent and Copyright Law*. Washington, DC: Public Affairs Press.

Eldred v. Ashcroft, No. 01-618, Brief of Intellectual Property Law Professors as *Amicus Curiae* Supporting Petitioners. http://cyber.law.harvard.edu/openlaw/eldredvashcroft/supct/amici/ip-lawprofs.pdf. Accessed September 20, 2015.

Goldstein, Paul. 2007. *Intellectual Property: The Tough New Realities that Could Make or Break Your Business*. New York: Portfolio.

Halbert, Debora J. 1999. *Intellectual Property in the Information Age: The Politics of Expanding Ownership Rights*. Westport, CT: Quorum Books.

Karaganis, Joe, and Lennart Renkema. 2013. *Copy Culture in the U.S. and Germany*. New York: The American Assembly.

Khan, B. Zorina. 2005. *The Democratization of Invention: Patents and Copyrights in American Economic Development, 1790–1920*. New York: Cambridge University Press.

Patterson, Lyman Ray. 1968. *Copyright in Historical Perspective*. Nashville: Vanderbilt University Press.

Story, Joseph. 1833. *Commentaries on the Constitution of the United States*, 3 vols. Boston: Hillard, Gray, and Company.

Walterscheid, Edward C. 2002. *The Nature of the Intellectual Property Clause: A Study in Historical Perspective*. Buffalo, NY: William S. Hein & Co.

9 THE POWER TO CONSTITUTE COURTS AND OTHER TRIBUNALS INFERIOR TO SUPREME COURT

Rebecca L. Keeler

Article I, section 8, clause 9
To constitute Tribunals inferior to the Supreme Court.

Article III, section 1
The judicial Power of the United States, shall be vested in one supreme Court,
and in such inferior Courts as the Congress may from time to time ordain and
establish.

KEY TERMS

Tribunals are entities with legal authority to resolve disputes using the law. They may be
courts in a judicial system or other tribunals such as administrative law judges or regulatory commissions which are separate from a judicial system. The term "tribunal"
does not exclusively refer to groups of individuals; often a single judge is referred to
as a court or tribunal. Note that the Constitution uses "courts" in Article III and "tribunals" in Article I. If Congress establishes a judicial authority and calls it a "court," it
will be regarded as an Article III court if its powers are those articulated in Article III.
If the "court" is assigned duties beyond the parameters in Article III, or if its decisions are subject to review by an authority outside of the Article III courts, or if its
judges have fixed terms of office, then it will be considered an Article I court.

    Other tribunals exist outside the judicial branch. Such tribunals and the officials
serving in them may be called quasi-judicial tribunals and officers. They perform

fact-finding and decision-making in a less formal, less independent manner than their judicial counterparts.

Jurisdiction refers to a tribunal's legal authority to decide based on geographic and subject matter parameters. For example, the District Court for Eastern Tennessee's jurisdiction extends to federal criminal cases and a limited range of civil legal disputes arising within the Eastern region of Tennessee.

Appellate jurisdiction refers to a tribunal's authority to review and ultimately affirm, modify, or reverse decisions of lower tribunals.

Original jurisdiction refers to a court's authority to decide a case for the first time in the judicial system. This is where parties first enter the judicial system for resolution of a legal dispute. Courts of original jurisdiction are where disputed facts are decided, and law is applied to arrive at a decision.

Diversity jurisdiction refers to the federal courts' authority to decide cases between parties from different states even if the disputes concern only state law.

Concurrent jurisdiction refers to authority to exercise judicial power over particular types of disputes that is accorded to more than one level or type of court. For example, whereas early U.S. circuit courts had exclusive jurisdiction to try serious federal criminal cases, in 1842 Congress relieved the heavy caseload of the circuit courts by granting concurrent jurisdiction to the district courts. This meant that serious federal criminal charges could then be brought in either the district court or the circuit court.

HISTORY AND DEVELOPMENT OF ARTICLE III COURTS

What follows is a brief account of the history and development of Congress's exercise of its power to constitute tribunals inferior to the Supreme Court. The chapter progresses in a somewhat chronological order concerning Article III courts, with minor digressions providing some context for historical developments. Non-Article III courts and tribunals are then discussed by tribunal rather than chronology.

Design of the judicial branch of U.S. government was not as challenging to the Framers as was design of the other branches. The Framers relied heavily on the judicial system in Britain as a model. Further, British legal principles were familiar to and used by the colonies. The biggest difference had to do with judicial independence. British courts possessed little independence. Their jurists served at the will of the king, and decisions of British courts could be overruled by Parliament. These distinctions were a source of great consternation in the Colonies, who included it among the grievances asserted against the king in the Declaration of Independence.

The American Framers wanted the U.S. courts to be more independent from the elective branches, to serve as an effective check on the other branches' possible abuse of constitutional authorities. To secure greater independence for the judiciary, Art. III §1 provided for federal judges' tenure to continue during good behavior, essentially until they die, retire, or are impeached and removed. The same section prohibits Congress from reducing judges' compensation. In these ways, judges serving in Article III courts are meant to be insulated from political pressures, thus able to render decisions that follow the law rather than popular political will.

Article V of the Constitution authorizes Congress to initiate constitutional amendments to overturn the courts' constitutional interpretations with which the Congress disagrees. Constitutional amendments can only take effect if sufficient states ratify or approve the amendments. However, the Court has emphatically claimed its authority to determine with finality what the Constitution itself means. On the other hand, Congress may also amend federal statutes to overcome a Supreme Court interpretation that was not consistent with Congress's intent.

Early debates over Constitutional provisions on the judiciary also focused on whether there would be federal courts below, or "inferior to," the Supreme Court. There were strong disagreements on whether there should be a robust federal judicial system or simply have state courts hear all cases until they are appealed to the U.S. Supreme Court. Some felt that a federal judiciary was essential to ensuring uniform application of federal laws and the Constitution across the country. They argued further that there are some types of disputes that can be tainted by bias or disregard for national interests if addressed in state courts, thus undermining the union. Others viewed all aspects of the federal government with concern and suspicion that it would overpower the states and deny states their autonomy.

Ultimately, Art. III §2 of the Constitution identified the particular types of controversies to which the federal judicial power could be applied. It did not, however, preclude state courts from addressing those same matters. Nor did the Constitution resolve the debate over the size of the federal judiciary. It simply granted Congress general authority to create tribunals inferior to the Supreme Court. But, Art. VI cl. 2 of the Constitution, commonly referred to as the supremacy clause, made it clear that federal law and the Constitution are the supreme law of the land, and that states are bound by it. The supremacy clause clearly put the federal government in charge of those matters assigned to it by the Constitution.

The first Congress convened on March 4, 1789, in New York City. That year Congress passed the Judiciary Act of 1789. The act established three types of courts: the Supreme Court, circuit courts, and district courts. The Supreme Court would consist of one chief justice and five associate justices and would convene twice a year to hear appeals from lower federal courts and state highest courts. In addition to appellate jurisdiction, the act authorized the Supreme Court to exercise original jurisdiction over "cases affecting ambassadors, other public ministers and consuls, and those in which a state shall be party" as required by Art. III, §2, cl. 2 of the Constitution. But the act also extended to the Supreme Court original jurisdiction to issue writs of *mandamus,* writs ordering public officials to perform ministerial or non-discretionary acts. This grant of original jurisdiction over writs of *mandamus* was later invalidated by the Supreme Court in its landmark 1803 case of *Marbury v. Madison.* The Court determined that Congress cannot add to the subjects over which the Constitution gave the Supreme Court original jurisdiction.

Marbury v. Madison set the precedent establishing in federal law the power of judicial review, which was not expressly recognized in the Constitution. The power of judicial review is certainly implied from the supremacy clause. It was also already in practice in several states. Judicial review was contemplated by the Framers of the Constitution, as illustrated in *Federalist* No. 78, wherein Alexander Hamilton wrote,

"Limitations [placed on the legislative authority by the Constitution] can be preserved in practice no other way than through the medium of courts of justice, whose duty it must be to declare all acts contrary to the manifest tenor of the Constitution void. Without this, all the reservations of particular rights or privileges would amount to nothing." It has since been extended to state legislative, judicial and executive actions as well as federal executive actions.

The Judiciary Act of 1789 established a three-tier system of federal courts, with a district court in each state, three circuit courts—each serving a geographic cluster of states: Eastern Middle, and Southern—and the Supreme Court, located in the nation's capital. The district courts were exclusively trial courts with jurisdiction over admiralty and maritime cases, petty federal criminal cases, and minor civil cases brought by the United States. Circuit courts exercised both appellate jurisdiction to review cases from the district courts, and original jurisdiction over major federal crimes, civil cases over a certain monetary value, suits involving the U.S. government, and suits between citizens of different states. It is significant to note that Congress allowed state courts to also decide federal civil cases involving disputes of high monetary value, those involving the U.S. government, and suits between citizens of different states. This shared jurisdiction was calculated to assuage the concerns of opponents of a large federal judiciary, as well as to manage the cost of the new federal judicial institutions.

All in all, the first federal court system largely reflected the desires of Federalists to create a strong national government that would hold the union together for the long run. But the design was also responsive to Anti-Federalists' concerns for retaining as much local autonomy as possible. The first federal court system was dispersed across the new nation, was served at the trial court level by local resident judges, and shared much of its trial court jurisdiction with state courts. Obviously the states did not retain the complete judicial autonomy they had enjoyed under the Articles of Confederation. As will be seen, state power would continue to erode as the nation and its federal courts grew.

Constitutional provisions for judicial independence from the elected branches do not totally insulate the courts from political forces emanating from those elected branches and beyond. One very early example of this dynamic surrounds the change of the majority party in both Congress and the Executive as a result of the elections in 1800. The Federalists who dominated both Congress and the Executive from the start were displaced by the Democratic-Republicans, led by Thomas Jefferson, in the election of 1800. On the eve of their departure in 1801, the Federalist Congress passed the Judiciary Act of 1801, with an eye toward packing the federal judiciary with life-term Federalist judges.

The Judiciary Act of 1801 reduced the Supreme Court to five members including the chief justice, expanded the circuit courts from three to six, established sixteen new circuit judge positions, and relieved members of the Supreme Court from their circuit-riding duties. In an effort to enhance the importance of the federal courts, Congress expanded their jurisdiction to all cases arising under the Constitution, thus giving people an option to pursue their legal disputes in federal courts, where they previously could only seek remedies in state courts. The 1801 act also made it easier to access the federal courts' diversity jurisdiction by reducing or even eliminating in some cases, the threshold monetary requirement to get into federal court. Had this legislative design survived, the judiciary would be substantially dominated by loyalists to the Federalist Party for some time to come.

However, the new Democratic-Republican Congress, with President Jefferson's support, promptly repealed the Judiciary Act of 1801 and passed the Judiciary Act of 1802 in April of that year. The 1802 act, in effect, amended the Judiciary Act of 1789; it was as if the 1801 act had never happened. In a bold exercise of political strategy, the 1802 act reduced the sessions of the Supreme Court to one per year, commencing in February. This ensured that the Court would not have an opportunity to find the repeal of the 1789 act unconstitutional until February 1803. By that time, the new judicial system would be in operation and would be costly if not impossible to dismantle. The Supreme Court ultimately capitulated by giving effect to the 1802 act in the 1803 case of *Stuart v. Laird*.

The Courts and the Country Expand

By 1803, Tennessee, Ohio, and Kentucky had joined the Union. To address growing caseload demands, in 1807 Congress created a seventh circuit that encompassed the three new states. It also increased the membership of the Supreme Court by one, to cover the circuit. This is the only legislation that actually required the justice to reside within the circuit—meant to minimize the hardship of traveling across the Appalachian Mountains.

Between 1807 and 1836, eight new states joined the Union. Pressure grew again for creation of more circuit courts (the real trial court workhorses of the federal judiciary) to handle the caseloads in these new states. Congress finally relented in 1837 by establishing the Eighth and Ninth circuits, reorganizing the Seventh Circuit, and adding two justices to the Supreme Court, for a total of nine justices. The circuits were arranged geographically to facilitate travel by the justices. Travel at the time was aided by the expanding system of railroads, though it remained crude by today's standards, particularly for elderly jurists.

In the meantime, Congress passed an increasing number of criminal laws to maintain order in the growing country, which in turn necessitated increased enforcement resources, including courts. Circuit courts bore the greatest burden from these new laws. Their caseloads continued to grow significantly. In 1842, Congress endeavored to alleviate the heavy criminal caseload by giving district courts concurrent jurisdiction over serious federal crimes. District courts thereby assumed responsibility for a share of the burgeoning serious criminal cases.

Inadequacies of the federal judicial system to efficiently manage caseloads across the country became undeniable as the Civil War approached. President Lincoln, in his first State of the Union message to Congress (1861), raised concerns that the judicial system was inadequate for the size of the country. Congress ignored the caseload concerns in 1862, but realigned circuits by annexing to existing circuits some of the areas not yet a part of any circuit.

Underlying proposals for change was a renewed debate over the role and strength of the American judiciary. One vision, drawn from arguments of the Anti-Federalists and still preferred by most Southerners, was a judicial system highly localized and served predominately by local judges who were familiar with and responsive to local conditions. They favored strong, fairly autonomous states and very limited power in the national government. Since the Judiciary Act of 1789, the federal judiciary was largely decentralized, though federal courts had become a very important venue for pursuit of justice across the country. The decentralized judicial system helped to preserve the importance of state court systems as well as the Southern agrarian economic and cultural model which relied heavily on the labor of slaves. But the forces of geographic, demographic, and commercial expansion supported by expanding congressional national policy legislation created more demand than the decentralized judicial system could satisfy.

The other predominant perspective, having roots in the ideas of Federalist Framers, viewed the judicial system as tasked with contributing to a national identity and unity by consistent interpretation and enforcement of the Constitution and a growing body of federal law. Its proponents also felt that some types of legal disputes should be left to the federal courts rather than state courts, particularly where national interests were at stake. This approach favored industrial/commercial interests, which relied upon consistent supportive laws across the nation to foster commercial expansion, in turn fostering prosperity across the country. Its proponents were less concerned about the closeness of the courts to the people. Proponents of this perspective instead offered the suggestion of creating a new tier of appellate courts to relieve the Supreme Court of the many cases presented to it for review. The proposal would disengage Supreme Court justices from circuit duties, removing the local connection between the high court and the people. If adopted, these proposals would tilt the balance of accommodations further in favor of the Federalist vision of the national judiciary.

In 1863 as the Civil War raged, Congress created the Tenth Circuit to cover California and Oregon. Supreme Court membership grew, accordingly, to ten—the highest membership the Court has ever seen. In light of the distance between the tenth circuit and the seat of the Supreme Court in Washington, D.C., Congress provided an annual allowance of $1,000 to the justice assigned to the tenth circuit, to cover travel expenses to Washington in order to sit with the Supreme Court. Still, the 1863 legislation did very little to alleviate the serious capacity challenges of the judicial system.

At the end of the war, Congress passed a very brief bill in 1866, which again reorganized the circuits. This time, however, the Republican majority Congress was focused on managing the influence of federal judges from southern states. In tandem with the state boundaries guiding the geographic jurisdiction of the district and circuit courts, it had become tradition to select Supreme Court justices from each circuit area. Before the war, five circuits were composed of slave states. The 1866 reorganization reduced the number of circuits to nine and reduced the number of circuits formed from slave states alone to two. When the dust settled, only one circuit encompassed only former confederate states. The geographic organization of circuits has since remained stable, except for splitting two large circuits and adding new states.

As the war ended and Reconstruction efforts began, the Republican Congress remained concerned about the Supreme Court being dominated by justices drawn from slave states. One artifact of this Southern strength on the Court was the 1857 case of *Dred Scott v. Sandford*. The Court had issued a strong pro-slavery decision, ruling that slaves were not citizens, so had no constitutional rights. The Court further found unconstitutional a law that limited the spread of slavery into new territories. To curb the potential of the majority power of Southern justices on the Court, Congress reduced membership to seven, setting a moratorium on new appointments until the current membership shrunk to that size through departures of justices. This had the added effect of denying President Andrew Johnson, a Democrat, then in a strained relationship with the Republican-dominated Congress, opportunity to fill a vacancy on the Court.

Another indicator of Congress's concerns about a Supreme Court unduly influenced by Southern interests was a law passed in 1868 that withdrew the Supreme Court's appellate jurisdiction over habeas corpus cases, even those already accepted by the Court for review. One such case presented the Court with an opportunity to find portions of the Reconstruction Act unconstitutional. It was an extraordinary action by Congress, not since repeated. The Court accepted Congress's action and dismissed the case. The action of Congress raised concerns about judicial independence and congressional intrusion on the courts' abilities to protect individual liberties. The Reconstruction era presented extraordinary challenges that had not been experienced before or since. However, the action was consistent with explicit terms of the Constitution granting Congress the power to define the scope of the Supreme Court's appellate jurisdiction (Art. III, §2, cl. 2).

The following year, Congress brought the court system a little closer to the modern model with the Judiciary Act of 1869. Congress returned the size of the Supreme Court to nine members, where it remains to this day. On the slow march toward eliminating circuit duties by Supreme Court justices, the 1869 law required justices to serve their assigned circuits a minimum of once every two years, even though the circuits were required to convene multiple times per year in most of the districts within the circuits. To facilitate processing of more cases, the law established dedicated circuit judgeships, and reduced the circuit court quorum to two.

The Judiciary Act of 1869 introduces a new topic: retirement benefits for judges and justices. The law was meant to clear a path to retirement for judges who were physically or mentally incapable of fulfilling their duties on the court. There is no constitutional power to forcibly remove an Article III judge who is disabled. Rather, informal pressure by colleagues has been the most effective means of encouraging a judge or justice's departure. This 1869 legislation authorized payment of federal judges' and justices' salary at the time of retirement for the remainder of the judge or justice's life if they reached age seventy and had served for at least ten years. During consideration of the bill, the Senate rejected the House provision for appointment of replacement judges for those who refused to retire, greatly limiting the impact of this law on reducing case delays. Congress would later relax the prerequisites for continuation of salary after retirement to the current requirement that the judge's age plus years of service add up to at least sixty-five. When a judge or justice, because of illness or disability cannot fulfill his or her duties but resists suggestions to resign or retire, Congress has authorized chief judges to reassign that judge to less critical work, and to temporarily assign other judges to fulfill the disabled judge's duties. If it is a Supreme Court justice who is disabled yet will not give up his or her seat, the options are more limited. Other justices may pick up some of the workload, and the justice may rely more heavily on his or her law clerks.

Returning to the Reconstruction era, the Jurisdiction and Removal Act of 1875 did much to expand the role of federal courts in the United States. Prior to this, state courts were handling most federal-law-based civil cases between residents of the same state. The 1875 act expanded federal court jurisdiction to hear all cases arising under the U.S. Constitution and laws of the United States. This meant that federal courts would have concurrent jurisdiction with the states with regard to those civil matters, except where another statute provided for exclusive federal jurisdiction. Congress also made it easier to have a case involving federal law or involving diversity of citizenship moved from state court to federal court. Before the 1875 act, only defendants sued outside their home states could claim diversity jurisdiction and have the case moved to federal court. The 1875 act allowed any party on either side of the case to get the case moved to federal court. This flung the doors to the federal courthouse wide open. This time, Congress's rationale had little to do with reintegration of Southern states, but much to do with advancing commercial interests by establishing a uniform system of justice in the federal courts. Still, though the 1875 legislation extended a big welcome mat to new litigation, Congress did not provide for corresponding increased resources for the judicial system to handle the new activity.

Between 1789 and 1875, Congress made many incremental, modest expansions of the judicial system, ever careful to retain the local engagement of federal judges and justices. It struggled to keep the judicial branch small and modestly effective. That trend changed dramatically with the 1891 Evarts Act. In this act, Congress finally took steps to address the growing capacity challenges faced by the courts. The most significant change was the creation of a new tier of appellate courts, called U.S. Circuit Courts of Appeals. These courts would function in panels of three judges drawn from an assigned Supreme Court justice and judges of respective circuits and districts. There was still no relief for Supreme Court justices riding circuit!

The 1891 Evarts Act took a significant step toward increasing the capacity of the judicial branch, by limiting the types of cases that could be appealed directly to the Supreme Court. Instead, most cases could be appealed only once, to the Circuit Court of Appeals, whose judgments would be final. The Circuit Court of Appeals could certify particular questions to the Supreme Court, for that Court's ruling. In such instances, the Supreme Court was given the discretion to either respond to the certified question or assume jurisdiction over the entire case to decide as if it had been appealed to the Supreme Court. Both measures (directing most appeals of trial court decisions to circuit courts of appeals for final decision, and providing discretion to the Supreme Court to decline to decide an entire matter) provided great relief to the burgeoning backlog of cases. Whereas in 1890, the Supreme Court opened its term with 1,800 cases on its docket and received 623 new cases, the number of new cases dwindled to 275 in 1892. Perhaps more importantly, this change in the court system placed a great portion of public policy responsibility at the circuit court of appeals level, in that many of their decisions were final—not subject to review by the Supreme Court.

Further adding capacity, Congress added a new circuit judge for each circuit, and repealed the circuit courts' appellate jurisdiction. The old circuit courts were left in place to continue as trial courts along with the district courts, but their productivity was increased with the addition of judges. In response to frequently expressed concerns, the 1891 act prohibited any justice or judge who participated in deciding a case at the trial level from participating in its review by the Circuit Court of Appeals. Although a full panel would consist of three judges, Congress authorized a quorum of two, meaning the Circuit Courts of Appeals could conduct business with only two judges/justices in attendance, again relieving Supreme Court justices of regular participation.

Completing the redesign of the judicial branch after the Evarts Act, Congress finally relieved Supreme Court justices of their circuit riding duties in the Judicial Code of 1911, some 122 years after circuit riding began with the Judiciary Act of 1789. No longer would members of the highest court of the land participate in trial or intermediate appellate court duties across the country. The influence of the early Republicans and their successors had receded, making way for greater implementation of Federalist policies toward a robust federal judicial system.

The Judicial Code of 1911 also finally eliminated circuit courts, leaving one trial court in the Article III judicial system, the district courts. The move simplified court administration. Congress charged a committee to thoroughly evaluate all existing judiciary laws that had been passed incrementally over many years, and to recommend changes to make them all consistent. Congress adopted those recommendations.

The Judges' Bill of 1925 greatly invigorated the Supreme Court's role as a national policy-making tribunal, by repealing much of its mandatory jurisdiction. Prior to 1911, most cases arrived at the Supreme Court for review of lower court decisions. By law, the Court had no choice but to decide those cases (thus, mandatory jurisdiction). The Court's backlog of cases grew well beyond its capacity to process in a reasonable amount of time. But the dramatic growth of the country and its economy, along with proliferation of federal laws, resulted in an explosion of litigation far beyond any efficiencies generated by Congress's incremental responses. Moving to discretionary power to accept or reject cases from among those presented for review empowered the Court to select the issues on which it would focus. For an interesting recent critique of the Supreme Court's discretionary review, see Hartnett (2000), listed in Further Readings at the end of the chapter.

Article III Specialized Courts, Judges, and Administration

Thus far we have discussed the largest components of the federal court system. There are a few more specialized courts, also created via Article III power, in existence today. There is a U.S. Court of Appeals for the Federal Circuit, created in 1982. It took over jurisdiction from the U.S. Court of Customs and Patent Appeals as well as the appellate jurisdiction of the U.S. Court of Claims. Both the U.S. Court of claims and the Court of Customs and Patent Appeals were abolished. The U.S. Court of Appeals for the Federal Circuit, situated in Washington, D.C., has nationwide geographic jurisdiction, unlike the limited geographic jurisdiction of other lower federal courts. The subject matter jurisdiction is specialized, focusing on international trade disputes, government contracts, patents, trademarks, certain money claims against the United States government, federal personnel, and veterans' benefits. It also handles appeals from decisions of many federal agencies.

Congress created another specialized trial court in 1980, the U.S. Court of International Trade, as successor to the U.S. Customs Court (1926–1980), following years of confusion over the earlier court's actual subject matter jurisdiction. With its primary offices in New York City, this trial court can convene anywhere in the country and even outside of the country. The court's focus is primarily on enforcement of trade agreements, although it can still hear disputes about tariffs, which were more frequent in the early days of the Customs Court.

One common theme throughout this story of building the federal court system is the perennial shortage of resources to meet an increasing demand for judicial services. Besides the slow incremental process of adding courts and judges to the system, Congress employs the policy tool of federal magistrates. Early predecessors to magistrates were called commissioners. Congress authorized trial courts to appoint commissioners for a variety of support duties such as issuing warrants, holding persons for trial, and accepting bail in federal criminal cases. Commissioners were compensated by fees for services until 1968, when the whole system for employing commissioners was revised. According to the Federal Magistrates Act of 1968, commissioners were to be called magistrates, and were to be paid salaries. They are authorized to dispose of minor offenses and to perform additional duties as assigned by district judges. Those duties may include conducting pretrial proceedings in civil and criminal cases, but district judges can assign other duties that are consistent with the Constitution and laws. Magistrate judges are not subject to judicial independence protections that district judges enjoy. Rather, they serve for a term of years that can be renewed. One benefit of the fixed term is that Congress has greater control over the number of magistrates serving over time. Congress expanded authority for magistrates, now called magistrate judges, to conduct civil and criminal misdemeanor trials with the consent of the parties. Interestingly, magistrate judges are not Article III judges, but because they serve the U.S. district courts, they function within Article III courts.

Bankruptcy judges occupy a place very similar to that of magistrate judges. That is, they are specialized, serve as adjuncts to the U.S. district courts, and serve for fixed terms. Bankruptcy judges are now appointed by U.S. Courts of Appeals, and serve terms of 14 years. District courts have exclusive, original jurisdiction over bankruptcy cases, and are authorized to refer the cases to bankruptcy judges. Previously, under the longest-lived prior bankruptcy law (1898–1978), district courts appointed referees to assist with bankruptcy cases. Referees were initially paid through fees; then in 1946 Congress provided for fixed salaries. In 1973, the Supreme Court changed the title of "referee" to "bankruptcy judge," for purposes of judicial administration. Then, in 1978, Congress authorized the president to nominate bankruptcy judges to be confirmed by the Senate, and to serve 14-year terms. However, administration of bankruptcy judges was located within the Department of Justice. The Supreme Court later expressed concern about the constitutionality of having judges outside the purview of federal courts' administration, with limited terms, deciding bankruptcy cases. Congress's response in 1984 was to place the bankruptcy judges squarely within the district courts' control, which is where they remain today. (See Chapter 5.)

In 1978, Congress created a controversial and secretive court called the Foreign Intelligence Surveillance Court (FISC). Congress was responding, in part, to a 1972 decision of the Supreme Court finding the executive had no constitutional authority to conduct warrantless domestic wiretap operations in the interest of national security. A special committee of Congress, the Church Committee, then conducted a study that revealed widespread unlawful, unconstitutional, overbroad, and unnecessarily intrusive surveillance of American citizens in the course of official intelligence gathering activities. The job of the specialized Article III Foreign Intelligence Surveillance Court is to issue warrants for U.S. intelligence-gathering operations within the United States. Eleven judges are selected by the Chief Justice of the United States from among district court judges, who serve only one term of up to seven years on the specialized court. Unlike any other court discussed here, the FISC usually hears from only one party, the government, in secret, with most records of proceedings classified, thus withheld from public examination.

Thirty-five years later, in 2013, a former defense contractor and Central Intelligence Agency employee, Edward Snowden, disclosed documents demonstrating that the FISC granted a broad order at the request of the Federal Bureau of Investigation, compelling Verizon Communications, Inc., to provide on a daily ongoing basis "'all call detail records or telephony metadata' for communications . . . both within the United States and between the U.S. and other countries." Revelation of the FISC's order for such broad surveillance of domestic phone calls triggered public outcry and renewed investigation by Congress. Congress responded with the USA FREEDOM Act of 2015, which places specific limits on domestic surveillance and other intelligence gathering that can be authorized by the FISC. It also directs (in some instances) that the FISC appoint *amicus curiae* to appear and provide legal arguments in support of individual privacy and civil liberties in the context of government applications for FISC warrants or orders. The 2015 law imposes obligations to make FISC decisions and orders public to the greatest extent possible. But those orders and decisions must pass a declassification review by the Director of National Intelligence. This preliminary review step by an executive branch official retains substantial limits on transparency. Of small comfort is the Foreign Intelligence Surveillance Court of Review, created by Congress to review decisions of the FISC. Few cases are appealed, because the vast majority of government applications are approved by the FISC. For what it is worth, further and final review may be had in the Supreme Court.

A part of the story yet untouched is court administration. In the earlier days of the federal judiciary, many administrative tasks were assumed by judges. But in 1922, Congress established the first formally recognized administrative structure within the judicial branch itself, the Conference of Senior Circuit Judges. The primary job of this group was to advise Congress on the needs of the federal courts. To aid in the process, the law required the senior judge in each district to provide annual reports to the Conference concerning the business of their districts.

Congress did, over time, build a supporting bureaucracy. Congress created the positions of court clerk, who manages court filings, correspondence, etc., and marshal, who was responsible for providing office and courtroom accommodations, to serve the early circuit and district courts. But much of the responsibility for court administration was assigned to the Treasury Department (1789–1849), then to the Interior Department (1849–1870), and then to the Justice Department (1870–1939). Finally, in 1939,

Congress strengthened the separation of powers by moving judicial administration out of the executive branch and into the judicial branch, establishing the Administrative Office of the U.S. Court. The act moved the functions of budgeting and personnel management into the judicial branch for the first time. The Administrative Office operates under the supervision of the Conference of Senior Circuit Judges, not the Supreme Court.

A more recent addition to judicial administration is the Federal Judicial Center, established by Congress in 1967. This agency is governed by its own board consisting of the chief justice, judges selected by the Judicial Conference, and the director of the Administrative Office. Its job is to conduct research on the judicial system and to provide educational services to the judicial system. A great deal of information on the federal judicial system, including its history, can be found on its agency website, at http://www.fjc.gov/public/home.nsf.

HISTORY AND DEVELOPMENT OF NON-ARTICLE III COURTS AND TRIBUNALS

The courts discussed above are regarded as Article III courts. Their primary distinctive features are that judges hold their positions during good behavior until they resign, retire, or die, and cannot have their salaries reduced. Also, they are limited by the jurisdictional constraints stated in Article III; functions that do not fall within Article III judicial powers cannot be assigned to Article III judges. In these ways, Article III judges are provided the greatest judicial independence available under the U.S. Constitution. The following courts were created by Congress, but have features that deprive them of the robust independence of Article III courts. These courts are often referred to as legislative courts, because Congress often draws its authority for the tribunals directly from Article I of the Constitution. Congress has used Article I power to create tribunals largely to provide specialized review of executive agency actions.

The oldest type of non-Article III federal court is the territorial court. Many of those areas outside the thirteen colonies participating in the Constitutional Convention started out as territories of the United States. As the nation acquired territories, Congress typically established at least one court with jurisdiction over both federal and local matters. It is this combination of local and federal jurisdiction which distinguished such courts from Article III courts. Territories on the North American continent have since become states, with their own state court systems, as well as extensions of the federal district and circuit courts. At the moment there are three territorial district courts, located in Guam, the Northern Mariana Islands, and the Virgin Islands. Congress set ten-year terms for the judges of these territorial courts. They exercise the same jurisdiction as U.S. district courts as well as local jurisdiction.

Another territory, Puerto Rico, currently has seven district court judges. Congress passed a law in 1966 declaring that any judges on Puerto Rico's U.S. District Court appointed after that time would be protected by Article III tenure and salary security. Congress allowed Puerto Rico to adopt its own constitution (subject, of course to Congress's approval), and to set up its own court system for local matters.

Four additional existing Article I courts were established by Congress: the U.S. Court of Federal Claims, the U.S. Tax Court, the U.S. Court of Appeals for the Armed

Forces, and the U.S. Court of Appeals for Veterans Claims. These specialized courts serve a number of important functions. Most importantly, they provide somewhat independent judicial review of federal agency actions alleged to violate individuals' rights. Dealing with very specialized laws and regulations, they help to ensure consistent decisions throughout the country, a result that cannot be realized through decision making by diverse district courts and courts of appeals. They relieve Article III courts of a huge volume of cases, many of them relatively small in terms of amounts in controversy, ensuring faster resolution. And they provide a less costly alternative to litigation in the district courts or courts of appeals, due to more streamlined procedures.

The U.S. Court of Federal Claims differs from the other three, in that it is administered within the Article III court system even though it is an Article I court. Congress created this court to hear money claims against the federal government. It conducts non-jury trials on such matters as government contracts, constitutional claims, tax refunds, Indian claims, civilian and military pay claims, patent and copyright claims, and vaccine injury claims. It also reviews agency decisions on compensation for Japanese-American internees during World War II. In an activity prohibited to Article III courts, this court also advises Congress on private claims against the government which are brought directly to Congress and for which Congress initiates private relief bills. The court will conduct a hearing on claims and make reports to Congress to aid in its decisions on the claims. Established in 1982, Congress called this the U.S. Claims Court; the name was changed to U.S. Court of Federal Claims in 1992. Its judicial decisions can be appealed to the U.S. Court of Appeals for the Federal Circuit. Judges are appointed by the president with consent of the Senate, but they serve fixed fifteen-year terms.

The U.S. Tax Court hears appeals from decisions of the Internal Revenue Service. It has national jurisdiction and operates around the country, with appeals from its decisions directed to the corresponding circuit court of appeals. Although Tax Court judges are appointed in the same manner as Article III judges, they serve for fixed fifteen-year terms. Tax Court judges are aided by special trial judges who are selected by the chief judge of the Tax Court. These special trial judges serve at the will of the chief judge. This provides a great deal of flexibility in managing the docket of cases. Placing appointment in the hands of the chief judge rather than some external executive official provides a greater degree of independence on the part of the special trial judges.

The U.S. Court of Appeals for the Armed Forces is the latest of a series of efforts to provide review of courts-martial proceedings against members of the armed forces. Art. I, §8, cl. 14 authorizes Congress "To make Rules for the Government and Regulation of the land and naval Forces." To this end, until 1920, courts-martial were conducted according to the Articles of War and the Articles for Government of the Navy, as will be discussed in a moment. Under these authorities, courts-martial were initiated by a military superior, and decisions were reviewed by that superior or the President, depending on the severity of the sentence or rank of the accused. Reacting to abuses during and after World War I, Congress required establishment of Boards of Review, for review of courts-martial convictions and sentences of members of the armed forces. The Office of the Judge Advocate General was to review other cases.

During and after World War II, though, additional weaknesses in the court-martial process were identified. Major concerns were the involvement and undue influence of military command in the process, exacerbated by lack of legal counsel for defendants or the presiding officers. In the course of addressing these and other concerns, Congress passed the Uniform Code of Military Justice in 1950. It established the Court of Military Appeals, which was eventually designated as the U.S. Court of Military Appeals in 1968. All five judges of this court sit together on all cases. To provide some level of independence from the military, judges are to be appointed "from civilian life" and do not qualify for appointment within seven years of retirement from active military duty. Judges are appointed by the president with the advice and consent of the Senate, and serve terms of fifteen years.

The Court of Appeals for Veterans Claims is a relatively new court, established in 1988 after claims of large numbers of veterans of the Vietnam War were denied by the Veterans Administration (VA). Before that, veterans who were dissatisfied with the VA's decisions concerning veteran disability, survivor, and education benefits had no access to judicial review. Advocates called for creation of the independent court. These advocates came largely from the Vietnam Veterans of America, who fought hard for the court in the face of resistance from more politically entrenched veterans services organizations. The Court of Appeals for Veterans Claims now has exclusive jurisdiction to review decisions of the Board of Veterans' Appeals, the final step in the intra-agency review process. Seven full-time judges plus two temporary judges are appointed by the president with the advice and consent of the Senate, and serve fifteen-year terms. The Chief Judge, in his March 18, 2015, testimony, asked Congress to permanently increase judgeships for the court to nine. He testified that the court's caseload has more than doubled in the past ten years. Decisions of the Court of Appeals for Veterans Claims are appealable to the Court of Appeals for the Federal Circuit. Although the legislation allows veterans to have legal or layperson representation in these tribunals, Congress has not authorized funding to provide legal counsel for veterans.

One last major group of specialized tribunals created by Congress is military tribunals, of which there are two general types. One type, court-martial, refers to the disciplinary process for members of the American military. In the early days of the Republic, the Continental Congress adopted the Articles of War, which Congress adopted and kept in place until 1950. In that year, Congress replaced the Articles of War with the Uniform Code of Military Justice (UCMJ). The Articles of War dealt with ordinary courts-martial—that is, discipline of American servicemen for offenses such as mutiny, insubordination, desertion, assistance to enemies, and sedition. The Articles also provided for court-martial prosecution of spies, an early precursor to military commissions. As early as 1802, Congress required that severe sentences imposed by courts-martial be subject to approval by the president. Besides the customary disciplinary offenses applicable to military personnel, today's UCMJ contains its own criminal code addressing a wide range of criminal behaviors.

Court-martial tribunals today and historically are assembled by and consist of military personnel. Unlike courts, a court-martial tribunal may be convened by the president, the secretary of defense, a military branch secretary, or any of a wide range of other military officials, depending on a number of circumstances. They are assembled as needed and may consist of only a military judge, or a military judge and a varying number of other members. The military judge presides over the trial, making rulings on legal issues, and instructing other members of the tribunal. But, unless the case is tried just to the military judge, s/he has no vote as to findings of fact, guilt or innocence, or sentence to be imposed. Instead, the other members function as a kind of jury to make these decisions.

Decisions by courts-martial are reviewed by the convening authority before becoming final, a step that would never occur in an Article III court proceeding. The convening authority can reduce, but not increase, the severity of findings and the sentence. From there, the decision may be reviewed by the court of appeals for the pertinent military service. The decision may then be appealed to the U.S. Court of Appeals for the Armed Forces, and may be reviewed by the U.S. Supreme Court. (See Chapter 13.)

The other major type of military tribunal is the military commission. Today, "military commission" refers to the tribunals involved in the process for prosecuting "unprivileged enemy belligerents," previously referred to as "enemy combatants," defined in the Military Commissions Act of 2009 as one who: "has engaged in hostilities against the United States or its coalition partners; has purposefully and materially supported hostilities against the United States or its coalition partners; or was a part of al Qaeda at the time of the alleged offense." Congress derives constitutional authority for this law from Art. 1 §8, cl. 10, "to define and punish Piracies and Felonies committed on the high Seas, and Offenses against the Law of Nations." (See Chapter 10.)

Use of military commissions to prosecute these stateless enemies since the events of September 11, 2001, has been controversial. As originally conceived by President George W. Bush, the accused were to be prosecuted before military tribunals without the involvement of federal courts. A 2006 Supreme Court decision found the president's military commission process deficient, in that it did not comport with the UCMJ or the Geneva Conventions. The president next turned to Congress for legislative authorization. Congress promptly enacted the Military Commissions Act of 2006 (MCA), which provided more structure for military commissions. Controversial provisions in the MCA of 2006 included limits on the access of the accused to habeas corpus and limits on rights to counsel. When the MCA of 2006 was challenged, the Supreme Court in 2008 concluded it was constitutionally insufficient in providing an accused meaningful access to habeas corpus review. Congress responded once again with the Military Commissions Act of 2009, which provides most of the protections extended to military personnel in court-martial proceedings. The MCA of 2009 omitted the 2006 act's limitations on access to habeas corpus review and remains intact at this time.

As with courts-martial, Congress provided that decisions of military commissions be initially reviewed by the convening authority, which can reduce but not increase seriousness of findings and sentences. The decision is then automatically reviewed by the U.S. Court of Military Commission Review, the last review within in the executive branch. The case can then be appealed to the U.S. Circuit Court for the District of Columbia Circuit.

Other Administrative Tribunals

Many of the tribunals discussed thus far have been "courts." But there are many tribunals authorized by Congress, which reside in executive agencies and independent regulatory commissions. Though far too numerous to detail in this chapter, they can be categorized as quasi-judicial boards, commissions, and individuals usually referred to as administrative law judges. These, too, are authorized by exercise of Congress's Article I powers. Quasi-judicial decision makers are not judges; they are usually specialists in the law and regulations specific to an agency or program. The Board of Veterans Appeals is one example that resides within the Department of Veterans Affairs; it provides a high level of review of agency decisions before those decisions may be subjected to review by the courts. These quasi-judicial tribunals serve to give the respective agencies one last shot at ensuring that an individual has been afforded a fair, error-free decision by the agency before the dispute may be taken to the courts. Cases before agency level quasi-judicial tribunals are decided by specialists in often-complex regulation, at a significantly lower cost than persons face in courts of law. Agencies generally prefer these tribunals because they help ensure consistency in rulings on agency policies and regulations. Congress and the courts like them because the alternative of having all those agency decisions reviewed in the courts would be tremendously expensive, requiring an extraordinary expansion of judicial resources.

FUTURE IMPLICATIONS

The foregoing account of Congress's exercise of its powers to create courts and tribunals reveals a historically reactive rather than proactive Congress in its attention to the judiciary. Today is no different. New laws passed to deal with changing technologies and expanding global interconnectedness are likely to further increase litigation, placing more pressure on very busy courts. If history is any indicator, Congress will not anticipate the impact of those laws on judicial capacity to deal with the litigation they bring. Courts, litigants, attorneys, and special interests will do what they have always done: encourage Congress to make legislative changes.

FURTHER READING

Dodge, Jaime. 2015. Reconceptualizing Non-Article III Tribunals. *Minnesota Law Review* 99 (February): 905-965.

Elsea, Jennifer K., and Michael John Garcia. 2010. Congressional Research Service Report RL33180, Enemy Combatant Detainees: Habeas Corpus Challenges in Federal Court. http://fas.org/sgp/crs/natsec/RL33180.pdf.

Hall, Kermit L. 1975. The Civil War Era as a Crucible for Nationalizing the Lower Federal Courts. *Prologue* 7: 3: http://www.archives.gov/publications/prologue/1975/fall/civil-war -courts.html.

Hartnett, Edward A. 2000. Questioning Certiorari: Some Reflections Seventy-Five Years after the Judges' Bill. *Columbia Law Review* 100: 1643–1738.

Holt, Daniel S. 2013. Debates on the Federal Judiciary: A Documentary History, Volume II: 1875–1939. Federal Judicial Center: http://www.fjc.gov/public/pdf.nsf/lookup/debates -federal-judiciary-vol-ii.pdf/$file/debates-federal-judiciary-vol-ii.pdf.

Ragsdale, Bruce A. 2013. Debates on the Federal Judiciary, Volume I: 1787–1875. Federal Judicial Center. http://www.fjc.gov/public/pdf.nsf/lookup/debates-federal-judiciary-vol-i .pdf/$file/debates-federal-judiciary-vol-i.pdf.

10 THE POWER TO PUNISH PIRACIES AND OTHER OFFENSES AGAINST THE LAW OF NATIONS

Cindy Galway Buys

Article I, section 8, clause 10
To define and punish Piracies and Felonies committed on the high Seas, and
Offenses against the Law of Nations

KEY TERMS

Piracy was defined by the U.S. Supreme Court in 1820 as "robbery upon the sea." Today, piracy has a broader meaning under international law and includes any illegal act of violence, detention, or depredation committed for private ends by the crew or passengers of a private ship and directed against another ship or persons on the high seas or outside any state's jurisdiction.

"Felonies on the high Seas" are different than piracies, although both are a type of felony. Historically, piracy could only be punished under the civil law of admiralty, while felonies were punished in common law courts. This distinction no longer exists today, as both types of crimes may be tried in federal courts of general jurisdiction. Piracy is considered a universal crime punishable by all nations, and the U.S. Supreme Court in *United States v. Smith* has deemed the pirate an "enemy of the human race."

"Offenses against the Law of Nations," in Roman times, were violations of the law of nations or *jus gentium*, which referred to a law common to all men that Roman courts could apply to foreigners. The law of nations was based on custom and thus was distinct from the law of treaties. In the seventeenth century, Hugo Grotius argued that the law of nations established legal rules for what is right and just among nations. In 1789, Jeremy Bentham coined the phrase "international law," which includes both customary international law and treaty law. Today, the terms law of nations and international law are often used interchangeably.

HISTORY AND DEVELOPMENT

The framers of the U.S. Constitution were concerned that the new federal government have the power to enforce international law to ensure its standing among foreign nations and to avoid negative foreign relations consequences. The 1777 Articles of Confederation had created a loose confederation of thirteen sovereign states and a weak federal government, with most of the power remaining in the states. Although Article IX of the Articles of Confederation gave the federal government the power to create courts to try piracies and other felonies committed on the high seas, it did not have jurisdiction over other crimes against the law of nations. Instead, crimes under international law were defined and punished by state law. And because not all of the states handled these crimes in the same way, problems arose. The leading example was the 1784 *Republica v. De Longchamps* case, in which the courts of Pennsylvania were asked to enforce the customary international law relating to diplomatic immunity following an assault on a French diplomat residing in Pennsylvania. There was some concern that if Pennsylvanian courts did not properly enforce the applicable international law, there could be negative foreign relations consequences for the fledging nation.

To address these concerns, clause 10 was included in the draft of the Constitution presented at the 1787 Constitutional Convention, to give the federal government the power to define and punish crimes under international law. There was very little debate over this clause at the Constitutional Convention. There was some discussion regarding whether it was necessary to include both the words "define" and "punish," and at least one delegate (James Wilson) thought it inappropriate for one nation to define crimes that should be determined by all nations. Ultimately, however, the delegates agreed to retain the words "define" and "punish" because they provided sufficient authority and certainty.

As adopted, Art. I, §8, cl. 10 gives Congress the power to define and punish three different types of behaviors: piracy, felonies on the high seas, and offenses against the laws of nations. Each type of conduct is discussed below.

Piracy

The seminal Supreme Court case interpreting this clause of the Constitution is *United States v. Smith*, an 1820 case that involved piracy. An 1819 act of Congress stated that if any person "shall, upon the high seas, commit the crime of piracy as defined by the law of nations," such an offender shall be convicted and punished with death. Thomas Smith was indicted for piracy after he and others seized the vessel, the *Irresistible*, and used it to attack and rob a Spanish vessel on the high seas. Thomas argued that the 1819 act of Congress was invalid because Congress must specifically define the crime of piracy before it may punish the offense. Here, Congress left the definition to the law of nations. The Court rejected the defense's argument, however, stating that Congress may define a crime by using "a term of known and determinate meaning." The Court then consulted the works of scholars writing about international law, the usage and practice of nations, and judicial decisions on the subject to determine whether piracy was defined in the law of nations with reasonable certainty. The Court easily concluded that piracy was well known as "robbery upon the sea." This case thus established the precedent that Congress could rely on international law when enacting statutes.

Today, piracy has resurged on the international scene, primarily as a result of the actions of Somali pirates in the Indian Ocean. In 2010, a United States court held the first piracy trial in the United States in over 100 years, in the case of *United States v. Hasan*. The current federal piracy statute, 18 USC §1651, continues to define piracy by reference to the law of nations, but has modified the sentence from death to life imprisonment. In *Hasan*, a group of Somali men set off in an oceangoing vessel carrying a rocket-propelled grenade and AK-47 assault rifles in search of a merchant ship to attack and plunder. They mistakenly attacked a U.S. Navy ship instead, which returned fire, then chased and captured the pirate vessel. The U.S. Navy took the pirates into custody and brought them to the United States for trial. The court reaffirmed that the federal piracy statute is not unconstitutionally vague and held that piracy includes acts of violence committed on the high seas without an actual taking constituting robbery. The court relied in part on the development of the law of piracy in international law over the last two centuries, including the codification of the crime in Article 15 of the 1958 Geneva Convention on the High Seas, and Article 101 of the 1982 United Nations Convention on the Law of the Sea, which have broadened the definition of piracy to encompass "any illegal acts of violence or detention, or any act of depredation, committed for private ends by the crew or the passengers of a private ship or private aircraft" on the high seas or otherwise outside the jurisdiction of any state.

Felonies on the High Seas

The power to define and punish felonies on the high seas has long been used to punish crimes such as murder or rape on the high seas. In more recent times, there have been several well-publicized cases involving possible criminal behavior aboard cruise ships, with physical or sexual assaults being the most common types of crime. Concern regarding these types of crimes led Congress to adopt the Cruise Vessel Security and Safety Act of 2010 under its Art. I, §8 authority to increase detection and record evidence of possible crimes on board vessels subject to the maritime jurisdiction of the United States.

Additionally, many of the current federal statutes that address felonious behavior on the high seas deal with drug trafficking. For example, Congress has relied on its clause 10 powers to enact statutes such as the Marijuana on the High Seas Act of 1980, the Maritime Drug Law Enforcement Act of 1980, 46 USC §70501 et seq., and the Drug Trafficking Vessel Interdiction Act (DTVIA), 18 USC §2285. The DTVIA is the most recent of the three, enacted in 2008 specifically to outlaw the operation of submersible or semi-submersible vessels without a nationality in international waters with the intent to evade detection, because such vessels were being used by drug traffickers to transport illicit drugs worldwide.

The Law of War

Congress also has long relied on the power to punish offenses against the law of nations to codify the international law of war into U.S. domestic law. In *Ex parte Quirin* (1942), the U.S. Supreme Court upheld Congress's "authority to define and punish offenses against the laws of nations by sanctioning, within constitutional limitations, the jurisdiction of military commissions to try persons for offenses which, according to the rules and precepts of the law of nations, and more particularly, the law of war, are cognizable by such tribunals." More recently, Congress relied in part on Art. I, §8, cl. 10 to enact the Uniform Code of Military Justice which, among other things, implements the Geneva Conventions on the Laws of War, and the War Crimes Act of 1996. However, one of the most controversial uses of Congress's power to punish offenses against the law of nations in recent years relates to its use of this power to sanction the arrest, detention, and trial of alleged terrorists or "unlawful enemy combatants" before military tribunals or commissions under various legal authorities, including the 2001 Authorization to Use Military Force, 50 USC §1541, and the Military Commissions Act.

In pursuing and prosecuting the persons responsible for the terrorist attacks of September 11, 2001, the U.S. government took the position that its war powers, combined with its power to define and punish offenses against the law of nations, gave it broad authority to subject war-related offenses to the jurisdiction of military commissions. While the U.S. Supreme Court upheld the government's power to create military commissions in *Hamdan v. Rumsfeld* (2006), it also held that such commissions can only try crimes recognized as war crimes under international law. Many of the alleged terrorists arrested and detained at Guantanamo Bay, Cuba, beginning in 2002 were charged with conspiracy to commit war crimes and were subject to trial by military commissions rather than being tried in federal courts in the United States. However, the U.S. Supreme Court in *Hamdan* found that conspiracy is not a crime under the international law of war, and thus these detainees could not be tried by military commissions. And in *Al Bahlul v. United States*, a federal court held that Congress cannot declare an offense to be an international war crime when the international law of war concededly does not. More specifically, the *Al Bahlul* court held that providing material support for terrorist activities was not a war crime prior to 2001 and vacated the conviction based on that charge because it violated the Constitution's ex post facto clause. This decision calls into question several other convictions based on the charge of providing material support to terrorists. (See Chapter 9.)

Congress also used its Art. I, §8, cl. 10 powers to adopt the Military Extraterritorial Jurisdiction Act of 2000, 18 USC §113(a), to reach criminal conduct by a person who was employed by or accompanying the Armed Forces, the U.S. Department of Defense, and its contractors and subcontractors outside the United States. In *United States v. Brehm*, the U.S. government brought charges against a citizen of South Africa who was accused of stabbing a British subject, J.O., during a fight at the Kandahar military base in Afghanistan. Brehm was employed by DynCorp, a U.S.-based private military contractor, which was supporting the NATO war effort in Afghanistan. Brehm claimed that the United States could not exercise jurisdiction over him because he had never set foot in the United States. The court disagreed, holding that Congress's powers under Art. I, §8 of the U.S. Constitution are sufficient to reach Brehm's conduct outside U.S. territory.

Other Criminal Offenses against the Law of Nations

It is important to remember that Art. I, §8, cl. 10 does not give Congress the power to punish felonies generally—only those that violate the law of nations. Despite that limitation, over the last two centuries, the power to punish offenses against the laws of nations has been used to punish many types of criminal behavior. Shortly after the *Smith* case, Congress renewed the federal piracy act and extended it to cover the slave trade as well, thus putting the slave trader into the same category as the pirate under the law of nations. Today, of course, slavery is prohibited by the Thirteenth Amendment to the U.S. Constitution.

Congress also relied upon its Art. I, §8, cl. 10 powers to punish the counterfeiting in the United States of notes, bonds, and securities of a foreign bank. (See Chapter 6.) In *United States v. Arjona* (1887), the defendant was convicted of having control and possession of a metallic plate for the purpose of printing counterfeit notes similar to notes issued by El Banco del Estado de Bolivar in Columbia. Arjona argued that Congress could not constitutionally make the offense of counterfeiting in the United States an offense against the law of nations. The U.S. Supreme Court rejected Arjona's argument, stating that the United States is responsible to foreign nations for all violations by the United States of international obligations and that it must protect intercourse between people of different nations. Hence, the United States has an obligation to punish those within its jurisdiction who counterfeit money of another nation. A refusal to do so would disturb the harmony between nations.

In modern times, the federal government often relies on the treaty power set forth in Art. II, §2, cl. 2 of the U.S. Constitution, in conjunction with its powers under Art. I, §8, cl. 10, and the necessary and proper clause, when enacting domestic legislation intended to implement international treaties relating to offenses against the law of nations. One example is Congress's enactment of the Torture Victim Protection Act of 1991 to implement the Convention Against Torture. Likewise, the U.S. government has relied on its clause 10 powers to implement international treaties relating to aircraft piracy and hostage taking. For example, in *United States v. Yunis*, the United States charged a Lebanese man, Fawaz Yunis, under the Hostage Taking Act and the Destruction of Aircraft Act, for his involvement in the hijacking of a Jordanian civilian aircraft in the Middle East. Yunis objected to U.S. jurisdiction, on the ground that the only nexus to the United States was the presence of several U.S. nationals on board the aircraft. The court held that Yunis's crimes are condemned by the world community and subject to prosecution under the universal principle of international law. Hence, Congress was within its powers in passing these two statutes to punish these crimes against the law of nations.

One of the Supreme Court's most recent cases challenging Congress's power to regulate criminal behavior is *Bond v. United States*, a 2014 case involving the reach of a federal statute implementing the Chemical Weapons Convention. In that case, Patricia Bond, a microbiologist, sought revenge against a woman with whom her husband was having an affair by spreading toxic chemicals on surfaces the other woman was likely to touch, such as her car, door handle, and mailbox. Bond was prosecuted under section 229 of the Chemical Weapons Convention Implementation Act of 1998, which forbids the possession or use of chemical weapons. Bond defended in part on the ground that the act was unconstitutional because it exceeded Congress's powers and was a violation of the Tenth Amendment to the U.S. Constitution, which reserved certain powers to the states. The Court avoided reaching the constitutional issue by adopting an interpretation of the act that did not cover Bond's simple assault, relying on the principle that Congress had not indicated its intention to intrude on states' traditional police powers. While this case did not rest explicitly on the basis of clause 10, it does illustrate the continuing tension between Congress's power to define and punish certain types of behavior and the states' power to do so.

Not all offenses against the law of nations are covered by international treaties, however. In some cases, no treaty covering the specific crime has yet been agreed upon by the international community. In other cases, a treaty may exist, but it may not be comprehensive. And in yet other cases, the U.S. government may not have ratified the relevant treaty. As a result, Congress has continued to rely on the power to define and punish offenses against the law of nations to address a wide variety of criminal behavior, including air pirates under the Federal Aviation Act (49 USCA Appx. §1472), human trafficking under the Trafficking Victim Protection Act (22 USC §7101), and the threat or use of certain weapons of mass destruction (18 USC §2232a).

Another growing area of congressional legislation with respect to offenses against the law of nations is terrorism. Anti-terrorism provisions have been incorporated into a number of federal statutes, including the Anti-Terrorism and Effective Death Penalty Act (AEDPA) of 1996 and the Uniting and Strengthening America by Providing Appropriate Tools Required to Intercept and Obstruct Terrorism Act of 2001 ("USA PATRIOT" Act). Many of these statutes rest their authority at least in part on Congress's power to define and punish offenses against the law of nations.

Pursuant to AEDPA, the U.S. secretary of state is empowered to designate certain organizations that threaten the security of the United States or its nationals as foreign terrorist organizations (FTOs). AEDPA then outlaws the provision of material support and resources to FTOs. This material support provision was at issue in *United States v. Ahmed*, involving a group of Somalis who were arrested in Djibouti, allegedly on their way to Yemen to join al Qaeda, another FTO. The Djibouti authorities turned the defendants over to the United States for questioning and prosecution. The Somali defendants argued that the U.S. government lacked jurisdiction to prosecute them because there was not a sufficient connection between their activities and the United States. The court held that U.S. jurisdiction was proper because Congress clearly intended for its terrorism-related statutes to have extraterritorial effect and that its power to define and punish offenses against the law of nations gave it constitutional authority to do so.

Civil Offenses against the Law of Nations

Although Art. I, §8, cl. 10 mentions "felonies" and the power to "punish," suggesting that it is intended to apply to criminal conduct, Congress has also relied on the clause to define and regulate civil offenses against the laws of nations. Congress has relied upon the clause to enact several statutes containing civil offenses as follows: first, in connection with a series of Neutrality Acts; second, in connection with the Alien Tort Statute, 28 USC §1350; third, in connection with the Torture Victim Protection Act, 28 USC §1350, note; and fourth, in connection with the Foreign Sovereign Immunities Act, 28 USC 1601 et seq.

From the very beginning of the nation, Congress relied on its clause 10 powers to enforce the international rules regarding neutrality. Congress adopted the first version of the Neutrality Act in 1794 "to secure the performance of the duty of the United States, under the law of nations, as a neutral nation in respect of foreign powers." Violation of the neutrality law could bring both criminal and civil penalties. The act and the international law of neutrality kept the United States out of the fighting between Cuban revolutionaries and Cuba's colonizing power, Spain, for several years. However, individuals in the United States who were sympathetic to the Cubans' cause attempted to supply the Cuban revolutionaries with vessels and arms. In 1896, the U.S. Navy intercepted one such vessel, the *Three Friends*, and placed it under arrest as it was leaving Florida waters bound for Cuba. The vessel's owner unsuccessfully challenged the forfeiture of the vessel, a civil penalty, due to its illegal activities. Another well-known series of Neutrality Acts were adopted by the U.S. Congress in the 1930s in an unsuccessful attempt to keep the United States out of World War II.

The Alien Tort Statute (ATS) permits civil suits in U.S. courts brought by an alien (i.e., a non-U.S. citizen) for a tortious act committed in violation of the law of nations or a treaty of the United States. It was originally part of the Judiciary Act of 1789. The ATS gained prominence in the 1980s when the Filartiga family, originally from Paraguay but then living in the United States, relied on the statute to sue Pena-Irala, the Inspector General of Police in Asuncion, Paraguay, for the torture and death of 17-year-old Joelito Filartiga in Paraguay. The family claimed that Joelito had been kidnapped, tortured, and killed because of his father's outspoken opposition to the Paraguayan government. The court held that torture is a tort in violation of the law of nations and awarded the Filartiga family a $10 million judgment against Pena-Irala. Victims of atrocities during the Bosnian civil war in the early 1990s were also successful in maintaining a civil action under the ATS in U.S. courts against the leader of the Bosnian Serb forces for genocide, war crimes, and crimes against humanity in *Kadic v. Karadzic*.

More recently, the ATS has been used by human rights activists to bring suit against corporations operating abroad, for their alleged complicity in serious human rights violations. For example, in *Almog v. Arab Bank*, approximately 1,600 plaintiffs brought suit against Arab Bank for knowingly providing banking and other administrative services to terrorist organizations, thereby aiding and abetting in terrorist bombings and other murderous attacks on civilians in Israel. The court found that the underlying activities constituted genocide and war crimes, as well as prohibited acts of terrorism under established norms of international law. The conduct alleged by plaintiffs was sufficiently specific and well-defined to be recognized as a claim under the ATS. The court further found that plaintiffs alleged facts sufficient to create liability for Arab Bank for aiding and abetting these violations of the law of nations. Corporate liability under the ATS has become more difficult to establish, however. In 2013, the

U.S. Supreme Court clarified in *Kiobel v. Royal Dutch Petroleum Co.* that corporations may only be subject to ATS suits in U.S. courts if the corporation has sufficient connections to the United States to overcome a presumption against the extraterritorial application of U.S. laws.

The third example of Congress's use of the "define and punish" clause to impose civil liability is the Torture Victim Protection Act (TVPA), enacted to implement the United States' international law obligation to prohibit and punish torture. The TVPA establishes a civil action for recovery of damages against an individual who, acting under actual or apparent authority, or color of law, of any foreign nation, engages in torture or extrajudicial killing. In *Aldana v. Del Monte Fresh Produce*, Guatemalan labor unionists successfully relied on both the ATS and TVPA to bring a claim against Del Monte, a U.S corporation and the owner of the Bandegua banana plantation in Morales, Guatemala. Plaintiffs were the officers of a national trade union of plantation workers known as SITRABI. They alleged that the Bandegua banana planation hired or established an agency relationship with a private armed security force. Plaintiffs further alleged that these security agents abducted plaintiffs, held them hostage, shoved them with guns, threatened to kill them, and forced them at gunpoint to sign papers resigning their positions and declaring the labor dispute to be over. Plaintiffs also alleged that a mayoral candidate and the current mayor of Morales participated in these activities. The court determined that the mayor's participation was sufficient to create state action as required by the statute and that plaintiffs had alleged sufficient facts to establish torture causing severe mental suffering under both the ATS and the TVPA.

On the other hand, in a case brought by the widow and sons of a United States citizen allegedly tortured and killed in Israel by intelligence officers of the Palestinian Authority, the court dismissed the action because it held that the TVPA does not impose liability on organizations such as the Palestinian Authority and the Palestine Liberation Organization (PLO). Only natural persons may be held liable for torture under the TVPA. Thus, corporations may be liable for torts in violation of the law of nations or treaties under the ATS if there is a sufficient connection to the United States, but cannot be held liable for torture under the TVPA.

The Foreign Sovereign Immunities Act (FSIA) is a fourth civil statute enacted under Congress's clause 10 powers. FSIA is intended to codify the general rule in international law that foreign states should not be subject to suits in the domestic courts of another state, except in certain circumstances. State immunity demonstrates respect for state sovereignty and assists in maintaining friendly foreign relations. FSIA begins with a presumption that foreign states are immune from suit in federal and state courts in the United States. However, there are several exceptions to this rule, such as when a foreign state consents to jurisdiction or is acting in a commercial capacity. In *Argentine Republic v. Amerada Hess Shipping Corp.*, a shipping company attempted to invoke one of these exceptions to obtain $10 million in damages from Argentina for bombing one of the company's vessels. The vessel was engaged in the transportation of oil between Alaska and the Virgin Islands when it was bombed by Argentine military planes approximately 500 miles from the Falkland Islands during the Falkland War, despite giving notice of its presence and peaceful, commercial purpose. Amerada Hess was unable to obtain any relief in Argentine courts, so it sued Argentina in the United

States under the ATS. The U.S. Supreme Court held that Amerada Hess must satisfy one of the exceptions in FSIA to maintain the suit, which Amerada Hess was not able to do. Accordingly, the court dismissed the case.

State immunity under FSIA does not extend to officials acting on behalf of a state, however. In *Samantar v. Yousuf*, the U.S. Supreme Court allowed an action to go forward against Mohamed Ali Samantar, who was at various times between 1980 and 1990 the first vice-president and minister of defense of Somalia and Somalia's prime minister. Plaintiffs in that case alleged that they were victims of torture and extrajudicial killings during Samantar's time in office and that he authorized the actions against plaintiffs. Although Samantar could not rely on the protection of state immunity under FSIA, the Supreme Court left open the possibility that Samantar may have other defenses at common law.

Limitations on Congressional Power

Congress's power under Art. I, §8, cl. 10 must be exercised consistently with international law and with other parts of the U.S. Constitution. As noted above, the clause only gives Congress power to define and punish piracies and felonies on the high seas and offenses that violate international law. States continue to retain the power to regulate domestic criminal behavior. Moreover, Congress's power must be interpreted consistently with international law limits on extraterritorial jurisdiction. For example, in a case brought under the Marijuana on the High Seas Act, a federal court in Florida held that Congress intended for the act to be applied consistently with international law limits on jurisdiction. In that case, the U.S. Coast Guard stopped a vessel, the *Island Merchant*, which was not flying the flag of any country, on the high seas about 400 miles from the United States. The Coast Guard discovered marijuana on board the vessel and arrested several crewmen who were Colombian nationals. The vessel was headed for the Bahamas, and there was no evidence that there was any intent to offload or distribute the marijuana in the United States. The court found, under those circumstances, that it lacked jurisdiction over the case, as there was no nexus to the United States.

On the other hand, U.S. jurisdiction does extend to crimes committed on U.S. flag vessels in navigable waters of another country and on the high seas, which are defined in UNCLOS as all parts of the sea that are not within the exclusive economic zone, territorial sea, or internal waters of the United States.

The extent of the connection to the United States required for the exercise of U.S. jurisdiction has been a matter of some controversy and has led to a split among the federal circuit courts. In particular, there has been a difference of opinion among the federal courts with regard to the scope of the Maritime Drug Law Enforcement Act (MDLEA). MDLEA was expressly enacted pursuant to Congress's power to define and punish felonies on the high seas and is intended to reach acts outside the territorial jurisdiction of the United States. The act makes it unlawful to manufacture, distribute, or possess controlled substances on a vessel subject to the jurisdiction of the United States. It is well established under international maritime law that when a vessel flies a U.S. flag, it is subject to U.S. jurisdiction. However, courts have had to grapple with the issue of when a vessel flying no flag or flying the flag of another country is subject to U.S. jurisdiction outside U.S. territorial waters.

In *U.S. v. Davis*, the Ninth Circuit Court of Appeals refused to find jurisdiction over a British-registered vessel operated by a non-U.S. citizen apprehended by the U.S. Coast Guard on the high seas. The court held that there was an insufficient nexus between the defendant and the United States to satisfy due process concerns. On the other hand, four other federal circuit courts have come to the opposite conclusion, upholding the extraterritorial application of MDLEA to non-U.S. citizens apprehended with drugs outside U.S. territorial waters when the flag nation of the vessel has consented to application of U.S. law to the defendants. These courts have found that the trafficking of narcotics is universally condemned by law-abiding nations, and thus it is within Congress's power to punish persons apprehended with narcotics on the high seas. This split of opinion regarding the extraterritorial application of U.S. law has not yet been resolved by the U.S. Supreme Court.

The Eleventh Circuit further limited MDLEA's reach in the case of *United States v. Bellaizac-Hurtado*. This case concerned an incident in which the U.S. Coast Guard observed a wooden fishing vessel operating without lights and without a flag in Panamanian waters. The Coast Guard informed the Panamanian authorities, who pursued the vessel. The occupants of the vessel abandoned it and fled into the jungle, where they were captured by Panamanian authorities. When the Panamanian authorities searched the vessel, they discovered a large amount of cocaine on board. After an exchange of diplomatic notes, the Republic of Panama consented to the prosecution of the suspects in the United States. The United States charged the defendants with possession with intent to distribute cocaine on board a vessel subject to the jurisdiction of the United States under MDLEA. The defendants challenged the constitutionality of MDLEA as applied to them because their vessel was not on the high seas and they were captured on land. The court agreed with the defendants that it did not have jurisdiction to decide their case under MDLEA because drug trafficking, while routinely criminalized under domestic law and prohibited by certain treaties, is not an offense under customary international law. Thus, the U.S. government could not rely on its power to define and punish offenses against the law of nations in prosecuting these defendants.

In addition, Congress cannot define and punish behavior that would be contrary to the United States Constitution. For example, in *Boos v. Barry* (1988), Congress had relied on its constitutional power to define and punish offenses against the law of nations when it enacted a statute making it unlawful to display any type of sign designed to "intimidate, coerce, or bring into public odium any foreign government" within 500 feet of any building occupied by a foreign government or its representatives. Petitioners wished to carry signs critical of the governments of the Soviet Union and Nicaragua and challenged the statute as unconstitutional infringement on their rights of free speech and assembly. The United States government claimed the statute was necessary to comply with its international law obligations which require the government to protect the premises of diplomatic missions against intrusion, damage, and disturbance of the peace or impairment of the dignity of the mission. While recognizing the importance of protecting diplomats, the U.S. Supreme Court struck down a portion of the statute as a violation of the First Amendment to the Constitution because it believed the statute was not sufficiently narrowly tailored to serve that purpose. Thus, when acting under Art. I, § 8, cl. 10, Congress must be careful not to otherwise exceed the limits of the U.S. Constitution or international law.

FUTURE IMPLICATIONS

Following World War II, the development of international law has been driven largely by written international agreements or treaties. As a result, the U.S. government has more often relied on its constitutional powers to make treaties and other international agreements, rather than the congressional power to define and punish offenses against the law of nations, when regulating international criminal behavior. However, Art. I, §8, cl. 10 will remain important for at least two reasons: (1) to implement international treaty obligations, and (2) to fill gaps in those treaties.

The international community continues to develop new treaties to address different types of criminal behavior. For example, the United Nations' International Law Commission has on its current agenda the study and development of additional rules regarding the immunity of state officials from foreign criminal jurisdiction and crimes against humanity. Historically, the United States has been an active participant in developing these new international rules and agreements, and often joins international agreements prohibiting international criminal activity. Thus, the United States will continue to rely on its power to define and punish piracy, felonies on the high seas, and offenses against the law of nations, to implement these new international treaties.

International treaties do not and likely never will address all aspects of undesirable behavior, however. Such treaties often take many years to negotiate, draft, and enter into force. They also are the product of compromise and, as a result, may contain vague language that reflects the lowest common denominator that could be agreed among the states that participated in the negotiation and drafting process. Thus, gaps in addressing specific international criminal behavior will inevitably remain. Moreover, with increased globalization, including the movement of persons, goods, and money across borders, and the creation and use of new technologies by criminal organizations, criminal behavior changes at a faster rate than international law. Accordingly, it is essential for Congress to have a tool to address problems arising from new types of international criminal behavior that is not dependent on the international community agreeing upon it in a treaty. As a result, it is likely that Congress will continue to find a need to rely on its constitutional power to define and punish offenses against the law of nations to address this rapidly changing environment.

FURTHER READING

Ken, Andrew J. 2007. Congress's Under-Appreciated Power to Define and Punish Offenses against the Law of Nations. *Texas Law Review* 85: 843.

Kontorovich, Eugene. 2009. The "Define and Punish" Clause and the Limits of Universal Jurisdiction. *Northwestern University Law Review* 103: 149.

Stephens, Beth. 2000. Federalism and Foreign Affairs: Congress's Power to "Define and Punish . . . Offenses against the Law of Nations." *William & Mary Law Review* 42: 447.

11 THE POWER TO DECLARE WAR

Brien Hallett

Article I, section 8, clause 11
To declare war, grant letters of marque and reprisal, and make rules concerning captures on land and water.

KEY TERMS

"**To declare war**" requires the declarer to exercise three functions or roles. First, the declarer must *draft* a "clear statement" of the grievances that justify the resort to war and the peace terms that will end the war. Second, the declarer must *decide* to go or not to go to war based upon the "clear statement." And, third, when the decision is to go to war, the declarer must *publish and declare* the "clear statement" that justifies and explains its decision. The exercise of these three functions is exemplified most clearly in the way the Second Continental Congress *drafted*, *decided* with a vote, and then *published and declared* the Declaration of Independence in 1776.

The *declaration of war* produced by the declarative speech act then functions as the public announcement of the end of the state and condition of peace and the beginning of the state and condition of war. The state and condition of war will end and the state and condition of peace will return with the conclusion of an eventual peace treaty.

What makes the declaring of war so confusing and controversial is that, historically, official declarations by legitimate declarers are the exception, not the rule. This is possible because, first, the declarer may exercise the three functions either *legitimately*, when possessed of a socially recognized power or right to declare war, or *illegitimately*, when not possessed of a socially recognized power or right to declare war.

Second, no need exists to declare war *officially*. This is the case because the three functions or roles required to declare war can be exercised in four basic patterns.

Three of the patterns are dominated by an individual decision-maker. The fourth is characterized by no individual decision-maker. Instead, a small assembly employs parliamentary procedures to make the decision, as the Second Continental Congress did in 1776.

With the first pattern, a king or emperor, who possesses a recognized prerogative right to declare war, legitimately *decides* to go to war. His privy council then *drafts* a "clear statement," which the king or emperor *publishes and declares* officially. This pattern is surprisingly infrequent in world history.

With the second pattern, a warlord or other commander-in-chief, without a recognized prerogative right to declare war, illegitimately *decides* to go to war. His assistants then *draft* a military order and a public announcement, which the warlord or commander-in-chief "*publishes and announces*" in a functionally equivalent declarative act. This pattern is the most frequent in world history. Presidents have initiated a large number of America's wars in this manner. Examples include President Harry Truman's initiation of the 1950 Korean War, and President Barack Obama's 2011 enforcement of a UN no-fly zone over Libya.

With the third pattern, a president as commander-in-chief, without a recognized prerogative right to declare war, illegitimately *decides* to go to war. His staff then *drafts* 1) a military order, 2) a presidential address, and 3) an "authorizing" resolution. The "authorizing" resolution is introduced into the Congress and passed, thereby *publishing and announcing* a first functionally equivalent declarative act. The president as commander-in-chief subsequently executes his military order and addresses the nation, thereby *publishing and announcing* a second functionally equivalent declarative act. Presidents have initiated a number of America's wars in this manner. Examples are President George H. W. Bush's 1991 Persian Gulf War or President George W. Bush's 2003 invasion of Iraq.

A variation on this pattern is for the State Department to draft a congressional declaration of war on the president's orders, for introduction and passage by the Congress. With this alternative Pattern Three, the president *decides*, the State Department *drafts*, and the Congress *publishes and declares*. This alternative pattern has been used for three American wars: the War of 1812, World War I, and World War II.

With the fourth pattern, a small assembly, possessing the recognized power to declare war, legitimately *drafts*, debates, and amends a "clear statement" justifying and explaining a resort to war. It then votes on the amended draft. If the vote is for war, that assembly has made the *decision* to go to war, which it simultaneously *publishes and declares* officially. The Declaration of Independence voted on by the Second Continental Congress in 1776 is the only example in American history of this pattern, of an assembly *drafting*, *deciding*, and *publishing and declaring* war.

In sum, while the second and third patterns have been the employed most frequently throughout both American and human history, only the first and fourth patterns declare war legitimately and officially.

"**[To] grant letters of marque and reprisal**": Edward I of England granted the first recorded letters of marque and general reprisal in 1295. The king's purpose was to regulate private war by granting licenses to his subjects to right private wrongs.

A subject, who had had property unjustly seized, applied to the king for a license to recover damages by armed force. With such a license, the subject was recognized under the laws of war and accorded prisoner of war status if captured. Without such a license, the subject was either a brigand on land or a pirate at sea, to be hanged accordingly.

The word "marque" derives from the Latin, *marca*, and indicates the right to cross boundaries to seize property in another realm. Reprisal does not carry this right of crossing into another realm. The permitted seizures are general but limited to the territory of the king who granted the right to reprisal. The advantages of acquiring both rights are obvious. Very quickly the two rights were conjoined into one, "letters of marque and reprisal."

By the fifteenth century, letters of marque and reprisal were more frequently issued as commissions to private ships to seize enemy ships under the laws of war and, hence, to avoid the charge of piracy. The term "privateer" was used to distinguish ships sailing under commission from true pirate ships sailing without commissions.

By granting commissions to private ships, a nation could augment its naval forces at no expense and wage war against the enemy's commerce. This *guerre de course* was very profitable, because the captured enemy ships and their cargo were of considerable value. To obtain this value, the privateer had to abide by the laws of war and the conditions of his commission, and bring any captured ships to port for adjudication as a "good prize" by an admiralty court.

Privateers were commissioned and prizes taken during the Revolutionary War and the War of 1812. Since then a few scattered commissions have been issued by the United States, but no captures made. The most recent case of this kind occurred during the first months of World War II. The Goodyear blimp, *Resolute*, was commissioned to conduct submarine patrols off Los Angles. Letters of marque and reprisal were issued because the civilian crew was armed with rifles.

Privateering was abolished among the major European powers under the Declaration of Paris, 1856. Although the United States has never signed the Declaration, it has abided by its terms. During the Civil War, the South issued letters of marque and reprisal to privateers, but not the North.

The present-day status of letters of marque and reprisal is unclear. Few can imagine ever again granting them. However, Jules Lobel (1986) has made a very strong case that modern-day covert and secret wars are essentially private wars. As such, they should not be initiated and fought under a presidential "finding." Instead, they should be initiated and fought under congressional letters of marque and reprisal.

"[To] make rules concerning captures on land and water": Since property of various kinds will be seized during war, Congress needs to establish rules to determine the status of the original owner, whether the seizure was legitimate or illegitimate, and the final disposition of the property. The main issue was whether sole ownership were to be transferred to the government to dispose of as it saw fit, or whether the capture were to be treated as a prize. If treated as a prize, additional laws had to be made so that admiralty courts might apportion the proceeds of all sales between the captors and the government.

HISTORY AND DEVELOPMENT

As recorded in James Madison's *Notes*, the Federal Convention took up the clause "To make war" just before the lunch break on Friday, August 17, 1787. Charles Pinckney of South Carolina began by suggesting that the House of Representatives "would be too numerous for deliberations," and so "The Senate would be the best depository, being more acquainted with foreign affairs." His colleague from South Carolina, Pierce Butler, then rose to object to vesting the power "To make war" in the legislature at all. "He was for vesting the power in the President, who will have all the requisite qualities, and will not make war but when the Nation will support it." Upon hearing Butler's objection, James Madison of Virginia and Elbridge Gerry of Massachusetts introduced an amendment, "to insert 'declare,' striking out 'make' war; leaving to the Executive the power to repel sudden attacks." Gerry then rebuked Butler, saying, "[I] never expected to hear in a republic a motion to empower the Executive alone to declare war." After a few more minutes of discussion, the Madison-Gerry amendment passed with seven "Ayes," two "Noes," and one abstention.

Needless to say, since 1787, much controversy has surrounded the Madison-Gerry amendment. Two points of universal agreement, however, do exist. All agree that the president, as commander-in-chief, may "repel sudden attacks" without an official, congressional declaration of war. In addition, all agree that the Congress and only the Congress may legitimately declare war officially. Both points are of great interest because of the way in which they demonstrate a misunderstanding of the power of the U.S. government to declare war.

With regard to the first, no president has ever had the need to "repel sudden attacks" without a congressional declaration or "authorization" in over 200 years. Hence, agreement that the president may do so is of only theoretical value, with no practical value. The most forceful example of this is President Franklin Roosevelt's response to the surprise attack on Pearl Harbor on Sunday, December 7, 1941. In response, President Roosevelt *decided* to go to war. He then initiated the alternative version of Pattern Three by convening a special joint session of the 77th Congress for the next day. Simultaneously, he ordered the State Department to *draft* a congressional declaration of war. The next day, at 12:30 PM, Monday, December 8, 1941, President Roosevelt gave information to the 77th Congress in the form of his famous "a date which will live in infamy" speech. The 77th Congress then voted and passed the State Department–drafted declaration in thirty-three minutes, thereby *publishing and declaring* the president's *decision* and the State Department's *draft*. In sum, "sudden attack" or no "sudden attack," time always exists to declare war both legitimately and officially.

With regard to the second point, agreement that the Congress and only the Congress may declare war both officially and legitimately means that the president is not a first-pattern king or emperor. He does not possess a constitutionally recognized prerogative right to declare war on his own authority. This last point of agreement, however, is where all the disagreements begin. Only the Congress may legitimately declare war officially, but an official and legitimate declaration is never needed to commence armed hostilities. Indeed, the vast majority of wars in world history—including American history—have commenced with second- or third-pattern, functionally equivalent, unofficial declarative acts, usually a military order and public announcement from the nation's commander-in-chief.

Interestingly, the frequency with which presidents have initiated armed hostilities in this way has increased significantly since World War II. Arthur Schlesinger wrote about this increase in a particularly influential 1973 book, *The Imperial Presidency*. Since then, "the imperial presidency" has become the standard way to describe second- or third-pattern, functionally equivalent, unofficial and illegitimate declarative acts by the president.

Be that as it may, since Friday, August 17, 1787, the main controversy has turned on a collision of these two universally recognized powers: the universally recognized power of the Congress to declare war officially and the universally recognized power of the president as commander-in-chief under Art. II, §2, cl. 1 to initiate armed hostilities unofficially. He does so with a second- or third-pattern, functionally equivalent declarative act. What is most significant about this collision between constitutional theory and actual practice is how it can be made to fit into to a larger constitutional debate over the relative powers of the Congress and the president. Did the Founding Fathers intend to create a strong executive, able to act with "energy and dispatch?" Or did they intend to create a weak executive that only executed the will of the legislature?

This question was debated most notably, for present purposes, in 1793. In order to avoid involvement in the first wars of the French Revolution, President George Washington acted with "energy and dispatch" and proclaimed American neutrality without recalling Congress, which was in recess. Alexander Hamilton, writing as *Pacificus*, defended Washington's "energy and dispatch" by arguing for a "strong executive." "The power of the Legislature to declare war," Hamilton wrote, "are *sic* exceptions out of the general 'Executive Power' vested in the President [as commander-in-chief], they are to be construed strictly—and ought to be extended no further than is essential to their execution." In response, James Madison, writing as *Helvidius*, opposed Washington's proclamation by arguing for a "weak executive." "Those who are to *conduct* a *war*," Madison asserted, "cannot in the nature of things, be proper or safe judges, whether *a war ought* to be *commenced, continued*, or *concluded*."

This two-hundred-year-old debate over a "strong" versus a "weak" executive has two salient features. First, it is endless. It is no closer to resolution today than it was two hundred years ago. Second, it ignores the comments of Charles Pinckney and Pierce Butler at the Federal Convention in 1787. To avoid getting bogged down in an endless debate, consider first how prophetic were Pierce Butler's remarks. Who can deny that successive presidents have not had "all the requisite qualities [to *commence*, to *continue*, and to *conclude* America's many wars]?" In addition, no president has made war "but when the Nation will support it." True, several American wars have turned sour and lost public support after they were begun. Vietnam and Iraq come to mind. But no president has ever *begun* a war without high levels of public and congressional support, a vocal opposition notwithstanding.

Speaking more concretely, "the requisite quality" that has enabled presidents "to *commence*, to *continued*, and to *conclude*" virtually all of America's wars on their own authority as commander-in-chief is the fact that they can. Presidents can do so because an official congressional declaration is never necessary. All the president as commander-in-chief has to do is to implement either pattern-two or pattern-three procedures. All he has to do is *decide* to go to war and *draft* a military order and his address to the nation. He then executes the order and *publishes* his address to the nation, either with or without consulting the Congress. These functionally equivalent declarative acts are much more efficient and effective than requesting an official declaration from the Congress.

The simplicity, efficiency, and frequency of presidential war-making brings one back to Charles Pinckney's observation that the House of Representatives "would be too numerous for deliberations" on the question of war or peace. His point, of course, is that deciding to go to war officially is a very complex foreign policy question. It requires a relatively small, dedicated body that is "more acquainted with foreign affairs." To entrust the declaring of war officially to a large body "more acquainted with *domestic* affairs" was not going to work—as it hasn't.

The pattern-four procedures that informed Pinckney's observation were, of course, the Second Continental Congress, which had declared war only eleven years before. In 1776, the fifty-five delegates to the Second Continental Congress were not "too numerous for deliberations." Of even greater importance, the fifty-five delegates were not merely "acquainted with foreign affairs"; these were their exclusive concern and business, as domestic affairs were the concern and business of the thirteen state legislatures. Consequently, the Second Continental Congress, unlike its successor, the United States Congress, was able to implement pattern-four procedures. Out of "a decent Respect to the Opinions of Mankind [which] requires that they should declare the causes which impel them to the Separation," the Second Continental Congress was able to *draft*, debate, and amend a "clear statement" of the justifications for the war and its peace terms—independence. Then, it was able to *decide*, on its own initiative, to transform an unofficially declared insurgency into an officially declared war. And, finally, it "*published and declared*" the "clear statement" of its decision, so as to "let Facts be submitted to a candid World."

Clearly, the small Second Continental Congress, with its exclusive focus on foreign affairs, is not the same thing as the large United States Congress, with its primary focus on domestic affairs. Still, the full effects of Pinckney's observation would not be felt until 1812. Between 1793 and 1812, President Washington's policy of neutrality kept the United States out of the French Wars of Revolution and Empire, 1792–1815. In August 1811, however, President Madison decided that British violations of American neutrality, symbolized by the impressment of America sailors, could no longer be tolerated. As Madison's Secretary of State, James Monroe, wrote to John Taylor on June 13, 1812, five days before the Twelfth Congress declared war against Great Britain officially:

> [Since n]othing would satisfy the present ministry in England, short of unconditional submission, which it was impossible to make. This fact being completely ascertained, the only remaining alternative, was to get ready for fighting, and to begin as soon as we were ready. This was the plan of the administration, when [the Twelfth] Congress met in November last [1811]; the President's message announced it; and every step taken by the administration since has led to it.

Madison's decision, needless to say, created a problem because the Congress did not see the situation in the same way. A majority still supported Washington's policy of neutrality. Consequently, the constitutionally mandated pattern-four procedures for self-initiated congressional decision-making would not work in 1812.

The pattern-four procedures had worked in 1776 for the Second Continental Congress, but they would not work in 1812 for the Twelfth Congress for the two reasons Charles Pinckney had observed: First, the House of Representatives was not sufficiently "acquainted with foreign affairs," at least from President Madison's perspective. Second, the House was "too numerous for [self-initiated] deliberations." In 1789, the First Congress had counted 65 members in the House, a number not too much greater than the 55 delegates in 1776. But by 1812, the House had already expanded to 143 members, on its way to the present 435 members. As a result, the collective action problems of the Congress had grown proportionally, and the ability of the House to set its own agenda and initiate its own decisions dwindled rapidly.

To compensate for these two problems, the House was rapidly abandoning its original committee-of-the-whole organization in favor of its modern standing-committee organization. The efficiency gained, however, was paid for by deceased congressional initiative. Standing committees meant that a president could more easily set the congressional agenda and pass his desired legislation whenever he could capture key standing committees. This, of course, is what happened in 1812. With the able assistance of Speaker Henry Clay, the Foreign Affairs, War, and Naval Committees were packed with "War Hawks." This set the stage for the alternative pattern-three procedures. Then, once Madison had set the precedent in 1812, pattern-two and -three procedures became the all-conquering patterns for presidential war-making ever since.

The Doctrinal Foundation of the War Powers Resolution of 1973

To restate the constitutional problem, the gap between constitutional theory and practice occurs because an official congressional declaration of war is never needed. A functionally equivalent military order and national address from the president as commander-in-chief is an even more efficient way to begin armed hostilities. In theory, this gap could have been closed had Art. I, §8, cl. 11 contained an explanatory phrase, such as "on all and every occasion"—that is, the Congress shall have power "to declare war *on all and every occasion*." Yet, even with such a phrase, the effects of Charles Pinckney's observation were sooner or later going to make congressionally initiated pattern-four procedures impossible. Presidential war-making employing a mix of pattern-two and pattern-three procedures would then become inevitable.

Curiously, as if he had had a premonition, James Madison had already written about this inevitable state of affairs in his 1793 *Letter of Helvidius*: With respect to the congressional power to declare war, "The executive has no other discretion than to convene and give information to the legislature." Possessing "no other discretion," President Madison put his own words into action during 1811 and 1812, as just described. But the description requires closer scrutiny.

As Secretary of State Monroe wrote to John Taylor, after President Madison had decided to go to war in August 1811, he "convened" the Twelfth Congress four months early, in November 1811. He next "gave them information" in "the President's message." And, finally, Secretary Monroe also obliged by drafting the text of the congressional declaration, which the Twelfth Congress passed on June 18, 1812. That is, all the Twelfth Congress had to do was to vote to *publish and declare* President Madison's *decision* and Secretary Monroe's *draft*.

Between November and June, Madison had also taken "every step" to ensure that the alternative pattern-three procedures moved along as expeditiously as possible. Of particular importance were Secretary Monroe's frequent meetings and dinners with Speaker Henry Clay at the "War Mess," which was the name given to the boarding house where the most prominent "War Hawks" lived. Of Secretary Monroe's numerous meetings with Speaker Clay at the War Mess, the one on Sunday, March 15, 1812, was especially fruitful. Not only did Speaker Clay agree to the president's final legislative strategy, but, in the left-hand margin of Clay's *aide-mémoire* of the meeting, the Speaker opined that

> Altho' the power of declaring War belongs to Congress, I do not see that it less falls within the scope of the President's constitutional duty to recommend such measures as he shall judge necessary and expedient than any other which, being suggested by him, they alone can adopt.

Two comments are in order: First, while it is theoretically true that the Congress "alone can adopt," as a practical matter, no Congress has every refused a presidential request either to declare or "authorize" war. Not only is the president as commander-in-chief very persuasive, but, more importantly, no politically astute president makes the request without assurance that it will be "adopted," as demonstrated by the infamous 1964 Gulf of Tonkin Resolution or the equally infamous 2003 authorizing resolution to invade Iraq. Second, but more significantly, the Congress has already lost the initiative. Employing pattern-four procedures, the Second Continental Congress always preserved its initiative and independent decision-making. Under the Madison–Clay doctrine, instead of *drafting* the text and *deciding* the question of war or peace on its own independent initiative, the Congress is now *adopting* a presidential decision and text. Neither "adoption" nor "authorizing," to state the obvious, is the same as "deciding," "drafting," and "declaring." But *deciding* and *drafting* are the two dynamos that put power into the power to declare war.

Oddly, the Madison–Clay doctrine was not codified until the end of the Vietnam War, when opposition to the "imperial presidency" had reached levels that would have surprised Pierce Butler. Riding this wave, the 93rd Congress passed the *War Powers Resolution of 1973* over President Richard Nixon's veto on Wednesday, November 7, 1973. As one would expect, the purpose of the Resolution is not to establish the independent congressional initiative found in pattern-four procedures. Instead, the Resolution codifies the two alternative pattern-three procedures, while doing nothing to diminish the president's power to employ the pattern-two procedures.

To begin, the Resolution does not define the Congress as an independent initiator possessed of the power to *draft* a declaration, to *decide* with a vote, and, when voted up, to "*publish and declare*" an official declaration. Instead, the Resolution codifies the two pattern-three procedures by defining the relationship between the president and the Congress as a theoretically co-equal participation in a "consultation" "to insure that the collective judgment of both the Congress and the President":

> Sec. 2. (a) It is the purpose of this joint resolution to fulfill the intent of the framers of the Constitution of the United States and insure that the collective judgment of both the Congress and the President will apply to the introduction of United States Armed Forces into hostilities, or into situations where imminent involvement in hostilities is clearly indicated by the circumstances, and to the continued use of such forces in hostilities or in such situations.

However, this theoretical co-equality is completely undermined in practice, because all initiative rests with the president:

> Sec. 3. The President in every possible instance shall consult with Congress before introducing United States Armed Forces into hostilities or into situations where imminent involvement in hostilities is clearly indicated by the circumstances . . .

That is, after the president has *decided* to go to war, but before he orders armed hostilities to begin—in that interval—he is to "consult" with the Congress. In other words, the Resolution codifies the Madison–Clay doctrine that "The executive has no other discretion than to convene and give information to the legislature," to repeat Madison's words.

But, of course, the Resolution undermines the theoretical co-equality of the Congress even further, because it requires the president to *draft* the text:

> Sec. 4 (a) (3) . . . the President shall submit within 48 hours to the Speaker of the House of Representatives and to the President pro tempore of the Senate a report, in writing, setting forth-
> > (A) the circumstances necessitating the introduction of United States Armed Forces;
> > (B) the constitutional and legislative authority under which such introduction took place; and
> > (C) the estimated scope and duration of the hostilities or involvement.

And, finally, the Resolution codifies a presidential preference for "statutory authorizations," also known as "Authorization for the Use of Military Force" resolutions (AUMF).

> SEC. 2. (c) The constitutional powers of the President as Commander-in-Chief to introduce United States Armed Forces into hostilities, or into situations where imminent involvement in hostilities is clearly indicated by the circumstances, are exercised only pursuant to (1) a declaration of war, (2) specific statutory authorization, or (3) a national emergency created by attack upon the United States, its territories or possessions, or its armed forces.

Number (3), of course, harkens back Elbridge Gerry's never-used presidential author-ity "to repel sudden attacks." Number (1) repeats the seldom-used alternative pattern-three procedures that lead to a State Department–drafted congressional declaration of war. And number (2) codifies the more frequently used pattern-three procedures that lead to a congressional "statutory authorization" of one sort or another. Ironically, perhaps, the War Powers Resolution does not outlaw the frequently used pattern-two procedures, when the president simply does not "consult" with the Congress. Outlaw-ing pattern-two procedures has never been a viable option, because the president never needs to "consult" with the Congress before he acts. As commander-in-chief, he can always issue a military order and make a national address on his own authority, as kings and emperors have always done.

In sum, whatever intentions James Madison and Elbridge Gerry might have had in proposing "to insert 'declare,' striking out 'make' war; leaving to the Executive the power to repel sudden attacks," the observations of Charles Pinckney and Pierce Butler were much more on point. For, to repeat, who can deny the evidence of American his-tory that the president has, "all the requisite qualities, and will not make war but when the Nation will support it?" And, is it not equally true that the Congress is "too numer-ous for deliberations," and not sufficiently "acquainted with foreign affairs" to exercise the power "to declare war" on its own independent initiative?

FUTURE IMPLICATIONS

Little foresight is needed to predict that war-making decisions will continue to lie primarily with the president in the years ahead. The two disabilities identified by Charles Pinckney will continue to prevent independent initiative on the part of the Congress. Consequently, many will say, what is needed is a better understanding of the politics, not of declaring war, but of the conditions under which *Congressional Checks on Presidential War Powers* are possible, to quote the subtitle of William Howell and Jon Pevehouse's excellent book. Such "checks," the authors discovered, "materialize under well-specified conditions, having to do with the institution's partisan composi-tion [*i.e.*, divided government], the size of a potential deployment, and the strength of international [mainly treaty] obligations" (223). Thus, the Congress will predictably attempt to "check" a president by holding oversight hearings, holding floor debates, passing resolutions, and otherwise contesting a president's decision 1) when the oppo-sition party controls at least one chamber, 2) when the size of the deployment is large enough to indicate a long, complex, and potentially controversial deployment, and 3) when international treaties have been invoked to justify the deployment.

When these three conditions are either not present or not present to a threshold level, the Congress will take little notice when a president does not "consult" with it and employs pattern-two procedures. For example, on Wednesday, February 11, 2015, President Barack Obama sent a White House drafted AUMF to the 114th Congress, "To authorize the limited use of the United States Armed Forces against the Islamic State of Iraq and the Levant." This should have initiated pattern-three procedures. However, his request met only one of Howell and Pevehouse's three conditions—the divided government condition. Republicans held a majority not only in one chamber but in both chambers. Obviously, the satisfaction of only one condition is not enough. No international treaty commitments were at stake, and the deployment was miniscule: 4,500 troops as trainers without combat roles.

As a result, on Tuesday, April 14, 2015, Speaker John Boehner announced that House would not even consider the president's request:

> Boehner blamed "artificial constraints" on the 4,500 American trainers and advisers to the Iraqi army [for his decision] . . . Without any action from Congress, Obama can continue to wage the fight however he sees fit. Which, Boehner has decided, is a better option than trying to work with the draft that White House officials sent up to Capitol Hill. "The president's asking for less authority than he has today. I've never seen any president, ever, do this," [Boehner] said, adding that he does not want his own committee chairmen to work up their own AUMF. "As much as I think Congress ought to speak on this issue, it's going to be virtually impossible to do that." (Kane, *Washington Post* 04/14/2015)

In sum, Howell and Pevehouse's research into how the government works in practice illuminates the three conditions that must be met before the Congress will agree to participate in either of the two alternative pattern-three procedures. The Congress participates, however, not to exercise its constitutionally mandated power "to declare war." Rather, it participates in order to "consult" with the president as commander-in-chief to "insure that the collective judgment of both the Congress and the President will apply to the introduction of United States Armed Forces into hostilities."

FURTHER READING

Fisher, Louis. 1995. *Presidential War Power*. Lawrence, KS: University Press of Kansas.

Hallett, Brien. 2012. *Declaring War: Congress, the President, and What the Constitution Says*. New York: Cambridge University Press.

Howell, William G., and Jon C. Pevehouse. 2007. *While Danger Gathers: Congressional Checks on Presidential War Powers*. Princeton, NJ: Princeton University Press.

Lobel, Jules. 1986. Covert War and Congressional Authority: Hidden War and Forgotten Power. *University of Pennsylvania Law Review* 134 (5) June, 1035–1110.

Torreon, Barbara Salazar. 2013. Instances of Use of United States Armed Forces Abroad, 1798–2013. Congressional Research Service (R42738, August 30).

Yoo, John. 2005. *The Powers of War and Peace: The Constitution and Foreign Affairs after 9/11*. Chicago, IL: University of Chicago Press.

Zeisberg, Mariah. 2013. *War Powers: The Politics of Constitutional Authority*. Princeton, NJ: Princeton University Press.

APPENDIX 1   HOW OFTEN HAVE PRESIDENTS DECIDED TO USE ARMED FORCE?

I. **Examples of Pattern-One Procedures**: No president has ever claimed or used his "royal" prerogative as commander-in-chief to declare war officially on his own authority. All presidential wars have been initiated with unofficial, functionally equivalent declarative acts.

II. **Examples of Pattern-Two Procedures**: Depending on how one counts, between 200 and 250 small U.S. military operations have occurred abroad from 1789 to 2013. Most of these occurred before World War II. During the nineteenth century, these actions were most frequently taken indirectly on the authority of the local commander, and not directly on presidential authority. The commander on the scene would land Marines or sailors to protect American citizens and property or to promote American interests.

Since World War II, the practice has continued—again, mostly for small operations abroad. But a good number have been large: most significantly, the Korean War, 1950–1953, and the War in Vietnam until 1964, when the Gulf of Tonkin Resolution was passed. President Lyndon Johnson's 1965 intervention in the Dominican Republic to protect American lives and property and to thwart a perceived Communist takeover is another example of a large operation without congressional authority.

III. **Examples of Pattern-Three Procedures**: Again, depending on how one counts, approximately 50 wars and small military operations of this type have occurred abroad, from 1789 to 2013.

Examples of wars and small operations that took place without a congressional "declaration of war," but with a congressional "authorization" of one sort or another include the Quasi-War with France, from 1798 to 1800; the First Barbary War, from 1801 to 1805; the Second Barbary War, of 1815; and many actions against foreign terrorists since September 11, 2001.

Since the Eisenhower Administration, presidents have drafted specific "Authorization to Use Military Force" resolutions, also known as AUMF resolutions:

1. Authorization for the President to Employ the Armed Forces of the United States for Protecting the Security of Formosa . . . , 1955
2. Promotion of Peace and Stability in Middle East, 1957
3. Maintenance of International Peace and Security in Southeast Asia (Gulf of Tokin Resolution), 1964
4. Multinational Force in Lebanon, 1983
5. Authorization of the Use of U.S. Armed Forces Pursuant to U.N. Security Council Resolution 678 with Respect to Iraq, 1991
6. Authorization of the Use of U.S. Armed Forces Against Those Responsible for the Recent Attacks Launched Against the United States, 2001
7. Authorization of the Use of Force Against Iraq Resolution, 2002

IV. **Examples of Alternative Pattern-Three Procedures**: The State Department has drafted nine congressional declarations for three separate wars:

1. The War of 1812 against Great Britain
2. World War I against Imperial Germany and Austria-Hungry in 1917
3. World War II against Imperial Japan, Nazi Germany, and Italy in 1941, and against Bulgaria, Hungary, and Rumania in 1942.

For the Mexican-American War in 1846, an appropriations bill was amended so as to become "An Act providing for the Prosecution of the existing War between the United States and the Republic of Mexico." Because this is an extraordinarily irregular procedure, the status of the Act as an official congressional "declaration of war" is dubious in the extreme. Among other provisions, the Act provided that "musicians and artificers, shall be allowed 40 cents per day for the use and risk of their horses."

Exceptionally, after he had made his decision, President William McKinley permitted the 55th Congress to draft the conditional declaration for the Spanish-American War in 1898 (Torreon 2013).

V.   **Examples of Pattern-Four Procedures**: The only example is the Second Continental Congress's Declaration of Independence, 1776.

APPENDIX 2   DRAFTING AMERICAN DECLARATIONS OF WAR

I.   When ordered by the president to draft a congressional declaration of war, the State Department has drafted unreasoned, absolute declarations on nine occasions for three wars: the War of 1812 and World Wars I and II. These declarations are unreasoned because they give neither justification for the resort to war, nor do they state the peace terms that will end the war. They are absolute because they simply and only "declare" war and "authorize" the president to use the armed forces. The declaration for the War of 1812 drafted by Secretary of State James Monroe is the epitome that has been copied by successive Secretaries of State:

> *Be it enacted by the Senate and House of Representatives of the United States in Congress assembled,* That war be and the same is hereby declared to exist between the United Kingdom of Great Britain and Ireland and the dependencies thereof, and the United States of America and their Territories; and that the President of the United States is hereby authorized to use the whole land and naval force of the United States to carry the same into effect, and to issue to private armed vessels of the United States commissions or letters of marque and general reprisal, in such form as he shall think proper, and under the seal of the United States, against the vessels, goods, and effects, of the Government of the said United Kingdom of Great Britain and Ireland, and the subjects thereof (Pub. L. No. 12-102, 2 Stat. 755).

II. When the Second Continental Congress decided to transform the insurgency that had been raging since April 1775 into an officially declared war in July 1776, they chose to draft a fully reasoned, absolute declaration. As such, the Declaration of Independence is a sophisticated and complex document that conforms to the traditional standards of Roman law. In outline:

A.   A *preamble* establishing the moral and philosophical basis for the war:
     WHEN in the Course of human Events, . . . a decent Respect to the Opinions of Mankind requires that they should declare the causes which impel them to the Separation.

B. A twenty-seven-item *indictment* of the *gravamina* that justify the resort to war: To prove this, let Facts be submitted to a candid World. He has refused his Assent to Laws, the most wholesome and necessary for the public Good . . . For quartering large Bodies of Armed Troops among us . . . He has abdicated Government here, by declaring us out of his Protection and waging War against us.

C. Evidence that war is the last resort: In every stage of these Oppressions we have Petitioned for Redress in the most humble Terms:

D. A *denunciation* of the war: We must, therefore, acquiesce in the Necessity, which denounces our Separation,

E. A *declaration of war*: and hold them, as we hold the rest of Mankind, Enemies in War, in Peace, Friends.

F. A *declaration of peace*: We, therefore, the Representatives of the UNITED STATES OF AMERICA, in General Congress, Assembled, appealing to the Supreme Judge of the World for the Rectitude of our Intentions, do, in the Name, and by Authority of the good People of these Colonies, solemnly Publish and Declare, That these United Colonies are, and of Right out (sic) to be, Free and Independent States;

G. Tellingly, the Declaration of Independence does not contain an "authorization" "to use the whole land and naval force of the United States."

12 THE POWER TO RAISE AND SUPPORT ARMIES AND TO PROVIDE AND MAINTAIN A NAVY

Robert C. Chalwell, Jr.

Article I, section 8, clause 12
To raise and support Armies, but no Appropriation of Money to that Use shall be for a longer Term than two Years;

Article I, section 8, clause 13
To provide and maintain a Navy;

KEY TERMS

Article I, §8, cl. 12 specifically imbues the United States Congress with powers formerly reserved for thirteen original states under the Articles of the Confederation (1781–1789). The clause meant that the army would be 1) strictly controlled by elected representatives in Congress, 2) limited in terms of duration, and 3) restricted in terms of the scope and duration of public expenditure. These powers were exercised by the Second Continental Congress (1775–1781) during the Revolutionary War as a means of effectively responding to a professional and numerically superior British military.

"To raise and support Armies": The power to "raise" an army means the ability of Congress to *directly* recruit citizens from within states, to serve under the command of the president of the United States of America as commander-in-chief of a unified armed force. The power to "support" an army means the authority to make budgetary allocations to pay for the military force raised. This power addressed lingering post-Revolution concerns over fiscal responsibility, accountability, and oversight. Further, the Federalists argued that the political and economic costs of war would deter congressional members from voting for war. The overarching assumption was that a declaration of war would be an option of last resort. As a democratically elected body, Congress would be heavily influenced by the average citizen's desire to avoid war taxes, the potential destruction to property, and the time away from productive labor and their families as requirements of military service. These commonly held reservations help explain the absence of large peacetime armies or a permanent weapons arsenal until after World War II.

"[N]o Appropriation of Money to that Use shall be for a longer Term than two Years": This language is clearly intended to restrict the duration of time for which the monies may be used. The deliberate inclusion of restrictive language goes to the heart of why the army clause was hotly debated at the Constitutional Convention. Temporal limitations on the funding and activities of an army were seen as key implements of control and oversight. As James Madison observed on April 20, 1795:

> Of all the enemies to public liberty war is, perhaps, the most to be dreaded, because it comprises and develops the germ of every other. War is the parent of armies; from these proceed debts and taxes; and armies, and debts, and taxes are the known instruments for bringing the many under the domination of the few.

Historically, standing armed forces, such as those commanded by Julius Caesar (July 100 BC–March 15, 44 BC), which overthrew the Roman Senate in 59 BC, and that of King George III (June 4, 1738–January 29, 1820), which was utilized to oppress British American colonists, were seen as unquestionable threats to republican government and civil liberties. Consequently the Founders saw standing armies as the principle danger to free government. To mitigate this danger, they sought to control both the amounts and the time money would be available to the army, but not to the navy.

"To provide and maintain a Navy," authorized in clause 13, was quite a departure from clause 12. In stark contrast to the restrictive language used to establish the U.S. Army, the raising of naval personnel, the procurement of equipment, weaponry, and ships, and the permanence of this institution can be assumed. The Founding Fathers agreed with Thucydides' view of naval forces as being central to trade and security and compatible with republican institutions. But robust armies were seen as threats to a republic.

HISTORY AND DEVELOPMENT OF THE ARMY

The early British American colonists considered the militia an important institution and necessary for defense and safety. Colonial legislatures would authorize a certain force level for seasonal campaigns, based on set recruitment quotas for each local militia. A Provincial Regular would serve in winter *or* spring garrisons, or be retained as need dictated for a specific campaign. Most units served for only a few weeks or months at a time. Militia members could legally be drafted by lot if volunteer recruitment resulted in inadequate forces; however, this was rare, as provincial regulars were incentivized by being better paid than their British Army counterparts and rarely engaged in combat.

At the beginning of the Revolution, neither the Second Continental Congress nor any state within the union maintained a professional military force. The recruitment of citizen volunteer militias was therefore necessary whenever matters of geographic security arose. These militias were funded and supervised by individual states, and were "adopted" by the Continental Congress in response to specific need. The force known as the Continental Army, which was formed on June 14, 1775, in response to the Battles of Lexington and Concord in April 1775 and the taking of the British Fort Ticonderoga in May 1775, was a combination of troops raised by the colonies of New Hampshire, Massachusetts, Rhode Island, and Connecticut. Ostensibly a regional force, they had been under the primary supervision and fiscal responsibility of the colonies that had raised them.

The first commander-in-chief of the Continental Army was Virginia Representative to the Continental Congress, General George Washington. Washington received broad and arguably vague orders to "proceed to Massachusetts, 'take charge of the army of the united colonies,' and capture or destroy all armed enemies." He was further ordered to send to Congress an "accurate strength return of that army." Instructions on managing, developing, and disciplining personnel were also rather vague. General Washington had the authority to determine how many men to retain, up to the set maximum, and he had the power to temporarily fill any vacancies below the rank of colonel. These powers are sometimes called the "dictatorial powers of Washington" and were not retained under the Articles of Confederation.

On June 15, 1775, the Second Continental Congress Committee of the Whole granted Washington authority to raise additional regiments from New York, Pennsylvania, Virginia, and Maryland to serve under his direct command. The ten companies of "expert riflemen" were intended to be a light infantry force for the ongoing siege at Boston (April 1775–March 1776). Each company included a captain, 3 lieutenants, 4 sergeants, 4 corporals, a drummer (or horn player), and 68 privates. Unlike the practice for the earlier provincial militias, the enlistment period was set at one year, a period that would expire on July 1, 1776.

On June 16, 1775, the Second Continental Congress authorized a variety of senior officers to support General Washington. Positions for five major staff officers were established: an Adjutant General, a Commissary of Musters, a Paymaster General, a Commissary General, and a Quartermaster General. For political and strategic purposes, six of the original companies of "expert riflemen" were enlisted—two from Pennsylvania, two from Maryland, and two from Virginia. This apportionment not only extended the formerly regional New England–based Continental Line, but also enfranchised the southern colonies to the economic benefits of accommodating professional regiments requiring locally procured uniforms, arms, and food, supplies, and quarters.

During the post-Revolution era, the U.S. Armed Forces were established in fits and spurts. Security and economic exigencies dictated some form of consistent and easily mobilized federal armed force. However, lingering distrust for a centralized institutions and a standing army remained exceptionally strong. As a result, the Continental

Army was quickly disbanded after the Revolutionary War. In addition, early executive and legislative leaders wrestled with a variety of logistical challenges, including provisioning soldiers, caring for the sick and injured, providing administrative support for the management of pensions, problems relating to finance, warship technology and design, infrastructure of shipyards and shipwrights, sources of raw materials and naval stores, determining deployment size, officering, and general personnel. These challenges were addressed within the context of complex geopolitical dynamics, concerns about constitutional authority, high tax burdens, cost overruns, and political corruption.

Lamenting this reality, on March 4, 1783, six months prior to the culmination of the Revolutionary War, General Washington expressed forebodings to Alexander Hamilton of "the sufferings of a complaining army on one hand, and the inability of the Confederation Congress and tardiness of States on the other." He communicated his fear to Hamilton that "unless Congress have powers competent to all general purposes, that the distress we have encountered, the expense we have incurred, and the blood we have spilt in the course of an eight years war, will avail us nothing."

Although many of the representatives to the Philadelphia Constitutional Convention had served with the Continental Line, with the exception of a few strident voices (Hamilton noteworthy among them), there was full agreement that a standing army would be counterproductive to the free, republican society being built. This full agreement prompted the cautious language of Art. I, §8, cl. 12, after much debate. But the cautious language did not satisfy all. At the Pennsylvania State Ratification Convention in 1787, delegate James Wilson found himself in the unenviable position of championing a strong national government while reassuring his constituents that a representative government, elected by citizens and restricted by separation of powers, would place "practical limitations on unnecessary wars and executive control over the military."

Later, President Washington complained in a private letter to a member of Congress about the state of finances and lack of power in Congress "competent to the great purposes of war." However, the American distrust of standing armies prevailed, and irregular state militias continued to serve as the nation's sole ground army. The only exception was a lone regiment to guard the Western Frontier and a battery of artillery to guard West Point's arsenal.

Continuing conflict with Native Americans soon made it imperative to raise and maintain a trained standing army. In response to the infamous defeat of General Arthur St. Clair, at the Battle of the Wabash by Blue Jacket and Little Turtle's tribal confederacy in November 1791, the Legion of the United States, was established in 1791. The Legion combined all land combat arms of the day (cavalry, heavy and light infantry, artillery) into one brigade-sized force, which could effectively split into stand-alone combined arms teams. Congress agreed with now-President Washington's proposal and augmented the small standing army until "the United States shall be at peace with the Indian tribes." Functioning as an extension of the U.S. Army from 1792 to 1796, members of the Legion served under the command of Major General Anthony Wayne of Pennsylvania, a former lieutenant of General Washington. The total standing armed force, at this time, numbered a mere 700 men.

Congress continued to neglect the army because it was satisfied with a minimal constabulary force on the frontier. On June 1, 1812, President James Madison became the first U.S. president to officially ask Congress for a declaration of war. In 1812, the regular army consisted of fewer than 12,000 men. Congress authorized the expansion of the army to 35,000 men, but support for the war was weak, particularly in New England. The forces granted to Madison were unprepared for serious or sustained campaigns. The result early on was the humbling surrender of Fort Detroit, after losing ground gained earlier by the occupation of southwestern Ontario, Canada.

The War of 1812 was a major turning point in the development of the U.S. military. Leadership remained a critical American weakness, resulting in the poor performance of several militia-based American armies during the war, particularly during the American invasions of Canada in 1812–13 and the 1814 defense of Washington. Congress was finally convinced of the need to focus on creating a more professional regular force. Greater numbers of military personnel were raised, expansible armies were organized, and standardized procurement systems were established.

With these changes, the two principal characteristics of the army were set until the end of the nineteenth century. First, the peacetime army would remain a small constabulary force of several tens of thousands, sufficient only to maintain the law and order on the frontier. Second, this constabulary force would then expand, accordion-like, in times of war, with a call for volunteers on short-term contracts and state militia forces that volunteered *en masse*. This mix of volunteers and volunteer militia units was sufficient for the Mexican-American War (1846–1848) and the Spanish-American War (1898), but insufficient for larger wars, when conscription was needed. Congress passed legislation authorizing a draft for the duration of the Civil War (the Enrollment Act of 1863) and World War I (the Selective Service Act of 1917). The first peacetime draft was the Selective Training and Service Act of 1940, in preparation for the American entry into World War II on December 8, 1941. This peacetime draft continued during the Cold War. By 1971, however, anti–Vietnam War protests forced President Richard Nixon to call for an end to the draft and a return to an all-volunteer army supported by an all-volunteer National Guard.

Like the War or 1812 before it, the Spanish-American War demonstrated the shortcomings of the nineteenth century constabulary army. The principal troubles were the lack of training and organization of the volunteers needed to expand the regular army. Recognition of these problems led to the Militia Act of 1902, also known as the Dick Act. (See Chapter 14.) Although the Militia Act was directed primarily at the reorganization and professionalization of the state militias, its greatest impact was on the regular army and its ability to expand and mobilize during World Wars I and II.

The 1902 act finally made the state militias a federal responsibility and transformed the militias into a National Guard. The federal government would now pay for National Guard payroll, training, and equipment. The act also clarified when the National Guard could be called to federal service and provided regular army officers to inspect and train guardsmen. A bureau in the War Department was also established to oversee the National Guard. In line with the reforms of the Militia Act, under President Theodore Roosevelt, Secretary of War Elihu Root redirected the army from its law and order mission as a small constabulary force, building it into a large modern force capable of waging war overseas.

The combination of the reorganization of the state militia into the National Guard and Secretary Root's recommissioning of the army prepared the way for the army's successful waging of World Wars I and II and the perhaps too many wars since 1945.

HISTORY AND DEVELOPMENT OF THE NAVY

As with the raising of armies during the colonial period prior to the adoption of the U.S. Constitution, the provision, maintenance, and supervision of naval forces were also the domain of individual colonies. On June 12, 1775, the Assembly of the Colony of Rhode Island authorized its navy to engage with the British as part of the Continental revolutionary forces. On October 13, 1775, the Second Continental Congress passed a resolution creating the Continental Navy, "adopting" the Rhode Island Navy, as had been the practice with provincial militias.

Subsequently, on November 10, 1775, a multi-purpose corps of fighters known as the Continental Marines was also established by the Second Continental Congress. This corps of sharpshooters were stationed in the tops of the ships' masts during battles, but their primary duty was to serve as onboard security forces, protecting the captain of a ship and his officers. As with the Continental Army, however, the Continental Navy and the Continental Marines were disbanded at the end of the Revolutionary War. The last ship of the Continental Navy, the frigate *Alliance*, was sold in 1785, and its commander, Captain John Barry, returned to civilian life.

Two years after the war, despite the capture of two American vessels in 1785 by Algiers-based Barbary pirates, and the urging of Thomas Jefferson—then ambassador to France—for a robust naval force to protect valuable trade assets, the Confederation Congress ignored these acts of piracy and refused to build a navy.

As already noted, the aversion of the Founders to a standing army did not apply to a navy. James Madison's original language for Art. I, §8, cl. 13, "to build and equip fleets," was amended to "to provide & maintain a navy" without debate "as a more convenient definition of the power." During the ratification debates, Federalists and Anti-Federalists both recognized the paramount importance of maritime trade and the necessity of a strong navy to protect it. Both factions additionally valued, to varying degrees, the importance of a federal navy to maintain American "independence of action" abroad. After ratification, however, the United States' only armed maritime service was the Revenue-Marines, commissioned in 1790 at the prompting of Alexander Hamilton (then secretary of the Treasury), to suppress smuggling. As with much of the Framers' debate over the federal government, both sides aggressively disagreed as to the scope and level of autonomy with which the naval institution should be endowed.

In the face of increased aggression from Barbary pirates in the Mediterranean, congressional debate on reviving the navy began near the end of 1793. Some thought that paying tribute would be wiser and cheaper than building a navy. One congressman even proposed the alternative of hiring the Portuguese navy to protect American commercial interests. Opponents to reviving the navy also questioned whether the requested six frigates would be adequate to the task, and if negotiation would not be a less costly, more effective means to assuaging the Barbary States. In his annual address to Congress on December 3, President Washington spoke in general terms of the nation's need to prepare to defend itself, "If we desire to avoid insult, we must be able to repel it; if we desire to secure peace . . . ; it must be known, that we are at all times ready for War." The threat in the Mediterranean, increased aggression from the British, and urging from Washington, led to the establishment of the U.S. Navy by the Naval Act of 1794. This act provided the foundation for a professional U.S. Navy.

Six ships were also commissioned for construction. However, so staunch was the Anti-Federalists' resistance to a permanent federal navy that the act contained a proviso that if peace were achieved between the United States and Algiers, the construction of the vessels would cease. The bill also provided compensation for naval officers and sailors, and outlined the manning and operation of each ship. Secretary of War Henry Knox, responsible for the construction of these ships, reported to Congress in December 1794 that the passing of the act

> created an anxious solicitude that this second commencement of a navy for the United States should be worthy of their national character. That the vessels should combine such qualities of strength, durability, swiftness of sailing, and force, as to render them equal, if not superior, to any frigates belonging to any of the European Powers.

When peace was agreed to between the United States and Algiers in 1796, in accordance with clause 9 of the Naval Act of 1794, construction on all six ships ceased. With support from President Washington, Congress conceded, however, to fund the continued construction of the three ships nearest to completion: the USS *United States* (1797), the USS *Constellation* (1797), and the USS *Constitution* (1797). The first ship completed, the USS *United States*, was nominally a 44-gun ship, but usually carried over 50. Like the USS *United States*, the remainder of these six vessels were designed to be fast, with interchangeable armaments, and a formidable hull meant to minimize damage from enemy canon fire. At the turn of the eighteenth century, French naval aggression directed at U.S. trade interests during the Quasi-War prompted congressional approval to complete the remaining three frigates: the USS *President* (1800), the USS *Congress* (1799), and the USS *Chesapeake* (1799). In addition, former merchant ships were purchased and recommissioned by the U.S. Navy, including the *Herald, Delaware, Enterprise, Montezuma, Norfolk,* and *Experiment.* Further acquisition of the *Pickering* and *Eagle,* part of the U.S. Revenue Cutter Service (formerly the Revenue-Marine), and the capture of the *Retaliation,* (formerly the French vessel *Croyable*), on July 7, 1798, off of New Jersey, rounded out what became regular coastal patrol squadrons.

The move toward a professional and robust military was furthered by Congress's passing a bill establishing the Department of the Navy, separate from the Department of War, and, on April 30, 1798, Benjamin Stoddert became the first secretary of the navy. Only a month later, the newly organized Department of the Navy was put to the test when, on May 28, Congress authorized the capture of armed French vessels off the coast of the United States and, in so doing, commenced the Quasi-War against France. The conflict galvanized passage of several pieces of naval legislation. On June 30, Congress gave President Adams the authority to borrow and arm ships from private citizens, who would then be paid with interest-bearing government bonds. On July 9,

U.S. naval vessels were authorized to capture armed French vessels anywhere on the high seas; Congress also sanctioned the issuing of privateering commissions, or letters of marque. Two days later, the United States Marine Corps was established, and on July 16, funds were appropriated to complete and equip the three remaining vessels begun under the Naval Act of 1794. By the end of the Quasi-War, naval forces included 30 vessels, 700 officers, and 5,000 seamen.

In 1800, the Democratic-Republicans took control of the executive and both houses of Congress, and increased their gradual control of state politics outside of New England. With the perception that a standing army and navy was part and parcel of expansive Federalism, President Jefferson began his tenure with plans to reduce the navy's budget as part of an overall plan of reining in national debt. However, renewed problems with the Barbary States in 1801 forced him to send a small squadron to the Mediterranean. As the Quasi-War neared its end, the Barbary States, particularly the Pasha of Tripoli, had expressed overt hostilities toward the United States. The continued payment of regular tribute to the Barbary States under the Peace Accords of 1795, long a thorn in Jefferson's side, was seen as a failure of Federalist foreign policy. With advice from U.S. Ambassador to Tripoli Cathcart, Jefferson dispatched frigates to the Mediterranean with a letter to Pasha Qaramanli. As Jefferson's secretary of state James Madison summarized the letter:

> "our sincere desire to cultivate peace and commerce with your subjects." Clearly disclosing the dispatch of "a squadron of observation, whose appearance [we hope] will give umbrage to no power." The letter communicated the innocuous purpose of the fleet was to "exercise our seamen" and to "superintend the safety of our commerce . . . [which] we mean to rest . . . on the resources of our own strength and bravery in every sea."

Additionally, Secretary Madison sent correspondence to American consuls in the Mediterranean that the president, convinced "of the hostile purposes of the Bashaw of Tripoli," was sending a naval squadron to protect U.S. commerce in the Mediterranean and to respond appropriately to any powers who declared war on the United States. As with the mobilization of naval forces for engagement with the French during the Quasi-War, Congress was willing and prepared to grant President-elect Jefferson support for his refusal to continue payment of the tribute under existing terms.

In sum, once authorized by the Naval Act of 1794, the navy quickly saw engagements in the Caribbean Sea and the Atlantic during the undeclared Quasi-War with France from 1798 to 1800, in the Mediterranean during the Barbary Wars from 1801 to 1805, with Britain during the War of 1812, and again from 1815 to 1816 on the Barbary coast. The building of this small fleet was a divisive issue in congressional politics of the day. From its embattled beginnings, the growth in importance, strength, and support of the navy was decisive in conflicts that shaped and expanded the United States throughout the nineteenth and twentieth centuries. Despite the liberal wording used to establish the U.S. Navy, congressional battles over funding, locations of naval bases, and indeed the specifics as to the makeup of the fleet have been waged almost ceaselessly, pitting military strategists against the purse-holders in Congress.

FUTURE IMPLICATIONS

The future course of the U.S. Army was set in 1902 and 1904. No longer would the army be a small constabulary force that inducted volunteers to expand to meet the needs of larger wars. Once the Militia Act of 1902 created the National Guard, and once Secretary of War Root transformed the army's mission to fighting the nation's wars overseas, the twentieth- and twenty-first-century character of the army was fixed. In contrast, the future of the U.S. Navy was set in 1794, when the Congress authorized a first fleet of six warships and a number of auxiliary ships. Since then, the navy has defended American commerce and fought her wars on the oceans of the world, as it does today and will do in the future.

Instead, economics has become the new challenge to congressional oversight and control of the army and the navy. Echoing President Dwight Eisenhower's 1960 "Military-Industrial Complex" speech, Rebecca Thorpe's 2014 book *The American Warfare State: The Domestic Politics of Military Spending* convincingly argues that a confluence of interests have aligned, simultaneously reducing the public cost of war and expanding the economic benefits of military industrialism (employment, revenue, and job security) to more regions of the country. In so doing, Thorpe asserts that the members of Congress with defense industries in their districts are more willing to adopt hawkish foreign policy stances that actually weaken "their institutional war powers" and enhance the president's ability to make military decisions independently. Thus, the checks and balances crafted by the Founders in Art. I, §8, cl. 12 and cl. 13 is now endangered not by the army or the navy, as they feared, but by economic interests.

FURTHER READING

Baer, George. 1994. *One Hundred Years of Sea Power: The U.S. Navy, 1890–1990*. Stanford, CA: Stanford University Press.

Edling, Max M. 2003. *A Revolution in Favor of Government: Origins of the U.S. Constitution and the Making of the American State*. Oxford, UK: Oxford University Press.

Kohn, Richard, ed. 1991. *The United States Military Under the Constitution of the United States, 1789–1989*. New York: New York University Press.

Stewart, Richard W., ed. 2004. *American Military History Vol. 1: The United States Army and the Forging of a Nation, 1775–1917*. Washington, D.C.: United States Army Center of Military History.

Symonds, Craig. 1980. *Navalists and Antinavalists: The Naval Policy Debate in the United States, 1785–1826*. Newark, DE: University of Delaware Press.

Thorpe, Rebecca. 2014. *The American Warfare State: The Domestic Politics of Military Spending*. Chicago, IL: The University of Chicago Press.

13 THE POWER TO REGULATE LAND AND NAVAL FORCES

Donald E. Heidenreich, Jr.

Article I, section 8, clause 14
To Make Rules for the Government and Regulation of the Land and Naval Forces

KEY TERMS

Rules for the Government: Congress has the power to pass laws to create the structure, organization, and leadership of the U.S. military.

Regulation of the Land and Naval Forces: Congress has the power to pass laws that create a legal system for the maintenance of good order and discipline in the U.S. military

HISTORY AND DEVELOPMENT

Civilian control of the military is central to the American understanding of the relationship between the military and the population. This dates to before the United States existed as a constitutional republic. In the colonial era, British forces were given their orders for general action from the civilian government in London, and colonial militias were both regulated and given orders from their civilian colonial governments. During the revolution, Washington continuously showed deference to the civilian authorities in areas in which his armies operated, and his act of surrendering his sword to Congress at the war's conclusion was the ultimate sign of military subservience. So, civilian regulation and governance of the military is central to the maintenance of the United States' constitutional republic.

When the Constitution was written, it was designed to ensure continued civilian control by giving the power to oversee all aspects of the military—except operational command—specifically to Congress, in section 8 of Article I. With regard to clause 14 of section 8, Congress passes the laws creating the military, establishing its size, organizing its system of supply, authorizing service members' pay and the purchase of equipment and supplies, organizing its leadership by creating the various ranks and positions, and creating professional schools. Further, the Congress passes legislation regarding the interaction of the different services, creating their command relationships, and writing the military legal code to which all service members are responsible. Congress also plays a critical role though the use of its oversight powers.

The center of Congress's role is handled by committees in both the House of Representatives and the Senate. Currently, both houses have Armed Services committees, which cover all aspects of the active military forces. The origins of the committees go back to the early nineteenth century. The Senate committee began its life as three separate committees in 1816: Military Affairs, Naval Affairs, and the Militia. Before the Civil War, the Committee on Militia was disbanded and its work moved to the Committee on Military Affairs. In 1946 the Committees on Naval Affairs and Military Affairs were merged to create the modern Senate Armed Services Committee. In the House of Representatives, the origins of the Armed Services Committee go back to 1822, when the House created separate Committees on Military and Naval Affairs. These two committees lasted until 1946, when they were merged to create the House Armed Services Committee.

The Congress has on occasion used special committees to perform its role of oversight of the military. When done well—like the Senate Committee to Investigate the National Defense Program, or "the Truman Committee," during World War II—it can have the important impact of saving both money and lives. On the other hand, if handled badly or for political purposes—such as the Joint Committee on the Conduct of the War, during the Civil War—it can be a serious hindrance to prosecution of military operations. The concept of congressional oversight of the military dates from 1792, when a House committee investigated the November 4, 1791, defeat of a force under General Arthur St. Clair at the Battle of Wabash River.

The Congress has a number of tools to carry out its responsibilities, including both the creation of and specific amendments to several of the titles of the U.S. Code and through annual appropriations bills. It has occasionally passed large structural legislation that has impacted the entirety of the U.S. military, as well as legislation that has impacted the military's relationship to U.S. society. Congress is constantly tinkering with the state and nature of the U.S. military. While much of this is done under its power of budgeting for the military (Art. §8, cl. 12 and 13), the Congress is always adjusting the laws governing the discipline, organization, and conduct of the military.

Military Titles in the U.S. Code

The Congress has regularly reorganized the structure of the U.S. military since the original creation of the army and navy by the Continental Congress in 1775. The

U.S. military currently consists of the army, navy, marine corps, air force, and federal reserve forces of the U.S., supplemented by the National Guard when in actual service of the national government and the Coast Guard in time of war.

The U.S. military is regulated through a number of titles in the U.S. Code. Title 10 covers the army, navy, air force, marines, and coast guard, as well as the uniformed services and the commissioned officers of the Public Health Service and National Oceanographic and Atmospheric Administration. Title 10 is divided into five subsections. Subtitle A deals with general military matters. Subtitle B deals with the army; C the navy and marines; D the air force; and E the reserve. Subtitle A, in effect, covers all aspects necessary to the organization of the Department of Defense and those laws general to the military as a whole, including the Uniform Code of Military Justice (UCMJ), which is contained in Chapter 47. Subtitles B, C, and D are all formatted the same way, as they cover each of the armed services. Subtitle E deals primarily with personnel issues, as far as the members of the Reserves are a part of the services' structures. Title 14 covers the Coast Guard; Title 32 covers the National Guard; Title 38 covers Veterans; and Title 51 covers War and National Defense, but much of this last has been repealed or transferred to other titles.

Creating the Modern System: The National Security Act of 1947

The nature of the governance of the U.S. military changed dramatically after World War II. The war had caused the army and navy to interact and cooperate in ways that had been outside of their experiences previously. These two services had each had their own separate places in the previous system; their interactions were often limited and their joint planning not as coordinated as possible. The requirement in both Europe and the Pacific for joint operations, and thus joint planning, made obvious the need for greater cooperation and coordination.

The current organization of the U.S. military was created in July 1947, with passage of the National Security Act. This legislation made a number of important changes to the military's organization and created a number of important new entities. The most important was the position of secretary of defense—which, in its initial incarnation, was not a particularly powerful position. In 1949 the act was amended and the military structure centralized under a Department of Defense.

The original 1947 act was not designed to meld the services, but was intended to create a coordinating agent known as the secretary of defense (SecDef). The act made the secretary of defense the "principle assistant to the President in all matters relating to national security." It gave the secretary of defense broad, general authority and responsibility for oversight of the services, but it also specified that the individual services would continue to "be administered as individual executive departments by their respective Secretaries and all powers and duties relating to such departments not specifically conferred upon the Secretary of Defense by the act shall be retained by each of their respective secretaries." This situation quickly became untenable.

The 1947 act also created the Joint Chiefs of Staff (JCS), made up of the three military service heads—the chief of staff of the army, the chief of naval operations, and the chief of staff of the air force—and the chief of staff (COS) to the president, if one had been appointed. The JCS was designated to be "the principle military advisors to the President and Secretary of Defense."

The 1947 act outlined, in broad terms, the nature of the relationships of the services to each other and their responsibilities. This division of responsibilities has been a source of contention between them ever since. The services, on more than one occasion, have had to renegotiate lines of demarcation in their respective responsibilities. The amendment gave to the army control over land combat, but also gave it control over such water and air elements as necessary to accomplish its mission. The navy was given responsibility for naval combat and granted control over such resources as needed to accomplish its mission, including its own air resources. The marine corps continued under the control of the navy, and was given responsibilities for land and air aerial combat, as well as protection of naval facilities. The act also created a new Department of the Air Force, breaking it out of the Army Air Forces, and gave it responsibility for aviation forces not otherwise assigned. This phrasing of their various missions in the legislation left enough room that the services themselves had to come to an agreement as to who would have which responsibilities, an agreement which is still debated among the services to this day. The act also added the Air National Guard to the U.S. reserve forces.

The act further created two non-military but important national security agencies: the National Security Council (NSC) and the Central Intelligence Agency (CIA). The NSC membership contained the new secretary of defense as well as the three service secretaries, in addition to other cabinet secretaries and the chairmen of the National Security Resources Board. The leader would be a civilian, keeping with the tradition of keeping matters involving the military under civilian control. In the CIA, by contrast, the director could be active duty military but would have no command authority.

In the 1949 Amendment to the National Security Act, the National Military Establishment was converted to the Department of Defense, and the three services were placed under its auspices. This change gave the secretary of defense more direct authority over the services. It also created a chairman for the Joint Chiefs of Staff—who was given limited powers, as he would not have command authority over the Chiefs of Staff of the service branches. The membership of the JCS has evolved over time as the missions of the parts of the military establishment have changed. In 1952, the marine corps commandant was authorized to participate when the JCS was dealing with marine corps issues. In 1978, the commandant of the marine corps was made a permanent member of the JCS. With the extensive use of National Guard forces, especially in the aftermath of 9/11, the chief of the National Guard Bureau was added to the JCS in 2011. In 1986 the Goldwater Nichols Department of Defense Reorganization Act created vice chairs and unified combatant commands. But the act continued to bypass the JCS in the chain of command by having the unified combatant commanders answering to the secretary of defense and ultimately the president.

A unified combatant command is an operational command that brings together all of the assets of all the services under a single commander in either a geographic or a functional area. At the moment, there are nine unified commands—six geographic and three functional:

Africa Command, covering sub-Saharan Africa
Central Command, covering the Middle East, North Africa, and Central Asia
European Command
Northern Command, covering North America
Pacific Command, covering Asia-Pacific
Southern Command, covering Latin America
Special Operations Command
Strategic Command, commanding the nuclear armed bombers and missiles of the
    Air Force and the Navy
Transportation Command, coordinating all military air, sea, and land transportation

The Articles of War and the UCMJ

The Second Continental Congress passed the first Articles of War, covering the U.S. military, on June 30, 1775. There were 69 provisions, which covered the conduct of officers and enlisted in and out of camp. For example, Article XI:

No Officer or soldier shall use any reproachful or provoking speeches or gestures to another, nor shall presume to send a challenge to any person to fight a duel . . . and all such offenders . . . shall be punished at the discretion of a general courts-martial.

On September 20, 1776, the Congress passed a more comprehensive Articles of War. It consisted of 18 sections, and the Congress required it to be read to the troops every two months. The rules were amended a number of times during the war.

During the Confederation period, the army saw some additional amendments to the Articles of War. The Articles of War were replaced in 1951 with the current military justice system, the Uniform Code of Military Justice (UCMJ). The UCMJ is a comprehensive legal code, which has at its heart the ideal of the maintenance of good order and discipline in all the branches of the military. The unification of the systems made the administration of military justice easier for courts above the trial court level. For the service member, the UCMJ is critical, since when a person enlists in the military they surrender most of their civil rights and liberties, but most of these protections are returned to them though the UCMJ.

The UCMJ is regularly updated, but occasionally those updates and changes can be controversial. "Don't ask, don't tell" was a political creation in response the controversy of the role of homosexuals in the U.S. military. Under the UCMJ, sodomy was a punishable crime, and this made it difficult for homosexuals to serve in the military. During the 1992 presidential campaign, Bill Clinton signaled his intention to change this policy to allow gays to serve in the military. After his election, however, this issue became a political firestorm that threatened to consume the first year of his first term. In order to put this issue behind him, Clinton agreed to a compromise policy that became known as "Don't ask, don't tell"—service members could not be asked whether they were homosexual, but gay service members were not to volunteer such information or otherwise reveal their sexual orientation. In September 2011, this policy was officially repealed. Finally, in 2014, the definition of sodomy in the UCMJ was changed to reflect a requirement that force or lack of consent on the part of one of the participants was necessary in order to it to be a criminal actively, but it still uses the term "unnatural carnal copulation" (Article 125(a)).

While most of the crimes enumerated in the code are similar to those that exist in the civilian world, some are particular to the military, such as the following:

Misbehavior of a sentinel (Article 113)
Malingering (Article 115)
Misconduct as a prisoner (Article 105)
Aiding the enemy (Article 104)
Mutiny (Article 94)
Insubordinate conduct toward warrant officer, noncommissioned officer, or petty officer (Article 91)
Contempt toward officials—meaning the President, Congress, or other civilian leaders (Article 88)

The primary purpose of these and other regulations like them are to ensure that good order and disciple is maintained in the military and subservient to the civilian authority. (See Chapter 9.)

The Constitution

The command structure of the U.S. military has been in an almost constant state of transition and transformation, with commands, units, and branches of the services coming in and out of existence on a regular basis as the threats to the U.S. and the technology available change.

The existence and nature of a national army was a major concern for the founding generation. The post-revolutionary army was kept intentionally small, as a large standing army was seen as antithetical to the concept of a free people. An important question was the necessity of a standing army and the role of the militia. The United States had a long tradition of the militia acting as the defense force for the colonies, through four colonial wars and numerous conflicts with the native population. Through three of those conflicts, regular British forces had played a limited role in the colonial defense, and when they did arrive in the colonies in any numbers, they were seen by the population as often repressive. The importance of a navy was also a question as at end of the war, as the Confederation government effectively closed down the navy by either selling or giving to other countries all the U.S. naval vessels as partial payment for the nation's debts.

Even under the best of conduct, standing armies were seen as a burden to the local community where they were located. The Continental Army was seen as no different. This history made the need for a standing army one of the most significant debates to occur during the Constitutional period. While this debate was important for the

Constitutional Convention, it would have an even greater impact on the state conventions that met to ratify the document. In a number of the states, suggestions were made to amend the Constitution to include changes making it as difficult as possible for the U.S. government to keep a standing army in peacetime. While none of the proposed amendments were ever added to the Constitution, they did show an attitude of concern over how such a military force would be constituted and governed.

The New Republic

Among the first acts required by any new government must be the creation of the means of self-defense. This was done by the First Congress, under the new Constitution, in relatively short order. The Congress first gained a quorum in April of 1789, and by August 7, passed a law establishing the Department of War. Its first secretary would be Henry Knox. For the first nine years of is existence, the Department of War would be responsible for all things military, because from 1789 to 1794, the army and militias were the only U.S. fighting forces; the navy and marine corps had not yet been revived. In September of that same year, the Congress passed an act that simply took the ordinances of the Confederation Congress, regarding the establishment of the U.S. military, and made them law under the new Constitution. The next year, Congress came back and passed a major reorganization.

In May of 1792, Congress passed "An Act to provide for calling forth the militia to execute the laws of the Union, to suppress insurrection and repel invasions." The state militias were brought into the U.S. military establishment when Congress passed this act, regularizing the process through which the president could call the militia into national service. Wishing to ensure its role in any use of the militias, Congress allowed the president to call the militia into national service for a period of only 30 days after the opening of the next session of Congress.

Then, a few days later, Congress passed "An Act more effectually to provide for the national defense by establishing an uniform militia throughout the United States," which outlined the nature of the militia. It was to be composed of white men between the ages of 18 and 45. It also required that all men be enlisted by the local unit commander. Each militia member was also required to provide his own weapon and equipment for potential campaigns. The states were required to divide their militias into units sized from division to company. The act further required that the militias also have artillery, cavalry, and light infantry units.

In 1794 the U.S. Navy was reestablished when Congress passed "An Act to provide naval armament," authorizing the construction of the first six new warships since the Revolution. Four of the ships would be 44-gun, and that other two, 36-gun vessels. The new navy would have six captains, but no admirals, as their senior leadership— and each ship would be assigned a lieutenant of marines. The navy was subject to the secretary of war. The reason for rebuilding the navy was to protect American merchant ships from piracy by the bey of Algiers. The bey captured American merchant ships sailing in the Mediterranean Sea and held the ships' crews for ransom. But, so fearful of the financial burden of the new navy was the Congress, that it required construction of the new ships to end if the United States was able to negotiate a settlement with the bey. Months later, Congress gave the president the authority to purchase or build up to ten galleys, which he could station where he felt necessary by passing "An Act to authorize the President of the United States, during the recess of the present Congress, to cause to be purchased or built, a number of vessels, to be equipped as galleys, or otherwise, in the service of the United States." With the success of the Washington administration in negotiating a treaty with the bey, the navy could well have once again gone into hibernation, but President Washington was able to convince Congress in 1796 to finish building three of the ships, thus reestablishing the U.S. Navy permanently.

Throughout the later 1790s, Congress continued to adjust the nature of the U.S. military. In the 1795 "Act for containing and regulating the Military Establishment of the United States, and for repealing sundry Acts," the army was structured with a corps of artillery and engineers as well as a "legion" of the United States, composed of over 4,800 men. The act discussed pay and rations as well as other personnel matters. Throughout the period, Congress passed a number of other acts that made often-small adjustments to the nature of the military. In 1798, the Congress expanded the military structure of the U.S. when it created the Department of the Navy. Benjamin Stoddert was appointed the first secretary by President John Adams. A few months later, Congress created a corps of 833 marines, headed by a major. This act left confusion in its early wake, as any marine on the land was subject to the control of the War Department, but those on ships were subject to the new Department of the Navy. The following year, 1799, the Congress passed "An Act for the government of the Navy of the United States," roughly the equivalent of the Articles of War. This was quickly replaced by an improved version a year later. In 1800, the commandant of the marine corps was raised from the rank of major to lieutenant colonel. The Congress continued to adjust the size scope and nature of the military during the period prior to the Civil war.

The Civil War

Congressional governance during the Civil War produced two innovations. The first was an important social landmark. The Militia Act of 1862 allowed blacks to perform any military duty they were deemed capable of performing. This began the slow process of reintegrating the U.S. Army for the first time since the Revolutionary War. The process ultimately required President Harry Truman to order full integration of the services in 1948. (See below.)

The second innovation was the passage of the first conscription law in America history. President James Madison had proposed conscription in 1814 for the War of 1812, but the war ended before Congress could enact a law. On March 3, 1863, Congress passed the Enrollment Act, allowing states to draft men when they could not meet their quota for volunteers. The act called for the enrollment of all men between twenty and forty-five years of age, but it allowed for exemptions from the draft if a substitute were willing to serve, or on payment of $300 (approximately $5,700 in 2015 dollars). The exemptions were controversial and led to the Draft Riots in New York City, July 13–16, 1863.

Post-Spanish-American War Reforms

The Spanish-American War exposed many serious deficiencies in the national defense system of the United States. The army was required to quickly expand its size from 28,000 to 223,000 in order to launch widespread operations in Cuba, Puerto Rico, and the Philippines. The expansion was possible because whole militia units volunteered, but the initiative was very chaotic. The Militia, or Dick, Act of 1903 was the response to that chaos. It was a major step forward in the regulation of the U.S. military. By repealing the Militia Acts of 1792 and 1862, the state militias now became an integral part of the regular military establishment. (See Chapter 14.)

The Dick Act and its 1908 amendments did a number of things that were important to incorporating the National Guard in the national military structure. It authorized the War Department to pay for National Guard encampments, as well as authorizing the secretary of war to buy equipment for the National Guard. The act also allowed the president to mobilize the Guard and use it outside of the boarders of the United States. The most important provision for the integration process was the War Department being given the authority to use Regular Army officers as trainers for the National Guard and for the War Department to pay for Guard officers to attend army schools. In addition, the National Guard was required to drill 24 times a year. The act also, in section 2, exempts those from "well recognized religious sect or organizations" with prohibitions against participating in wars from military service.

Other significant reforms occurred in the military leadership of the services. In 1903, the "Act to increase the efficiency of the Army" replaced the position of commanding general of the army with a chief of staff of the army, and created a General Staff Corps. In 1915, the Congress established the position of chief of naval operations to replace the system of aides created by Navy Secretary George von Meyer in 1909.

World War I

With the coming of the First World War, the National Defense Act of 1916 led to further reforms of the U.S. military structure. A new national volunteer army was created in order for the military to have its own militia force, the Federal Reserve. The act also laid out the organization of the various types of divisions in the army. It set the size of the peacetime army at 175,000 and a wartime level of 300,000. It outlined the general structure of the army and its major corps, even designating the unit organization down to the company, troop, and battery level. It put aviation under the control of the signal corps. The act also created the Reserve Officer Training Corps (ROTC). The National Guard saw a significant increase to potentially over 430,000, while requiring drilling 48 times a year.

A year later, the Selective Service Act of 1917 reinstituted a draft for the first time since the Civil War. Unlike the Civil War draft, the 1917 act made exemptions illegal. A substitute could not serve in the place of a draftee. According to the U.S. Selective Service statistics, of the 4.8 million Americans who served during World War I, approximately 2.8 million were draftees.

The end of the war brought more changes. The government ended the draft and reduced the size of the regular force to 280,000, along with return to a volunteer force.

The role of the General Staff in planning for future operations was strengthened. John J. Pershing's success in the Great War lead the 66th Congress in 1919 to "revive" the rank, as opposed to the title, of General of the Armies of the United States, in such a way that effectively allowed for only Pershing's appointment to the rank.

World War II

For many Americans, World War II began with the Selective Training and Service Act of 1940, which was the first peacetime draft in America history. It lasted until 1973, when the draft was ended and the military returned to an all-volunteer force. During World War II, approximately 10 million men were conscripted into the services, and 6 million volunteered. The major structural change in the U.S. military was the way in which the Army Air Corps (1926–1941) developed into the United States Army Air Force (1941–1947), and then became an independent service—the United States Air Force—as part of the National Defense Act of 1947.

In 1944, the Congress changed the rank structure of the U.S. military with the creation of the five-star ranks of general of the army and fleet admiral for the navy—and, after its split from the army, general of the air force. The five-star rank was created because other Allied armed forces had long had the five-star rank of "marshal." In terms of rank, this lack put American generals and admirals in an inferior position during combined operations with Allied countries. All of the officers who have held this rank have done so because of their service in World War II, the last being Omar Bradley, who died in 1981.

Desegregation

Segregation had been the standard in the army since the Civil War. In the summer of 1862, Congress passed the Second Confiscation Act and Militia Act, which give the president the authority to raise black troops into the U.S. military in an organized way that had not been true since the Revolutionary War. The Militia Act of 1862 allowed blacks to perform any military duty they were deemed capable of carrying out. This led to approximately 189,000 African Americans serving in the Union Army during the war. This was an important social landmark because it began the slow process of integrating the U.S. Army for the first time since the Revolutionary War. These two acts led to the creation of a whole subsystem of units designated as the United States Colored Troops (USCT). After the Civil War, the army had six black regiments, two cavalry and four infantry. Segregated units continued to be the norm in the army during World Wars I and II. In the summer of 1948, President Harry Truman, as commander-in-chief, issued Executive Order 9981, ordering an end to segregation in the military, a process that would take years to complete.

Women in the Armed Forces

Women have served in all of America's wars—but either in the capacity of nurses or disguised as men. The role of women in the U.S. military would begin to be formalized with the creation of the U.S. Army Nurse Corps in 1901. During World War I the army refused to enlist women except as nurses. On the other hand, the navy and marines enlisted a limited number of women for other duties. During World War II, 350,000 women served, and, in addition to military nurses in the army and navy, each service had its own women's corps: the Women's Army Corps (WAC), the navy's Women Accepted for Volunteer Emergency Service (WAVES), and the Women's Air Force Service Pilots (WASPs). Both the army and the navy had decided by the conclusion of World War II that keeping women in the peacetime military would be beneficial. The woman's corps were bought permanently into the U.S. military by the passage of the Women's Armed Services Integration Act of 1948, but women were barred from combat positions. In 1978 the separate corps for women in each service were closed down, and women were integrated into the regular services. Gradually, women service members were admitted to more and more combat roles. By 2016, the issue of women in combat positions reached a point where the secretary of defense recommend elimination of the combat exclusion altogether.

FUTURE IMPLICATIONS

Congress has and continues to act regularly to carry out its responsibilities under Art. I, §8, cl. 14. In every session of Congress, subtle changes to the organization of the military and adjustments to the UCMJ continue not only to make the military better for the defense needs of the republic, but to better reflect the society it protects.

FURTHER READING

Hewes, James E., Jr. 1975. *From Root to McNamara: Army Organization and Administration, 1900–1963*. Washington, D.C.: Center of Military History. http://www.history.army.mil /html/books/040/40-1/cmhPub_40-1.pdf.

Judge Advocates General School. 1945. *Laws of Land Warfare*. Ann Arbor, MI.

MacGregor, Morris J., Jr. 2001. *Integration of the Armed Forces*. Washington, D.C.: Center of Military History. http://www.history.army.mil/html/books/050/50-1-1/cmhPub_50-1-1.pdf.

Morden, Bettie J. 1990. *The Women's Army Corps, 1945–1978*. Washington, D.C.: Center of Military History. http://www.history.army.mil/html/books/030/30-14-1/cmhPub_30-14.pdf.

Naval History and Heritage Command. 1997. *Rules for the Regulation of the Navy of the United Colonies of North-America [28 November 1775]* http://www.history.navy.mil/browse-by -topic/organization-and-administration/regulations-and-policy/navy-regulations-1775.html.

Stewart, Richard, ed. 2009. *American Military History, Volumes 1 and 2*. Washington, D.C.: Center of Military History. http://www.history.army.mil/books/AMH-V1/index.htm#HTML http://www.history.army.mil/books/AMH-V2/index.htm#HTML.

United States. 1914. *Rules of Land Warfare*. Washington, D.C.: Government Printing Office.

United States Selective Service. History and Records. https://www.sss.gov/About/History-And -Records/Induction-Statistics. (Accessed November 2015.)

14 THE POWER TO CALL FORTH AND REGULATE THE MILITIA

Paul Lorenzo Johnson

Article I, section 8, clauses 15 and 16
To provide for calling forth the militia to execute the laws of the union, sup-
press insurrections and repel invasions; [and] To provide for organizing, arm-
ing, and disciplining, the militia, and for governing such part of them as may
be employed in the service of the United States, reserving to the states respec-
tively, the appointment of the officers, and the authority of training the militia
according to the discipline prescribed by Congress . . .

KEY TERMS

A **militia** embodies a civic republican tradition with roots stretching back to Britain, Switzerland, Renaissance Italy, and ancient Rome and Greece. It has several
basic components. First, its *martial role*: although perhaps useful for certain types
of police duty, the militia is ultimately a military force. Second, it is *organized*:
the militia is an actual body, as opposed to an unorganized mass of individual
citizens with guns. Third, the militia is *government-sponsored*: this institution not
only operates with legal sanction but is established, funded, and directed by the
government.

Fourth, the militia is composed of *citizen soldiers*: militia members in times of
peace are not employed as full-time soldiers, which makes the militia a reserve force,
as opposed to an active-duty force. Fifth, it employs *peacetime training*: this is what
separates militia members from other kinds of citizen soldiers, such as wartime volunteers or draftees who enter military service with no prior training. Sixth, a case could
also be made for *localism* as a distinguishing feature of the militia: traditionally, the

militia is organized at, and operates at, the local level, which distinguishes it from other kinds of military-reserve forces.

These components are sufficient to describe the militia as it exists today in the form of the National Guard, but there was a *seventh* component, *universal obligation*, that was critical to the original understanding of the militia at the time of the framing of the U.S. Constitution. For most Americans, the only frame of reference available in recent memory for compulsory military obligation is the Selective Service conscription that was used in both World Wars and eventually replaced with the all-volunteer force during the Vietnam War. However, militia duty was very different than serving under a national military draft. The militia system that the English settlers brought with them in the early 1600s to the American colonies and which lasted until the mid-1800s, was universal, not selective, since in theory every able-bodied adult male citizen owed this duty to the state. The militia system required military training measured in days, not years, and except in the case of national emergency, militia members were not required to travel outside of their state, let alone perform foreign tours of duty.

Calling forth denotes legally requiring the militia to mobilize and deploy for service under the full jurisdiction of the federal government. Prior to this calling forth, the militia operates primarily under the jurisdiction of the state government.

The militia clauses of Art. I, §8 of the Constitution resolved a debate between the Federalists and the Anti-Federalists at the Philadelphia Convention in 1787. Federalists had urged full national control of the militia to create what would amount to a full-fledged army reserve force to complement the full-time regular army that they also intended to provide to the federal government, while Anti-Federalists vehemently opposed both nationalization of the militia and any provision for a regular army. The Federalist side eventually won most of the disputed ground on this issue, although they had to accommodate Anti-Federalist opposition by providing for continued state oversight of the militia during peacetime.

Paradoxically, as described below, this dual state–federal ownership of the militia was the reason why the American universal militia system completely died by the mid-1800s—but also the reason why the militia was fully resurrected over the next century and a half, this time in all-volunteer form.

Organizing, arming, and disciplining: "Organizing" first means recruiting personnel to serve. This requires addressing the questions of who will be prohibited from serving and who will be allowed (or required) to serve. Next, the responsibility to organize means creating a hierarchical structure that locates military units within larger command structures. Organizing also involves specifying the support components and specialized tactical groups necessary to round out a naturally infantry-dominated force.

"Arming" means to provide with *military-grade* weaponry. Before gunpowder became known in Europe, militias were armed with pikes and swords. In the seventeenth, eighteenth, and nineteenth centuries, militias were armed with muskets and rifles. Today, the National Guard of the United States is armed with the same kind of modern weaponry that the active army enjoys.

"Disciplining" means to provide with sufficient preparation to ensure combat readiness, in the event that the militia is called into service. This includes specifying what sanctions will be used to make the service obligation enforceable, in order to make sure that militia members show up for duty and follow orders from their officers, and to make sure that militia officers faithfully perform their duties. Another aspect of the responsibility to discipline is to provide the militia with useful training in preparation for actual military service.

HISTORY AND DEVELOPMENT

Wholesale Shirking of Constitutional Duty, 1792

After the Revolutionary War, the Continental Congress commissioned General George Washington to put together a plan for the post-war military establishment. The militias were in a sorry state on the eve of the Revolutionary War, with organization and discipline at a historical nadir. Since the military threat from Native Americans had gradually declined, the well-regulated militias of the 1600s had declined as well, as the colonials came to rely on British and British-sponsored regulars to provide for their defense. Washington's experience with the militias during the Revolutionary War, most especially their tendency to abandon the cause at the end of their short enlistment terms, reinforced his prejudices against basing the new national system of defense on citizen-soldiers.

In writing his May 1783 reply to the Confederal Congress, which was titled *Sentiments on a Peace Establishment*, Washington carefully took into account the prevailing public sentiment against maintaining standing armies during peacetime. He advocated a middle-ground approach that would provide for both a small force of regulars to guard the nation's frontier and a well-regulated universal militia. The militia was to be based on the principle of *classification*—specifically, classified into ready and reserve components based on age group, an approach that every subsequent president for the next few decades would advocate (unsuccessfully) to Congress. In Washington's plan, the ready component of the militia, intended for rapid response in national emergencies, was to consist of a corps of young men 18–25 years old in every state. These young men would receive 10 to 25 days of training per year and be paid for their training and time spent in actual service. The reserve component of the militia was to consist of all other adult males up to 50 years old, with a few legal exemptions, and be required to train once or twice a year. They would be provided with uniform arms by the national government, to be inspected annually.

Washington's proposal received short shrift in the Confederal Congress at the time. The war over, the state militias were allowed to sink back into disrepair. After the ratification of the Constitution, then-President Washington transmitted another defense plan to Congress in 1790, drafted by his secretary of war, Henry Knox, and entitled the *Plan for the General Arrangement of the Militia of the United States*. This plan again proposed a small standing army, supplemented by a militia. The militia would be grounded on the principle of universal obligation for all citizens and divided into three components: an "advanced corps" of all young men 18–20 years old, who would train for 10 to 30 days per year and form a rapid-response force; a "main corps" of all men 21–45 years old, who would train for four days per year and be liable to be called out in any national emergency that the advanced corps was not large enough to handle; and a "reserved corps" of all men 46–60 years old, who would assemble twice a year for inspection of arms, and who would only be liable for service in the most dire of emergencies, such as invasion by a foreign army. In that plan Knox justified his proposal in terms of military readiness: "In cases of necessity, an army may be formed of citizens, whose previous knowledge of discipline will enable it to proceed to an immediate accomplishment of the designs of the State, instead of exhausting the public resources, by wasting whole years in preparing to face the enemy."

Washington and Knox recognized that one, two, or even four days of training per year would not provide nearly enough time to acquire enough military skill or familiarity with arms to be useful on the battlefield. The purpose of classification by age was to ensure that at least the young men entering the system would receive at least a minimally sufficient degree of training, and then over time that age cohort would move up to the main corps and then the reserve corps, gradually diffusing basic military experience throughout the whole citizenry.

Unfortunately for Washington, Knox, and the militia as an institution, Congress rejected the principle of classification in the Militia Act of 1792. Although later presidents, including Jefferson and Madison, urged Congress to reform the system by adopting classification, the legislative branch was recalcitrant. The 1792 act also reenacted the Continental Congress's mistake of capping service terms at only three months per year; this provision would soon go a long way toward rendering the militia fairly useless as federal forces in the War of 1812, just as similarly short terms of service had done in the Revolutionary War.

The 1792 Militia Act represented a complete shirking of congressional duty to organize, arm, and discipline the militia. Instead of arming, Congress placed that responsibility on the individual militia member, who would be required obtain his own musket or rifle at his own expense, as well as ammunition and other necessary accouterments. For officers, this even included a sword. These requirements were a heavy financial burden for many, not to mention a logistical one: in certain parts of the country, especially along the western frontier, there was no industrial capability for weapons manufacture and few guns to be had for purchase. It took years before the states could import them from Europe or begin to manufacture them domestically.

In theory, the 1792 act provided for militia discipline. The law declared the 1779 manual *Regulations for the Order and Discipline of the Troops of the United States*, which Baron von Steuben had compiled for the Continental Army, to be the basis of the militia's training. However, since there was no accountability established, the states allowed their militias to train however they saw fit. For the most part, this consisted of nothing more than basic parade maneuvers. The only method of oversight was to require each state to appoint an "adjutant general," who would compile returns (summaries) of the number of men under state command and the condition of their weapons and forward this report to the governor and the president.

The 1792 law's primary—or only—achievement was in keeping the principle of universal military obligation alive by its declaration that every able-bodied white male

U.S. citizen ages 18–45 was required to be enrolled in the local militia company. Some occupations would be permanently exempt, but this short list covered only those necessary to keep the country running. Because the law also allowed the states to add their own lists of exemptions, the universal aspect quickly broke down. Local politics vitiated the institution over the next few decades, as the states gradually and steadily expanded the list of exempted occupations. The main effect of this trend was to make it very easy for the well-to-do to avoid militia service entirely.

The new militia system was first put to federal use during the 1791 Whiskey Rebellion. When rebels in western Pennsylvania took up arms in response to federal attempts to collect taxes on whiskey, Washington used his authority under the law to call out the militia to put down insurrections. Despite that 1792 act's lofty declarations and admonitions, the condition of militia organization and discipline at that time had remained very poor in every state called upon to provide militiamen. The force of 13,000 men that the states eventually fielded in response to their quotas was primarily comprised of bounty-seeking volunteers and paid substitutes, rather than enrolled members of the militia.

Subsequent legislation in 1798, 1803, and 1808 made some improvement, although only slight. The July 6, 1798, act authorized the president to sell 30,000 guns to the states. The March 2, 1803, act allowed the U.S. secretary of war to create a standard template for the adjutant generals to use in submitting their returns to the federal government. These actions were mainly symbolic gestures. The April 23, 1808, act was the first real, although limited, step toward arming the militia. It was also the first-ever grant-in-aid from the federal government to the states. The 1808 act authorized an annual appropriation of $200,000 to purchase arms that would be given to the states proportionally on the basis of the number of militia members they had enrolled, as reported in the annual returns.

This annual grant of arms to the states fell far short of actually arming the militia. At a contemporary price of about $12–$14 per gun, the appropriation was only enough for about 14,000–16,000 arms, or enough to accommodate about 2 percent of the national enrollment of militiamen. This annual grant did not come with any requirement to ensure that the weapons would be maintained in good condition, and at the state level there was rarely any degree of oversight. Occasionally, states created their own public armories, where the weapons could be stored and occasionally loaned to individuals, but much more often, governors were delighted at the chance to distribute this form of political patronage at the federal government's expense; they issued the guns directly to favored militia companies. For their part, militia companies lobbied their governor intensely for a share of the arms grant, but in the end the majority of these guns eventually ended up rusted or beyond repair due to poor maintenance, negligence, and even abuse on the part of militia members, such as using the musket's ramrod as a fire poker. Volunteer companies, which were usually formed and maintained solely on the energy of an enterprising would-be officer, often did not last more than a few years. There were many occasions where a disbanded company's arms were found rusting years later in a damp warehouse.

Still, this very limited effort by Congress was the single greatest factor in prolonging the existence of the universal militia during the nineteenth century. It provided states with a real incentive to do their part to maintain their militia systems, since in order to get their share of muskets from the federal government, they had to do the difficult work of keeping track of their citizens—and in a period of American history where weak government bureaucracy coincided with exceptional population mobility—in order to keep them enrolled in the militia.

The Antebellum Universal Militia in Practice

The only full-time roles in the militia system included the governor as commander-in-chief of the state militia, the adjutant general, and in some states, a quartermaster general, who had the care of any publicly owned weapons in state armories. Like the enlisted men in each militia company, all of the officers of every rank, the ones who kept the whole system running, were private citizens who performed their duties on a part-time basis.

The militia was organized locally at the company level, usually consisting of several dozen men. Companies were grouped into regiments, then battalions, then divisions. Each organizational unit was commanded by officers who oversaw the submission of returns regarding the number of men enrolled, the extent of training-day attendance, and the numbers and working condition of all the militia's weapons. Besides notifying militia members of upcoming training days, conducting inspections and drills at training days, and assessing fines for non-attendance or indiscipline, the officers' most important and time-consuming responsibility was maintaining enrollment lists for the militia companies by keeping tabs on all individuals moving into or out of the community. However, the lack of support and lack of pay from the state and local governments—and the awkward nature of assessing fines against militia members who may also be the officer's neighbors, friends, and business partners—meant that even well-meaning officers had a very hard time carrying out their duties.

Two methods were used to select officers: election by the militia members being the most common method, and appointment by the state legislature or governor, which was primarily used for high-ranking officers. The practice of election of officers by the enlisted men they oversaw made it rather difficult to enforce discipline, since the officers elected had to continually curry the men's favor to stay in office. Consequently, there was more pleading than commanding on training days.

Despite the threat of fines that undergirded the system, the only real force that allowed it to keep running was the universal-obligation norm, as well as officers' sense of duty. In places and at times where the citizen-soldier ideal waned, or when few officers took their duties seriously, no amount of fines or other legal coercion could keep the system functioning. When that norm dissipated, even a vigorous and dedicated officer willing to assess fines could not enforce the payment of fines assessed.

At training days, militia members showed up to have their weapon inspected to ensure that it was in working condition, and then to be led through elementary drill exercises as a company, using a crash-course version of European-style field tactics. Training days generally took place two or three times a year, one or two of them being company-level events, and one event taking place at a higher organizational level such as the regiment, where multiple militia companies would participate together.

Realistically, the little training that could be condensed into two or three days annually could not make its participants battle-ready. Evaluating the institution on this basis, military theorists over the years condemned militia training as useless. While partly true, this perspective misses a very important aspect: the role of training days as civic rituals. Each participant took part in the ancient tradition, renewed for himself the connection between citizenship and soldiering, and reaffirmed his obligation to defend his liberty and the political institutions that preserved that liberty.

Training and muster days also served the community as a whole. For an agrarian society, these were the largest and most celebrated social gatherings of the year. Politicians and candidates for office attended and always gave speeches to the militias and the spectators. The entire community turned out in a setting that resembled a county fair rather than boot camp. Hundreds or even thousands of spectators would gather and watch the training and inspection of the militia companies in the mornings. The most popular event was the mock battle or target practice competition that took place in the afternoon. In the same way that muster days served as civic rituals for the individual militiaman, musters were likewise a ritual for the community at large, allowing the community to collectively reaffirm its support for the militia.

Death of the Universal Militia

After the War of 1812, Congress effectively washed its hands of the whole matter of regulating the militia. Widespread poor performance by militiamen called into federal service, combined with the extreme difficulty faced in merely trying to keep the militia in the field long enough to win a battle or two, made it apparent that the ill-regulated militia that Congress had sanctioned twenty years earlier *could not* contribute in any degree to national defense. The poor state of discipline and short terms of service were compounded by the refusal of many to go an inch beyond U.S. borders, on the grounds that attacking British positions in Canada did not technically constitute "repel[ling] invasions." This complaint obviously refused to acknowledge military realities about good offenses making the best defenses. As long as the federal government did not have the kind of access and oversight required to really regulate the militia in peacetime, nor the degree of control necessary to make good use of it in wartime, it would never again take the militia seriously. As a result, presidents eventually gave up trying to talk Congress into reforming the militia by introducing classification, and the tiny amount of annual funding for arming the militia remained stagnant until long after the Civil War. Left to their own devices, the states exacerbated the existing degree of inequality, and then by increasing neglect, they allowed the whole system to collapse under its own weight.

The burdens that this system imposed on individual militia members included the cost of furnishing arms, ammunition, and subsidiary supplies; the opportunity cost of lost wages or work on training days and while traveling to training days, as well as the expense of required travel for training, which was greater in rural areas; any fines incurred from absence at trainings or indiscipline, including not having a weapon in nonworking condition; and, for many, jail time in debtor's prison, the result of financial inability to pay the fines assessed. During wartime or national emergencies, there were additional burdens on the families of militiamen who were called up for duty, including loss of the sole wage-earner or of the manpower necessary for harvesting crops. The requirements of arming oneself, attending unpaid trainings, and serving when called up, operated as a highly regressive form of taxation.

The burden of militia duty was especially heavy for those living on the western frontiers. By definition, frontier areas tended to be very sparsely settled, so militia companies covered a larger geographical area, implying long distances to travel to attend training day. Whereas a militia member in a New England city would have to give up a day of labor to attend his local training, a militia member on the frontier might lose a few days. Frontiersmen tended to be poorer than city-dwellers on average, which made it harder to bear any fines imposed for non-attendance, and since most frontier dwellers were farmers, the lost labor could result in an entire crop dying from neglect by the time they returned. Finally, the ever-present threat of raids by hostile Indians made it so that militia members in the western territories, when called into active service, sometimes had to choose between defending a neighboring community they were ordered to march to and defending their own wives and children back home.

The gradual exemption of the well-to-do from militia service created a negative feedback loop that hastened the militia's demise. Those left to bear the burden of service resented the system for its inequality and lobbied for an end to their burden as well, and when they could not effect a change in the law, they employed civil-resistance tactics ranging from foot-dragging to savage burlesque. Overwhelmed officers attempted to compensate by further watering down trainings and increasing the volume of alcohol they used at these events to ply obedience from the enlisted men. By the 1830s and 40s, musters had degenerated into debauched, drunken festivals, which attracted greater scorn and determination by men of any means to avoid service. Temperance crusaders, debtor's prison abolitionists, and working-class groups successfully lobbied the states to end training days and the militia fine. By the time that the states began responding to the first tremors of oncoming civil war and seriously assessing their state forces' preparedness for the first time since 1812, there was basically nothing left to revive: militias had to be put together for Union and Confederate service from scratch by drawing upon a motley assortment of volunteer organizations.

Resurrecting the Militia in an All-Volunteer Format

While from the 1700s onward the universal militia never achieved anything close to the ideal of a "well-regulated militia" that the Second Amendment holds as essential to the security of the republic, the volunteer militia organizations that eventually won federal patronage and a prominent place in the constellation of national defense policy *did* achieve that ideal. Once the federal government recognized the National Guard as a professional and militarily useful reserve force, including its willingness to submit to federal standards and oversight for organization and discipline, Congress became an eager patron.

The tradition of the American volunteer militia units goes back to the beginning of British colonization in America. These units were originally created to serve as rapid-response teams, formed on the model of the British "trained bands." By the time of the

Revolutionary War, they were called "minutemen." Besides their ready-reserve role, the volunteer militia units also provided the cavalry and artillery units for the colonial and state militias.

Ironically, although the dual-control system had previously contributed to the collapse of the militia by allowing the state and the federal governments to each avoid the duty to arm, organize, and discipline, now dual control was what allowed the new militia system to succeed as a militia. Federal sponsorship gave the volunteer organizations a military purpose. If these forces had continued only at the state level, they would have either morphed into a state police force, perhaps like state highway patrols, or their state sponsors would have stopped funding them after the threat from militant labor had declined by the end of the 1800s. On the other hand, if all control and sponsorship had passed to the federal government, the militia would have been wholly absorbed into the national army reserve, with the local-control aspect completely gone, and uncertain prospects about whether it would be continued each time there was a war draw-down.

The volunteer militia organizations tended to be formed from the socially elite, who had greater leisure time available for military activities. Some members served in these units to avoid serving in the common militia, since volunteer-unit service counted as meeting the legal obligation for militia service. However, most volunteer militiamen were eager to perform, rather than avoid, military duty. Similar to modern concerns about the effect of private schools on their public counterparts, the volunteer companies tended to siphon off the most committed, most talented, and best resource-endowed individuals in the community away from the common militia.

The volunteer organizations had a statutory role. Although under the 1792 Militia Acts the majority of the manpower would operate as infantry, the acts also provided for artillery and cavalry companies. These specialized companies would be composed of volunteers from within the division, who had to provide themselves uniforms at their own expense. The 1792 Militia Acts therefore formalized the dual system that had more or less always existed of practice, with elite companies of volunteers operating alongside the ordinary or common militia.

Following the Civil War and demobilization on each side, volunteer organizations reconstituted themselves in the states. They continued to recruit on the basis of the social events and civic prestige that came with membership, but they quickly found a useful role as state constabulary forces. The states had continued to distribute their shares of the annual $200,000 federal grant of weapons to the volunteer organizations, and the volunteers had proven themselves useful for quelling urban riots in the years before the Civil War. When the Great Railroad Strike of 1877 broke out across the country, the afflicted states called their volunteer militia units into service. The enlisted men in these units were not wealthy, although their officers tended to be, and the states worried that they might sympathize with the strikers, but the volunteer militias loyally (and violently) put down the revolt as directed. As a result of this performance, state funding for the volunteer militias increased dramatically, especially in states that were particularly hard-hit by repeated and widespread labor strikes.

This improved sponsorship gave the militias a role other than as civic clubs, though the role and reputation for strikebreaking made recruitment among working-class individuals much more difficult. Still, the militias aspired to a different role: military service for their country. To this end, the volunteer organizations began holding state-sponsored summer training camps. The states were happy to pay for these trainings, as riot duty formed part of the curriculum, but the volunteer militias and the states also sought for supervision and inspection by the U.S. Army at these events to ensure that the organizations would begin to achieve some proficiency in more purely military matters.

The federal government began to take note of these reconstituted militia organizations. In 1887, Congress increased the annual grant in aid for militia arms for the first time since 1808, doubling it to $400,000, and then further increasing the grant to $1,000,000 in 1900. In 1897, Congress created an exchange program that allowed the militias to begin to trade in their old rifles and muskets for more modern rifles. The main event that convinced the federal government to take the new state militias seriously was the Spanish-American War. Although the militias who entered service in the war were woefully inadequate in their training and preparation—though the army was not much better at the time—militia members served with distinction, including serving extended tours to perform the thankless task of putting down a native Filipino independence-seeking rebellion in America's newfound colony.

Soon after that war, federal support for the militias was solidified through the passage of the 1903 Dick Act, named after Representative Charles Dick of Ohio, a war veteran and militia member himself. This act formally repealed the 1792 Militia Acts and the principle of universal obligation. While it still declared that the militia consisted of the whole mass of able-bodied male citizens between the ages of 18 and 45, this was no more than lip service to tradition. The act recognized the volunteer militias as the "organized militia," with everyone who was not serving in the volunteer militia considered part of the "reserve militia"—or, in other words, non-existent militia. Federal control was greatly increased: the Dick Act set the annual service cap at nine months instead of three, subjected the militia to the same discipline and organization as the army, and required 24 separate drills (training days) and one 5-day summer training camp annually for all militia members. For the first time in U.S. history, Congress allowed militia officers and enlisted men to be paid for attendance at training. The militia was also allowed to train together with the army. One of the most important features of the Dick Act was that it mandated that states could only receive their annual appropriation for weapons if they had enrolled at least 100 militiamen per each senator and representative for that state in Congress. This provision spurred states that had not yet formed a state militia organization to do so.

The next few decades were marked by a pattern of steadily increased funding for the militia, which was named the National Guard by the 1916 National Defense Act, combined with steadily increased federal control. Congress expanded training to 48 drill days per year plus a 15-day summer training camp and fully subjected the Guard to the army's supervision and tutelage. Far from the climate of state jealousy of federal power that, a century earlier, had prompted them to view the militia as a potential counterbalance against the army, the states welcomed federal sponsorship and regulation for this organization—provided that the National Guard remain at least predominantly under state control during peacetime—since federal funding lightened their financial burden as the militia's co-sponsor. Eventually, the federal government assumed the vast majority of that burden of supporting the Guard.

Guardsmen also welcomed and pushed zealously for the move toward federal sponsorship; their main fear was that the National Guard might somehow fail to secure a role as the nation's primary military reserve organization. This fear was justly founded. The army, out of traditional contempt toward the militia, sought to create its own reserve organization under the "raise and support armies" clause of the Constitution (Art. I, §8, cl. 12); this new reserve was intended to displace the National Guard. The Army Reserve was established by the 1916 National Defense Act, but it remained a comparatively small and politically weak competitor for decades.

The interwar movement toward universal military training (UMT) also threatened the Guard's existence. UMT is a military system that consists of a small regular army combined with a large citizen-soldier reserve operating entirely under federal control. Advocates of UMT pushed for the National Guard to give up its constitutional role under the Militia Clauses and begin a new institutional life solely under the "raise and support armies" clause. This threat did not materialize out of the blue: in order to ensure that the National Guard could serve outside of the country, the 1916 act had required all Guard officers and enlisted men to swear a dual oath to obey both the governor and the president, and it had provided that individual Guardsmen, when called into federal service, would be discharged from the militia and enter the army, resuming their militia status after the national emergency ended. Similarly, the 1933 amendments to the 1916 act had formally designated that there would be two National Guards, and each Guardsman would belong to both: one, the state National Guard, which would continue to operate under the Militia Clauses, and the other, the "National Guard of the United States," which would fall under the "raise and support armies" clause and form an official part of the Army Reserve.

However, the movement toward federal control did not result in the demise of the National Guard, whether as a militia or otherwise. Thanks to a skilled lobby, the creation of a sympathetic bureau within the War Department, and a strong network of support at the state level and within Congress, which was largely the result of already civic-minded Guardsmen naturally migrating into state and federal political office, the Guard managed to fend off army plans that would have absorbed or disbanded the state militias.

Today, the National Guard has been thoroughly integrated into the U.S. military structure but still preserved as a militia organization. Each state has its own National Guard organization, and in peacetime the Guard remains largely under state control, often doing disaster-response and occasionally riot-control duty. The United States maintains both the Guard and the Army Reserve as its two reserve components of the land-based forces.

The federal government has full jurisdictional control over the National Guard when called into service. Its ability to extend that call was expanded in 1952 to include non-emergency duty and training with the governor's consent, and in 1987 to remove the gubernatorial-consent requirement. Because Guard members belong to both their state's National Guard and the National Guard of the United States, in the words of the Supreme Court in *Perpich v. DOD* (1990), "In a sense, all of them now must keep three hats in their closets—a civilian hat, a state militia hat, and an army hat—only one of which is worn at any particular time."

FUTURE IMPLICATIONS

The National Guard has been a success where the universal civic militia was not, because the federal government was now able to subject the militia to proper military regulation and training. The volunteer militias that became the National Guard were willing to submit to this because they were eager to be taken seriously as military organizations. The states were willing to submit to this because the federal government was going to shoulder a much larger share of the financial responsibility. The federal government was willing to sponsor these militia organizations because it had a real prospect of turning them into a militarily useful reserve organization—not only because it finally had full access to these militias, but because by this point in U.S. history there existed a sufficiently large, stable, and professional regular military that could provide the kind of oversight necessary to ensure battle-readiness in the militia.

Now that the militia is fully a part of the federal force structure, its contribution to national defense is secured. A separate and useful question to ask is whether the National Guard (and the Army Reserve) can play any role in *restraining* the civilian leadership from resorting to unpopular military action, due to the political costs they might face from the citizenry over requiring the citizen-soldiers to mobilize, fight, and die in a given military conflict.

The architects of the Vietnam War deliberately avoided calling up the National Guard and the Army Reserves during the war, anticipating that doing so would force a greater accountability for the country's military policy, since the reserve forces had extensive middle-class participation. Instead, they adopted a selective draft with plenty of exemptions, which disproportionately placed the manpower burden on racial minorities and lower-class whites. This meant that the war could produce a larger number of casualties before political pressure could mount to force an end the war, compared to relying on fully mobilized reserves. After the war, the military closely integrated the active forces and the reserve component in a "Total Force" concept, ensuring that the reserves, including the Guard, would be called up if the military was employed for anything larger than a minor police action. Opponents of unilateral executive power lauded this shift as a useful check on the president, to make sure that the nation would not fight another unpopular war. However, the wars in Iraq and Afghanistan show that instead of serving as a check on the president's ability to conduct unlimited military operations, the Total Force concept's heavy reliance on the reserves allowed the nation's civilian leaders to subject the reservists to multiple tours of duty with little breathing space in between, with debilitating physical and psychological results from this strain. The experience of the National Guard so far in the War on Terror suggests that these hopes may have been misplaced.

Since America has a longer history of universal military obligation in peacetime, extending from the early 1600s to the mid-1800s, than of all-volunteer service, it is worth asking what place the idea of universal obligation has in this country into the future. With the advent of nuclear weapons and the disappearance of territorial threat and of great-power challenge to U.S. hegemony, the idea of conventional total war appears to have become obsolete. The U.S. maintains a relatively small but technologically sophisticated force that is quite sufficient for any purpose short of actually invading other countries. Occasional calls surface in Congress to reinstate the draft, but public opinion is so far decidedly against it.

Draft proponents are not thinking in terms of a militia-type model, but if the national security situation ever changed such that military conscription became a serious option, a universal militia system established in peacetime theoretically holds distinct advantages over a wartime draft. As Henry Knox had pointed out, if done right, a universal militia requires much less time and expenditure in order to raise a very large army, since—after it has been around for enough years—a large proportion of the populace has some degree of military training. Any attempt to re-establish a universal militia, though, would require figuring out how to overcome the list of problems highlighted in this chapter, such as how to provide sufficient training, make the burden equitable for rich and poor, establish effective mechanisms for enforcement, and ensure full federal control in wartime.

FURTHER READING

Cooper, Jerry. 1993. *The Militia and the National Guard in America since Colonial Times: A Research Guide*. Westport, CT: Greenwood Press.

Cooper, Jerry. 1997. *The Rise of the National Guard: The Evolution of the American Militia, 1865–1920*. Lincoln, NE: University of Nebraska Press.

Cornell, Saul. 2006. *A Well-Regulated Militia: The Founding Fathers and the Origins of Gun Control in America*. New York: Oxford University Press.

Cress, Lawrence Delbert. 1982. *Citizens in Arms: The Army and the Militia in the American Society to the War of 1812*. Chapel Hill, NC: University of North Carolina Press.

Derthick, Martha. 1965. *The National Guard in Politics*. Cambridge, MA: Harvard University Press.

London, Lena. 1951. The Militia Fine, 1830–1860. *Military Affairs*, 15 (Autumn): 133–144.

McCreedy, Kenneth Otis. 1991. Palladium of Liberty: The American Militia System, 1815–1861. Ph.D. diss. University of California, Berkeley.

Palmer, John McAuley. 1979 [1941]. *America in Arms: The Experience of the United States with Military Organization*. New York: Arno Press.

Pitcavage, Mark. 1995. An Equitable Burden: The Decline of the State Militias, 1783–1858. Ph.D. diss. Ohio State University. https://etd.ohiolink.edu/rws_etd/document/get/osu1217 271550/inline

Riker, William H. 1957. *Soldiers of the States: The Role of the National Guard in American Democracy*. Washington, D.C.: Public Affairs Press.

15 THE POWER TO EXERCISE AUTHORITY OVER THE DISTRICT OF COLUMBIA AND FEDERAL PROPERTY

Mary M. Cheh

Article I, section 8, clause 17
To exercise exclusive Legislation in all Cases whatsoever, over such District
(not exceeding ten Miles square) as may, by Cession of particular States, and
the Acceptance of Congress, become the Seat of the Government of the United
States, and to exercise like Authority over all Places purchased by the Consent
of the Legislature of the State in which the Same shall be, for the Erection of
Forts, Magazines, Arsenals, dock-Yards and other needful Buildings . . .

Article I, section 8, clause 17, is the source of Congress's power to govern the District of Columbia, the nation's capital, and places ceded by the states to the federal government for the erection of military bases and other federal buildings. The clause is not as well-known as other sources of congressional powers, such as the war power or the power to regulate interstate commerce. Yet the clause does explain the anomalous political condition of the District of Columbia and illustrates the delicacy and complexity of allocating powers between the national government and the states in our federal system.

KEY TERMS

"To exercise exclusive Legislation in all Cases whatsoever . . ."
Congress may create and exercise power over the District of Columbia and places ceded by states to the United States *exclusive* of any power the states may otherwise exercise.

The importance of this grant must be understood in terms of federalism, that is, the balance of power created by the Constitution between the federal government and the states. Generally speaking, under the Constitution, Congress exercises specific powers relating to national interests while states retain authority over purely local matters such as domestic relations, local crime, and zoning. But this clause gives Congress extraordinary, sweeping, and plenary power over the District for every proper purpose of government, whether the interest be national or of entirely local nature. Thus, so far as the District (and ceded property) is concerned, Congress may legislate on any subject even beyond its specified grants of power and including even those of a hyper-local nature, such as prescribing parking rules or setting standards for the collection of stray dogs.

"Over such District (not exceeding 10 Miles square) as may, by Cession of particular States, and the Acceptance of Congress, become the Seat of the Government of the United States . . ."

Under the Residence Act of 1790, Congress tasked President George Washington with selecting a site, a District, along the banks of the Potomac River to serve as the seat or capital of the United States government. The land selected was legislatively granted, or ceded, ("Cession") by the states of Maryland and Virginia and legislatively accepted by Congress. President Washington chose the area of the current District of Columbia, as well as additional land since ceded back to Virginia. The land included the incorporated towns of Georgetown and Alexandria and other smaller settlements.

A portion of the land was designated as the federal district and called the City of Washington, to honor George Washington, while the land surrounding it was called the Territory of Columbia. In 1871 Congress merged the City of Washington and the Territory into the current District of Columbia.

"[E]xercise like Authority over all Places purchased by the Consent of the Legislature of the State in which the Same shall be, for the Erection of Forts, Magazines, Arsenals, dock-Yards, and other needful Buildings"

The "like authority" is the full, plenary, and sweeping authority that Congress may exercise over the District of Columbia, and the "Places" are any lands ceded to the United States government by legislation of the granting state. The purposes to be served by obtaining these places is stated to be for things such as "Forts," "Magazines" (places to store ammunition), "Arsenals," and "dock-Yards," thus suggesting what seems to be purposes limited to military-type installations. But the language is expanded by the reference to "other needful Buildings," and, in fact, the federal government has acquired property from states for any number of purposes such as prisons, parks, or wildlife refuges. Thus, the purposes of the acquisitions are not limited.

HISTORY AND DEVELOPMENT

In the Beginning

The District clause was not in the original draft of the Constitution, and the idea for it was instead referred to a committee, which reported favorably upon it. The Convention adopted it with an insignificant amendment and apparently without objection.

This rather uncontroversial acceptance by the Convention delegates contrasts with a rather tumultuous event that occurred a mere four years earlier and which provided the impetus for creating a separate enclave for the national government, an area completely controlled by Congress and freed of any influence or dependence on any state.

In June 1783, the Congress of Confederation, the precursor legislative body operating under the Articles of Confederation, was sitting in session at Independence Hall in Philadelphia. The Congress was forced to adjourn after being menaced by a mob of former Continental Army soldiers seeking back pay and debt relief. The mutinous soldiers insulted the delegates, blockaded the doors, and prevented the delegates from leaving until Alexander Hamilton was able to negotiate their exit. The Congress, fearing for its very safety, asked Pennsylvania for protection, but the state did nothing. Under these circumstances, Congress adjourned to Princeton, New Jersey, whose residents promised to protect them. The National legislature remained there without insult or attack, until for the sake of convenience; they adjourned to Annapolis, Maryland. As Justice Story noted, "the degrading spectacle of a fugitive congress [was] sufficiently striking to produce this remedy" (i.e., the creation of a special federal enclave).

During the 1789 constitutional ratifying convention in North Carolina, delegate James Iredell captured the concerns directly:

> What would be the consequence if the seat of government of the United States, with all the archives of America, was in the power of any one particular state? Would not this be most unsafe and humiliating? Do we not all remember that, in the year 1783, a band of soldiers went and insulted the Congress? The sovereignty of the United States was treated with indignity. They applied for protection to the state they resided in, but could obtain none. It is to be hoped such a disgraceful scene will never happen again; but that, for the future, the national government will be able to protect itself.

Opponents of the Constitution offered multiple objections to clause 17, some quite fantastic. Opponents said that the District might become some sort of sanctuary providing various privileges and immunities to those within it. The District might become a base for maintaining an aristocracy, or for planning and launching tyranny, and that the aristocrats and oppressors would be answerable to no laws except those Congress might adopt. A powerful standing army might be kept in such a District. And Congress might pass oppressive laws to govern the people of the District. A further objection, which was not fanciful and which did ripen into the most serious shortcoming of the District clause, was that the people of the District of Columbia, far from enjoying special privileges and immunities, would not enjoy full democratic rights, a voice in the national legislature, or direct control over their own affairs.

The arguments in favor of a capital separate from any state—a District under the exclusive legislative authority of Congress—included protecting the legislature of the Union and the property of the United States, including its archives; eliminating dependency on any state for its orderly operations; and avoiding jealousies among the states or claims of undue influence by the state where the capital was located. Opposition views that state sovereignty would somehow be impaired by the very existence of the

District were dismissed as baseless and further answered by noting that a District of ten miles square was a tiny space and that any property used to comprise the District could only come from states which gave consent.

As for protecting the democratic rights of the people who would live in the District, supporters of the Constitution acknowledged that District residents would not be citizens of any state and not entitled to the privileges of citizens of a state. Nor would they have any direct representatives in the Congress or even, as of the immediate creation of the District, a local legislature. Yet the supporters of the Constitution and the District clause anticipated that the states which ceded the land to create the federal capital—Maryland and Virginia—would make provisions as part of that cession to ensure that their former citizens were represented in the federal government. James Madison, in *Federalist* No. 43, referring to the states whose citizens were to be removed into the new capital, assumed that, "the State will no doubt provide in the compact for the rights and consent of the citizens inhabiting it." And he was right, at least temporarily. Between 1790 and 1800, residents of the District continued to vote in local, state, and national elections in their respective states. Then, in 1800, the residents were disenfranchised as part of the congressional law transferring full authority from the states to the federal government. This loss of voting rights was viewed as benign, on the assumption that the residents of the capital would still be well represented, even lucky, because they would be represented by all of the Members of Congress, who would be attentive to their wants and responsive to their needs. And District residents would be able to directly mingle with and lobby members Congress.

In 1801, Representative John Dennis (MD) speaking of District residents said, "from their contiguity to, and residence among the members of the General Government, they knew that though they might not be represented in the national body, their voice would be heard." This may have made some sense at the time, given that the House of Representatives had scarcely over 100 members and the District's population was fewer than 15,000 residents. The Framers and the early Congress could not have foreseen that, by 1960, the population of the District would swell to over 760,000 people. Over time the complete disenfranchisement of District residents became less and less defensible.

Opponents of the new Constitution also took aim at exclusive congressional control over places ceded by states to the federal government. They denounced the authority as a violation of state sovereignty and state prerogatives. As with the creation of a District, they claimed that the ceded places could become sanctuaries for fugitives and that, from these enclaves, malevolent persons could cause harm to state and local interests in the state where they were located. The supporters of the provision argued that it was imperative for the public safety and convenience that the money spent on such places and the public property kept there be exempt from the authority of the particular state where they may be located. This is particularly evident with military installations, since places on which the security of the entire Union may depend should not be dependent in any degree on a particular state of the Union. A basic principle of political accountability and the supremacy of federal law also inhere in this position; that is, a part of the Union (a state) in which only the citizens of that state are represented may not control the interests of the whole (the nation). Furthermore, the supporters argued, the state wherein the ceded property is located is protected because the state must consent to the cession. And the ceding state need not cede unqualified control, but may transfer the property with restrictions.

The idea that ceded property may be conveyed with restrictions or qualifications was once contested but is now settled. Indeed in the decades following the ratification of the Constitution, states have made many cessions for federal military facilities, prisons, and other purposes. And in most cases, states routinely reserved the right, for example, to serve state civil and criminal process on persons found within the ceded areas, thus contradicting the idea that these places would be sanctuaries for fugitives. It should be noted, however, that a state's reservation of authority is not deemed an exercise of state power over the United States, an impermissible principle under the doctrine of the supremacy of federal law. Rather it is deemed an exercise of Congress's exclusive power, which includes Congress's power to permit the states this latitude.

Moreover, even if Congress accepts a reservation of some authority to the ceding state, Congress may always rely on its general powers—such as those over interstate commerce or taxation—to eliminate the effects of a state reservation of power. For example, a Pennsylvania school district wanted to impose occupation and per capita taxes on employees who lived in the Lewisburg Federal Penitentiary, a ceded federal enclave. A federal court held that such a tax was valid because although the state had ceded its power to tax the lands and buildings in the enclave, it had not ceded its power to tax individuals who lived there. However, if the United States thereafter passed legislation pursuant to its general Art. I, §8, cl. 1 *taxing* power and its Amendment XVI *power to tax incomes*, and exempted from taxation all persons living on federal property or in federal prisons, it could do so. Then a conflict would be created between federal and state law, and, under the doctrine of supremacy of federal law, the Pennsylvania tax would have been invalid as applied.

Creation of the District

In 1789, the people ratified the new Constitution with the District clause intact. The land that would become the District was not immediately selected, however, so Congress met at temporary capitals, including the last temporary capital in Philadelphia. Where the permanent capital should be located was a controversial issue that was not resolved until Congress passed the Residence Act of 1790. The law assigned President Washington the job of selecting a site along the banks of the Potomac River and appointing three commissioners to oversee its development. Washington selected ten square miles of land ceded from property in Maryland and Virginia. It included the modern-day District of Columbia, Georgetown, Alexandria, and other small European settlements. As the federal buildings were constructed, President Washington referred to that area of the District as the Federal City. Thereafter the Commissioners named that part of the District the "City of Washington" in honor of the president, and the remaining part was named the Territory of Columbia. In 1846, the area of Alexandria and Alexandria County (now Arlington County) was retroceded, or given back, to Virginia. The Alexandria merchants were disappointed that they did not realize the economic growth they expected from being part of the District, and residents had lost the right to vote and representation in Congress as a result of joining the District. And, although it did not explicitly say so, Alexandria desired retrocession to protect its bustling slave trade from congressional control. Alexandria voters petitioned Congress and the Virginia legislature, and both agreed to the retrocession. In 1871, on the land remaining after retrocession, the city of Washington and the territory of Columbia were incorporated into what is today the District of Columbia.

Congressional Control over Local Affairs

Congress has always claimed its clause 17 exclusive power over the District of Columbia and its constitutional authority to adopt legislation "in all Cases whatsoever, over such District." At times, Congress's exclusive power and dominion over the people of the District of Columbia has been questioned as itself unconstitutional, but none of these challenges have been successful. And yet, under clause 17, Congress is not *required* to exercise its power or to exercise it to its fullest extent. Congress could choose to create a government for the District and vest in it a wide range of lawmaking power just as it has done under Art. IV, §3, cl. 2 with the territories of the United States. And, in fact, the form and powers given to local government in the District have varied considerably over the last 200 years, as Congress has shifted between quite extensive and direct control and a more hands-off approach.

When Congress took possession of the District in December 1800, it divided it into two counties: that of Alexandria on the west side of the Potomac, and that of Washington on the east side. The laws of Virginia were carried over to the Alexandria portion and continued the municipal government of Alexandria, and the laws of Maryland were carried over to the Washington portion and continued the municipal government of Georgetown. To this preexisting local government structure, Congress continued all other corporate bodies and created a court system (the Levy Court) with judicial and administrative functions. In 1802 Congress passed legislation to incorporate the City of Washington with a Mayor and Council invested with typical municipal powers, including the power to pass laws and regulations and impose taxes. The members of the Council were elected by the white male inhabitants of the City. Other officers such as the members of the Levy Court were appointed by the president of the United States and the Senate.

During the first year of the Civil War, because of the exigencies associated with that conflict, Congress created a special Metropolitan Police area and took from the mayor and council of Washington various police functions and placed them under the control of five commissioners appointed by the president, the Senate, and the mayors of Washington and Georgetown. Despite this, the general system of local municipal government, with an increasing expansion of local self-government, continued for decades. During that time the federal government took little part in local affairs except to protect its own public buildings and property. Indeed in 1871 Congress acted to create significant home rule authority in the residents of the District. It merged Washington City, Georgetown, and Washington County, and passed an Organic Act providing for a District Governor appointed by the president and an elected legislature with significant municipal powers.

The expansion of home rule for the District came to an end less than ten years later, primarily because of massive overspending by a prominent local figure, Alexander "Boss" Shepherd. Shepherd was the unelected chief of the public works department and, for a time, governor of the Territory of Washington. He managed or mismanaged the spending of millions of dollars to reshape what was a sleepy, backwater town into a modern city. Congress's investigation and subsequent firing of Shepherd led the body to end the governorship and instead impose a commission system to govern the District. In 1878, Congress repealed the home rule provisions of the Organic Act altogether and disbanded the territorial government entirely. The District was thereafter to be governed by a three-person commission appointed by the president. As noted by the United States Supreme Court in 1889, under the new system, "Legislative powers . . . ceased, and the municipal government [was] confined to mere administration." For almost 100 years thereafter, Congress exercised its clause 17 plenary power via direct legislation over the District, with very little involvement of District residents.

Home rule finally returned in 1973. No doubt some members of Congress were moved to grant more local control out of a sense of fairness to the growing number of residents or in response to local agitation, but the primary motivation appeared to be congressional fatigue with responsibility for local District affairs. Under the 1973 District of Columbia Self-Government and Governmental Reorganization Act (the "Home Rule Act"), Congress expressed its intent to relieve itself to "the greatest extent possible, of the burden of legislating upon essentially local District matters." The grant of authority to the District was broad but far from complete, and Congress retained full authority to override, or veto, any District legislation and to prescribe legislation for the District on any matter. Under this latter authority, local residents have chafed at the use of the District to advance pet policies of congressional members such as school vouchers or certain novel tax policies.

Congress retains ultimate legislative authority over the District chiefly by providing that local legislation passed by the District government becomes law only after its review. This review takes two forms. Non-budgetary laws must be sent to Congress for "passive" review; that is, a law is sent to Congress and if, after 30 days (60 for criminal laws), Congress does not affirmatively disapprove of the legislation, it becomes law. By contrast, the District's budget requires active congressional approval. A locally approved budget must be transmitted by the mayor to the president, who then submits it to Congress as part of the national budget. Congress must enact affirmative legislation to allow the District to spend any money, whether the money comes from federal sources or is part of the billions of dollars raised locally. Additionally, Congress can line-item veto any expenditure that, for any reason, it does not like. And Congress has done this in many instances—including, for example, prohibiting spending locally raised money to pay for poor women's abortions.

The Home Rule Act also explicitly prohibits local legislation in nine enumerated areas. The District may not, for example, tax, or even pass laws concerning, any federal property or functions. And unlike even the Territories of the United States, the District may not tax non-residents on any income they earn in the District, a dramatic financial loss since approximately two-thirds of the people who work in the District do not live there.

At the same time, it should be noted that congressional control of District affairs and finances has included certain benefits. In the 1990s, the federal government bailed out the District when its bonds were rated below junk and bankruptcy loomed. The federal government took over the District's pension liabilities at that time as well. And the federal government continues, to the present day, to pay for the local court system and its related costs (though, as a consequence, local judges are not selected locally but are nominated by the president and confirmed by the Senate).

The Home Rule Act was a welcome return of authority to District residents. Yet the essential defect of Congress–District relations is maintained. That is, anything the local government is empowered to do is at sufferance of Congress, and whatever District residents gained under the Home Rule Act can be snatched back as readily as in the 1870s. Indeed, Section 601 of the Home Rule Act states quite clearly:

> the Congress of the United States reserves the right, at any time, to exercise its constitutional authority as legislature for the District, by enacting legislation for the District on any subject, whether within or without the scope of legislative power granted to the Council by this Act, including legislation to amend or repeal any law in force in the District prior to or after enactment of this Act and any act passed by the Council.

National Voting Rights and Representation in Congress

Once the cession of land from Virginia and Maryland was finalized, and accepted in 1801, Congress invoked its clause 17 authority and officially established the District of Columbia. The residents thereby lost their right to vote in their former states and acquired no rights to vote for members of Congress or have a representative in either house. Almost immediately residents began seeking representation in the national legislature. As early as 1801, citizens voiced concern about their political disenfranchisement. In that year for example, a prominent citizen, Augustus Woodward, stated:

> This body of people is as much entitled to the enjoyment of the rights of citizenship as any other part of the people of the United States. There can exist no necessity for their disenfranchisement, no necessity for them to repose on the mere generosity of their countrymen to be protected from tyranny, to mere spontaneous attention for the regulation of their interests. They are entitled to participation in the general councils on the principles of equity and reciprocity.

At the time, members of Congress were largely indifferent to these complaints. As mentioned previously, many believed that District residents were in fact represented by all members of Congress—and well represented, at that. As to any prospect for statehood or representation akin to statehood, Representative Randolph of Virginia expressed a common sentiment that, "the other states can never be brought to consent that two Senators, and at least three electors of the President, shall be chosen out of this small spot, and by a handful of men."

Over two hundred years later, however, the "handful of men" now stands at over 650,000 residents, a population larger than Wyoming and Vermont and close to the populations of Alaska and North Dakota. Residents of the District of Columbia serve in the military and comply with other obligations of United States citizenship, such as the payment of federal taxes. District residents often point out that paying millions and millions of annual federal taxes without a vote in the national legislature conflicts with a major reason the original colonists fought the Revolutionary War against Great Britain: no taxation without representation. District license plates carry the message "Taxation Without Representation" to remind others of their situation. Beyond taxation, residents invoke a more fundamental principle as well: consent of the governed.

Through all of the variations in home rule, Congress never successfully used its power over the District of Columbia to grant District residents voting rights in Congress. And to this day, around the world, District citizens remain the only residents of a democratic capital who have no vote in their country's national legislature. In 1970 Congress did provide the District with a delegate to the House of Representatives, elected every two years by the people of the District. But while this delegate may participate in debates, he or she has no vote. At one time, from 1996 to 2007, the House permitted the delegate to vote in the Committee of the Whole—with the proviso, however, that if the vote were ever decisive, it would not count. The position is held in such low esteem by other Representatives that on several occasions, the District's delegate has been denied the opportunity to testify before a House subcommittee on legislation directly affecting the District.

Under its Article V power, Congress also successfully proposed to the states two constitutional amendments to expand District residents' right to vote. One survived the state ratification process (approval of 3/4 of states), and one did not. On March 29, 1961, the states ratified the 23rd Amendment, allowing the District to elect the same number of electors for president and vice president as it "would be entitled if it were a State, but in no event more than the least populous State." Thus, District residents could now vote in presidential elections and select three electors.

Since the late 1880s, members of Congress have introduced almost 200 constitutional amendments to grant District residents voting rights in Congress. These proposals have taken a number of forms, such as allowing the District to elect one, two, or no Senators and one Representative, or as many representatives to which it would be entitled as if it were a state. Only one proposal, The D.C. Voting Rights Amendment, made it through the process to be presented to the states for ratification. In 1978, the Senate, joining an earlier House vote, approved a proposal providing that, for the purpose of electing Senators, Representatives, presidential electors, and ratifying amendments, the District would be treated as if it were a state. Like all proposed amendments, this amendment required approval of 3/4 of the states to become effective. Congress, as it often does, put a time limit on the ratification process, specifying a period of seven years. The amendment was ratified by 16 states but died in 1985, failing to get the required approval of 38 states within the required time.

Apart from constitutional amendments, Congress has considered three kinds of *legislative* options for giving District residents voting representation in Congress: (1) legislatively define the District as a state for the purpose of voting for federal officials (sometimes referred to as "nominal statehood"), (2) retrocede, or return, the District back to Maryland or simply allow District residents to vote in Maryland for federal officials; (3) *legislatively* grant the District statehood.

Nominal Statehood

From the early days of the Republic, there have been debates over whether the District is "nominally" a state. Proponents of nominal statehood argue that because certain words in the Constitution do not have rigid or fixed meanings, use of the word "state" in the Constitution can encompass the District. The Supreme Court initially rejected this view but, later in 1820, endorsed it, saying that the District could be treated as a state at least for the purposes of imposing taxes pursuant to Art. I, §2.

The Court later extended this view to other clauses, saying that, "Whether the District of Columbia constitutes a 'State or Territory' within the meaning of any particular statutory or constitutional provision depends upon the character and aim of the specific provision involved." Those arguing that Congress could confer "nominal statehood" on the District say that Congress could rely on its legislative power over the District and other constitutional powers and simply declare that "state, or "states," wherever those words appear in Art. I, §2, or §3 or both (e.g., "The House of Representatives shall be composed of Members chosen every second Year by the People of the several States") shall also mean the District of Columbia.

This approach has not found favor for many reasons, not the least of which is a Supreme Court opinion affirming a federal district court decision that rejected it outright. After a careful review of the relevant text, history, and precedents, the federal district court in *Adams v. Clinton* agreed with the defendant that, "the Constitution leaves no doubt that *only* the residents of *actual states* are entitled to representation." In particular, the majority noted that an examination of the language of Article I "makes clear just how deeply Congressional representation is tied to the structure of statehood."

Retrocession or Virtual Retrocession

Another avenue to secure voting rights and the benefits of statehood for District residents would be to retrocede District land to Maryland. Just as Congress retroceded Arlington and Alexandria back to Virginia in 1846, some commentators advocate for retrocession of the District, save for the National Capital Service Area, to Maryland. This would grant District residents the rights and privileges of living in a state without actually forming a new state. With this plan, Congress would retain dominion over land left as the national capital.

Following the precedent established by the Virginia retrocession, retroceding to Maryland would entail approval of the retrocession by District and Maryland voters and an act of Congress. Congress would shrink the national seat of government to a federal enclave comprising the Capitol, the White House, the Supreme Court, national monuments, and adjacent federal buildings. The Constitution places a maximum size for the seat of government ("not exceeding ten Miles square"), but it does not place a minimum size on the District. Some critics advance the "fixed form" argument to oppose this reading, arguing that a strict construction of the District clause means "once the cession was made and this 'district' became the seat of government, the authority of Congress over its size and location seems to have been exhausted." However, the Virginia precedent, and the Court's approval of that retrocession in *Phillips v. Payne*, fatally weakens this as a viable argument.

The 23rd Amendment presents another possible obstacle to retrocession. The amendment provides for at least three electoral votes for presidential elections for the District. Retroceding this land would make this amendment redundant because Maryland already has its own electoral votes as provided under the Constitution; but the remaining federal enclave, according to critics, would also continue to have its three electoral votes, even though, presumably only the First Family would now live in the nation's seat of government. Critics argue that an act of Congress cannot repeal a constitutional amendment. The rejoinder is that statehood would likely make the 23rd Amendment moot, either by making it no longer applicable to the District or by impliedly repealing it, but not explicitly doing so.

Since 1838, various bills have been introduced in Congress to retrocede all or part of the District to Maryland. None have passed. And if any were to pass, it is unclear whether Maryland would embrace the opportunity to annex the District or whether District residents would agree to the change. Both Maryland and the District would have to agree to retrocession for such a change to take place.

Statehood by Legislation

Aside from any attempt to legislatively grant voting representation to the District, Congress may have the power to create the state of New Columbia out of District land. Under this scenario, Congress could shrink the seat of government to an area containing only the Capitol building, the White House, the Supreme Court, national monuments, and adjacent federal buildings. The remaining District land could become the state of New Columbia via Congress's power to admit new states to the Union under Art. IV, §3. The only constitutionally required steps for the process of admitting a new state would be an admission bill passed by Congress and presentment of that bill to the president.

Some commentators have questioned whether creating a new state out of the District would destroy the original concept of the seat of government being independent of any state. The response is that Congress would still maintain exclusive control of the area designated as the capital. There is precedent for shrinking the size of the District. Again, however, such an approach could run afoul of the 23rd Amendment. But, as with retrocession, creating this new state would make the 23rd Amendment either moot or no longer applicable because, except perhaps for the First Family, there would not be any actual residents remaining in the federal enclave.

But, as with retrocession, the true obstacle to this approach is political; to pass an enabling act to create the state of New Columbia, the legislation must have bipartisan support, and it is quite unclear whether that support exists or can be mustered.

FUTURE IMPLICATIONS

Because of events that transpired well over 200 years ago, hundreds of thousands of residents in the District of Columbia have no vote in the Congress of the United States, even as to matters affecting entirely local interests. And because clause 17 vests Congress with the power to "exercise exclusive legislation in all cases whatsoever" over the District, Congress is empowered to pass all laws to govern the District, even ones entirely local in nature. The fact that District residents exercise any local authority at all arises from permission granted to them by Congress—permission that can be, and sometimes has been, readily withdrawn. Because of Congress's complete dominion over District residents, the late Senator Edward Kennedy and others have referred to the District as "the last colony."

Under these circumstances, it is quite likely that District residents and those who sympathize with their plight will continue to press for change. On the local governance front, there will likely be continued efforts by residents to attain control over the budgeting of local dollars. And, with respect to voting representation in Congress (and broader rights and responsibilities enjoyed by the citizens of other states) the matter of statehood or other paths to democratic reform are likely to arise. The political success of these efforts is difficult to predict, and some of the legal questions associated with them are complex and remain unsettled.

Budget Autonomy

Ever since the congressional passage of the Home Rule Act in 1973, local District of Columbia officials and District residents have chafed under provisions that require affirmative congressional approval for the District to spend its own local funds. This is not a trifling sum. Over half of the District's budget, approximately six billion dollars, comes from local fees and locally raised income, property, and sales taxes. And the Home Rule Act prescribes a specific process and timetable for District officials to create and approve its local budget, a timetable that prevents the District from adopting the calendar year as its fiscal year and which causes gaps in making timely expenditures, necessitating "bridge funding" until congressional approval takes place.

In 2012, the Council of the District of Columbia unanimously enacted the Local Budget Autonomy Act of 2012. It was signed by the mayor and ratified by the voters of the District of Columbia in an April 2013 referendum. Nevertheless the mayor and the chief financial officer of the District refused to implement the law, saying that they believed it was invalid under the Home Rule Act. The law provided that the District could spend its own fee and tax revenues without getting an affirmative annual appropriation from Congress. Rather, the Council would send its budget to Congress as it does with ordinary legislation and, as in such cases, the budget would become law after a 30-day *passive* review period unless Congress specifically rejected it. The question is whether the 2012 Budget Autonomy Act is a valid exercise of the amending process set out in the Home Rule Act or whether that amending action actually violated the limits placed on the amending authority in the Home Rule Act. A chief limit is that no amendment can change the respective roles of Congress, the president, and the federal

Office of Management and Budget in the enactment of the District's total budget. A federal District Court agreed that the Budget Autonomy Act was invalid but that ruling was vacated when the matter was later deemed moot. The issue remains unsettled. What is perfectly clear, however, is that Congress, if it chose to do so, could specifically grant the District the local budget autonomy it so clearly desires. The issue will remain less a matter of law and more a matter of politics.

Statehood and Intermediate Steps to Full Voting Rights

The only way for District residents to secure equal representation and full and *permanent* voting rights in Congress is statehood. But statehood via congressional legislation (shrink the District and create a state from the remainder) or a straightforward constitutional amendment has proven to be a very hard political sell. Supporters of statehood believe the key is educating the public about the District's plight and engaging in a vigorous political campaign akin to the civil rights struggles of the 1960s. This is likely to be a difficult and long-term project, and, in the meantime, supporters face a strategic dilemma: should residents pursue an incremental approach of increasing local autonomy over District affairs and some greater representation in Congress, or should they hold out for statehood exclusively?

Under an incremental approach, the end goal would remain statehood, but advocates would pursue a step-by-step approach, gradually posturing the District as if it were a state. This has already been happening in actions real and symbolic. The District exercises many powers of a state under the Home Rule Act, and it has pressed to assume autonomy over its local budget. The District's lawyer is no longer referred to as "corporation counsel" but as "attorney general," and some elected officials have suggested that the mayor and Council be called the governor and legislature. The advantages of incrementalism are that it might positively change public perceptions of the District's ability to govern itself, that Congress would ultimately see statehood as more palatable and less threatening, and that, in the meantime, the residents would, in fact, acquire greater autonomy and control over their local affairs.

But incrementalism carries disadvantages and risks. The first is the frustration that will come if greater autonomy is conferred and then snatched back by a new set of congressional leaders. Second is the danger of the compromises the District may be forced to make for modest and always contingent advances. To illustrate, legislation was proposed in the late 2000s that would have secured a voting representative in the House of Representatives for the District. On April 18, 2007, the House passed the District of Columbia Voting Rights Act of 2007, which would have provided for a single congressional district for the District of Columbia. To appease those who worried this would throw off the political balance in the House, the bill would have increased the House from 435 to 437 seats, adding an extra seat for Utah as well. Because the District is reliably Democratic and Utah is reliably Republican, this would have preserved the balance. The Senate version of the bill failed to pass, however.

The bill was introduced again in the House and Senate in 2009. This time it passed the Senate, but it included a hastily added amendment repealing most of the District's gun control laws. Although moderate House Democrats were willing to pass the bill with the amendment, D.C. voting rights advocates demanded a clean bill. Eventually, District Delegate Eleanor Holmes Norton, who introduced the bill, agreed with then-Majority Leader Steny Hoyer to table the bill, finding the amendment to be too difficult to accept.

A final disadvantage of incrementalism is that its success may sap the fervor for statehood and dilute the arguments that may, in purer form, ultimately win. This is particularly true of the effort to secure a vote for the delegate in the House of Representatives. If such a vote were recognized, opponents of statehood could then argue that the District does have a vote and one, in their opinion, more commensurate with the District's geographic size and population. Supporters of statehood would thereby lose perhaps their greatest rhetorical weapon—taxation without representation. It's much easier to make one's case by saying, "We have no vote in Congress," than it would be to say, "We have a vote, but we want more votes."

What is clear is that the status of the District and Congress's exclusive, plenary power over it will continue to be a contentious political issue.

FURTHER READING

Boyd, Eugene. 2007. *District of Columbia Voting Representation in Congress: An Analysis of Legislative Proposals* (CRS Report No. RL33830). Washington, D.C.: Congressional Research Service. http://assets.opencrs.com/rpts/RL33830_20070130.pdf.

Cheh, Mary M. 2014. Theories of Representation: For the District of Columbia, Only Statehood Will Do. *William & Mary Bill of Rights Journal* 23: 65–87.

Garg, Arjun. 2007. A Capital Idea: Legislation to Give the District of Columbia a Vote in the House of Representative. *Columbia Journal of Law and Social Problems* 41: 1–51.

Lois E. Adams v. William Jefferson Clinton, 90 F. Supp. 2d 35 (D.D.C.), affirmed 531 U.S. 941 (2000).

Raven-Hansen, Peter. 1975. Congressional Representation for the District of Columbia: A Constitutional Analysis. *Harvard Journal on Legislation* 12: 275–96.

Schrag, Philip G. 1990. The Future of District of Columbia Home Rule. *The Catholic University Law Review* 39: 311–71.

16 THE POWER TO APPROPRIATE MONEY AND TO BUDGET

Craig Goodman

Article I, section 9, clause 7
No Money shall be drawn from the Treasury but in Consequence of Appropriations made by Law; and a regular Statement and Account of the Receipts and Expenditures of all public Money shall be published from time to time.

KEY TERMS

Appropriations provide the legislative branch with the power of the purse. This requires Congress pass a bill in order to spend money from the federal treasury. These bills must be passed annually by September 30, because if they are not, the government does not have the ability to continue funding for various programs. The bills represent the fiscal policy of the federal government. (See "Fiscal policy" below.)

The **Budget and Accounting Act (1921)** required the president to submit a budget to Congress each year. The initial agency requests for funding would be reviewed by the president's staff rather than made directly to Congress. The legislation also established a Bureau of the Budget (renamed the Office of Management and Budget in 1970) as well as the Government Accounting Office, as the financial and performance audit institution of the Congress. It was renamed the Government Accountability Office in 2004.

The **Congressional Budget and Impoundment Control Act (1974)** established a formal budgetary process in Congress via the establishment of Budget Committees in each chamber. Each year, the committees are required to create a budget resolution by April 15 that provides a total amount of money available to the Appropriations

Committees for the coming fiscal year. The budget resolution is not subject to a presidential veto, and it does not specify how the appropriations dollars should be spent, but it sets out the total amount of spending for the Appropriations Committees in the fiscal year. It is designed to provide a clear statement of government spending priorities for the fiscal year. The legislation also established the Congressional Budget Office. (See "Impoundment" and "Fiscal year" below.)

Continuing resolutions are resolutions that extend the appropriations bills from the previous fiscal year when Congress is unable to pass appropriations bills by the September 30 deadline. Many of these continuing resolutions (CRs) are short-term extensions that might last a few days or weeks until congressional negotiators can finalize details. However, a CR can be extended for a full year by simply extending the previous appropriations act rather than passing a new one.

Discretionary spending is the portion of the budget controlled by the annual appropriations process. Defense spending is the largest share of discretionary spending, but overall discretionary spending only comprises one-third of all federal spending. This includes spending on programs supporting education, scientific research, and public lands. (See "Mandatory spending.")

Earmarks refer to specific provisions inserted in appropriations bills that direct federal spending to a specific project. Earmarks were prohibited from 2011. For individual members of Congress, earmarks were valuable because they allowed for credit-claiming and often generated positive publicity for the congressman who inserted the earmark. The use of earmarks was part of legislative strategy, whereby congressional leaders could offer benefits to individual members in exchange for support on other pieces of legislation. Rank-and-file members also had a greater incentive to support appropriations bills because, if the bills did not pass, the funding contained in the earmark would not arrive in their districts.

Fiscal policy is the way the government influences the nation's economy by raising or lowering its spending or the taxes. Fiscal policy is different than monetary policy, which is how the Federal Reserve Bank influences the economy by adjusting the supply of money in the economy.

The **fiscal year** is the federal government's "accounting" year. For budget and accounting purposes businesses and governments do not usually use the "calendar year," but some other convenient "year." Since 1974, the federal fiscal year has started on October 1 and ended on September 30 of each year.

Impoundment occurs when the president refuses to spend money appropriated by the Congress. The president usually says that the appropriation unnecessarily increases the national debt.

Mandatory spending is also known as entitlements, and the continued growth of this category of spending has crowded out discretionary spending. Spending on these entitlement programs makes up the largest share of the federal budget. These programs, such as Social Security and Medicare, are funded through permanent laws that create a legal obligation to pay benefits to an individual who meets the requirements established by law. Instead of the annual appropriations process, the Treasury Department is authorized to spend these funds without Congress acting on an annual basis. (See "Discretionary spending," above.)

Reconciliation is a process that allows the passage of a bill changing existing laws with a simple majority, but the bill must follow fairly restrictive procedural requirements. Reconciliation is especially critical in the Senate to get around a filibuster.

Regular order is orderly and deliberative lawmaking without unusual or tricky procedures. The majority rules, but the minority has its opportunity for input.

A **rider** is a provision added to a bill that has little or nothing to do with the subject matter of the bill. When the underlying bill is passed, the added "rider" is also becomes law.

An **omnibus bill** combines two or more appropriations bills into a single bill. Packaging multiple pieces of legislation together is designed to minimize potential objections from the floor.

Sequester/sequestration is an automatic decrease in all federal spending, except Social Security and interest payments.

HISTORY AND DEVELOPMENT

One of the most important powers available to the legislative branch of the United States government is the power of the purse. The power of the purse gives Congress the responsibility for making decisions about spending in the United States and offers an important check on the other branches of government. Not only does Congress have responsibility for passing legislation detailing how federal monies should be spent, Congress also shares responsibility with the president for establishing a budget for the United States for each fiscal year.

The First Congress in 1789 appropriated a total of $639,000 to cover the expenses of the federal government. The first appropriations bill had four classes of expenditures and was covered in 13 lines of statute. Today, the federal government spends sums like that in a matter of seconds, but new programs cannot occur until Congress appropriates funds for their operation. In addition, Congress has the power to eliminate funds, which can serve as a powerful check on executive action. In exercising its appropriation power, Congress requires that agencies justify their existence and their various programs, actions, policies, and initiatives on an annual basis. Congress thus has regular opportunities to bring an allegedly wayward agency in line by threatening to change or reduce the amount of money appropriated to that agency.

The Constitution vested both chambers of the legislature with responsibility for appropriations, but the differences in size and composition between the House and Senate make finding annual agreement on levels of spending a significant challenge, especially when the respective legislative bodies are controlled by different parties. Strategic bargaining between the two houses on funding is thus commonplace. The concept of budgeting, meanwhile, is not formally specified in the Constitution, and the idea was introduced in the United States more than 100 years after the Constitution was ratified. Despite hopes that it would get federal spending under control, the process has not worked as intended.

During the Colonial era, settlers asserted that the power of the purse rested with the legislative branch, and control over spending was one of the bulwarks of legislative power. When deliberations began at the Constitutional Convention, the fifth resolution from the Committee of the Whole was that each branch should have the right of originating acts. The first mention of exercising control over appropriations bills occurred on June 13, 1787, as Elbridge Gerry offered a motion that such bills should originate in the first branch of the government—the House of Representatives. Gerry argued that the House was elected directly by the people and should hold the purse strings. Pierce Butler objected, asserting that the Senate should not be discriminated against, because it would not be like the English of House of Lords. Furthermore, Butler argued that if the Senate did not have a role, talented men would not be interested in serving in that body, and the Senate would be more likely to attach other clauses to money bills. Later in the debate, Charles Pinckney and Roger Sherman discussed the question in the context of the structure of the Senate since no decision had been made about proportionality. The Convention voted against Gerry's resolution 3–8 with only Delaware, New York, and Virginia in favor. The issue of appropriations briefly occurred on June 30, 1787, as Benjamin Franklin raised the issue in context of the proper structure of the bicameral legislature. Franklin argued that when Congress appropriated money the delegates should have suffrage in proportion to the sums they contribute to the Treasury as a means of finding compromise because otherwise he argued that the smaller states would have the power of giving away money from the larger states.

On July 5, 1787, Gerry reported a recommendation from the Committee of the Whole House that all bills that involved raising or appropriating money should originate in the lower house and no money shall be withdrawn from the Treasury except through appropriations first passed by the first house. James Madison argued that such a concession was not especially worthwhile and the historical record suggested that depriving the Senate of the ability to originate or alter appropriations bills would negate the idea of checks and balances. Furthermore, Madison argued that it would probably not be too hard to find a member of the House who would be willing to offer amendments to spending bills on behalf of a senator.

On July 6, 1787, the Convention continued the debate over the proper responsibility for appropriations. Gouverneur Morris suggested that it was right to deprive the second branch of the legislature the opportunity to develop proposals. It would provide a valuable point of comparison. But James Wilson could not see any reason for such discrimination. Hugh Williamson suggested that, if both branches did not have the power, the responsibility should be confined to the second branch because they would be watched more carefully than in the first branch. However, George Mason raised concerns about Senate control because they were not close to the people and could forget from where the money originated, and this could contribute to the development of an aristocracy. As the Convention continued the debate on July 6, 1787, the delegates continued to frame the question of origination of appropriations bills in the context of representation as well as whether it would effectively lead to gridlock if the two branches could not agree on bills. The motion that eventually carried restricted appropriations bills to the House. The vote was confusing, however, with five states in favor (Connecticut, Delaware, Maryland, New Jersey, and North Carolina), three states opposed (Pennsylvania, South Carolina, and Virginia), and three states divided (Georgia, Massachusetts, and New York). Given these divisions, the Convention was compelled to vote whether the question of restricting appropriations bills to the House had passed with a majority and the vote was affirmative, 9–2.

On July 14, 1787, John Rutledge called for a reconsideration of money bills in the first branch of government. Not surprisingly, Gerry was against any reconsideration because he believed that it was the cornerstone of accommodation between the delegates. During the course of this new debate, the delegates suggested that compromise was essential, and a committee had already been appointed to find one. If the delegates could not accept the committee's proposal, perhaps it would be time to consider the Convention at an end. Caleb Strong suggested that the smaller states had made quite a concession on money bills originating in the House so they might expect some consideration, such as equality in the Senate. The Convention would continue discussing matters on July 16, 1787, but there were no votes or detailed discussions on the matter of money bills. Still, the Convention voted 5–4–1 to adopt the report of the committee.

On August 8, 1787, Pinckney moved to strike Art. I, §5 of the draft that allowed only the House to originate and amend appropriations bills, arguing that it could clog the government's operations and asserting that if the Senate could be trusted with other great powers, it could be trusted to originate money bills. Ghorum [Gorham] opposed allowing the Senate to originate money bills, but decided that they should be permitted to amend them. Gouverneur Morris suggested the Senate should have the right to originate money bills because they would sit constantly and had a smaller number so they could prepare bills correctly as well as preventing delays. Colonel Mason did not wish to cover this ground again at the Convention because striking Section 5 would undermine the broader compromises that had been made concerning representation in the legislative branch. Furthermore, he believed the Senate was an aristocratic body that should never be permitted to handle the purse strings. As with many things, the delegates were divided over whether giving the House sole responsibility for appropriations was such a great advantage that it nullified the concept of equality in the Senate, while Ellsworth believed the clause was of no consequence. Madison favored striking the clause, and the Convention voted 7–4 to strike it. New Hampshire, Massachusetts, Connecticut, and North Carolina were opposed, while New Jersey, Pennsylvania, Delaware, Maryland, Virginia, South Carolina, and Georgia were in favor.

The following day, August 9, 1787, Randolph and Williamson expressed concerns about the decision of the Convention to strike responsibility for appropriations bills from the House of Representatives and suggested that the move endangered the success of the plan. Franklin noted that the origination of money bills in the House and the equality of votes was connected by compromise, but other delegates suggested that giving the House sole responsibility might be an important source of tension between the two chambers. As the delegates debated the powers of the legislative branch, several members of the Convention, including Mason, Randolph, and Gerry, struggled to protect the right of the House to originate national spending and taxing plans without Senate amendment because their states of Virginia and Massachusetts would exercise more power in the House of Representatives. Allowing the House sole responsibility for controlling revenues and appropriations would mean that simple majorities in the House would make these critical decisions, but Madison in particular expressed concern about giving the House so much power. As the Committee of Detail hammered out provisions, its approach was consistent with the original compromise, whereby the Senate would not have the ability to alter or amend bills for appropriating federal dollars.

After the Committee of Detail reported to the Convention, the delegates struck the clause over the opposition of the New England states and North Carolina. Not surprisingly, some of the delegates fought to overturn this decision. Williamson described the Senate as a "House of Lords," while Madison argued that the origination of money bills in the House would limit the role of the Senate. Two efforts to restore House control over appropriations bills failed 4–7. Wilson argued that war, commerce, and revenue were the great objects of government, and that all three were closely connected with money. He thus reasoned that prohibiting the Senate from originating bills would mean that chamber would not be able to craft necessary and important bills. Gerry suggested that the plan would fail to gain popular support if the Senate was not restrained from originating appropriations bills, because the people would only accept their immediate representatives from meddling with their purses. John Dickinson suggested that experience in the states should be a guide, and eight states allowed the other branch to amend while vesting responsibility for origination in the popular branch.

On August 15, 1787, Strong offered an amendment stating that appropriations bills should originate in the House of Representatives, but that the Senate could propose or concur in amendments as they would in other bills. The motion was seconded by Colonel Mason so the power of the Senate would be limited and Ghorum [Gorham] argued this amendment was important because without it the Senate would acquire the habit of preparing money bills and this would eventually develop into an exclusive responsibility.

On September 8, 1787, the Convention finally voted on the final language that appeared in the Constitution concerning appropriations bills. The vote was 9–2, with Delaware and Maryland casting the only votes in the negative. The effect of this compromise was a rule that provided the House with little bite because of the unlimited authority of the Senate to propose amendments, and gave the Senate equal authority over the federal budget. The decision allowing the Senate nearly equal influence over the budget at the expense of the House helped contribute to the opposition of the Constitution from Mason, Randolph, and Gerry.

From the Early Congresses to the Civil War

While the Constitution granted the legislative branch the responsibility for appropriations in Art. I, §9, cl. 7, it did not provide any specific instructions as to how Congress should exercise those powers. After the Constitution was ratified, responsibility for crafting appropriations bills rested with the House Ways and Means Committee and the Senate Finance Committee. In the earliest Congresses, the executive branch would develop a proposal and the House would consider the request in the Committee of the Whole. Following this debate, the House would appoint a select committee to work on the specific items in the bill (Stewart, 1989). Such simplicity did not last. By 1794, Congress was considering two appropriations (also known as supply) bills: one for the government and one for the military. During the first few decades of the nineteenth century, the number of annual appropriations bills increased to include bills for fortifications (1823), rivers and harbors (1826), post offices (1844), and the legislative, executive, and judicial branches (1856). One aspect of simplicity that remained was the general practice that these appropriations bills should be free of policy-related matters and only provide specific sums of money for a fixed period of time.

Federal spending during the early years of the republic remained relatively stable, but by the 1840s the rivers and harbors bills had become a prime vehicle whereby House members could funnel federal dollars into their districts. President James K. Polk actually vetoed two of these bills in 1846 and 1847 as too costly. Pension fraud relating to the Revolutionary War and the War of 1812 was another issue. Besides the challenges of spending bills, the antebellum Congresses struggled with riders—that is, policy measures on appropriations bills. Members embraced legislative riders as tactics to pursue their own policy preferences. With the increased frequency of riders, the House adopted rules preventing expenditures that were not authorized by law. However, it also softened the rule to allow appropriations for public works projects. House members soon found ways to get around the rules.

While Congress struggled with the specific amounts of money to appropriate, no significant increases in spending occurred except during periods of war. Such events often increased the debt, but it was often paid down, as peacetime revenues from tariffs were normally sufficient to cover expenditures. Generally speaking, it would be an accurate assessment to describe federal spending as contributing very little to the overall economy. The Civil War marked a fundamental change, as the federal government spent more than $1.3 billion dollars during the last year of the war and accumulated a debt of nearly $2.5 billion dollars.

Appropriations after the Civil War

One of the major changes in the appropriations process following the Civil War was the creation of separate appropriations committees in the House and Senate. The House created their committee in 1865, and the Senate followed suit in 1867. The decision to cleave appropriations from Ways & Means was prompted by a growing concern that the committee was overworked. Little public discussion or rancor surrounded the proposed change. Some of the members, notably Thaddeus Stevens (R-PA), noted that the change could decrease coordination between spending and taxing, but the short-term demands of workload took priority in the decision to create the Appropriations Committees.

Congress again faced the heavy use of legislative riders in the 1870s. In 1876 the House adopted the Holman Rule, which permitted substantive amendments to appropriations bills so long as they reduced federal spending. President Rutherford B. Hayes, a Republican, was especially opposed to the rule, because he believed that it threatened to strip him of his veto power. Over time, the rule became a mechanism that allowed House Democrats to advance their policy interests. For example, Democrats in the South, eager to establish Jim Crow laws, used the rule to defund federal elections laws. But in 1885, the House returned to the 1838 rules regarding riders, with the exception of appropriations for public works. The return of a Democratic president,

Grover Cleveland, meant there was less of a need to control spending, and the Holman Rule was eliminated. However, the rule would subsequently be reinstated on several occasions during periods of divided government that pitted Democratic majorities in the House against Republican presidents.

Another major development was decentralization of control over appropriations to the legislative committees. In the 49th Congress (1885–1887), the Rules Committee created a proposal that would allow Appropriations to retain control over bills that overlapped committee jurisdictions (examples included fortifications and the District of Columbia) while giving legislative committees, such as Military Affairs, Rivers and Harbors, and Agriculture, control over their own spending bills. While Samuel Randall (D-PA) filed a minority report arguing that Appropriations served as a guardian of the Treasury, the House overwhelmingly adopted the measure because it gave more members influence over government spending decisions. While not the only cause of increased federal spending in the late nineteenth century, the decentralization of the appropriations process has nonetheless been frequently cited as a factor. By the close of the 1800s, the entire process of determining a budget had become uncoordinated and decentralized to such an extent that many lawmakers expressed concern that it was hindering the nation's ability to responsibly budget for its needs.

An Executive Budget

By the early part of the twentieth century, Congress was struggling with deficits because congressional committees made recommendations for agency budgets. Congress considered those committee recommendations in a piecemeal fashion without any consideration for aggregate levels of spending. The solution to the problem was allowing the president to prepare a national budget. By thinking about expenditures and revenues at the same time, the president would provide an opportunity for investigating the trade-offs between spending and taxing. Before World War I, President William Howard Taft called for an executive budget because the president was responsible for managing the executive branch. Reformers during the early part of the twentieth century wanted "executive leadership," where the president would rely on experts to help create a federal budget.

However, it was not until World War I, which brought a dramatic increase in federal spending and significant expansion of the federal debt, that Congress would consider including the president in the budgetary process. The challenge, then, was to find a reform proposal that would allow the president some latitude to set the agenda while also retaining Congress's authority to make appropriations. This challenge was met when Congress passed the Budget and Accounting Act of 1921. While granting the president the ability to make recommendations, Congress also responded by restoring the role of the Appropriations Committees so there would be a counterweight to the president. During the 1920s, the federal budget was reduced, as there was general agreement on the need for balanced budgets.

The efficiencies gained in the 1920s disappeared when the Great Depression started in 1929. In two years, federal revenues were reduced by 50 percent, and demands for federal intervention to relieve poverty and hunger soared. The Roosevelt administration was initially committed to balanced budgets, but it gradually came to embrace the ideas of John Maynard Keynes, who argued that governments should run deficits to stimulate economic demand. While the New Deal programs implemented by Roosevelt did not represent an organized and comprehensive set of proposals, federal expenditures increased dramatically, as did federal spending as a share of the gross national product. In terms of the bigger picture, the lasting consequence of the New Deal was that the federal government came to bear a much greater responsibility for the health of the economy.

The Modern Appropriations Process

The Appropriations Committees occupy a challenging spot in the congressional hierarchy because they need the support of a majority of members if their recommendations regarding federal spending are going to make it into law. When the Appropriations Committees overstep their bounds, the rest of the chamber can restrict their powers, as happened in the House in the late nineteenth century, when the legislative committees favored higher levels of spending than Appropriations. The power and influence of the Appropriations Committee reached its peak in the middle of the twentieth century. No longer present in the committees were the old norms of restraint and protecting the federal treasury. Members often used their positions on the committee to serve as advocates for programs they favored.

One of the classic studies of the appropriations process in Congress is Richard Fenno's *The Power of the Purse*. Fenno's study occurred against a very different backdrop for the Appropriations Committees than before World War II. Federal revenues generated through higher wartime taxes made it much less painful to support the expansion of various forms of federal spending. Fenno noted that power was dispersed to the subcommittees, and one of the common practices was universalism, where benefits were distributed to all members of the committee regardless of party status, in order to build as large a coalition as possible in support of the appropriations bills.

Not long after Fenno concluded his study of the appropriations process, the broader economic environment soured, and this created new pressures on the federal government. Besides the economic factors, internal pressures had eroded the status of the Appropriations Committees. Rank-and-file members had larger staffs, and power was no longer vested as strongly within committee chairmen. The majority Democrats had empowered subcommittees and the caucus more generally. The event that triggered a new change in structure, however, was the decision of President Richard Nixon to impound funds and not spend money the Congress had decided to allocate to different programs. In addition, Congress realized that it did not have the capacity or authority to develop an independent budget plan. The Budget and Accounting Act of 1921 was good for the executive branch, but not for Congress. In 1974, Congress passed the Congressional Budget and Impoundment Control Act (CBICA), which expanded the budgetary capacity of the legislative branch to compete with the president.

After the CBICA, two budgets are introduced each year, one in the House and one in the Senate, although neither is binding. The two chambers are supposed to complete the consolidated budget resolution by April 15 each year. This budget resolution is designed to bring recommendations for appropriations and revenue into a single document and make a conscious decision about funding priorities, the federal deficit, and the total public debt of the United States. Once the budget resolution, which is not subject to a presidential veto, has passed, the Appropriations Committees can start their work based on the allocations provided.

In addition to the budget resolution that established a general framework for spending, CBICA established the Congressional Budget Office (CBO) to provide Congress with nonpartisan, quality budgetary and economic information comparable to what the president received from the Office of Management and Budget. Generally speaking, CBO maintains a fairly low profile on Capitol Hill, as it generates estimates of the costs associated with pieces of proposed legislation. Under a rules change pushed through by Republicans in the 114th Congress (2015–2017), however, the CBO will be required to implement "dynamic scoring" for pieces of legislation in order to capture the broader economic effects of a proposed piece of legislation. The idea behind the rules change is that legislation has broader impacts beyond simple dollars and cents, and analysts should attempt to determine the relationship between legislation and those effects. Critics have suggested that so-called dynamic scoring creates misleadingly rosy economic forecasts for cutting taxes and other conservative economic policy goals. While this fight over scoring legislation may appear arcane, estimates from the CBO can influence strategy on the floor in both chambers of Congress.

One of the other tools available to Congress under the Congressional Budget and Impoundment Control Act of 1974 is reconciliation. The process of reconciliation allows the passage of a bill changing existing laws with a simple majority (especially critical in the Senate), but the bill must follow fairly restrictive procedural requirements. For example, it cannot increase the federal deficit beyond a ten-year window. While reconciliation can be a powerful tool to change existing federal laws on spending (entitlements, for example), the possibility of a filibuster remains.

While passed with good intentions, there is little evidence that the new CBICA budgetary structure plays much of a role in reducing spending. Moreover, the new structure created conflict with other Congressional actors, who were not especially interested in following the Budget Committees' guidelines.

The changes that started in 1974 also altered federal budgets. They are now a very complex undertaking, requiring the participation of the president and members of Congress. Another challenge is that funds do not flow into a single account. In addition to the general account, there are special funds and trust funds where the revenues are reserved for specific purposes, such as for the Social Security Trust fund. This increases the challenges to developing a unified plan linking revenues and expenditures.

Struggling with Polarization

Another consequence of a more centralized budget process was that it became vulnerable to growing political polarization. Because the new process highlighted totals at the beginning of the process and established clear winners and losers, Democrats and Republicans found themselves on opposite sides. Adding to the polarization, deficits emerged as a significant issue during the 1980s. Both sides expressed desires for a balanced budget, but disagreed on the best way forward to accomplish that, and neither side was particularly interested in engaging in bargaining and compromise.

Congress eventually passed the Balanced Budget and Deficit Control Act of 1985 (Gramm-Rudman-Hollings, GRH), which required annual spending cuts until the deficit was reduced. The purpose of the bill was to bring congressional negotiators to the table to find spending cuts and/or increased revenues; otherwise sequestration would occur. Sequestration is an automatic decrease in all federal spending, except Social Security and interest payments. The bottom line is that not all federal spending was subject to restrictions. Only slightly more than a quarter of all Federal spending was fully subject to sequestration. Some scholars have characterized GRH as an example of Congress abdicating its power and admitting that the budgetary process had spun so far out of control that the only solution was surrendering the power of the purse to a mechanical rule (Wildavky and Caiden, 1997). In the end, GRH was a failure because it did not produce the bargaining and compromise needed to find reasonable solutions. The proposed cuts mandated under GRH were unpalatable—more than 30 percent in both defense and non-defense programs. GRH was a blunt object for finding budgetary savings, and much of the budget was not fully available for sequestration.

The combination of structural problems with GRH and economic problems ranging from recessionary conditions to a crisis in the Savings and Loan industry, led Congress to pass the Budget Enforcement Act (BEA) in 1990. One of the most notable changes in the BEA was the creation of separate categories for different types of discretionary spending, so that if spending *within* a category exceeded the target for the fiscal year, spending would be reduced in that category the following year to avoid increasing the deficit. The second change was the adoption of PAYGO (Pay As You Go), which required Congress to pay for any changes to programs or establishment of new programs that increased spending. In effect, PAYGO discouraged spending because it transformed budgeting into a zero-sum game, where new dollars for one program had to be offset with cutting dollars from another program.

The new Republican majority in the 104th Congress (1995–1997) ushered in a new era in appropriations politics. The new majority attempted to grant the president a line-item veto. This is another example of Congress abandoning its power of the purse by transferring responsibility to the president to make decisions over cutting spending. The Line Item Veto Act allowed the president to sign the bill and then go back and eliminate taxing and spending items. After the president identified measures that would be removed, Congress could overturn presidential rescissions with a two-thirds vote. The Supreme Court in a 6–3 vote struck down the legislation because it violated the presentment clause (Art. I, §7, cl 2 and 3), since the president could unilaterally strike items from legislation passed by Congress.

Changing the Appropriations Committee was essential if the GOP wanted to follow through on its promises to reduce spending. Speaker Newt Gingrich picked Representative Robert Livingston (R-LA) as new chairman of the committee and required committee members to support efforts to cut the federal budget. In addition to reducing the size of the federal budget, the new Republican majority also wanted to use appropriations bills as a vehicle for substantive legislating—using riders to affect policy. Despite House prohibitions on such tactics, the Republicans controlled the

Rules Committee, which was responsible for setting terms of debate on the House floor. Republicans in control of the Rules Committee allowed the strategy to proceed. Naturally, partisanship grew within the Appropriations Committee, as the Democratic minority no longer had much of an incentive to support the work of the committee. The use of riders contributed to the shutdown of the federal government in 1995 and 1996.

While the budget shutdowns in 1995–1996 were not a preferred solution, there was a silver lining to the confrontations. President Clinton and the Republican leadership in Congress recognized the need for compromise and negotiated deficit reduction acts in 1995 and 1997, which generated fiscal improvements and produced budgetary surpluses. This short-term period of cooperation would not last, and significant budgetary challenges would emerge in the first two decades of the twenty-first century.

Upon his election in 2000, President George W. Bush made cutting taxes one of his major domestic priorities. He succeeded in reducing marginal tax rates through the budget reconciliation process. The tax cuts would expire after ten years, if not reauthorized. Following the September 11, 2001, terrorist attacks, federal spending on defense rapidly increased, and, combined with the Bush tax cuts, the size of the budget deficit increased as well. One of the consequences of the increased deficit was a fiscal crisis that led Republicans to call for significantly restricting entitlement and domestic discretionary spending—the so-called "starve the beast" strategy that David Stockman had articulated during President Reagan's administration. But after President Barack Obama's inauguration in 2009, he worked with congressional Democrats to pass the American Recovery and Reinvestment Act, an $800 billion economic stimulus package designed to push the United States out of its so-called Great Recession. The passage of the stimulus bill and the Affordable Care Act (also known as Obamacare) ranked among the greatest triumphs of Obama's first term, but they came at a significant political cost, as the 2010 midterm elections produced a Republican majority in the House and reintroduced divided government.

The Republican majority in the House changed the political calculations, and the growing size of the federal deficit forced negotiations between the two sides. In 2010, President Obama established the Fiscal Responsibility Commission (Bowles-Simpson), but it failed to produce a plan that would generate bipartisan support. As Republicans and Democrats struggled to find a solution to raising the debt ceiling in 2011, Congress passed the Budget Control Act of 2011. This legislation established annual caps on domestic and defense discretionary spending over ten years and required a "super-committee" of twelve members to find another $1.2 trillion dollars in spending cuts; otherwise the cuts would occur through sequestration and fall evenly on defense and domestic discretionary spending (much like Gramm-Rudman, most of the largest special fund, like Social Security, could not be cut). The super-committee failed to produce a plan, and Representative Paul Ryan (R-WI) and Senator Patty Murray (D-WA) negotiated a two-year agreement (the Bipartisan Budget Act of 2013) that would lift the sequester budget caps, but in the absence of a longer agreement, that agreement would expire, and Congress would face tighter budgetary caps for the upcoming fiscal year, 2016. Republicans and Democrats have drawn lines in the sand, with Republicans wanting to adhere to the budgetary caps, but agreed to increase defense spending by designating it as emergency spending and not subject to the sequester caps. President Obama has threatened to veto any bills that do not provide a comparable increase in funding for domestic programs.

In September 2015, Speaker John Boehner made a dramatic announcement that he was resigning from Congress to avoid subjecting rank-and-file Republicans to a fight over his leadership with members of the more conservative House Freedom Caucus. In the days after his resignation, Speaker Boehner announced his intentions to "clear the barn" for the next speaker by negotiating agreements on spending and raising the debt ceiling, and he was able to follow through on that commitment. However, the budget deal raised the sequester caps for the next two years, allowing Congress to spend more money—but it does not guarantee that a government shutdown will not occur, because Congress still must write the actual appropriations bills, and some Republicans have pledged to use those individual appropriations to push policy riders that President Obama will certainly oppose and possibly veto.

In sum, fights over appropriations and the budget have become increasingly partisan affairs. Even the adoption of a budgetary process in 1974 was not enough to force legislators to make decisions on the basis of neutral criteria. Further, the breakdown in the process has empowered the executive branch to exert more control. The inability to create a workable process for resolving difficult choices means future Congresses will need to confront the consequences of forty years of partisan polarization and budgetary failure.

Other issues and considerations are likely to weigh on Congress's ability to exercise its power of the purse as well. For example, the establishment of the 1974 budgetary process, coupled with other statutory changes, created new obstacles for Congress in exercising its power of the purse. The process of shaping appropriations bills is heavily influenced by certain norms. The first of these norms is that the House of Representatives generally acts first in writing the spending bills and the Senate acts second. Each chamber considers their appropriations bills, and the differences are usually resolved via a conference committee. However, this regular order has broken down, as both chambers routinely miss the April 15 deadline for the budget resolution, and many appropriations bills are not brought to the floor. The absence of individual appropriations bills denies rank-and-file members in both chambers the ability to offer amendments and vote. This means fewer opportunities to engage in position-taking and credit-claiming (Oleszek 2011).

In recent years, Congress has also been unable to pass the thirteen annual appropriations bills and has been forced to rely on a series of continuing resolutions and omnibus bills in order to keep the federal government operating. A continuing resolution means that Congress effectively abandons the effort to pass a new set of appropriations bills for the next fiscal year. Alternatively, Congress may choose to combine two or more appropriations bills into a single legislative vehicle, called an omnibus bill. Packaging multiple pieces of legislation together is designed to minimize potential objections from the floor.

In sum, as the appropriations process has broken down, nearly 60 percent of the time since 1975, Congress has abandoned the use of regular order and relied on large omnibus packages in order to fulfill constitutional obligations. Some of the changes stem from the Republican insistence on using the Appropriations Committee as a means of securing policy goals, and since the House can no longer serve as the anchor, it has encouraged the Senate Appropriations Committee to take a more active role by writing complete bills rather than waiting for the House. This way of doing business has served to increase institutional tension, and the executive branch is no longer as deferential to Congress on matters of appropriations.

One of the first promises Senator Mitch McConnell (R-KY) made, after becoming Majority Leader in the Senate in 2015, was to return to regular order for appropriations. But scholars such as Peter Hanson have argued that while Senator McConnell may favor such a change, it is highly unlikely to occur in the near future, for several reasons. While the Senate may write their own appropriations bills, the tradition is that the Senate does not consider bills not passed in the House. In addition, the Senate is generally at a bill-crafting disadvantage, because the rules of the Senate make it much easier for a single senator to filibuster an appropriations bill or offer an unlimited number of amendments. As a result, Senate leaders become more likely to pull appropriations bills from the floor and look to package as many as possible in an omnibus bill, which further restricts opportunities available to rank-and-file senators. Combine the rules of the Senate with high levels of polarization, and the roots of congressional failure to work through appropriations bills in regular order are clear (Hanson 2014).

In addition to the tensions between the House and Senate and the inability to follow regular order, the elimination of earmarks fundamentally changed the nature of appropriations politics, even though they only comprised a tiny fraction of all federal spending. The chairman of the House Appropriations Committee used to be an especially valuable gavel because of his ability to distribute favored spending to members in the form of earmarks. However, the House banned the use of earmarks in 2011, and that has reduced the clout of the chairman. In some respects the absence of earmarks has served to reduce the ability of Congress to engage in bargaining and compromise because there is nothing to grease the wheels. Earmarks were important for members because they allowed members to respond to their districts and gave the legislature greater control over federal spending rather than leaving as much discretion in the hands of bureaucratic agencies. While earmarking remains prohibited, members of Congress have found a workaround—lettermarking (Mills et al., forthcoming). This practice involves legislators writing to the heads of an agency requesting that specific projects in their district be retained. The evidence suggests, however, that this practice is not nearly as effective as earmarking.

FUTURE IMPLICATIONS

Despite the efforts of reformers to improve the process, Congress continues to struggle with its responsibilities to complete the annual appropriations process and pass a budget in a timely fashion. The budget establishes a framework, but much of the total federal spending is effectively on autopilot because of entitlements. As a result, the annual appropriations bills that are supposed to provide for control over federal agencies are significantly weakened. This is an effect of a disjointed pluralism, where members add new institutional forms, such as the Budget Committees, without dismantling the existing institutions, such as the Appropriations Committees, and fail to provide a rational overall structure. The end result is that contradictory objectives promote battles rather than stable and coherent solutions.

The combination of polarized political parties, a constitutional system that separates responsibility between the legislative and executive branches, fundamental differences over the scope of the national government, and relatively close margins of control, suggest that Congress will likely not be able to truly fulfill its responsibilities regarding the power of the purse for some time to come. Instead, showdowns over appropriations bills are likely to remain common in the near future, as is the reliance on using omnibus bills to package multiple appropriations bills in a single legislative vehicle. This fragmented budgetary process will not be sufficient to help provide clarity, and so Congress is likely to lurch from manufactured crisis to manufactured crisis, further cementing its reputation as the least-liked branch of the national government.

FURTHER READING

Evans, Diana. 2004. *Greasing the Wheels: Using Pork Barrel Projects to Build Majority Coalitions in Congress*. New York: Cambridge University Press.

Fenno, Richard. 1966. *The Power of the Purse: Appropriations Politics in Congress*. Boston: Little, Brown and Company.

Fisher, Louis. 1975. *Presidential Spending Power*. Princeton, NJ: Princeton University Press.

Hanson, Peter. 2014. *Too Weak to Govern: Majority Party Power and Appropriations in the U.S. Senate*. New York: Cambridge University Press.

Kiewiet D. Roderick and Mathew D. McCubbins. 1991. *The Logic of Delegation: Congressional Parties and the Appropriations Process*. Chicago: University of Chicago Press.

Mills, Russell W., Nicole Kalaf-Hughes, and Jason A. MacDonald. Forthcoming. Agency Policy Preferences, Congressional Letter-Marking, and the Allocation of Distributive Policy Benefits. *Journal of Public Policy*.

Oleszek, Walter J. 2011. *Congress Procedures and the Policymaking Process* (8th edition). Washington, D.C.: CQ Press.

Schick, Allen. 1995. *The Federal Budget: Politics, Policy, and Process*. Washington, D.C.: The Brookings Institution.

Stewart, Charles H., III. 1989. *Budget Reform Politics: The Design of the Appropriations Process in the House of Representatives, 1865–1921*. New York: Cambridge University Press.

Wildavsky, Aaron, and Naomi Caiden. 1997. *The New Politics of the Budgetary Process* (3rd edition). New York: Longman.

17 THE POWER TO ADVISE AND CONSENT (TREATIES)

Jeffrey S. Peake

Article II, section 2, clause 3
The President . . . shall have the Power, by and with the Advice and Consent
of the Senate, to make Treaties, provided two thirds of the Senators present
concur.

KEY TERMS

"Treaty" is a term that differs depending on whether one is considering international law or U.S. domestic (i.e., constitutional) law. Under international law, treaty simply means a formal agreement between two or more sovereign states establishing a legal commitment. Thus, the term is quite broad and encompasses all formal international agreements completed by the United States, including all forms of executive agreements (See below). Under U.S. domestic law, however, the term has a more narrow definition. Also referred to as "Article II treaties," the more narrow domestic law definition includes only those international agreements signed by the president or his agent and submitted to the Senate for advice and consent. Synonyms for "treaty" include convention, agreement, compact, and protocol.

Krutz and Peake summarize the significance of treaties to American foreign policy when they write, "Making international agreements lies at the core of foreign policy, as such agreements affect a vast range of American foreign policies" (2009, 3), including every area of policymaking in the international domain, ranging from trade to human rights to arms proliferation.

The ambiguity regarding the definition of "treaty" under domestic and international law has led to significant legal and political controversy. Given the high hurdle of advice and consent (two-thirds of voting senators) and the president's option to complete their international agreements as executive agreements, it would seem the attractiveness of altogether avoiding the super-majority requirement in the Senate would limit the use of treaties vis-à-vis executive agreements. While the United States has completed about 300 international agreements annually since 1949, only about 6 percent are treaties submitted to the Senate for advice and consent. The vast majority are completed as executive agreements. As a legal instrument, treaties are still regularly used to complete the most significant and far-reaching international agreements, at least until very recently. In one analysis of *significant* international agreements from 1949 to 2000, two scholars found that about 40 percent were submitted to the Senate as Article II treaties, suggesting that modern presidents do not evade the Senate on a large share of significant agreements (Krutz and Peake 2009, 88).

While the Constitution's Framers did not explicitly define the term, treaties are mentioned elsewhere in the document. In Art. I, §10, the Constitution provides that the treaty power is in the domain of the national government, and not the states: "No state shall enter into any treaty, alliance, or confederation." The judiciary's role is extended to treaties in Art. III, §2, where it states that the "judicial power shall extend to all cases, in law and equity, arising under this constitution, the laws of the United States, and treaties made, or which shall be made under their authority." Finally, the Constitution elevates treaties as supreme law, when it states in Article VI that "all treaties made, or which shall be made, under the authority of the United States shall be the supreme law of the land."

HISTORY AND DEVELOPMENT

The historical record is clear that the Framers intended to share the treaty power between the president and Senate. Alexander Hamilton, an advocate for broad interpretation of presidential powers, stated in several essays published in the *Federalist Papers* his belief that the treaty process should include the legislature. For example, in *Federalist* No. 69, Hamilton clearly states that treaties and "every other species of convention usual among nations" require joint action by the president and two-thirds of the Senate. James Madison went even further in his writings, considering treaty making as more of a legislative function. In *Federalist* No. 64, John Jay argues against delegating the treaty power to the president, laying out a strong case for the Senate's inclusion in the advice and consent stage of the treaty process, while excluding the House of Representatives.

Despite what is seemingly clear constitutional language on the role of the president and Senate in treaty making, significant ambiguities emerged in practice early in the history of the republic. For example, did advice and consent preclude Senate involvement in the treaty-making stage of the process, or did it require it? Two competing views of the roles that should be played by the president and Senate in the treaty process emerged. The first view, which has won out, is that the treaty-negotiating process (i.e., the point prior to presidential submittal to the Senate for advice and consent) is a presidential monopoly. In the words of Justice Sutherland, the president "alone negotiates" treaties. Given the president's initiative in foreign policy, he can present the Senate with *faits accompli*, but to which that body is under no obligation to approve (Krutz and Peake 2009, 27).

On the other hand, Louis Fisher argues that the Framers clearly intended for Senate involvement during all stages of the treaty process. Rather than possessing just a veto on the president's international agreements, this line of reasoning suggests that Senate advice is appropriate throughout. Senate inclusion, according to Fisher, is wise and in line with the Framers' intent, given that body's role in advice and consent. He also notes that there are numerous cases throughout history where senators were included as part of the negotiating team (1985, 256–57). While Fisher's arguments are persuasive, it is clear that the presidential monopoly view was swiftly adopted: as early as the Jay Treaty of 1794, presidents began skirting senatorial advice during the negotiation stage of the process. The exclusion of the Senate from the negotiation stage in 1794 was a sign of things to come, as presidents began to altogether coopt and circumvent the Senate's role in the treaty process through the use of executive agreements in place of treaties.

The Treaty Process

The modern treaty process follows a five-stage process. The executive first negotiates and signs the treaty. Second, the president submits the treaty to the Senate for advice and consent. Presidents will sometimes sign a treaty but then decide not to submit the treaty to the Senate, as was the case for President Bill Clinton and the Kyoto Protocol. The process in the Senate formally starts when the president transmits the treaty to the Senate, via a memorandum that requests advice and consent and lays out the president's reasons for seeking ratification of the agreement. As explained above, the first two stages are effectively presidential monopolies.

Upon transmittal, a treaty is referred to the Senate Foreign Relations Committee, which must first act on a resolution of ratification before the full Senate can take up the treaty for advice and consent. During the committee stage of the process, the committee may decide to attach conditions to the treaty, which will become part of the resolution considered on the floor. These amendments may be reservations, understandings, or declarations (RUDs). They are significant tools of the Senate. RUDs can alter the language and meaning of treaty provisions, and may require renegotiation with treaty partners. Moreover, they sometimes address a broader set of policies than those considered in the treaty, and if attached to the treaty, which is then ratified, become the law of the land and only require a simple majority vote on the floor for approval.

Once the committee reports the treaty, Senate leaders must seek approval of the resolution for the treaty to move forward, which requires the constitutionally mandated two-thirds vote of present senators. Should the treaty fail to make it to a vote on the floor (or fail on the floor vote), it is returned to the committee, where it sits indefinitely until the committee sees fit to report it once again. The Senate may also return the treaty to the president by simple resolution, whether or not the treaty ever makes it to the floor for a vote. In some cases presidents will withdraw a languishing treaty from Senate consideration. Upon such requests, the Senate will return the treaty to the president via simple resolution. Presidents typically make such requests when they transmit a treaty that supersedes an existing treaty that is currently awaiting Senate consent. During the final stage, the president ratifies the treaty, as amended, by signing the instrument of ratification, which is then exchanged with treaty partners (or deposited with the requisite international organization), having the effect of entering the treaty into force for domestic and international law.

The House of Representatives is not altogether excluded from the treaty process. While most treaties are self-executing, many require implementing legislation or obligate the United States to spend sums of money. When this is the case, the House has a formal role, as such actions require normal legislative action. An example includes the Panama Canal Treaties, which were ratified by the thinnest of margins in the Senate in 1978. The treaties could have effectively been scuttled in the House, had it not narrowly passed the implementing legislation required to put the treaties into effect.

What is clear is that the modern treaty process as described above is both procedurally and politically cumbersome, especially given the requirement for super-majority consent in the Senate. It was not long before presidents began looking for an alternative means to complete international agreements, and they found it in the executive agreement, as discussed below.

Presidents have two other important treaty powers: treaty interpretation and treaty termination. Under domestic law, presidents are free to terminate or withdraw from existing treaties unilaterally, as President George W. Bush did with the Anti-Ballistic Missile Treaty in 2001. This is uncommon, of course, as doing so may have serious domestic and international political ramifications. The Congress can check the president here via statute, but in the two times treaty termination has been controversial, opponents in Congress lacked the wherewithal to generate a congressional majority. While presidents have claimed an exclusive power to interpret existing treaties, recent case law suggests that both the executive and legislative branches together interpret the meaning of treaties (see *Hamdan v. Rumsfeld*, 126 U.S. 2749 [2006], involving interpretation of the Geneva Conventions). This is especially the case when the Senate has attached accompanying RUDs to ratification documents, indicating their express interpretation.

Executive Agreements

Executive Agreements are a form of international agreement holding the same legal authority as a treaty under international law but completed domestically using processes that differ from the Article II process described above. The State Department's Office of the Assistant Legal Advisor for Treaty Affairs categorizes Article II treaties as treaties and all other international agreements as agreements other than treaties, or executive agreements. Executive agreements can be broken down into three categories with important distinctions: (1) congressional-executive agreements, which are pursuant to a previous act of Congress and may require congressional approval via joint resolution; (2) agreements pursuant to an existing treaty; and, (3) presidential agreements, or sole executive agreements, completed pursuant to the president's plenary foreign policy powers—that is, expressly stated Article II powers.

Congressional-executive agreements are further broken down into three subtypes: (1) agreements where Congress provides *ex ante* authorization to the president to negotiate an agreement on a specific matter; (2) agreements where Congress legislates on a foreign policy matter, instructing the president to verify certain facts before the agreement can take effect; and, (3) agreements where the president seeks *ex post* approval by submitting the agreement to Congress (rather than just the Senate) for legislative approval via joint resolution. This category requires only majority approval from both chambers, rather than the two-thirds Senate majority required by the Treaty Clause. Major trade agreements (e.g., NAFTA) are typically completed using the third subtype.

As noted above, executive agreements make up the vast majority of international agreements completed by modern presidents, and they are also commonly used to complete consequential international agreements. For example, the U.S. commitment to Afghanistan's security is governed entirely by executive agreements completed by the Bush and Obama administrations. Other key examples include the Paris Peace Accords, ending U.S. participation in the Vietnam War, and the U.S.-Israeli agreements that made Israel the largest recipient of U.S. foreign aid.

From 1789 to 1839, executive agreements made up just 31 percent of all international agreements signed by the president. Over the next fifty years (1840–1889) that percentage increased to 53, and from 1890 to 1939 it stood at 64 percent. Since 1940, just over 94 percent of all international agreements signed by the president are completed as executive agreements. What is lost in these numbers, however, is the fact that most executive agreements receive congressional authorization in some fashion. In one accounting, nearly 87 percent of executive agreements were either congressional-executive agreements or agreements pursuant to a treaty. Thus, while the vast majority of international agreements are executive agreements, the vast majority of these executive agreements involve Congress in some fashion, whether through *ex post* or *ex ante* approval.

While the Framers did not envision international agreements other than Article II treaties, the Supreme Court has consistently upheld the legal authority of executive agreements. In *United States v. Pink* (315 U.S. 203 [1942]), the Court found that "all international compacts and agreements" are to be treated "with similar dignity" as treaties. Some important distinctions do exist for the purposes of domestic law, however, placing duly ratified treaties as more significant, legally, than executive agreements. Executive agreements do not supersede existing treaties or federal law, nor can they violate the constitutional rights of American citizens. Executive agreements trump state laws (as would a treaty), as also established in *Pink*. Congress retains authority to resist executive action where its powers are clear, should it decide to act.

When one compares the cumbersome treaty process outlined above with the much simpler executive agreement process, the attractiveness of executive agreements becomes quite apparent. Most executive agreements enter into force upon the executive's signature. As noted above, some may require approval by Congress or subsequent spending or implementing legislation. When such a requirement is necessary, normal legislative majorities are required, not the two-thirds constitutionally mandated Senate super-majority, as is the case for treaties. Executive agreements are a foreign policy tool that provide presidents and Congress with an efficient and expedient mechanism to complete international agreements. Executive agreements are "a rational adaptation by modern presidents, in conjunction with Congress, to the complex foreign policy environment unforeseen by the framers of the Constitution" (Krutz and Peake 2009, 187).

This argument rests on notions of constitutional construction—the idea that interpretations of constitutional provisions change through joint action and practice on the part of the political branches in response to constitutional ambiguities and changing political contexts. Thus, executive agreements can be viewed "as a significant adaptation on the part of the political branches" to the highly complex international environment.

One obvious question that arises, given the apparent freedom presidents have in choosing how to complete their international agreements, is why would they ever use the formal treaty process at all? After all, executive agreements afford presidents the opportunity to circumvent the noisome and often gridlocked treaty process, so why not always use executive agreements? The answer to this question is twofold and has more to do with domestic and international politics than with law.

In terms of domestic politics, political science scholarship suggests that presidents are constrained by the willingness of legislators to check executive action. In other words, presidents are less free to act unilaterally, using executive agreements, when legislative opponents are in a position to check their actions or make them pay a price for their behavior. Thus, presidents do not appear to evade the Senate on treaties by using executive agreements instead when the other party has majority control of the Senate. There are numerous examples where a president considered completing an agreement as an executive agreement rather than as a treaty, but went the treaty route in response to pressure from leading senators. Such was the case in 1997 when President Bill Clinton agreed to submit the Flank Document Agreement to the Conventional Forces Europe to the Senate for advice and consent. In terms of international politics, agreement partners often have a strong preference that an agreement with the United States be a treaty rather than an executive agreement. International relations scholars, in particular Lisa Martin (2000), persuasively argue that treaties send more credible signals of commitment to agreement partners than executive agreements. One example is Russian president Putin's request that President George W. Bush submit the Moscow Treaty, a nuclear arms agreement, to the Senate for advice and consent rather than complete it on his own authority.

Another consideration is the degree of congressional support for the use of executive agreements during the modern era. In order to have its say on significant international agreements, Congress has enacted legislation mandating a specific process to complete certain types of agreements. For example, the Atomic Energy Act of 1954 requires the president to submit agreements on nuclear cooperation to Congress for approval, either via the treaty process or through legislation. Similar laws require presidents to submit trade agreements to Congress for bicameral approval, and others allow Congress to effectively veto executive agreements on fisheries within a specific time window. Thus, executive agreements may also benefit the House of Representatives, as they might provide for direct involvement by the lower chamber, something the treaty clause precludes.

While Congress has largely acquiesced to their use, there were times during the last century when the use of executive agreements became controversial. During the 1950s, the Senate debated the so-called "Bricker Amendment," a constitutional amendment that, if enacted, would have amended the treaty clause to require that all international agreements become effective only upon the passage of legislation. The amendment failed by just a single vote in the Senate. In response to abuses of the executive agreement process during the 1960s and 1970s, Congress again attempted to curtail their use. The most they could muster, however, was the procedural requirement that the executive report all executive agreements to Congress, the so-called Case-Zablocki Act of 1972. In 2008, significant constitutional questions arose surrounding President Bush's agreements with Iraq, committing the United States to Iraq's security for several years beyond the U.N.-mandated withdrawal date. Democrats charged that the president needed congressional approval to complete such a significant agreement, but Bush completed the agreement on his own authority as a sole executive agreement.

The 2015 nuclear accord with Iran, known as the Joint Comprehensive Plan of Action, is a more recent and controversial case pitting the Republican Congress against President Obama in his efforts to broker a deal in which Iran would give up its efforts toward nuclear weapons in exchange for elimination of economic sanctions. When the pending deal prompted a Republican backlash in March 2015, officials at the State Department initially claimed that the accord was a nonbinding agreement typically referred to in the literature as a political agreement. This all changed, however, when Congress enacted the Iran Nuclear Agreement Review Act in May. The agreement would not go into effect if Congress enacted a resolution of disapproval, subject to a presidential veto; however, a Democratic filibuster in September thwarted the Republican attempt for such a resolution in the Senate.

Political Agreements

A Political Agreement is often referred to as a "gentlemen's agreement." Political agreements are neither a treaty nor an executive agreement, and are not considered a formal treaty under international law and thus are nonbinding. Hollis and Newcomer define a political agreement "as a nonlegally binding agreement between two or more nation-states in which the parties intend to establish commitments of an exclusively political or moral nature." The breach of treaties and executive agreements (i.e., binding legal agreements) "can generate both political and legal consequences . . . only politics governs the political commitment so its breach will only produce political consequences" (2009, 517; 520).

Political agreements are part of the president's plenary foreign policy powers as chief diplomat, and Congress has no constitutional authority in this matter. It is often unclear whether the executive intends to complete a binding agreement (e.g., an executive agreement or treaty) or a political agreement, as was the case during the Iran nuclear accord controversy discussed above, so there is often confusion among relevant domestic actors in the process, in particular members of Congress. Examples of significant political commitments include the Shanghai Communiqué, which established a new relationship between the People's Republic of China and the United States during the Nixon Administration; the Helsinki Accords, which established a forum for human rights and other disputes that was the precursor to the Organization for Security and Cooperation in Europe; and several recent climate change accords, including the 2008 Group of Eight Declaration on the Environment and Climate Change and the 2014 U.S.–China Joint Announcement on Climate Change. (The Department of State provides guidance on nonbinding agreements, including their proper naming and terms to avoid, here: http://www.state.gov/s/l/treaty/guidance/. Accessed 25 September 25, 2015.)

Costs of Presidential Monopoly on Stage-One Negotiations

Soon after the Constitutional Convention, Pierce Butler of South Carolina remarked that treaties should "be gone over, clause by clause, by the president and the Senate together." His colleagues shared this perspective, including President George Washington when he brought a treaty he was negotiating with the Creek Indians to the Senate in 1789. Washington sent the Senate thirteen questions about the treaty and even appeared on the floor of the Senate to hear senators' concerns regarding the treaty. The meeting did not go well, and the president reportedly vowed that "he would be damned if he ever went there again" (Krutz and Peake 2009, 31–32). While Washington continued to seek Senate advice prior to submitting treaties to the Senate for consent, as discussed above, his successors soon ended the practice. The practice had the effect of cutting the Senate out of the advice part of the advice and consent role described in the treaty clause.

Excluding the Senate from the first stage of the treaty process had its costs. Beginning in the early nineteenth century, the Senate began providing its advice through the amendment process during debate over the resolution of ratification for the treaty. This practice proved problematic, as the executive would negotiate a treaty and submit it to the Senate, only to have the Senate make significant changes, thus endangering final ratification, as treaty partners might not go along with the changes. Examples include the King-Hawkesbury Convention of 1803 and the Hay-Pauncefote Treaty of 1900. As a result of such changes, between 1789 and 1992, the president or U.S. treaty partners eventually rejected 43 treaties that were amended during the Senate stage of the process. This is double the number of treaties rejected on the floor of the Senate over the scope of U.S. history. The dominant view among senators during the nineteenth century is reflected in the famous remark by Senator Henry Cabot Lodge (R-MA), "that a treaty sent to the Senate is not properly a treaty but merely a project" (Krutz and Peake 2009, 32).

The Senate of Lodge's time was considered a graveyard for treaties. Not a single significant treaty received Senate consent between 1869 and 1898. Of the 22 outright Senate rejections of proposed treaties in the scope of U.S. history, 14 occurred between 1860 and 1935. This frustrated presidents significantly, of course, and President Teddy Roosevelt once remarked, "Individual Senators evidently consider the prerogatives of the Senate as far more important than the welfare of the country." President Woodrow Wilson's largest domestic political defeat involved the Treaty of Versailles, the peace treaty that ended World War I, which failed on the Senate floor in a defeat engineered by Senator Lodge. Krutz and Peake explain that "one reason treaties were so endangered . . . is the fact that the Senate was prodded to defend its foreign policy prerogatives through the only means available to it, since presidents had so often excluded the Senate from the first phase of the treaty process" (2009, 33). Furthermore, the conflict over treaties was marked by partisanship exacerbated by heightened ideological polarization between the two parties. Such a conclusion is also apparent during the early twenty-first century, as discussed below.

Since 1935, the conflict surrounding the treaty ratification process has been much less severe, at least until very recently. In fact, since 1935, only four treaties were rejected outright in a floor vote in the Senate, suggesting to some that the Senate is accommodating when it comes to treaties. The floor defeats include the Law of the Sea Convention in 1960; the Montreal Protocol No. 4 in 1983; the Comprehensive Nuclear Test Ban Treaty in 1999; and the U.N. Convention for the Rights of the Disabled in 2012. However, measuring conflict based on floor failures underestimates the severity of political conflict surrounding treaties during the modern era. This is partly a result of the rise of executive agreements, the modern president's alternative to Article II treaties. As described above, starting with President Franklin Roosevelt, presidents started to routinely use executive agreements to finalize their international agreements instead of Article II treaties. Moreover, Senate consent to treaties is commonly subject to considerable delay, often proving costly to the president and to U.S. foreign policy. Perhaps the best example is the Genocide Convention, first submitted to the Senate by President Truman. It was not ratified until 1986, a delay of nearly forty years. Today, numerous treaties languish in the Senate, some for decades. Many of these treaties include significant multilateral human rights, arms control, and environmental conventions.

FUTURE IMPLICATIONS

In conclusion, the president and the Senate have effectively struck an institutional bargain to change the meaning of the treaty clause. The bargain allows for the use of the more expedient executive agreement process for a vast majority of international agreements as long as presidents continue to send the most significant agreements to the Senate as treaties, particularly when the Senate is on record as preferring a treaty. Such a bargain benefits both institutions, as it has made foreign policy more efficient, made agreements more credible, and reserved the Senate process for the most significant and far-reaching agreements or those agreements that specifically deal with the Article I powers of Congress (e.g., tax treaties) or the powers of the states (e.g., extradition). If the Senate were to approve the 300 or so agreements completed annually, it would get little else done.

However, the bargain underpinning the evolution of the treaty process has been under considerable stress in recent years. Treaty politics during the presidency of Barack Obama have been particularly conflict-ridden, and the president has largely avoided the treaty instrument altogether. Since entering office in January 2009, Obama has submitted just twenty-three treaties at the halfway point through the 114th Congress, averaging a paltry three treaty transmittals per year, compared to the annual average of fifteen per year for his modern predecessors (Truman through George W. Bush). If you include the treaties Obama has submitted with the pending treaties that he has supported, his success rate on getting treaties ratified is significantly lower than his predecessors, about 38 percent—compared to an average success rate of just over 80 percent for other modern presidents. Much of the blame for this poor treaty record rests with the Senate, as conservative Republicans have managed to block many of Obama's significant treaties, including agreements that have broad domestic political support (e.g., the U.N. Law of the Sea Convention and the U.N. Disabilities Convention). At the same time, Obama's use of executive agreements has continued apace, and he is using executive agreements to complete a host of significant international agreements. David Kaye summarizes the problem for U.S. foreign policy:

> The U.S. Senate rejects multilateral treaties as if it were sport. Some it rejects outright . . . Others it rejects through inaction: dozens of treaties are pending before the Senate, pertaining to such subjects as labor, economic and cultural rights, endangered species, pollution, armed conflict, peacekeeping, nuclear weapons, the law of the sea, and discrimination against women. Often, presidents don't even bother pushing for ratification, since they know the odds are long . . . The United States' commitment problem has grown so entrenched that foreign governments no longer expect Washington's ratification or its full participation in the institutions treaties create. The world is moving on; laws get made elsewhere, with limited (if any) American involvement. (2013, 113)

Whether future presidents will continue the trend of treaty disuse that Obama has started may depend on two factors that raise important questions for the president's unilateral powers and joint action on the part of the president and Congress when it comes to some of the United States' most significant foreign policies. First, scholars of unilateral presidential powers and the imperial presidency point to the role of Congress in checking presidential abuse. The Congress's ability to check the president is severely undermined by partisan polarization. The beauty of unilateral presidential action is that the president acts first and Congress must react in order to check the president if a majority disagree with the president's actions. Doing so typically requires a legislative act, which the president can veto. However, when the president acts alone, against the wishes of a majority of Congress, his actions lack legitimacy, and while legal, may not be as credible, as the opposing party might vow to contravene the president's action upon attaining office, as appears to be the case with the 2015 Iran nuclear accord.

Second, the super-majority requirement of the treaty clause makes it very difficult to have joint, credible action on the part of the president and the Senate on important international commitments, leaving presidents in a precarious position vis-à-vis world partners. Some legal scholars argue that the treaty clause is unworkable as a modern instrument and call for an end to treaties, citing the congressional-executive agreement as a superior model. Clearly their more limited use in recent years leads to justifiable empirical claims that U.S. political actors find treaties less useful as a practical diplomatic tool.

Of course, for many, expediency is not a sufficient justification for ignoring the clear dictate of the Constitution—that joint action by the president *and* Congress is necessary for the United States to make legally binding international commitments. One hopeful consideration is that in the scope of history, the use (or disuse) of treaties appears to relate to a number of contextual factors, including both in international politics (i.e., the need for treaties) and in domestic politics (i.e., partisan polarization).

It is quite plausible that when, in the future, the Congress is less hampered by rampant partisan polarization, it will be in a better position to check the president's proclivity for unilateral action on international agreements and to act jointly with the president on treaties, decreasing the attractiveness of unilateral action. Retention of the legislative's advice and consent authority requires a healthy legislative institution—one cannot rely on the good will of future presidents in entirety.

FURTHER READING

Fisher, Louis. 1985. *Constitutional Conflicts between Congress and the President.* Princeton, NJ: Princeton University Press.

Grimmett, Jeane. 2001. International Agreements and U.S. Law. In *Treaties and other International Agreements: The Role of the United States Senate.* Congressional Research Service Report. Washington, D.C.: Library of Congress.

Hollis, Duncan B., and Joshua J. Newcomer. 2009. "Political" Commitments and the Constitution. *Virginia Journal of International Law* 49 (3): 507–584.

Johnson, Loch K. 1984. *The Making of International Agreements: Congress Confronts the Executive.* New York: New York University Press.

Kaye, David. 2013. "Stealth Multilateralism." *Foreign Affairs* 92 (5): 113–24.

Krutz, Glen S., and Jeffrey S. Peake. 2009. *Treaty Politics and the Rise of Executive Agreements: International Commitments in a System of Shared Powers.* Ann Arbor, MI: University of Michigan Press.

Martin, Lisa L. 2000. *Democratic Commitments: Legislatures and International Cooperation.* Princeton, NJ: Princeton University Press.

Peake, Jeffrey S. 2015. The Domestic Politics of U.S. Treaty Ratification: Bilateral Treaties from 1949–2012. *Foreign Policy Analysis,* forthcoming

Peake, Jeffrey S., and Glen S. Krutz. 2014. President Barack Obama, Partisanship, and the Politics of International Agreements. *2014 Annuaire Français des Relations.* English version available at http://papers.ssrn.com/sol3/papers.cfm?abstract_id=2587806.

18 THE POWER TO ADVISE AND CONSENT (APPOINTMENTS)

Mitchel A. Sollenberger

Article II, section 2, clause 2
The President . . . shall nominate, and by and with the advice and consent
of the senate, shall appoint ambassadors, other public ministers and con-
suls, judges of the supreme court, and all other officers of the United States,
whose appointments are not herein otherwise provided for, and which shall
be established by law. But the Congress may by law vest the appointment of
such inferior officers, as they think proper, in the president alone, in the courts
of law, or in the heads of departments. The president shall have power to fill
up all vacancies that may happen during the recess of the senate, by granting
commissions which shall expire at the end of their next session.

KEY TERMS

**"The President . . . shall nominate, and by and with the advice and consent of the
senate, shall appoint ambassadors, other public ministers and consuls, judges of
the supreme court, and all other officers of the United States . . . [but] Congress
may by law vest the appointment of such inferior officers"**: There are two primary
appointment methods contemplated by this clause. First, the president may nominate
by and with the advice and consent of the Senate several named positions and all other
principal officers of the United States. This appointment process is referred to as presidential appointed and Senate confirmed (PAS). The second method permits Congress
to establish "inferior officers" that can be appointed either by the default PAS process;
or by the president alone (PA); or by federal courts; or by department and agency heads
(Schedule C and noncareer SES [Senior Executive Service]).

Determining what type of process should be used for a particular office is difficult. What is a principal or inferior officer? There is also the issue of distinguishing an officer from an employee, as many people who work for the federal government are not considered Article II officers. In 1823 Chief Justice John Marshall, sitting as a circuit court judge, presented one of the first statements on the distinction between officers and employees: "Although an office is an employment, it does not follow that every employment is an office. A man may certainly be employed under a contract, express or implied, to perform a service without becoming an officer." More recently the Supreme Court has stated that the term "officers" does not encompass everyone employed by the federal government. Instead, the Court reasoned, "[e]mployees are lesser functionaries subordinate to officers of the United States."

Despite the lack of clarity for the term "employee," the focus for this clause has been the defining of the principal and inferior officer appointments. The most relevant and current elaboration on the subject comes from the Supreme Court, which stated that "the term 'inferior officer' connotes a relationship with some higher ranking officer or officers below the President: Whether one is an 'inferior officer' depends on whether he has a superior . . . we think it evident that 'inferior officers' are officers whose work is directed and supervised at some level by others who were appointed by President nomination with the advice and consent of the Senate." The Court's distinction between principal and inferior officers leaves questions to resolve. For example, to what extent would direction and supervision need to be given to make an officer inferior? And how are an employee, principal officer, and inferior officer different if the critical factor for all appears to be the level of supervision/subordination of the position?

Regardless of the lingering questions, most appointment studies focus primarily on the PAS appointment system, which includes two stages: the pre-nomination process and the confirmation process. The first stage, depending on the type of appointment, is often centered on the president and includes a number of administrative review mechanisms. It begins when a position is created; a federal official resigns, announces his or her retirement, or dies in office. By tradition, judicial appointments at the district and circuit court level and various state-based positions are usually selected based on the recommendation of the home-state senator of the president's party. Once a nomination is made, the second stage begins; this involves a number of steps and review measures that include committee referral, staff investigation, committee hearings and vote, before Senate floor debate and final action.

"The president shall have power to fill up all vacancies that may happen during the recess of the senate, by granting commissions, which shall expire at the end of their next session": In creating this provision, the framers provided a way for presidents to staff the federal government when the Senate would not be in session. However, the framers gave little guidance in interpreting its meaning at the Constitutional Convention. That is important because a broad interpretation could provide the president with near-unlimited ability to act without Senate involvement. Subsequently the bulk of recess appointments have hinged on words such as "recess" (how long the Senate has to be on break to be considered in recess) and "happen" (does the vacancy have to have occurred during the recess of the Senate for the president to make a recess appointment).

It is with the interpretation of word "recess" that more recent inter-branch disputes have occurred. In these cases presidents have used their recess power to bypass the confirmation process to secure an appointment. President George W. Bush used his recess appointment power to place Fifth Circuit nominee Charles W. Pickering and Eleventh Circuit nominee William H. Pryor on the federal bench after Democratic senators successfully prevented confirmation votes from being taken.

President Bush made Pickering's recess appointment on January 16, 2004, during an intersession recess of Congress. Pickering's service on the federal bench expired on December 8, 2004, at which time he told Bush he did not want to be renominated. Pryor's case was more controversial, in that Bush made the appointment on February 20, 2004, during a 10-day intrasession adjournment of Congress. As scholar Louis Fisher explained, the "seemingly technical distinction between inter- and intrasession recess appointments has a practical effect. Someone who receives an intersession appointment serves until the end of the next session, or about a year. An individual with an intrasession appointment made early during the session serves close to two years" (Fisher 2014, 45). Pryor's appointment was unsuccessfully challenged in the Eleventh Circuit.

More recently the Senate has acted to prevent presidents from abusing their recess appointment power by holding pro-forma sessions every third day. The Senate's refusal to go into a prolonged adjournment seemingly meant that the president could not use the recess power to place individuals into executive and judicial positions without senatorial consent. The Senate began holding pro-forma sessions during the 2007 Thanksgiving recess, after President Bush had made two recess appointments. For nearly one and half years the Senate held over two dozen pro-forma sessions to prevent Bush from making recess appointments. Senate Historian Donald A. Ritchie said he believed this was the first time the Senate used pro-forma sessions to block recess appointments.

Starting in the fall of 2011, Senate Republicans began holding pro-forma sessions to prevent President Barack Obama from making recess appointments as well. As had been the case under Bush, the Senate usually only convened for a few minutes or less, without taking action. Based on legal advice from the Office of Legal Counsel, which determined that pro-forma sessions did not bar the president from making recess appointments, Obama went ahead and made four recess appointments—three to the National Labor Relations Board (NLRB) and one to be the director of the Consumer Financial Protection Bureau in early January 2012.

A lawsuit against the recess appointments challenging the authority of President Obama to take such action was promptly filed. In January 2013; the D.C. Circuit Court ruled that Obama could not make intra-session recess appointments, as the term "the recess" does not contemplate such a power being used within a session of the Senate. The appellate court also held that any recess appointment made could only apply to vacancies that occurred during the actual recess. The case next went to the Supreme Court. Although the Court rejected both points made by the D.C. Circuit, it concluded that the Obama administration could not unilaterally decide when a "recess" occurs. The Court reasoned that it was willing "to interpret the Clause as granting the President the power to make appointments during a recess," but it would not offer a construction that would give "the President the authority routinely to avoid the need for Senate confirmation."

The Court therefore permitted the use of intra-session recess appointments but not in cases where the recess is for less than ten days. The rationale behind the ten-day threshold centered on the lack of any precedent. The Court also dismissed the Obama administration's view that the Senate's pro-forma sessions were makeweight attempts to prevent the president from exercising his constitutional powers. Instead, the Court deferred to the Senate's authority to conduct its business as it determines, with special emphasis placed on its capacity to act on legislation and nominations at any time during a pro-forma session.

Congress has used other mechanisms to weaken the president's recess appointment power, such as passing funding restrictions. The original law, passed in 1863, prohibited the use of funds to "be paid out of the Treasury of the United States to any person appointed during the recess of the Senate, to fill a vacancy in any existing office . . . until such appointee is confirmed by the Senate." In 1940, Congress revised its overly strict prohibition on salary payments for recess appointees. The law retained the prohibition on payments to "an individual appointed during a recess of the Senate to fill a vacancy in an existing office, if the vacancy existed while the Senate was in session and was by law required to be filled by and with the advice and consent of the Senate, until the appointee has been confirmed by the Senate."

However, Congress created three exceptions, which still exist today, to make it easier for recess appointees to receive a salary. First, payments can be made "if the vacancy arose within 30 days before the end of the session of the Senate." This exception recognized the lack of time the president and Senate have to consider a judicial replacement, let alone confirm that person. Second, payments are permitted if, at the end of a session, a nomination has been pending before the Senate (unless that nomination had already received a recess appointment). Given the limited time the Senate has at the end of a session, the provision is a reasonable concession for the circumstance. Third, payments can be made if a nomination "was rejected by the Senate within 30 days before the end of the session." (This does not apply if the president nominates the person rejected.) This final exception is the Senate's attempt to ensure that presidents will not make recess appointments of rejected nominations. All three exceptions are subject to the qualification that a nomination must be sent to the Senate no later than 40 days after the next session begins.

HISTORY AND DEVELOPMENT

Under the British system in place during the American colonial era, the king had absolute control over appointments. As Alexander Hamilton explained in *Federalist* No. 69, the "king of Great Britain is emphatically and truly styled the fountain of honor. He not only appoints to all offices, but can create offices." The framers of the Constitution rejected that model for making federal appointments and settled on a system where power would be shared. That was no accident, as the shared structural arrangement over appointments had historical significance. The colonial experience taught the Framers that the power to make appointments should not be given solely to the executive, as royal governors used their appointment authority as a way to bribe others and control the colonies.

During the Revolution, most state governments began with strong legislative bodies, as the colonists took the appointment power from royal governors. Delaware, Pennsylvania, and South Carolina did not even create a governor position and instead gave most executive authority to a president appointed by the legislative body. In Virginia, apart from the governor selecting justices of the peace upon the advice of a Privy Council, the legislative body made all appointments. In Georgia, New Jersey, and North Carolina, the governor had little or no involvement in appointments. Only in Maryland was the governor authorized to appoint a number of officeholders.

Not until the passage of the New York Constitution of 1777 did an independent executive emerge that was on equal footing with the legislative body, or governor's council, in making appointments. The New York Constitution gave the governor, with the "advice and consent" of the Council of Appointments, the power to make appointments. This shared appointment power was the first of the pre-1787 state constitutions. Two other state constitutions in Massachusetts and New Hampshire followed New York's model of giving the executive enhanced authority.

At the national level, a similar experience occurred. The only governing institution was the Continental Congress. There was no executive branch or executive officers to even exercise appointment authority. By the summer of 1775, however, the Congress realized that it needed administrative help. As a result, Congress established a post office department under the direction of a postmaster general. Although not a truly independent executive agent, the postmaster general was given much-needed administrative power to conduct postal affairs, including authority to appoint as many deputies at such places as he believed proper. Later on, executive officers were created for the Foreign Affairs (January 10, 1781), War, Marine, and Finance Departments (February 7), and the office of Attorney General (February 16). Apart from giving these officers administrative responsibilities, Congress empowered them to make appointments within their power as well.

The Revolutionary experience set the stage for how the appointment power would be shaped at the Constitutional Convention. At the state and national levels, the movement was in the direction of a shared appointment responsibility. The Constitutional Convention would solidify the existing practice of moving toward a shared appointment responsibility, while creating a truly independent executive branch. The record of the Convention, however, is mixed when it comes to determining how the Framers believed the Article II appointment power should be exercised.

Initially Edmund Randolph proposed that "the National Legislature" be given total control over appointments, but that idea was rejected. Still, the unease with an independent executive remained. John Rutledge cautioned against executive-controlled appointments, reasoning it might be "leaning too much towards Monarchy." Eventually Alexander Hamilton offered a compromise in which the president appointed or nominated and the Senate rejected or approved the individual. The bulk of the remaining discussion over appointments centered on the benefits of various appointment methods. Some asserted that an executive-centered approach ensured that responsibility would be taken for making good appointments. Others believed that lawmakers would have greater familiarity with qualified candidates for federal offices.

The extensive debates over appointments resolved some of the more significant questions about whether the appointment power would be placed in the legislative branch or shared between Congress and the presidency. The Convention, however, left unanswered some of the more practical issues for making appointments. How should the president nominate? How should the Senate carry out its "advice and consent" duty? What does "advice" mean, and upon what offices should it be given?

Only after the Convention would those questions began to slowly be addressed, as each branch began to craft its own customs and rules for vetting individuals considered for federal offices. Early on, presidents chose to consult and solicit recommendations from lawmakers—particularly senators, governors, and other prominent officeholders of the president's political party. This practice is referred to as senatorial courtesy and is maintained with judicial (federal judges, U.S. attorneys, and marshals) and other appointments to this day. Senatorial courtesy traces its origins to George Washington's administration, when the Senate rejected the nomination of Benjamin Fishbourn to be the naval officer for the Port of Savannah, Georgia. In that instance, senators deferred to objections to Fishbourn raised by at least one of Georgia's home-state senators.

Consultation also occurs with executive branch offices, including department-level, cadet/midshipman, and postmaster appointments (until 1970 when President Richard Nixon transformed the Post Office Department into a government corporation). Appointments to cabinet-level positions experience fewer cases of lawmakers recommending specific candidates. However, as political scientist G. Calvin Mackenzie has noted: "The President rarely announces a [cabinet] nomination without first assessing the sentiments of those individuals and interests most likely to be affected by the nomination"—namely members of Congress (Mackenzie 1981, xix). One former presidential aide put the issue into practical terms: "The president has got to realize that cabinet secretaries and some other major appointments have got to pass Senate scrutiny . . . So it's very important along the way . . . that he's got to be talking to the leadership as to whether or not there is a particular problem or difficulty with a particular individual."

From the first president until today, the default position has been cooperation, not conflict or isolated action. The pre-nomination process functions as a sort of conflict-mitigation mechanism that can do much to ensure that disagreements between the president and Congress are resolved long before a nomination is made. The fact is that confirmation fights—until recent decades—have been the exception, not the rule, to governing. Such disputes represent a symptom of greater underlying problems, which are not the subject of this chapter. The important point to remember is that it is in the interest of the president and Congress to maintain a friendly, productive long-term relationship. Negotiating during the pre-nomination process helps to alleviate tensions and increase the likelihood of a smooth confirmation process.

Confirmation Process

As with the pre-nomination stage, the confirmation process has largely been shaped through practice, as the text of the Constitution provides few details on how "advice and consent" should function. Because the confirmation history and pathway used for other types of nominations tracks well with how judicial candidates are reviewed and confirmed, this section will provide details on the development of the Judiciary Committee involvement with appointments.

The formal structure used today to review and confirm nominations was slow to take hold in the Senate. From 1789 to 1816, the Senate had no standing committee system. Instead, it would usually review nominations as a collective body. Not until December 10, 1816, did the Senate adopt a resolution establishing the Judiciary Committee as one of its original standing committees. Even with this change, judicial nominations were only occasionally referred to committee, because the custom remained that the entire Senate should take part in the vetting process.

During James Monroe's presidency (1817–1825), the Senate referred one of the 21 lower court nominations to committee. In that case, the Judiciary Committee received the name of South Carolina district court nominee, Thomas Lee, on February 12, 1823. For six days the committee reviewed Lee's nomination before reporting it to the Senate floor. That same day the Senate voted for confirmation by voice vote. In 1829, Anti-Jackson Senator Josiah S. Johnston of Louisiana explained how the Senate investigative process worked in the early nineteenth century: "It had been usual to lay the nominations for some days on the table, and when called up for consideration, the members of the State interested in the appointment gave the Senate the information which they might possess with regard to the character and qualifications of the person in nomination; other members sometimes gave their opinions, and upon these statements the Senate relied." Only if there were charges against the nominee or the person was unknown, Johnston went on to state, would the Senate make a committee referral.

As the federal courts expanded and the duties of the Senate increased, it became nearly impossible for senators to manage the increased workload without utilizing the committee system more fully. By 1868, the Senate adopted a rule that automatically referred all nominations to the appropriate standing committee. Since that time every judicial nomination has been referred to committee, except in unusual cases in which the nominee was a sitting senator or a former president.

The custom of presidents consulting with lawmakers during the pre-nomination process has meant that often the confirmation process goes smoothly, since the two branches confer with each other before a nomination is officially made. But the Judiciary Committee does not shy away from its responsibilities to investigate nominations. Dating back to at least 1845, the Senate Judiciary Committee has requested presidential administrations to provide documents for judicial nominees. By at least the 1890s, the committee had created a form letter to request similar information.

More recently, every judicial nomination is evaluated by the American Bar Association's Standing Committee on the Federal Judiciary. First consulted by the Judiciary Committee in 1947, the ABA judges each nominee on their professional competence, integrity, and judicial temperament. They are rated as "Well Qualified," "Qualified," or "Not Qualified."

In 1979, Chairman Edward Kennedy greatly strengthened the existing investigative procedures by assigning additional committee staff to conduct background checks on judicial nominations. This has allowed the committee to more closely scrutinize the qualifications and fitness of judicial nominations.

To aid in the investigation, the committee sends each judicial nominee a questionnaire designed to supply information on the nominee's background, including education, employment record, draft status, bar association memberships, published writings, public statements, court cases (if a judge), public offices held, political affiliations, legal career, financial holdings, and various other concerns. The questionnaire, first instituted in the late 1970s by Chairman Kennedy, has given the committee an added tool to scrutinize judicial nominations without the aid of the executive branch or the need to rely solely on home-state senators. No committee action is permitted until the questionnaire is returned.

Over the years, important information on nominees has come from outside interest groups as well. Interest group participation in judicial appointments dates at least to the 1881 opposition of President Rutherford B. Hayes's nomination of Stanley Matthews to the Supreme Court. At the time of his selection, Matthews served as chief counsel to railroad tycoon Jay Gould. Along with other business leaders, Gould lobbied Hayes for the nomination. However, populist farming groups led by the National Grange waged a successful campaign against Matthews by exposing his ties to big business. Matthews's nomination died in the Judiciary Committee without legislative action.

Despite the success of this lobbying effort, Hayes's successor, President James Garfield, decided to again nominate Matthews. This time Gould and other big business supporters mounted a major effort to confirm Matthews, which succeeded by a one-vote margin of 24 to 23.

In recent years, interest groups have redoubled their involvement in the judicial appointment process. Instead of advancing a purely economic agenda, as was the case with the Matthews nomination, these groups divide along many ideological and partisan grounds. On the conservative side, members of the Federalist Society have worked within the executive branch to support the selection of Republican judicial nominations. Other conservative organizations include the Committee for Justice, Coalition for a Fair Judiciary, and the Judicial Confirmation Network. Liberal organizations, including the Alliance for Justice, the People for the American Way, the NAACP Legal Defense & Education Fund, and the National Organization for Women, are equally involved in the judicial appointment process. These groups have many techniques to influence judicial appointments, including direct and indirect appeals to senators by organizing media campaigns, oral or written efforts of persuasion, campaign contributions, and formal testimony at confirmation hearings.

Another important aspect of the committee system and the review of judicial nominations is the "blue slip," so called because of its color. The committee counsel or nomination clerk will send out a blue slip to the senators of the state where the president has nominated an individual to seek their assessment concerning appellate court, district court, U.S. marshal, and U.S. attorney nominations. Blue slips do not apply to Supreme Court, Attorney General, Solicitor General, or other positions of a "national" nature. At times they have been used to gain information about a nominee or by home-state senators to block action on a nomination.

Created in the 1910s, blue slips first operated as a means to gain information about a judicial nominee from their home-state senators. For the first forty years, blue slips did not stop committee action. In 1956, however, newly appointed committee Chair James O. Eastland (D-MS) rewrote blue-slip policy to give senators absolute control to prevent confirmation of home-state nominees of which they disapproved. Eastland's policy allowed a senator from the home state to prevent committee action either by submitting a negative blue slip or by failing to return it. In 1979, during the Carter administration, Senator Edward Kennedy (D-MA) took over as chair and modified the blue-slip policy. He implemented a provision whereby the full committee would vote on whether to proceed if a senator failed to return a blue slip. When announcing this policy change, Kennedy acknowledged the traditional role of blue slips in the judicial appointment process and said that even he could not discard the tradition. Since that time the blue-slip policy has been strengthened and weakened depending on the political control of the Senate and presidency. By all accounts current Judiciary Chair Charles Grassley (R-IA) requires the return of a positive blue slip before moving on a nomination.

Confirmation hearings are not required by Senate or committee rules. Hearings for Supreme Court nominees were rare in the nineteenth century. However, they became more frequent by the start of the twentieth century. In 1916, the Judiciary Committee held its first open hearings to consider the nomination of Louis Brandeis. In 1925, Harlen F. Stone became the first Supreme Court nominee to appear and testify before the Judiciary Committee. A continuous practice of Supreme Court nominees appearing before the Judiciary Committee, however, did not begin until 1955 with the nomination of John M. Harlan.

Only in recent decades have lower court nominations been subject to hearings by the full committee. During Chairman Eastland's tenure from 1956 to 1978, a subcommittee managed all hearings for judicial nominations. These were often little more than perfunctory affairs. Over the last thirty-five years the committee hearing has increased in importance, but highly contentious confirmation hearings are the exception, not the norm. As Eighth Circuit Judge Richard S. Arnold once stated: "if you're a nominee for one of the lower courts and a lot of senators show up at your hearing, you're in trouble."

Depending on the nominee, a hearing is often the only time s/he is able to publicly address charges made against her/him. If there are concerns about a nominee, then a hearing also gives senators a chance to ask questions, which might help them determine the fitness of a candidate. If answers are not forthcoming or the senators feel that a nominee is not qualified to sit on the federal bench, the committee may decide not to act or the president may be forced to withdraw the nominee.

At the Supreme Court level many nominees, like John Roberts, Samuel Alito, and Sonia Sotomayor, go through a rather smooth process with only moments of intense questioning. For nominees like Robert H. Bork and Clarence Thomas, the hearings have proved to be painful affairs. Only hours after Bork was nominated by Republican President Ronald Reagan in 1987, Senator Edward Kennedy took to the floor of the Senate and gave his "Robert Bork's America" speech. In it, Kennedy said that if the Senate confirmed Bork "women would be forced into back alley abortions, blacks would sit at segregated lunch counters, rogue policemen could break down citizen's doors in midnight raids, school children could not be taught about evolution, writers and artists could be censured at the whim of government." At his hearing, Bork's scholarly-like responses to senators' questions did not win him any votes. Bork came across at best as overbearing and at worst as a rightwing ideologue who would take the Supreme Court back to the nineteenth century. The Judiciary Committee reported Bork's nomination unfavorably by a 9 to 5 vote, and the Democratic-controlled Senate rejected him 42 to 58.

Mindful of what had happened to Bork, Thomas said very little during his confirmation hearings. At times he appeared to be evasive toward questions on such well-known topics as abortion rights. Despite the lack of forthcoming answers, Thomas' nomination was reported without recommendation by a 13 to 1 vote to the Senate. However, before a confirmation vote could be held, news reports surfaced that a former employee of Thomas, Anita Hill, had alleged that he had sexually harassed her. The Judiciary Committee decided to hold additional hearings. Thomas did not admit to harassing Hill and denounced the committee's handling of the matter: "How would any member on this committee or any person in this room or any person in this country like sleaze said about him or her in this fashion or this dirt dredged up and this gossip and these lies displayed in this manner? How would any person like it?" He explained that there "was an FBI investigation" into the allegations. "This is not an opportunity to talk about difficult matters privately or in a closed environment," Thomas said. "This is a circus. It is a national disgrace. And from my standpoint . . . it is a high-tech lynching for uppity blacks."

In response to the Thomas confirmation hearing and the manner in which the sexual harassment allegations were reviewed, the Judiciary Committee established special procedures, whereby it now holds a closed session with each Supreme Court nominee to inquire about any charges made. Both the majority and minority counsels brief the committee about any charges or concerns.

Hearings on nominees to lower courts tend to be less intense and have not traditionally included the same preparation procedures as with Supreme Court nominees. However, the increased scrutiny of lower court nominees has caused recent administrations to undergo more intense preparations for these positions. Some of the additional aid involves providing nominees with transcripts of previous hearings, but a more important benefit has been a briefing on committee hearing procedures. In addition, the administration preps nominees by reviewing the potential questions senators might ask on particular legal concerns or distinctive parts of a nominee's legal career.

The last step at the committee stage is a vote, with all nominations being required to receive a positive vote to report to the Senate. However, even if such a vote occurs, a combination of Senate procedures, political compromises, and timing issues must all come together to ensure that a confirmation vote occurs. The Senate floor stage is perhaps the most trying, because the scheduling of floor time for debates and voting must be negotiated between the majority and minority parties. Often the Senate does not have the luxury of focusing only on nominations. The confirmation process is only one small, albeit important, part of what the Senate does. Aside from voting on nominations, the Senate has to manage oversight, appropriations, treaties, trade agreements, presidential vetoes, and other matters of public policy concern.

Scheduling is therefore always a pressing concern and a difficult aspect of the confirmation process. All nominations reported from committee are listed on the Executive

Calendar, with no assumption that a vote will be held. At this point the majority leader has the discretion to determine when and even whether a nomination will receive a confirmation vote. Senate rules do not require the majority leader to schedule a nomination for consideration.

Senators may resort to "holds" to delay or prevent a confirmation vote. Unlike blue slips, holds are not normally publicly disclosed and have not been made available on a government or private website. Although nowhere mentioned in the rules of the Senate, holds are informal devices that block action on measures scheduled for floor consideration. The majority leader, through his ability to set the Senate's agenda, decides whether and for how long he will honor a hold. Generally, holds are honored because they are linked to the power of a senator to filibuster or to object when the majority leader asks for unanimous consent. Without the consent of all its members, no measure can easily pass in the Senate. As a result, each senator has the ability to create a lot of mischief.

Holds are not absolute veto devices. Majority leaders have acted on nominations and bills "in the face of a senator's hold, in effect challenging the senator to object and obstruct Senate consideration of a measure." According to political scientist Steven S. Smith, often "the weight of opinion and the concern about retribution from alienated senators usually are great enough to suppress objection" (Smith 1989, 110). Yet holds are usually respected. At the end of a legislative session, when floor time is precious, their use means that a nomination or measure will likely not pass the Senate.

Holds came into existence out of a necessity to ensure that the Senate could conduct its business in a timely manner and still respect the rights of individual senators. For the most part, the Senate operates under compromises between the majority and minority party in what are known as unanimous consent agreements (UCA). To obtain a UCA, the Senate created holds to give senators the ability to object to particular nominations or measures before they were scheduled for a vote. Holds became a key part of the legislative process. Traditionally, holds were not used on judicial nominations, but in recent years they have become an important tool in confirmation battles. Usually a hold is a delaying tactic, but if used effectively it can prevent confirmation of a judicial nomination. By permitting a delay, a senator has time to review a nominee's record before making a decision on confirmation. A senator can also use a hold to block a nominee whose views he disagrees with. In disputes with a president or even with another senator, a hold can be used as strategic leverage to ensure passage of preferred legislation or confirmation of a favored nominee.

There have been occasional calls to abolish or modify the practice of holds. In 1985, a group of 60 senators agreed on changes, but no substantial modifications were adopted. Twelve years later, in 1997, Senators Ron Wyden (D-OR) and Charles Grassley (R-IA) failed in their effort to make holds public information. In 2002, the two senators again introduced a resolution to end secret holds. However, the Senate did not act. A year later, Senate leadership established a limited disclosure of holds, but it did not change formal rules. The Senate agreed to a similar reform measure in 2007 as part of the Honest Leadership and Open Government Act. Section 512 of the act, titled "Notice of Objecting to Proceeding," encouraged more openness but did not force senators to make holds known. At most, the new policy is treated as a voluntary requirement and carries with it no enforcement mechanism. In short, senators conclude that holds are a useful procedural tool.

A hold is an effective tool, but its power is founded on the threat of senators to speak as long as they wish—thus bringing to a halt Senate business and, in the case of judicial nominations, preventing an up-or-down vote. The filibuster is the source of every senator's power and has done much to shape the Senate's customs and traditions. The right to debate is based on Senate Rule XIX, which states that "No Senator shall interrupt another Senator in debate without his consent." Unlike the House, senators are not recognized to speak for a set number of minutes. Senators are not accustomed to cede the floor or even be interrupted without their consent. Couple this right with the lack of time limits on debate, and this creates the possibility of filibusters that senators can use to delay or block action on judicial nominations. The only exception is if Senate Rule XXII, referred to as cloture, is invoked. The rule permits a senator to submit a motion, signed by at least 16 senators, "to bring to a close the debate." A vote on a cloture motion cannot be held until two days after it is presented. At that point, the Senate can vote to end debate, but it takes three-fifths of the Senate, or 60 senators, to invoke cloture.

The first successful filibuster of a judicial nomination occurred in 1968, when President Lyndon B. Johnson nominated Associate Justice Abe Fortas for Chief Justice. Several senators opposed Fortas because of his friendship with Johnson, liberal views, ethical concerns over payments received for lectures given at American University, and the hope of giving Richard Nixon (running for president that year) the opportunity to make the selection. Republican and southern Democratic senators mounted a filibuster to block Fortas's confirmation. After an unsuccessful attempt to cut off debate failed 45 to 43, Fortas asked that his name be withdrawn, thus marking the first time the Senate filibustered a judicial nomination.

More recently, President Barack Obama has experienced partisan battles over filibusters. After he had been in office less than a year, Senate Republicans tried to block the confirmation of Seventh Circuit nominee David Hamilton through the use of the filibuster, but the Senate would eventually confirm. In 2010 Senate Republicans filibustered three more of Obama's judicial nominations. Democrats grew frustrated. Senator Patrick Leahy attacked the use of filibusters by Republicans, calling them a baseless means to merely "delay and obstruct of President Obama's nominations."

Filibusters of lower court nominations are not new. Early in his presidency, six of George W. Bush's nominations were filibustered. By 2004 Senate Republicans were insisting on "up-or-down" votes for their stalled judicial nominations and even threatened a "nuclear option." Under this procedure, the presiding officer of the Senate would declare filibusters of judicial nominations unconstitutional and thus out of order. If the minority party challenged the ruling, the majority party would need only a simple majority to prevail. A procedural move of this magnitude would have limited the power of the Senate minority to block a confirmation vote. Instead of Senate leadership coming together, a bipartisan group of 14 senators (known as the "Gang of Fourteen") agreed to a plan that put an end to most of the filibustering and promoted greater cooperation between the two parties.

During Obama's presidency, Democrats began to propose similar measures. In early 2010, Democratic Senator Tom Harkin of Iowa introduced a resolution to amend

Senate rules to decrease the votes necessary to stop a filibuster. After the first cloture vote, the threshold required to end debate would be reduced from 60 to 57. If that vote failed, on the third try 54 votes would be needed, until finally cloture could pass with only 51 votes. Another Senate resolution, offered by New Mexico Senator Tom Udall, would fix that problem by abolishing the two-thirds requirement in making Senate rules changes.

For over three years Senate Majority Leader Harry Reid did not move on the idea of weakening the filibuster. However, in the fall 2013 tensions rose as Democratic senators increasingly viewed Republicans as obstructing President Obama's nominations and overall agenda. In particular, Democratic Senator Jeff Merkley noted that the failed cloture vote on Mel Watt's nomination to be the director of the Federal Housing Finance Agency in late October restarted talks of using the nuclear option. Within a month of that vote, Reid decided to use the nuclear option and change Senate rules to allow all executive-branch nominations and most judicial nominations, except for Supreme Court candidates, to be confirmed by simple majority votes.

FUTURE IMPLICATIONS

One cannot address the future of the appointment process without focusing on the significant change to the filibuster rule ushered into the Senate by Democratic lawmakers. The most logical feature of the rule change is that a greater number of nominations will be confirmed when the same political party controls both the White House and Senate. At least immediately after the filibuster rule change, this assumption has proved true. Speaking a year after the rule change took place, Majority Leader Reid boasted: "Senate Democrats were able to overcome political gridlock and confirm the highest number of district and circuit court judges in a single Congress in over thirty years." Considering that Senate Democrats accomplished this feat in only one year, that number is remarkable.

When the presidency and Senate are not controlled by the same political party, the most likely outcome will be continued ideological battles, delays, and fewer confirmed nominations. If that assumption proves correct, then there will also likely be a greater variation in the confirmation rates, based on whether there is unified or divided government. It is still too soon to tell how the appointment process will play out with Republicans back in control of the Senate. However, it appears that the quick confirmation pace that the Obama administration enjoyed when Democrats led the Senate has slowed and stopped completely for high-profile nominations, especially for positions to the U.S. circuit courts, with a Republican-controlled Senate.

Some believe that the filibuster rule change will expand to include Supreme Court nominees, and perhaps even legislation, so those measures can be decided by a simple majority vote. Currently only executive-branch and lower court nominations are exempted from the filibuster. Conservative pundit Charles Krauthammer was one of the first to publicly declare that Republicans should use the nuclear option to push legislation through the Senate. Republican Senator Mike Lee has also come out in support of such a move. If this occurs, there are likely to be fundamental changes in how the Senate operates, not only when managing nominations but in all legislative matters. If the filibuster is completely removed, there will be little incentive to run the institution in a way that promotes deliberation and dialog. Instead, the Senate will likely become a clone of the House of Representatives, where the majority can control the debate and pass legislation without support from the minority political party.

FURTHER READING

Abraham, Henry J. 2007. *Justices, Presidents, and Senators: A History of the U.S. Supreme Court Appointments from Washington to Bush II*. New York: Rowman & Littlefield Publishers.

Binder, Sarah A., and Forrest Maltzman. 2009. *Advice & Dissent: The Struggle to Shape the Federal Judiciary*. Washington, D.C.: Brookings Institution Press.

Fisher, Louis. 2014. *Constitutional Conflicts between Congress and the President*. Lawrence, KS: University Press of Kansas.

Gerhardt, Michael J. 2000. *The Federal Appointment Process: A Constitutional and Historical Analysis*. Durham, NC: Duke University Press.

Graves, Scott E., and Robert M. Howard. 2009. *Justice Takes a Recess: Judicial Appointments from George Washington to George W. Bush*. Lanham, MD: Lexington Books.

Harris, Joseph P. 1953. *The Advice and Consent of the Senate*. Berkeley: University of California Press.

Mackenzie, G. Calvin. 1981. *The Politics of Presidential Appointments*. New York: The Free Press.

Rutkus, Denis Steven. 2010. Supreme Court Appointment Process: Roles of the President, Judiciary Committee, and Senate. *CRS Report*, Feb. 19.

Smith, Steven S. 1989. *Call to Order: Floor Politics in the House and Senate*. Washington, D.C.: Brookings Institution Press.

Sollenberger, Mitchel A. 2011 *Judicial Appointments and Democratic Controls*. Durham, NC: Carolina Academic Press.

19 THE POWER TO ENFORCE THE CIVIL WAR AMENDMENTS

Jesse Merriam

Article XIII

Sect. 1. Neither slavery nor involuntary servitude, except as a punishment for crime whereof the party shall have been duly convicted, shall exist within the United States, or any place subject to their jurisdiction.

Sect. 2. Congress shall have power to enforce this article by appropriate legislation.

Article XIV

Sect. 1. All persons born or naturalized in the United States, and subject to the jurisdiction thereof, are citizens of the United States and of the State wherein they reside. No State shall make or enforce any law which shall abridge the privileges or immunities of citizens of the United States; nor shall any State deprive any person of life, liberty, or property, without due process of law; nor deny to any person within its jurisdiction the equal protection of the laws.

Sect. 2. Representatives shall be apportioned among the several States according to their respective numbers, counting the whole number of persons in each State, excluding Indians not taxed. But when the right to vote at any election for the choice of electors for President and Vice President of the United States, Representatives in Congress, the Executive and Judicial officers of a State, or the members of the Legislature thereof, is denied to any of the male inhabitants of such State, being twenty-one years of age, and citizens of the United States, or in any way abridged, except for participation in rebellion, or other crime, the basis of representation therein shall be reduced in the proportion which the number of such male citizens shall bear to the whole number of male citizens twenty-one years of age in such State.

Sect. 3. No person shall be a Senator or Representative in Congress, or elector of President and Vice President, or hold any office, civil or military, under the United States, or under any State, who, having previously taken an oath, as a member of Congress, or as an officer of the United States, or as a member of any State legislature, or as an executive or judicial officer of any State, to support the Constitution of the United States, shall have engaged in insurrection or rebellion against the same, or given aid or comfort to the enemies thereof. But Congress may by a vote of two-thirds of each House, remove such disability.

Sect. 4. The validity of the public debt of the United States, authorized by law, including debts incurred for payment of pensions and bounties for services in suppressing insurrection or rebellion, shall not be questioned. But neither the United States nor any State shall assume or pay any debt or obligation incurred in aid of insurrection or rebellion against the United States, or any claim for the loss or emancipation of any slave; but all such debts, obligations and claims shall be held illegal and void.

Sect. 5. The Congress shall have power to enforce, by appropriate legislation, the provisions of this article.

ARTICLE XV

Sect. 1. The right of citizens of the United States to vote shall not be denied or abridged by the United States or by any State on account of race, color, or previous condition of servitude.

Sect. 2. The Congress shall have power to enforce this article by appropriate legislation.

KEY TERMS

The Civil War Amendments are the 13th, 14th, and 15th Amendments. They were ratified in 1865, 1868, and 1870 respectively and created a new constitutional device for securing civil rights. Each amendment provided in its final section that Congress shall have the authority "to enforce . . . by appropriate legislation" the guarantees provided in that amendment, thereby giving Congress the power to enforce the 13th Amendment prohibition on slavery, the 14th Amendment guarantees of due process and equal protection of law against state governments, and the 15th Amendment protection of voting rights against both the federal and state governments. These provisions have come to be known as "enforcement provisions."

Since the ratification of the Civil War Amendments, similar enforcement provisions have been a part of every constitutional amendment guaranteeing individual rights, but at the time of the ratification of the Civil War Amendments, enforcement provisions were entirely novel to the American constitutional system. Indeed, none of the rights enumerated in the first twelve amendments mention which branch of government is responsible for their enforcement. Moreover, the rights and procedures guaranteed in those first twelve amendments were intended solely to *limit* congressional power. But the Civil War Amendments explicitly limited state authority, while also expanding federal authority, over various subject matters relating to race and civil rights.

This difference between the Civil War Amendments and the preceding constitutional amendments is due to the dramatically different political contexts in which these amendments arose. At the time of the Founding, citizens generally had more faith in their local governments than in the newly formed union. Responding to this concern, the Founders sought to limit federal but not state authority via the Bill of Rights. After the Civil War, however, this faith had been reversed, especially with regard to the ability and willingness of states to treat their black residents fairly. The Framers of the Civil War Amendments created this new enforcement authority to give Congress a broader power over national governance, an expansion that many saw as necessary to protect African Americans.

Two questions are central to understanding Congress's enforcement power under the Civil War Amendments. The first is a *who* question: Who is subject to Congress's enforcement power? Only state officials who have violated the underlying guarantee? Or private actors as well? This public/private distinction is significant because the 13th Amendment, in prohibiting slavery, is the only one of the Civil War Amendments that explicitly constrains private as well as public actions. The 14th and 15th Amendments, by contrast, prohibit only governmental action: the 14th Amendment prohibits states from denying any person within their jurisdictions due process or equal protection of the law, and the 15th Amendment prohibits states, as well as the federal government, from denying citizens the right to vote on the basis of race.

A major issue arising under this *who* question is whether the 14th and 15th Amendments give Congress a power over *private* action, even though the substantive guarantees in those amendments apply only to *governmental* action. Progressives have often argued that *all* of the enforcement powers under the Civil War Amendments reach private actions. According to this argument, even a private citizen's racial discrimination—say, a waiter's denying a black person service at a restaurant—is subject to congressional regulation, as part of Congress's power to enforce the 14th Amendment's guarantee that states may not deny citizens an equal protection of the law. This interpretation holds that Congress, in prohibiting the waiter's discrimination against a black patron, would be enforcing the same principle of equal protection enshrined in the 14th Amendment. Conservatives, however, have sought to limit the scope of each respective enforcement provision according to the reach of the substantive guarantee it is designed to enforce. Under this view, Congress may use its 13th Amendment enforcement power to regulate private conduct, because that amendment deals with private action (i.e., private individuals enslaving other private individuals), but Congress may use its 14th Amendment enforcement power only to regulate state action, because that amendment constrains only the actions of the several states.

The second issue is a *what* question: What does it mean to enforce the Civil War Amendments? This question turns on whether the enforcement provisions give Congress the independent power to define the meaning of the substantive guarantees contained in these amendments, exclusive of any judicial or executive opinions on what these guarantees might mean. This raises the role of judicial review under the Civil War Amendments. Judicial review refers to the power of courts to determine the validity of laws according to some higher-level norm, such as the constitutional text. The Constitution does not specifically provide for the power of judicial review, but in the landmark case of *Marbury v. Madison* (1803), the Supreme Court found a robust power of judicial review in various parts of the Constitution, thus giving the federal judiciary the authority to invalidate laws it deems in violation of the Constitution. The Supreme Court has come to interpret this power to mean that it has the ultimate authority in the Republic to determine what the Constitution means.

But if the enforcement provisions were to give Congress the power to define what constitutes a violation of the underlying guarantee, this could substantially undermine the power of judicial review. It could mean, for example, that Congress could define the 13th Amendment's ban on slavery as including *any form of discrimination* against people of African descent—no matter what the Supreme Court has said on the subject. Thus, even if the Supreme Court were to rule that the 13th Amendment simply prohibits a person from actually enslaving another person, Congress still could invoke its 13th Amendment enforcement power to prohibit restaurants from discriminating on the basis of race, as part of its independent determination that such discrimination is part and parcel of the entire institution of slavery.

Advocates of a broad enforcement power argue that courts should not second-guess how Congress seeks to enforce the Civil War Amendments. Instead, courts should simply make sure that the enactment in question is reasonably related to the constitutional guarantee it purports to enforce. This interpretation of the enforcement power is bolstered by the fact that, in debating the Civil War Amendments, several proponents of the amendments explicitly compared the enforcement provisions to the necessary and proper clause in Art. I, §8, cl.18. The necessary and proper clause gives Congress the power "[t]o make all Laws which shall be necessary and proper for carrying into Execution the foregoing Powers" in Art. I, §8, as well as "all other Powers vested by the Constitution in the Government of the United States, or in any Department or Officer thereof." In *McCulloch v. Maryland* (1819), the Supreme Court, in one of Chief Justice Marshall's most famous opinions, established that the necessary and proper clause adds to, rather than limits, the scope of Congress's enumerated powers. More specifically, the Court held in that case that Congress could charter a national bank in the State of Maryland, because even though creating a national bank there would not be technically necessary for Congress to exercise its enumerated powers, the bank would be "appropriate" in facilitating Congress's exercise of these powers. Under the *McCulloch* Court's reading of the necessary and proper clause, courts need not subject congressional determinations about what is "necessary and proper" to close scrutiny. Rather, courts must inquire only into whether Congress has acted *reasonably* in seeking to effectuate one of its enumerated powers. Proponents of a broad enforcement power claim that, by using the term "appropriate" in the enforcement clauses, the framers of the Civil War Amendments were invoking Chief Justice Marshall's reasoning in *McCulloch*, which interpreted the phrase "necessary and proper" to mean "appropriate" to the effectuation of Congress's enumerated powers.

Proponents of a narrower interpretation of the enforcement power point to two important differences between the necessary and proper clause and the enforcement provisions. One, whereas the broad interpretation focuses on the similarity between "necessary and proper" and "appropriate legislation," the narrow interpretation emphasizes the difference between "carrying into Execution" other laws and "enforcing" constitutionally guaranteed rights. Enforcement seems to require a tighter fit between Congress's enactment and the meaning of the relevant guarantee the enactment seeks to secure. Proponents of this narrow view of the enforcement authority often argue that the power to *enforce* a constitutional guarantee is simply the power to provide *remedies* for violations of that guarantee. Under this interpretation, Congress may create civil or criminal actions against slaveholders as part of its 13th Amendment enforcement power, but it may not *define* the meaning of slavery under the 13th Amendment however it pleases. This position gives a distinct status to courts in defining the meaning of the substance of the Civil War Amendments, leaving Congress only with the power to create remedies against those who violate these judicial interpretations.

Two, while it is true that the framers of the Civil War Amendments directly compared the enforcement provisions to the necessary and proper clause, they did not end up using the same language of "necessary and proper." And given that the Framers of these amendments were well aware of how the necessary and proper clause had been interpreted by the Supreme Court, one would expect them to use identical language in the Civil War Amendments if they wanted to give Congress the same broad power over their meaning.

This issue regarding Congress's enforcement power to define constitutional meaning is one of those rare issues in which liberals tend to argue for a narrower interpretation and conservatives for a broader version of judicial review. This division has been particularly striking when Congress and the Supreme Court have disagreed over the meaning of the Civil War Amendments. The discussion that follows, concerning the history and development of the enforcement power, addresses these *who* and *what* questions through a summary of the leading congressional debates and Supreme Court opinions on the subject.

HISTORY AND DEVELOPMENT

During the Reconstruction Era, generally thought to cover the years 1863–1877, Congress passed several important civil rights laws under its new enforcement powers, arousing significant constitutional controversy, as part of the much larger controversy over the entire enterprise of Reconstruction. The period involved intense discord between Northern Republicans—often referred to as the "Radical Republicans" for their zealotry in advancing black civil rights—and Southern Democrats, many of whom had supported the Confederacy. The Radical Republicans were outraged by the possibility of these former Confederates representing the South in Congress and making political decisions on behalf of the very country they had just rebelled against. The Radical Republicans believed that the Confederates had to be punished for their rebellion. Moreover, they contended, winning war should give the victor certain privileges, and the North should use its war victory to uplift African Americans and facilitate their assimilation into general society. And if this required some coercive legal tactics, such as the disenfranchisement of Southern whites or military control over the South, then so be it. Racial equality was worth the price.

Many Southern Democrats, however, saw this period as one of unrivaled corruption, bare partisanship, and crude opportunism. Southern Democrats argued that Reconstruction was designed to maximize financial and political gain for the exploitive coalition of "Carpetbaggers" (Northern whites who traveled South to run various enterprises), "Scalawags" (Southern whites who welcomed Republican rule, often times for self-interested reasons), and black freedmen—all at the expense of the conquered Southern whites.

Just as Reconstruction divided the North and South, it has similarly divided scholars, often in politically charged ways. For a long time, historians tended to agree with the Southern account, finding that Reconstruction politics were characterized by an unusual amount of corruption and incompetence. This account received its strongest intellectual support in the early twentieth century from the Dunning School (named after Columbia University Professor William Archibald Dunning), and for much of the twentieth century it had a strong hold of public opinion, as is evident in the popularity of such Southern-sympathetic accounts of the era as the 1939 film *Gone with the Wind*.

In the 1960s, however, many historians and political scientists began challenging the Dunning School, charging that it was based on cynical and racist suppositions about the possibilities of interracial political coalitions and the capacities of black governance. Much of this revisionary literature not only defended Reconstruction as legitimate but also argued that, if the era had any shortcomings, it was that the period was insufficiently aggressive in promoting black progress. Reconstruction was, in Eric Foner's words, "America's unfinished revolution."

Historians today generally accept that although Reconstruction did involve significant corruption and opportunism, it was not an unusually bad period for politics, especially in light of the exigency following the war. Coinciding with the historic election of President Barack Obama in 2008, there has been a movement to reform the national understanding of Reconstruction and to redirect attention on how the period ushered in many of the laudable civil rights goals that we continue to pursue in the twenty-first century.

Regardless of one's political position, one thing is certainly clear about Reconstruction: It transformed federal-state relations. This is what makes the period so controversial as a constitutional matter. In many ways, our contemporary debates over the *who* and *what* questions relating to Congress's enforcement powers represent continuing disagreement over how to reconcile Reconstruction's tremendous expansion of federal authority with the original Constitution's guarantee of state sovereignty and limited federal powers.

Reconstruction and the Creation of Congress's Enforcement Powers

The first major constitutional debate over Congress's enforcement power appeared in the Senate Debate over the Civil Rights Act of 1866, one year after the 13th Amendment's ratification and two years before the 14th Amendment's ratification. The Civil

Rights Act of 1866 sought to eradicate the so-called "black codes." After the Civil War, many Southern states had replaced their slave codes (laws restricting the lives of slaves) with nearly identical black codes (laws imposing similar burdens on the freedmen in seeking employment, using property, and testifying in court).

In passing the Civil Rights Act of 1866, a question arose over Congress's authority to reach into such local matters. President Andrew Johnson, a Democrat and staunch opponent of the Republican-led Reconstruction, vetoed the bill, claiming that it was outside of Congress's authority and therefore unconstitutional. As Johnson put it, "Slavery has been abolished," and only if slavery were resuscitated would it "become the duty of the General Government to exercise" its power under the newly created 13th Amendment enforcement authority. Johnson was thus raising the *what* question discussed above, concerning whether Congress may define the meaning of slavery in enforcing the 13th Amendment. According to Johnson, the 13th Amendment enforcement authority gave Congress only the power to create remedies against people who violated the prohibition against slavery.

Johnson's veto, however, was promptly overridden by the necessary two-thirds of Congress, marking the first time in the nation's history that Congress had trumped a presidential veto on a major piece of legislation. Given this historic moment, many of the Radical Republicans took the time to detail how the bill fit within Congress's 13th Amendment enforcement power. Senator Charles Sumner, one of the most radical of the Republicans, defended the bill on the ground that "the protection of the colored race in civil rights is essential to complete the abolition of Slavery."

Some moderate Republicans, however, disagreed with this interpretation of the 13th Amendment. For example, Senator Edgar Cowan argued that because the Civil Rights Act of 1866 applied to *all* African Americans, whether they had been slaves or not, the bill was actually an enforcement of a prohibition on racial discrimination, not an enforcement of a prohibition on slavery. On this point, Representative John Bingham, though a Radical Republican himself, agreed that the Civil Rights Act of 1866 was not justified under the 13th Amendment. Bingham argued that a new constitutional amendment, prohibiting state-sanctioned racial discrimination, was necessary to authorize such an enforcement power. To create such a power, Bingham drafted the 14th Amendment.

Ratified two years after the Civil Rights Act of 1866, the 14th Amendment was intended to provide the necessary constitutional support for the Act by prohibiting states from depriving persons within their jurisdictions of due process or equal protection of the law. The ratification process was a highly contentious affair, reaching resolution only after the Republicans (1) denied Southern representation in Congress until the amendment was ratified, (2) dissolved through military force the ten Southern state legislatures that initially voted against the amendment, and (3) finally held new votes for the amendment in these ten states but with a newly formed electorate that included black men but excluded former Confederate soldiers (i.e., most white men in the states). Although there were claims that the 14th Amendment was not properly ratified in compliance with the amendment process specified in Article V of the Constitution, these complaints quickly dissipated, and within a few years the 14th Amendment became largely accepted as giving Congress the authority to regulate racial discrimination engaged in by the states, such as the type of discrimination banned in the Civil Rights Act of 1866.

But did the 14th Amendment also constrain *private* affairs? This question was brought before the Court in *U.S. v. Cruikshank* (1875), where the Court held that the 14th Amendment's guarantees of due process and equal protection constrain only state actors, not individuals acting in a private capacity. That case involved charges under the Enforcement Act of 1870, as well as various constitutional provisions, including the recently ratified 14th Amendment, against several white men involved in the Colfax Massacre. This massacre was the single most violent clash between whites and blacks in Reconstruction, involving the deaths of three whites and an estimated 150 blacks. The violence erupted over the disputed 1872 Louisiana election, leading to a stand-off at the Colfax, Louisiana, courthouse between a group of white insurgents who had gathered together to raid the courthouse and transfer power to the Democrats, and a group of freedmen and black state militia who were occupying the courthouse in an effort to secure the offices for the Republicans.

After the United States brought charges under the Enforcement Act of 1870 against several white insurgents for violating the constitutional rights of the black victims, a lower court quashed the indictment for failing to state a valid legal claim, and the U.S. Supreme Court affirmed this ruling. According to the Court, the Act could not provide a basis for prosecution against the white insurgents, because "The power of the National Government is limited to the enforcement" of the 14th Amendment guarantees of equal protection and due process, and this amendment does not constrain private individuals. In hewing closely to the 14th Amendment's applicability to state actors, the Court infuriated the Radical Republicans, who saw it as a reactionary retreat from Reconstruction.

The Radical Republicans had bigger problems outside of the Supreme Court, however, as many members of their own party started to feel that, after a decade of federal intervention, Reconstruction had gone too far in punishing Southern whites. Despite this growing resistance, the Radical Republicans pushed ahead, finally passing the Civil Rights Act of 1875, after being proposed by Senator Charles Sumner five years earlier. This Act was the boldest piece of Reconstruction legislation to date, surpassing the Civil Rights Act of 1866 by banning *private* racial discrimination engaged in by "inns, public conveyances on land or water, theaters, and other places of public amusement."

But the tide continued tugging against the Radical Republicans, eventually leading the federal government in 1877 to withdraw troops from the South. This withdrawal was part of the Compromise of 1877, an informal deal between Democrats and Republicans in resolving the contested Hayes-Tilden presidential election of 1876. Samuel J. Tilden (the Democrat candidate) had won the popular vote, but there were 20 contested electoral votes. The Republicans agreed that, in exchange for these votes, making Rutherford B. Hayes (the Republican candidate) the victor, they would cede authority over the South to the local Democrats, signaling the end of Reconstruction.

If there were any lingering doubts about Reconstruction's survival after the withdrawal of federal troops, the Court put such doubts to rest six years later with the *Civil Rights Cases* (1883). These were five consolidated cases involving constitutional challenges to the Civil Rights Act of 1875, arising from all around the country—California, Kansas, Missouri, New York, and Tennessee—a vivid reminder that racial segregation was not just a part of Southern life. In each of these cases, the private parties had clearly violated the Civil Rights Act of 1875 by denying African Americans access to public accommodations because of their race, making the only issue, once the cases reached the Supreme Court, whether Congress had the authority under its enforcement powers to pass the Act.

The Supreme Court, 8–1, held that neither the 13th nor the 14th Amendment enforcement authority warranted the Act. As for the 13th Amendment enforcement authority, the Court held that it gave Congress only the power to regulate *slavery*, not acts only tangentially related to that institution. In Justice Bradley's words, to interpret the 13th Amendment enforcement authority to encompass all forms of discrimination against African Americans would require "running the slavery argument into the ground," as this would give Congress a plenary authority over all aspects of personal race relations, something that the Court did not find to be part of the purpose or text of the 13th Amendment. Likewise, the Court flatly rejected the 14th Amendment argument on the ground that inter-personal relations are "not the subject-matter of the Amendment."

The Court concluded the opinion with now-infamous language expressing its frustration with Reconstruction's preoccupation with the upliftment of African Americans: "When a man has emerged from slavery, and, by the aid of beneficent legislation, has shaken off the inseparable concomitants of that state, there must be some stage in the progress of his elevation when he takes the rank of a mere citizen and ceases to be the special favorite of the laws, and when his rights as a citizen or a man are to be protected in the ordinary modes by which other men's rights are protected."

Dissenting alone, Justice Harlan took issue with the majority's patronizing language, finding that less than twenty years after the abolition of slavery it was "scarcely just to say that the colored race has been the special favorite of the laws." Harlan also challenged the two major premises in the majority's holdings on the scope of Congress's 13th and 14th Amendment enforcement authority. According to Harlan, the 13th Amendment gave Congress authority over private racial discrimination, because such discrimination is part of the "badges of slavery and servitude." The 13th Amendment enforcement power therefore authorized Congress to pass the Civil Rights Act of 1875 as part of its authority over the "the eradication not simply of the [slavery] institution, but of its badges and incidents." As for the 14th Amendment enforcement authority, Harlan claimed that it authorized Congress to regulate private businesses that opened themselves up to the public, since these businesses are licensed by law and are therefore places of "quasi-public employment."

Although President Chester Arthur supported Harlan's position and pushed Congress to pass new civil rights legislation, Congress did not comply, as the Radical Republicans had lost their sway over the party, which had largely lost interest in the Reconstruction enterprise. The legacy of Reconstruction's failures loomed over the Republic for the next century. Indeed, until the Civil Rights Movement, nearly a century after Reconstruction, Congress did not employ its enforcement power to protect blacks from Jim Crow legislation.

Although many civil rights gains were made during this period, these battles were not fought through Congress, but rather through the federal judiciary, which, as a life-tenured and unelected body, was more receptive than Congress to such claims. One of the principal goals of this litigation was to desegregate public education, and after a long and arduous battle, led by the NAACP, this goal was finally realized in the Court's landmark decision of *Brown v. Board of Education* (1954).

The *Brown* decision, however, incited significant resistance throughout the South, agitating extraordinary acts of brutality against African Americans. Re-igniting unresolved issues from Reconstruction, many Southerners claimed that they could not be subject to the *Brown* decision, because the 14th Amendment was ratified under Northern coercion. The Georgia State Legislature even passed a resolution declaring that the 14th and 15th Amendments were essentially ratified "at the point of the bayonet," thus making them "null and void and of no effect." It was this Southern backlash against *Brown* that inspired a sizable political majority, especially among Democrat voters in the Northern part of the country, to get back on board with the Reconstruction agenda that the Radical Republicans had initiated a century earlier. In what is often referred to as the Second Reconstruction, Congress again sought to use its enforcement authority over the Southern states to empower black political representation, enhance black financial and educational achievement, and eradicate private racial discrimination.

The Civil Rights Movement and the Expansion of the Enforcement Powers

The Civil Rights Act of 1964 and the Voting Rights Act of 1965 created significant constitutional controversies over the scope of Congress's enforcement power under the Civil War Amendments. Unlike 100 years earlier, however, when the Court was a reluctant, and sometimes even hostile, participant in Congress's Reconstruction agenda, this time the Court, veering leftward under the guidance of Chief Justice Earl Warren, was on board—and at times led the march.

Title II was one of the most controversial provisions in the Civil Rights Act of 1964, as this provision was nearly identical to the Civil Rights Act of 1875 in banning racial discrimination in places of public accommodation (e.g., restaurants). Given the *Civil Rights Cases* (1883), Congress realized that Title II was vulnerable to a constitutional challenge as exceeding its enforcement power. But Congress was also well aware that since Reconstruction there had been a significant change in the Court's interpretations of the commerce clause, thereby offering a new path, outside of the Civil War Amendments, for Congress's authority to pass Title II. To understand this path requires some background on the development of the Court's commerce clause jurisprudence in the early twentieth century.

In the 1930s, President Franklin D. Roosevelt pushed for the Court to interpret the Constitution broadly to accommodate the New Deal. After much resistance, the Court eventually capitulated, and in several important cases in the late 1930s and early 1940s, the Court started interpreting Congress's power under the commerce clause to permit Congress to regulate not simply channels of interstate commerce (e.g., roads, bridges) and objects in interstate commerce (e.g., goods passing from one state to another), but also *intrastate activities* that have a substantial effect on the national economy (e.g., wheat produced by a local farmer). (See Chapter 3.)

Drawing from these precedents, the proponents of the Civil Rights Act of 1964 framed racial discrimination in economic rather than moral terms, in an attempt to justify Title II as an invocation of Congress's commerce rather than enforcement power. As Senator Hubert Humphrey, the lead author of the legislation, contended in congressional debate, the commerce clause gave Congress the authority to prohibit racial discrimination in places of public accommodation, because "Discrimination and segregation on racial grounds have a substantial adverse effect on the interstate flow of goods, capital, and of persons."

Two Supreme Court cases that year—*Heart of Atlanta Motel Inc. v. United States* (1964), involving a large Atlanta, Georgia, motel that refused to rent rooms to blacks, and *Katzenbach v. McClung* (1964), involving a Birmingham, Alabama, barbecue restaurant that refused to serve blacks—validated Title II under the commerce clause. Unlike the *Civil Rights Cases* (1883), where the Court was nearly unanimous in invalidating the Civil Rights Act of 1876, the Court was now unanimous in *upholding* nearly identical legislation. The only disagreement within the Court in these cases was over whether to use the commerce clause or Section 5 of the 14th Amendment to uphold Title II.

Justice Clark, writing for the majority of the Court, opted to use the commerce clause, thereby accepting how the Court in the *Civil Rights Cases* interpreted the 13th Amendment enforcement authority to apply only to the subject of slavery and the 14th Amendment enforcement authority to apply only to state actions. In concurrence, however, Justice Douglas argued that the Court should have used the 14th Amendment as the basis for upholding the Civil Rights Act of 1964, thus overruling the Court's decision in the *Civil Rights Cases*. According to Douglas, overruling that precedent "would have a more settling effect, making unnecessary litigation over whether a particular restaurant or inn is" part of interstate commerce. Justice Goldberg agreed with Douglas that the 14th Amendment should have provided the basis for upholding the Civil Rights Act of 1964, because notwithstanding Congress's invocation of the commerce clause in passing the act, it was clear that the "primary purpose of the [law] . . . is the vindication of human dignity and not mere economics."

Continuing the steady march of the Second Reconstruction, President Lyndon B. Johnson proposed the Voting Rights Act of 1965, which sought to eliminate the racially discriminatory voting practices that pervaded much of the South. Whereas the *Civil Rights Cases* had presented an obstacle to Congress's using its enforcement authority to ban private racial discrimination in the Civil Rights Act of 1964, there was no direct obstacle under Supreme Court precedent preventing Congress from using its enforcement authority to extend voting rights. For this reason, in contrast to its commerce-centered debate over the Civil Rights Act of 1964, in debating the Voting Rights Act of 1965 Congress explicitly relied on its enforcement authority under the 14th and 15th Amendments.

Within a year of the passage of the Voting Rights Act, the Court heard two major challenges to its constitutionality. In *South Carolina v. Katzenbach* (1966), South

Carolina invoked the Court's original jurisdiction over cases involving lawsuits between states and the United States. South Carolina challenged various provisions in the Act, focusing in particular on the preclearance requirement. Under this requirement, if the federal government determined that a state had "engaged in the use of tests or devices for the purpose or with the effect of denying or abridging the right to vote on account of race or color," that state would no longer be allowed to change its voting procedures without first getting federal approval that the changes would not have racially discriminatory effects. For many Southerners, this requirement bore many of the unsavory features of Reconstruction, with the federal government, under Northern control, once again exercising authority over the political process in Southern states.

In an 8–1 opinion, written by Chief Justice Earl Warren, the Court upheld this preclearance requirement on the ground that the 15th Amendment enforcement authority means that "Congress may use any rational means to effectuate the constitutional prohibition of racial discrimination in voting." According to the Court, the preclearance requirement satisfied this low standard, because it was perfectly reasonable for Congress to focus the federal government's limited resources on those states that historically had the most serious problems with regard to racial discrimination and voting rights.

Justice Hugo Black, a native Alabaman, concurred with most of the Court's opinion, but dissented, alone, from the part of the opinion upholding the preclearance requirement. Recalling some of the Southern outrage over Reconstruction, Justice Black wrote that "the inevitable effect of any such law which forces any one of the States to entreat federal authorities in far-away places for approval of local laws before they can become effective is to create the impression that the State or States treated in this way are little more than conquered provinces."

Within a month of deciding the South Carolina case, the Court heard oral arguments in *Katzenbach v. Morgan* (1966), another major challenge to the Act. This case did not turn on the preclearance requirement but rather Section 4(e). This provision sought to protect the voting rights of New York City's growing Puerto Rican population by providing "that no person who has completed the sixth grade in a public school, or an accredited private school, in Puerto Rico in which the language of instruction was other than English shall be disfranchised for inability to read or write English." A key precedent in this challenge was *Lassiter v. Northampton County Board of Elections* (1959), holding that literacy tests for voting do not violate the 15th Amendment. Given the *Lassiter* ruling, how could Section 4(e), banning the use of a particular type of literacy test, be an *enforcement* of the 15th Amendment?

The Court, 7–2, held that this was a valid enforcement, because Congress has the independent power to determine the scope of the meaning of the constitutional guarantee it is seeking to enforce. Writing for the Court, Justice Brennan explained, in what has become known as his "ratchet theory," that the enforcement power functions as a one-way ratchet, giving Congress the power to strengthen, but not weaken, constitutional protections beyond judicial determinations. In advancing this ratchet theory, Brennan explicitly compared the enforcement provisions to the necessary and proper clause, claiming that "the draftsmen sought to grant to Congress, by a specific provision applicable to the Fourteenth Amendment, the same broad powers expressed in the Necessary and Proper Clause."

Justice Harlan, joined by Justice Stewart, took issue with this claim, contending that treating the enforcement provision as just another necessary and proper clause would simply give "Congress the power to define the substantive scope of the [relevant] Amendment." Moreover, Harlan criticized Brennan's ratchet theory as being unprincipled in allowing for the use of congressional discretion only to *strengthen*, and not *weaken*, judicial determinations. Discretion must be allowed to go *both ways*.

Two years later, the Court pushed this enforcement theory even further in *Jones v. Alfred H. Mayer Company* (1968). That case involved a refusal by Alfred H. Mayor Company, a large housing development corporation, to sell a recently created planned community property to an interracial couple in St. Louis, Missouri, which at the time prohibited interracial marriage. Because the case arose shortly before passage of the Fair Housing Act, the couple turned to an old statute as its basis for relief, 42 USC § 1982, originally passed as Section 1 of the Civil Rights Act of 1866.

There were several questions before the Court, two of which are significant for our purposes here in investigating the scope of Congress's enforcement authority. One was whether the Civil Rights Act of 1866 not only constrained public but also private actors, like the Alfred H. Mayer Company, in selling property. The other question was whether, if the Act did indeed reach such private action, Congress had the enforcement authority to pass the Act.

The Court, again 7–2, but with Justice Stewart writing the opinion this time, answered both questions in the affirmative, interpreting the legislative history surrounding the Civil Rights of 1866 to indicate that the Act was designed to apply not only to public but also to private actors, and that Congress had the power to pass this law as part of its enforcement of the 13th Amendment. By interpreting the 13th Amendment enforcement power this way, the Court asserted that it should be highly deferential to how Congress construes the meaning of slavery: "Surely Congress has the power under the Thirteenth Amendment rationally to determine what are the badges and the incidents of slavery, and the authority to translate that determination into effective legislation." The Court found a ban on private racial discrimination in the context of real estate transactions to be rationally related to Congress's enforcement of the 13th Amendment ban on slavery, because "when racial discrimination herds men into ghettos and makes their ability to buy property turn on the color of their skin, then it too is a relic of slavery."

Justice Harlan dissented, repeating his concern that this broad interpretation of the enforcement power would unduly expand federal authority. Harlan challenged the majority's understanding of the relevant legislative history and reminded the Court that the 14th Amendment was adopted precisely due to a concern that the 13th Amendment would not generate an enforcement authority broad enough to encompass the 1866 Act's application to racial discrimination falling short of slavery.

The *Jones* case completed a remarkable turnaround between the First and Second Reconstructions, with the only consistent Warren Court critic of Justice Harlan's *Civil Rights Cases* dissent being his grandson and namesake, Justice John Marshall Harlan II. Adding to this irony, what in 1866 ignited the first constitutional controversy over the enforcement power turned out to generate the Supreme Court's farthest-reaching enforcement decision, the *Jones* decision, almost exactly 100 years later, with the

Supreme Court coming full circle, now on the side of the Radical Republicans—thus giving a sense of resolution to those who had labored so long for racial equality.

But this resolution would be short-lived, making *Jones* the high-water mark in Congress's enforcement authority. The changing tide in the Supreme Court, largely due to the rise of the legal conservative movement in the 1980s, led to a diminished view of the enforcement power in two major Rehnquist Court cases, *City of Boerne v. Flores* (1997) and *U.S. v. Morrison* (2000), thereby resuscitating the enforcement vision enunciated in the *Civil Rights Cases*.

The Legal Conservative Movement and the Weakened Enforcement Powers

The *Boerne* case arose out of the Religious Freedom Restoration Act, an extraordinary act in several respects. The legislation was not only passed by an overwhelming bipartisan majority, commanding a nearly unanimous House and Senate, but this bipartisanship also enjoyed support from strange bedfellows, including liberal advocacy groups like the American Civil Liberties Union (ACLU) as well as many conservative Christian organizations. These groups united for the explicit purpose of overruling the Supreme Court's decision in *Employment Division v. Smith* (1990), which they believed had been an erroneous interpretation of the free exercise (of religion) clause (Bill of Rights, Art. I, cl. 2). Although a few major pieces of legislation have enjoyed such bipartisan support, and some statutes have sought to alter Supreme Court opinions, never before had a major piece of legislation done both. That is all to say: The *Smith* decision was *that* unpopular. But why?

The *Smith* decision overruled, or at least substantially narrowed the scope of, the Court's decision in *Sherbert v. Verner* (1963), which at the time was the governing test under the free exercise clause. Under the *Sherbert* test, if a law "substantially burdened" a religious practice, the law was invalid unless the government could show that the law was "narrowly tailored" to achieve a "compelling interest." The *Smith* decision held that the Court had often applied this religion-protective doctrine in diluted ways to rule for the government. According to the *Smith* majority, the real test that the Court had been implicitly applying in these cases was that the free exercise clause prohibits laws that are either not generally applicable or not religiously neutral, whether or not the laws substantially burden religious practices.

This new test infuriated divergent religious communities and rights-advocacy organizations, which had looked to the *Sherbert* test for protection from government regulation. Congress passed RFRA to require courts to go back to the old *Sherbert* test and apply it in all cases in which a federal or state law substantially burdens a religious practice.

The question quickly arose as to what constitutional authority Congress had to impose RFRA on the states. This clearly was not permissible under the commerce clause, because it subjected *all* state and local governmental actions that had a substantial burden on religious practices to the *Sherbert* test, whether or not those practices were economic in nature. But it was plausible that Congress could invoke its 14th Amendment enforcement power as its constitutional authority for passing RFRA, because the statute sought to enforce Congress's understanding of the free exercise clause, a constitutional provision that had been "incorporated" by the Supreme Court to apply to the states via the 14th Amendment. In other words, because the free exercise clause constrained state action only because of the 14th Amendment (i.e., the free exercise clause, as well as the other provisions in the Bill of Rights, constrained only federal action), and because Congress passed RFRA to restore the Supreme Court's *Sherbert* understanding of the free exercise clause, RFRA was an enforcement of the 14th Amendment.

This was the argument that Patrick Flores, the Catholic Archbishop of San Antonio, Texas, made in *City of Boerne v. Flores* (1997). The case arose after Flores sought a building permit to enlarge the St. Peter's Church in Boerne, Texas, because, at its current size, the church was unable to accommodate many of its parishioners for Sunday masses. Because the church was a 1923 mission-style building located in a historic district, the local zoning authorities denied the request. Flores then sued the city, on the ground that this denial violated the free exercise clause as well as RFRA.

Under the free exercise clause, as interpreted in *Smith*, Flores had a weak claim, because it was clear that the city was not targeting churches through its historic preservation laws. But under RFRA, Flores had a strong case. By limiting the number of parishioners the church could accommodate, the denial of the permit substantially burdened the church's religious practices, and the city's interest in preserving the integrity of this particular building did not appear sufficiently strong to override that burden on religious worship.

But the Supreme Court, 6–3, ruled against Flores, on the ground that Congress lacked the authority to impose RFRA on the state and local governments. Writing for the majority, Justice Anthony Kennedy held that RFRA was not a valid use of the enforcement authority. The Court explained that the *Katzenbach v. Morgan* decision was different, in that the facts at issue in that case involved Congress banning a state law that likely would have violated the 14th Amendment anyway; indeed, the New York State literacy voting requirement likely violated the equal protection clause because it targeted Puerto Ricans. That case, therefore, involved something much more like Congress's enforcement—i.e., a remedy—of a state violation of the 14th Amendment. Flores's challenge to Boerne's historic preservation laws, however, involved a challenge to the very type of religiously neutral and generally applicable law that the Supreme Court had just declared in *Smith* to be in compliance with the free exercise clause. RFRA thus presumptively banned a state act that the free exercise clause clearly permitted.

Justice Kennedy rejected the rationality standard applied in the Warren Court enforcement cases, and announced in its place a new standard, the "congruence and proportionality" test. Under the Warren Court enforcement decisions, Congress simply had to establish a *rational* connection between the challenged law and the 14th Amendment injury that the law sought to cure. But under the "congruence and proportionality" test, Congress must show that the remedy closely fits the violation. Thus, while RFRA would seem to satisfy the Warren Court rationality test, since it seemed perfectly rational for Congress to protect religious individuals and organizations from state acts that would have been unconstitutional under the *Sherbert* ruling, RFRA was invalid as applied to the state and local governments under this tougher "congruence and proportionality" test, because there is not a sufficiently close remedy-injury fit when Congress seeks to *change* a constitutional standard, as it sought to do in RFRA by rejecting the *Smith* test. As Justice Kennedy explained, "Congress does not enforce a constitutional right by changing what the right is."

The Court thus resuscitated in *Boerne* the *Civil Rights Cases'* answer to the *what* question: The judiciary, and not Congress, has the final say over *what* the Constitution means, and that meaning, and only that meaning, is what Congress may enforce. Three years later, in *U.S. v. Morrison* (2000), the Court also affirmed that the *Civil Rights Cases'* answer to *who* is subject to the enforcement power: The enforcement power tracks the subject of the relevant amendment, and therefore the 14th Amendment enforcement authority does not reach private action.

The *Morrison* case involved a constitutional challenge to the Violence Against Women Act (1994), which, among other things, created a federal civil cause of action for women who had been victims of gender-motivated violence. In September 1994, Christy Brzonkala, at the time a freshman at Virginia Tech University, was allegedly gang raped by Antonio Morrison and James Crawford, both members of the Virginia Tech football team. After Brzonkala filed a complaint with the university, Virginia Tech found insufficient evidence to discipline Crawford but found Morrison guilty of sexual assault and suspended him for two semesters. This sentence incited significant campus controversy, with Morrison threatening to sue the University on the ground that he had been denied due process as a black man accused of raping a white woman. In the midst of this controversy, Virginia Tech decided to reduce Morrison's sentence. When Brzonkala discovered that Morrison would be returning to campus in fall 1995, she withdrew from the university and sued Morrison in federal court for damages under VAWA, becoming the first woman to bring a suit under the Act.

By a 5–4 vote, the Court held that Congress had exceeded its constitutional authority in creating a federal civil action for gender-motivated violence, and thus Brzonkala's suit against Morrison could not prevail. The Court explained that the commerce clause did not authorize her lawsuit against Morrison, because gender-motivated violence is not an economic activity. Nor did the 14th Amendment's enforcement clause authorize her lawsuit, because although a *state's* discrimination on the basis of gender violates the 14th Amendment, and thus would warrant Congress's creating legal remedies against offending states, a *private individual's* discrimination on the basis of gender cannot violate the 14th Amendment, and thus cannot be the basis for congressional action under the 14th Amendment's enforcement authority. The four liberal Justices on the Court dissented, focusing on the commerce clause point, but Justice Breyer took the time to explain in his dissenting opinion why he also disagreed with the majority's holding as to the enforcement authority. According to Breyer, the states' *inaction* in protecting women from gender-motivated violence could constitute the necessary state *action* under Congress's 14th Amendment enforcement authority.

The *Morrison* decision, in limiting the application of the enforcement authority to protect from legal liability a black man in a Southern state accused of raping a white woman, represents a peculiar turnaround in the enforcement authority's functionality, which, of course, had traditionally focused on protecting blacks from Southern white violence. This turnaround stems from the fact that the enforcement power, though arising out of the particular political and social context surrounding the Civil War and Reconstruction, is not simply about protecting one racial group from another, or empowering one political party over another, or subjecting one geographic region to another. Rather, at its essence, the enforcement power is about the type of constitutional system we want. Do we want a system whereby the federal government has broad authority over local matters, allowing the federal government to trump state power when it deems state action (or inaction) insufficient? Do we want a system where the federal government can use this power to reach into private, interpersonal relations? And do we want a system in which Congress, rather than the Supreme Court, is the ultimate source of constitutional meaning, at least when it comes to the meaning of the rights guaranteed in the Civil War Amendments? The Constitution created in 1787 would answer these questions quite differently from the Constitution amended under Reconstruction. The question for us is which Constitution we want to live under today.

FUTURE IMPLICATIONS

The scope of the enforcement provisions may be of great significance in the coming decades, especially if the Roberts Court seeks to continue the Rehnquist Court's efforts to restrict federal authority. So far, the Roberts Court's federalism jurisprudence has been mixed, with Chief Justice Roberts often seeking a middle-ground position between the conservative and liberal justices on the breadth of federal authority under the commerce clause.

As for the future of enforcement power doctrine, the "congruence and proportionality" test announced in the *Boerne* case continues to be the governing standard, but it has been used by the liberal justices in several cases after *Boerne* to justify a broad enforcement power. This prompted Justice Scalia in later years to urge the Court to reject the test, in favor of a more restrictive standard focusing on whether the congressional enactment functions as a remedy against actual, as opposed to merely hypothetical, constitutional violations. Even Justice Scalia, however, conceded that due to cases like *South Carolina* and *Morgan*, he felt obligated under *stare decisis* to accept Congress's broad enforcement power to enact prophylactic legislation against racial discrimination. It remains to be seen whether the Court will take up Scalia's proposal to change the "congruence and proportionality" standard, and whether the Court will carve out a special exception for Congress's enforcement power over race issues. Such doctrinal niceties, of course, will be relevant only if the Civil War enforcement provisions are not mooted by an all-encompassing federal power under the commerce clause.

FURTHER READING

Ackerman, Bruce. 1998. *We the People, Volume 2: Transformations*. Cambridge, MA: Harvard University Press.

Calabresi, Steven G., and Nicholas P. Stabile. 2009. On Section 5 of the Fourteenth Amendment. *University of Pennsylvania Journal of Constitutional Law* 11: 1431.

Foner, Eric. 1988. *Reconstruction: America's Unfinished Revolution, 1863–1877.* New York: Harper and Row.

McConnell, Michael. 1997. Institutions and Interpretation: A Critique of *City of Boerne v. Flores. Harvard Law Review* 111: 153.

Zietlow, Rebecca. 2006. *Enforcing Equality: Congress, the Constitution, and the Protection of Individual Rights.* New York: New York University Press.

APPENDIX A

THE ARTICLES OF CONFEDERATION AND PERPETUAL UNION

To all to whom these Presents shall come, we the undersigned Delegates of the States affixed to our Names send greeting.

Articles of Confederation and perpetual Union between the states of New Hampshire, Massachusetts-bay Rhode Island and Providence Plantations, Connecticut, New York, New Jersey, Pennsylvania, Delaware, Maryland, Virginia, North Carolina, South Carolina and Georgia.

I.

The Stile of this Confederacy shall be **"The United States of America"**.

II.

Each state retains its sovereignty, freedom, and independence, and every power, jurisdiction, and right, which is not by this Confederation expressly delegated to the United States, in Congress assembled.

III.

The said States hereby severally enter into a firm league of friendship with each other, for their common defense, the security of their liberties, and their mutual and general welfare, binding themselves to assist each other, against all force offered to, or attacks made upon them, or any of them, on account of religion, sovereignty, trade, or any other pretense whatever.

IV.

The better to secure and perpetuate mutual friendship and intercourse among the people of the different States in this Union, the free inhabitants of each of these States, paupers, vagabonds, and fugitives from justice excepted, shall be entitled to all privileges and immunities of free citizens in the several States; and the people of each State shall free ingress and regress to and from any other State, and shall enjoy therein all the privileges of trade and commerce, subject to the same duties, impositions, and restrictions as the inhabitants thereof respectively, provided that such restrictions shall not extend so far as to prevent the removal of property imported into any State, to any other State, of which the owner is an inhabitant; provided also that no imposition, duties or restriction shall be laid by any State, on the property of the United States, or either of them.

If any person guilty of, or charged with, treason, felony, or other high misdemeanor in any State, shall flee from justice, and be found in any of the United States, he shall, upon demand of the Governor or executive power of the State from which he fled, be delivered up and removed to the State having jurisdiction of his offense.

Full faith and credit shall be given in each of these States to the records, acts, and judicial proceedings of the courts and magistrates of every other State.

V.

For the most convenient management of the general interests of the United States, delegates shall be annually appointed in such manner as the legislatures of each State shall direct, to meet in Congress on the first Monday in November, in every year, with a power reserved to each State to recall its delegates, or any of them, at any time within the year, and to send others in their stead for the remainder of the year.

No State shall be represented in Congress by less than two, nor more than seven members; and no person shall be capable of being a delegate for more than three years in any term of six years; nor shall any person, being a delegate, be capable of holding any office under the United States, for which he, or another for his benefit, receives any salary, fees or emolument of any kind.

Each State shall maintain its own delegates in a meeting of the States, and while they act as members of the committee of the States.

In determining questions in the United States in Congress assembled, each State shall have one vote.

Freedom of speech and debate in Congress shall not be impeached or questioned in any court or place out of Congress, and the members of Congress shall be protected in their persons from arrests or imprisonments, during the time of their going to and from, and attendence on Congress, except for treason, felony, or breach of the peace.

VI.

No State, without the consent of the United States in Congress assembled, shall send any embassy to, or receive any embassy from, or enter into any conference, agreement, alliance or treaty with any King, Prince or State; nor shall any person holding any office of profit or trust under the United States, or any of them, accept any present, emolument, office or title of any kind whatever from any King, Prince or foreign State; nor shall the United States in Congress assembled, or any of them, grant any title of nobility.

No two or more States shall enter into any treaty, confederation or alliance whatever between them, without the consent of the United States in Congress assembled, specifying accurately the purposes for which the same is to be entered into, and how long it shall continue.

No State shall lay any imposts or duties, which may interfere with any stipulations in treaties, entered into by the United States in Congress assembled, with any King, Prince or State, in pursuance of any treaties already proposed by Congress, to the courts of France and Spain.

No vessel of war shall be kept up in time of peace by any State, except such number only, as shall be deemed necessary by the United States in Congress assembled, for the defense of such State, or its trade; nor shall any body of forces be kept up by any State in time of peace, except such number only, as in the judgement of the United States in Congress assembled, shall be deemed requisite to garrison the forts necessary for the defense of such State; but every State shall always keep up a well-regulated and disciplined militia, sufficiently armed and accoutered, and shall provide and constantly have ready for use, in public stores, a due number of filed pieces and tents, and a proper quantity of arms, ammunition and camp equipage.

No State shall engage in any war without the consent of the United States in Congress assembled, unless such State be actually invaded by enemies, or shall have received certain advice of a resolution being formed by some nation of Indians to invade such State, and the danger is so imminent as not to admit of a delay till the United States in Congress assembled can be consulted; nor shall any State grant commissions to any ships or vessels of war, nor letters of marque or reprisal, except it be after a declaration of war by the United States in Congress assembled, and then only against the Kingdom or State and the subjects thereof, against which war has been so declared, and under such regulations as shall be established by the United States in Congress assembled, unless such State be infested by pirates, in which case vessels of war may be fitted out for that occasion, and kept so long as the danger shall continue, or until the United States in Congress assembled shall determine otherwise.

VII.

When land forces are raised by any State for the common defense, all officers of or under the rank of colonel, shall be appointed by the legislature of each State respectively, by whom such forces shall be raised, or in such manner as such State shall direct, and all vacancies shall be filled up by the State which first made the appointment.

VIII.

All charges of war, and all other expenses that shall be incurred for the common defense or general welfare, and allowed by the United States in Congress assembled, shall be defrayed out of a common treasury, which shall be supplied by the several States in proportion to the value of all land within each State, granted or surveyed for any person, as such land and the buildings and improvements thereon shall be estimated according to such mode as the United States in Congress assembled, shall from time to time direct and appoint.

The taxes for paying that proportion shall be laid and levied by the authority and direction of the legislatures of the several States within the time agreed upon by the United States in Congress assembled.

IX.

The United States in Congress assembled, shall have the sole and exclusive right and power of determining on peace and war, except in the cases mentioned in the sixth article — of sending and receiving ambassadors — entering into treaties and alliances, provided that no treaty of commerce shall be made whereby the legislative power of the respective States shall be restrained from imposing such imposts and duties on foreigners, as their own people are subjected to, or from prohibiting the exportation or importation of any species of goods or commodities whatsoever — of establishing rules for deciding in all cases, what captures on land or water shall be legal, and in what manner prizes taken by land or naval forces in the service of the United States shall be divided or appropriated — of granting letters of marque and reprisal in times of peace — appointing courts for the trial of piracies and felonies commited on the high seas and establishing courts for receiving and determining finally appeals in all cases of captures, provided that no member of Congress shall be appointed a judge of any of the said courts.

The United States in Congress assembled shall also be the last resort on appeal in all disputes and differences now subsisting or that hereafter may arise between two or more States concerning boundary, jurisdiction or any other causes whatever; which authority shall always be exercised in the manner following. Whenever the legislative or executive authority or lawful agent of any State in controversy with another shall present a petition to Congress stating the matter in question and praying for a hearing, notice thereof shall be given by order of Congress to the legislative or executive authority of the other State in controversy, and a day assigned for the appearance of the parties by their lawful agents, who shall then be directed to appoint by joint consent, commissioners or judges to constitute a court for hearing and determining the matter in question: but if they cannot agree, Congress shall name three persons out of each of the United States, and from the list of such persons each party shall alternately strike out one, the petitioners beginning, until the number shall be reduced to thirteen; and from that number not less than seven, nor more than nine names as Congress shall direct, shall in the presence of Congress be drawn out by lot, and the persons whose names shall be so drawn or any five of them, shall be commissioners or judges, to hear and finally determine the controversy, so always as a major part of the judges who shall hear the cause shall agree in the determination: and if either party shall neglect to attend at the day appointed, without showing reasons, which Congress shall judge sufficient, or being present shall refuse to strike, the Congress shall proceed to nominate three persons out of each State, and the secretary of Congress shall strike in behalf of such party absent or refusing; and the judgement and sentence of the court to be appointed, in the manner before prescribed, shall be final and conclusive; and if any of the parties shall refuse to submit to the authority of such court, or to appear or defend their claim or cause, the court shall nevertheless proceed to pronounce sentence, or judgement, which shall in like manner be final and decisive, the judgement or sentence and other proceedings being in either case transmitted to Congress, and lodged among the acts of Congress for the security of the parties concerned: provided that every commissioner, before he sits in judgement, shall take an oath to be administered by one of the judges of the supreme or superior court of the State, where the cause shall be tried, 'well and truly to hear and determine the matter in question, according to the best of his judgement, without favor, affection or hope of reward': provided also, that no State shall be deprived of territory for the benefit of the United States.

All controversies concerning the private right of soil claimed under different grants of two or more States, whose jurisdictions as they may respect such lands, and the States which passed such grants are adjusted, the said grants or either of them being at the same time claimed to have originated antecedent to such settlement of jurisdiction, shall on the petition of either party to the Congress of the United States, be finally determined as near as may be in the same manner as is before prescribed for deciding disputes respecting territorial jurisdiction between different States.

The United States in Congress assembled shall also have the sole and exclusive right and power of regulating the alloy and value of coin struck by their own authority, or by that of the respective States — fixing the standards of weights and measures throughout the United States — regulating the trade and managing all affairs with the Indians, not members of any of the States, provided that the legislative right of any State within its own limits be not infringed or violated — establishing or regulating post offices from one State to another, throughout all the United States, and exacting such postage on the papers passing through the same as may be requisite to defray the expenses of the said office — appointing all officers of the land forces, in the service of the United States, excepting regimental officers — appointing all the officers of the naval forces, and commissioning all officers whatever in the service of the United States — making rules for the government and regulation of the said land and naval forces, and directing their operations.

The United States in Congress assembled shall have authority to appoint a committee, to sit in the recess of Congress, to be denominated 'A Committee of the States', and to consist of one delegate from each State; and to appoint such other committees and civil officers as may be necessary for managing the general affairs of the United States under their direction — to appoint one of their members to preside, provided that no person be allowed to serve in the office of president more than one year in any term of three years; to ascertain the necessary sums of money to be raised for the service of the United States, and to appropriate and apply the same for defraying the public expenses — to borrow money, or emit bills on the credit of the United States, transmitting every half-year to the respective States an account of the sums of money so borrowed or emitted — to build and equip a navy — to agree upon the number of land forces, and to make requisitions from each State for its quota, in proportion to the number of white inhabitants in such State; which requisition shall be binding, and thereupon the legislature of each State shall appoint the regimental officers, raise the men and cloath, arm and equip them in a solid-like manner, at the expense of the United States; and the officers and men so cloathed, armed and equipped shall march to the place appointed, and within the time agreed on by the United States in Congress assembled. But if the United States in Congress assembled shall, on consideration of circumstances judge proper that any State should not raise men, or should raise a smaller number of men than the quota thereof, such extra number shall be raised, officered, cloathed, armed and equipped in the same manner as the quota of each State, unless the legislature of such State shall judge that such extra number cannot be safely spread out in the same, in which case they shall raise, officer, cloath, arm and equip as many of such extra number as they judge can be safely spared. And the officers and men so cloathed, armed, and equipped, shall march to the place appointed, and within the time agreed on by the United States in Congress assembled.

The United States in Congress assembled shall never engage in a war, nor grant letters of marque or reprisal in time of peace, nor enter into any treaties or alliances, nor coin money, nor regulate the value thereof, nor ascertain the sums and expenses necessary for the defense and welfare of the United States, or any of them, nor emit bills, nor borrow money on the credit of the United States, nor appropriate money, nor agree upon the number of vessels of war, to be built or purchased, or the number of land or sea forces to be raised, nor appoint a commander in chief of the army or navy, unless nine States assent to the same: nor shall a question on any other point, except for adjourning from day to day be determined, unless by the votes of the majority of the United States in Congress assembled.

The Congress of the United States shall have power to adjourn to any time within the year, and to any place within the United States, so that no period of adjournment be for a longer duration than the space of six months, and shall publish the journal of their proceedings monthly, except such parts thereof relating to treaties, alliances or military operations, as in their judgement require secrecy; and the yeas and nays of the delegates of each State on any question shall be entered on the journal, when it is desired by any delegates of a State, or any of them, at his or their request shall be furnished with a transcript of the said journal, except such parts as are above excepted, to lay before the legislatures of the several States.

X.

The Committee of the States, or any nine of them, shall be authorized to execute, in the recess of Congress, such of the powers of Congress as the United States in Congress assembled, by the consent of the nine States, shall from time to time think expedient to vest them with; provided that no power be delegated to the said Committee, for the exercise of which, by the Articles of Confederation, the voice of nine States in the Congress of the United States assembled be requisite.

XI.

Canada acceding to this confederation, and adjoining in the measures of the United States, shall be admitted into, and entitled to all the advantages of this Union; but no other colony shall be admitted into the same, unless such admission be agreed to by nine States.

XII.

All bills of credit emitted, monies borrowed, and debts contracted by, or under the authority of Congress, before the assembling of the United States, in pursuance of the present confederation, shall be deemed and considered as a charge against the United States, for payment and satisfaction whereof the said United States, and the public faith are hereby solemnly pleged.

XIII.

Every State shall abide by the determination of the United States in Congress assembled, on all questions which by this confederation are submitted to them. And the Articles of this Confederation shall be inviolably observed by every State, and the Union shall be perpetual; nor shall any alteration at any time hereafter be made in any of them; unless such alteration be agreed to in a Congress of the United States, and be afterwards confirmed by the legislatures of every State.

And Whereas it hath pleased the Great Governor of the World to incline the hearts of the legislatures we respectively represent in Congress, to approve of, and to authorize us to ratify the said Articles of Confederation and perpetual Union. Know Ye that we the undersigned delegates, by virtue of the power and authority to us given for that purpose, do by these presents, in the name and in behalf of our respective constituents, fully and entirely ratify and confirm each and every of the said Articles of Confederation and perpetual Union, and all and singular the matters and things therein contained: And we do further solemnly plight and engage the faith of our respective constituents, that they shall abide by the determinations of the United States in Congress assembled, on all questions, which by the said Confederation are submitted to them. And that the Articles thereof shall be inviolably observed by the States we respectively represent, and that the Union shall be perpetual.

In Witness whereof we have hereunto set our hands in Congress. Done at Philadelphia in the State of Pennsylvania the ninth day of July in the Year of our Lord One Thousand Seven Hundred and Seventy-Eight, and in the Third Year of the independence of America.

Agreed to by Congress 15 November 1777 In force after ratification by Maryland, 1 March 1781

Source: Records of the Continental and Confederation Congresses and the Constitutional Convention, 1774–1789, Record Group 360; National Archives.

APPENDIX B

THE CONSTITUTION OF THE UNITED STATES OF AMERICA

WE, the People of the United States, in order to form a more perfect union, establish justice, insure domestic tranquility, provide for the common defence, promote the general welfare, and secure the blessings of liberty to ourselves and our posterity, do ordain and establish this Constitution for the United States of America.

ARTICLE I.

Sect. 1. ALL legislative powers herein granted shall be vested in a Congress of the United States, which shall consist of a Senate and House of Representatives.

Sect. 2. The House of Representatives shall be composed of members chosen every second year by the people of the several states, and the electors in each state shall have the qualifications requisite for electors of the most numerous branch of the state legislature. No person shall be a representative who shall not have attained to the age of twenty-five years, and been seven years a citizen of the United States, and who shall not, when elected, be an inhabitant of that state in which he shall be chosen. Representatives and direct taxes shall be apportioned among the several states which may be included within this Union, according to their respective numbers, which shall be determined by adding to the whole number of free persons, including those bound to service for a term of years, and excluding Indians not taxed, three-fifths of all other persons. The actual enumeration shall be made within three years after the first meeting of the Congress of the United States, and within every subsequent term of ten years, in such manner as they shall by law direct. The number of representatives shall not exceed one for every thirty thousand, but each state shall have at least one representative; and until such enumeration shall be made, the state of New-Hampshire shall be entitled to chuse three, Massachusetts eight, Rhode-Island and Providence Plantations one, Connecticut five, New-York six, New Jersey four, Pennsylvania eight, Delaware one, Maryland six, Virginia ten, North-Carolina five, South-Carolina five, and Georgia three.

When vacancies happen in the representation from any state, the Executive authority thereof shall issue writs of election to fill such vacancies.

The House of Representatives shall chuse their Speaker and other officers; and shall have the sole power of impeachment.

Sect. 3. The Senate of the United States shall be composed of two senators from each state, chosen by the legislature thereof, for six years; and each senator shall have one vote. Immediately after they shall be assembled in consequence of the first election, they shall be divided as equally as may be into three classes. The seats of the senators of the first class shall be vacated at the expiration of the second year, of the second class at the expiration of the fourth year, and of the third class at the expiration of the sixth year, so that one-third may be chosen every second year; and if vacancies happen by resignation, or otherwise, during .he recess of the Legislature of any state, the Executive thereof may make temporary appointments until the next meeting of the Legislature, which shall then fill such vacancies.

No person shall be a senator who shall not have attained to the age of thirty years, and been nine years a citizen of the United States, and who shall not, when elected, be an inhabitant of that state for which he shall be chosen.

The Vice-President of the United States shall be President of the senate, but shall have no vote, unless they be equally divided.

The Senate shall chuse their other officers, and also a President pro tempore, in the absence of the Vice-President, or when he shall exercise the office of President of the United States.

The Senate shall have the sole power to try all impeachments. When sitting for that purpose, they shall be on oath or affirmation. When the President of the United States is tried, the Chief Justice shall preside: And no person shall be convicted without the concurrence of two-thirds of the members present.

Judgment in cases of impeachment shall not extend further than to removal from office, and disqualification to hold and enjoy any office of honor, trust or profit under the United States; but the party convicted shall nevertheless be liable and subject to indictment, trial, judgment and punishment, according to law.

Sect. 4 The times, places and manner of holding elections for senators and representatives, shall be prescribed in each state by the legislature thereof; but the Congress may at any time by law make or alter such regulations, except as to the places of chusing Senators.

The Congress shall assemble at least once in every year, and such meeting shall be on the first Monday in December, unless they shall by law appoint a different day.

Sect. 5. Each house shall be the judge of the elections, returns and qualifications of its own members, and a majority of each shall constitute a quorum to do business; but a smaller number may adjourn from day to day, and may be authorized to compel the attendance of absent members, in such manner, and under such penalties as each house may provide.

Each house may determine the rules of its proceedings, punish its members for disorderly behaviour, and, with the concurrence of two-thirds, expel a member.

Each house shall keep a journal of its proceedings, and from time to time publish the same, excepting such parts as may in their judgment require secrecy; and the yeas and nays of the members of either house on any question shall, at the desire of one-fifth of those present, be entered on the journal. Neither house, during the session of Congress, shall, without the consent of the other, adjourn for more than three days, nor to any other place than that in which the two houses shall be sitting.

Sect. 6. The senators and representatives shall receive a compensation for their services, to be ascertained by law, and paid out of the treasury of the United States. They shall in all cases, except treason, felony and breach of the peace, be privileged from arrest during their attendance at the session of their respective houses, and in going to and returning from the same; and for any speech or debate in either house, they shall not be questioned in any other place.

No senator or representative shall, during the time for which he was elected, be appointed to any civil office under the authority of the United States, which shall have been created, or the emoluments whereof shall have been encreased during such time; and no person holding any office under the United States, shall be a member of either house during his continuance in office.

Sect. 7. All bills for raising revenue shall originate in the house of representatives; but the senate may propose or concur with amendments as on other bills.

Every bill which shall have passed the house of representatives and the senate, shall, before it become a law, be presented to the president of the United States; if he approve he shall sign it, but if not he shall return it, with his objections to that house in which it shall have originated, who shall enter the objections at large on their journal, and proceed to reconsider it. If after such reconsideration two-thirds of that house shall agree to pass the bill, it shall be sent, together with the objections, to the other house, by which it shall likewise be reconsidered, and if approved by two-thirds of that house, it shall become a law. But in all such cases the votes of both houses shall be determined by yeas and nays, and the names of the persons voting for and against the bill shall be entered on the journal of each house respectively. If any bill shall not be returned by the President within ten days (Sundays excepted) after it shall have been presented to him, the same shall be a law, in like manner as if he had signed it, unless the Congress by their adjournment prevent its return, in which case it shall not be a law.

Every order, resolution, or vote to which the concurrence of the Senate and House of Representatives may be necessary (except on a question of adjournment) shall be presented to the President of the United States; and before the same shall take effect, shall be approved by him, or, being disapproved by him, shall be repassed by two-thirds of the Senate and House of Representatives, according to the rules and limitations prescribed in the case of a bill.

Sect. 8. The Congress shall have power

To lay and collect taxes, duties, imposts and excises, to pay the debts and provide for the common defence and general welfare of the United States; but all duties, imposts and excises shall be uniform throughout the United States;

To borrow money on the credit of the United States;

To regulate commerce with foreign nations, and among the several states, and with the Indian tribes;

To establish an uniform rule of naturalization, and uniform laws on the subject of bankruptcies throughout the United States;

To coin money, regulate the value thereof, and of foreign coin, and fix the standard of weights and measures;

To provide for the punishment of counterfeiting the securities and current coin of the United States;

To establish post offices and post roads;

To promote the progress of science and useful arts, by securing for limited times to authors and inventors the exclusive right to their respective writings and discoveries;

To constitute tribunals inferior to the supreme court;

To define and punish piracies and felonies committed on the high seas, and offences against the law of nations;

To declare war, grant letters of marque and reprisal, and make rules concerning captures on land and water;

To raise and support armies, but no appropriation of money to that use shall be for a longer term than two years;

To provide and maintain a navy;

To make rules for the government and regulation of the land and naval forces;

To provide for calling forth the militia to execute the laws of the union, suppress insurrections and repel invasions;

To provide for organizing, arming, and disciplining, the militia, and for governing such part of them as may be employed in the service of the United States, reserving to the States respectively, the appointment of the officers, and the authority of training the militia according to the discipline prescribed by Congress;

To exercise exclusive legislation in all cases whatsoever, over such district (not exceeding ten miles square) as may, by cession of particular States, and the acceptance of Congress, become the seat of the government of the United States, and to exercise like authority overall places purchased by the consent of the legislature of the state in which the same shall be, for the erection of forts, magazines, arsenals, dockyards, and other needful buildings; — And

To make all laws which shall be necessary and proper for carrying into execution the foregoing powers, and all other powers vested by this constitution in the government of the United States, or in any department or officer thereof.

Sect. 9. The migration or importation of such persons as any of the states now existing shall think proper to admit, shall not be prohibited by the Congress prior to the year one thousand eight hundred and eight, but a tax or duty may be imposed on such importation, not exceeding ten dollars for each person. The privilege of the writ of habeas corpus shall not be suspended, unless when in cases of rebellion or invasion the public safety may require It.

No bill of attainder or ex post facto law shall be passed. No capitation, or other direct, tax shall be laid, unless in proportion to the census or enumeration herein before directed to be taken.

No tax or duty shall be laid on articles exported from any state. No preference shall be given by any regulation of commerce or revenue to the ports of one state over those of another: nor shall vessels bound to, or from, one state, be obliged to enter, clear, or pay duties in another.

No money shall be drawn from the treasury, but in consequence of appropriations made by law; and a regular statement and account of the receipts and expenditures of all public money shall be published from time to time.

No title of nobility shall be granted by the United States: — And no person holding any office of profit or trust under them, shall, without the consent of the Congress, accept of any present, emolument, office, or title, of any kind whatever, from any king, prince, or foreign state.

Sect. 10. No state shall enter into any treaty, alliance, or confederation; grant letters of marque and reprisal; coin money; emit bills of credit; make any thing but gold and silver coin a tender in payment of debts; pass any bill of attainder, ex post facto law, or law impairing the obligation of contracts, or grant any title of nobility.

No state shall, without the consent of the Congress, lay any imposts or duties on imports or exports, except what may be absolutely necessary for executing its inspection laws; and the net produce of all duties and imposts, laid by any state on imports or exports, shall be for the use of the Treasury of the United States; and all such laws shall be subject to the revision and controul of the Congress. No state shall, without the consent of Congress, lay any duty of tonnage, keep troops, or ships of war in time of peace, enter into any agreement or compact with another state, or with a foreign power, or engage in war, unless actually invaded, or in such imminent danger as will not admit of delay.

ARTICLE II.

Sect. 1. The executive power shall be vested in a president of the United States of America. He shall hold his office during the term of four years, and, together with the vice-president, chosen for the same term, be elected as follows.

Each state shall appoint, in such manner as the legislature thereof may direct, a number of electors, equal to the whole number of senators and representatives to which the state may be entitled in the Congress: but no senator or representative, or person holding an office of trust or profit under the United States, shall be appointed an elector.

The electors shall meet in their respective states, and vote by ballot for two persons, of whom one at least shall not be an inhabitant of the same state with themselves. And they shall make a list of all the persons voted for, and of the number of votes for each; which list they shall sign and certify, and transmit sealed to the seat of the government of the United States, directed to the president of the senate. The president of the senate shall, in the presence of the senate and house of representatives, open all the certificates, and the votes shall then be counted. The person having the greatest number of votes shall be the president, if such number be a majority of the whole number of electors appointed; and if there be more than one who have such majority, and have an equal number of votes, then the house of representatives shall immediately chuse by ballot one of them for president; and if no person have a majority, then from the five highest on the list the said house shall in like manner chuse the president. But in chusing the president, the votes shall be taken by states, the representation from each state having one vote; a quorum for this purpose shall consist of a member or members from two-thirds of the states, and a majority of all the states shall be necessary to a choice. In every case, after the choice of the president, the person having the greatest number of votes of the electors shall be the vice-president. But if there should remain two or more who have equal votes, the senate shall chuse from them by ballot the vice-president.

The Congress may determine the time of chusing the electors, and the day on which they shall give their votes; which day shall be the same throughout the United States.

No person except a natural born citizen, or a citizen of the United States, at the time of the adoption of this constitution, shall be eligible to the office of president; neither shall any person be eligible to that office who shall not have attained to the age of thirty-five years, and been fourteen years a resident within the United States.

In case of the removal of the president from office, or of his death, resignation, or inability to discharge the powers and duties of the said office, the same shall devolve on the vice-president, and the Congress may by law provide for the case of removal, death, resignation or inability, both of the president and vice-president, declaring what officer shall then act as president, and such officer shall act accordingly, until the disability be removed, or a president shall be elected.

The president shall, at stated times, receive for his services, a compensation, which shall neither be encreased nor diminished during the period for which he shall have been elected, and he shall not receive within that period any other emolument from the United States, or any of them.

Before he enter on the execution of his office, he shall take the following oath or affirmation:

"I do solemnly swear (or affirm) that I will faithfully execute the office of president of the United States, and will to the best of my ability, preserve, protect and defend the constitution of the United States."

Sect. 2. The president shall be commander in chief of the army and navy of the United States, and of the militia of the several States, when called into the actual service of the United States; he may require the opinion, in writing, of the principal officer in each of the executive departments, upon any subject relating to the duties of their respective offices, and he shall have power to grant reprieves and pardons for offences against the United States, except in cases of impeachment.

He shall have power, by and with the advice and consent of the senate, to make treaties, provided two-thirds of the senators present concur; and he shall nominate, and by and with the advice and consent of the senate, shall appoint ambassadors, other public ministers and consuls, judges of the supreme court, and all other officers of the United States, whose appointments are not herein otherwise provided for, and which shall be established by law. But the Congress may by law vest the appointment of such inferior officers, as they think proper, in the president alone, in the courts of law, or in the heads of departments.

The president shall have power to fill up all vacancies that may happen during the recess of the senate, by granting commissions which shall expire at the end of their next session.

Sect. 3. He shall from time to time give to the Congress information of the state of the union, and recommend to their consideration such measures as he shall judge necessary and expedient; he may, on extraordinary occasions, convene both houses, or either of them, and in case of disagreement between them, with respect to the time of adjournment, he may adjourn them to such time as he shall think proper; he shall receive ambassadors and other public ministers; he shall take care that the laws be faithfully executed, and shall commission all the officers of the United States.

Sect. 4. The president, vice-president and all civil officers of the United States, shall be removed from office on impeachment for, and conviction of, treason, bribery, or other high crimes and misdemeanors.

ARTICLE III.

Sect. 1. The judicial power of the United States, shall be vested in one supreme court, and in such inferior courts as the Congress may from time to time ordain and establish. The judges, both of the supreme and inferior courts, shall hold their offices during good behaviour, and shall, at stated times, receive for their services, a compensation, which shall not be diminished during their continuance in office.

Sect. 2. The judicial power shall extend to all cases, in law and equity, arising under this constitution, the laws of the United States, and treaties made, or which shall be made, under their authority; to all cases affecting ambassadors, other public ministers and consuls; to all cases of admiralty and maritime jurisdiction; to controversies to which the United States shall be a party; to controversies between two or more States, between a state and citizens of another state, between citizens of different States, between citizens of the same state claiming lands under grants of different States, and between a state, or the citizens thereof, and foreign States, citizens or subjects.

In all cases affecting ambassadors, other public ministers and consuls, and those in which a state shall be party, the supreme court shall have original jurisdiction. In all the other cases before mentioned, the supreme court shall have appellate jurisdiction, both as to law and fact, with such exceptions, and under such regulations as the Congress shall make.

The trial of all crimes, except in cases of impeachment, shall be by jury; and such trial shall be held in the state where the said crimes shall have been committed; but when not committed within any state, the trial shall be at such place or places as the Congress may by law have directed.

Sect. 3. Treason against the United States, shall consist only in levying war against them, or in adhering to their enemies, giving them aid and comfort. No person shall be convicted of treason unless on the testimony of two witnesses to the same overt act, or on confession in Open court.

The Congress shall have power to declare the punishment of treason, but no attainder of treason shall work corruption of blood, or forfeiture except during the life of the person attainted.

ARTICLE IV.

Sect. 1. Full faith and credit shall be given in each state to the public acts, records, and judicial proceedings of every other state. And the Congress may by general laws prescribe the manner in which such acts, records and proceedings shall be proved, and the effect thereof.

Sect. 2. The citizens of each state shall be entitled to all privileges and immunities of citizens in the several states.

A person charged in any state with treason, felony, or other crime, who shall flee from justice, and be found in another state, shall, on demand of the executive authority of the state from which he fled, be delivered up, to be removed to the state having jurisdiction of the crime.

No person held to service or labour in one state, under the laws thereof, escaping into another, shall, in consequence of any law or regulation therein, be discharged from such service or labour, but shall be delivered up on claim of the party to whom such service or labour may be due.

Sect. 3. New states may be admitted by the Congress into this union; but no new state shall be formed or erected within the jurisdiction of any other state; nor any state be formed by the junction of two or more states, or parts of states, without the consent of the legislatures of the states concerned as well as of the Congress.

The Congress shall have power to dispose of and make all needful rules and regulations respecting the territory or other property belonging to the United States; and nothing in this Constitution shall be so construed as to prejudice any claims of the United States, or of any particular state.

Sect. 4. The United States shall guarantee to every state in this union a Republican form of government, and shall protect each of them against invasion; and on application of the legislature, or of the executive (when the legislature cannot be convened) against domestic violence.

ARTICLE V.

The Congress, whenever two-thirds of both houses shall deem it necessary, shall propose amendments to this constitution, or, on the application of the legislatures of two-thirds of the several states, shall call a convention for proposing amendments, which, in either case, shall be valid to all intents and purposes, as part of this constitution, when ratified by the legislatures of three-fourths of the several states, or by conventions in three-fourths thereof, as the one or the other mode of ratification may be proposed by the Congress; Provided, that no amendment which may be made prior to the year one thousand eight hundred and eight shall in any manner affect the first and fourth clauses in the ninth section of the first article; and that no state, without its consent shall be deprived of its equal suffrage in the senate.

ARTICLE VI.

All debts contracted and engagements entered into, before the adoption of this Constitution, shall be as valid against the United States under this Constitution, as under the confederation.

This constitution, and the laws of the United States which shall be made in pursuance thereof; and all treaties made, or which shall be made, under the authority of the

United States, shall be the supreme law of the land; and the judges in every state shall be bound thereby, any thing in the constitution or laws of any state to the contrary notwithstanding.

The senators and representatives beforementioned, and the members of the several state legislatures, and all executive and judicial officers, both of the United States and of the several States, shall be bound by oath or affirmation, to support this constitution; but no religious test shall ever be required as a qualification to any office or public trust under the United States.

ARTICLE VII.

The ratification of the conventions of nine States, shall be sufficient for the establishment of this constitution between the States so ratifying the same.

Done in Convention, by the unanimous consent of the States present, the seventeenth day of September, in the year of our Lord one thousand seven hundred and eighty-seven, and of the Independence of the United States of America the twelfth. In witness whereof we have hereunto subscribed our Names.

GEORGE WASHINGTON, President,
and Deputy from Virginia.

Delaware
George Read
    Gunning Bedford, Junior
    John Dickinson
    Richard Bassett
    Jacob Broom

Maryland
    James M'Henry
    Daniel of St. Tho. Jenifer
    Daniel Carrol

Virginia
    John Blair
    James Madison, Jr.

North Carolina
    William Blount
    Richard Dobbs Spaight
    Hugh Williamson

New-Hampshire
    John Langdon,
    Nicholas Gilman

Massachusetts
    Nathaniel Gorham
    Rufus King

Connecticut
    William Samuel Johnson
    Roger Sherman

New York
    Alexander Hamilton

New Jersey
    William Livingston
    David Brearley
    William Paterson
    Jonathan Dayton

South Carolina
    John Rutledge
    Charles Cotesworth Pinckney
    Charles Pinckney
    Pierce Butler

Georgia
    William Few
    Abraham Baldwin

Pennsylvania
    Benjamin Franklin
    Thomas Miffin
    Robert Morris
    George Clymer
    Thomas FitzSimons
    Jared Ingersoll
    James Wilson
    Gouverneur Morris

Attest, William Jackson, SECRETARY.

AMENDMENTS TO THE CONSTITUTION

On September 25, 1789, the First Congress of the United States therefore proposed to the state legislatures 12 amendments to the Constitution that met arguments most frequently advanced against it. The first two proposed amendments, which concerned the number of constituents for each Representative and the compensation of Congressmen, were not ratified. Articles 3 to 12, however, ratified by three-fourths of the state legislatures, constitute the first 10 amendments of the Constitution, known as the Bill of Rights.

ARTICLES in addition to, and Amendment of the Constitution of the United States of America, proposed by Congress, and ratified by the Legislatures of the several States, pursuant to the fifth Article of the original Constitution.

ARTICLE I

Congress shall make no law respecting an establishment of religion, or prohibiting the free exercise thereof; or abridging the freedom of speech, or of the press; or the right of the people peaceably to assemble, and to petition the Government for a redress of grievances. (Submitted to states September 25, 1789. Ratified December 15, 1791: 2 years, 4 months, and 20 days.)

ARTICLE II

A well regulated Militia, being necessary to the security of a free State, the right of the people to keep and bear Arms, shall not be infringed. (Submitted to states September 25, 1789. Ratified December 15, 1791: 2 years, 4 months, and 20 days.)

ARTICLE III

No Soldier shall, in time of peace be quartered in any house, without the consent of the Owner, nor in time of war, but in a manner to be prescribed by law. (Submitted to states September 25, 1789. Ratified December 15, 1791: 2 years, 4 months, and 20 days.)

ARTICLE IV

The right of the people to be secure in their persons, houses, papers, and effects, against unreasonable searches and seizures, shall not be violated, and no Warrants shall issue, but upon probable cause, supported by Oath or affirmation, and particularly describing the place to be searched, and the persons or things to be seized. (Submitted to states September 25, 1789. Ratified December 15, 1791: 2 years, 4 months, and 20 days.)

ARTICLE V

No person shall be held to answer for a capital, or otherwise infamous crime, unless on a presentment or indictment of a Grand Jury, except in cases arising in the land or naval forces, or in the Militia, when in actual service in time of War or public danger; nor shall any person be subject for the same offence to be twice put in jeopardy of life or limb; nor shall be compelled in any criminal case to be a witness against himself, nor be deprived of life; liberty, or property, without due process of law; nor shall private property be taken for public use without just compensation. (Submitted to states September 25, 1789. Ratified December 15, 1791: 2 years, 4 months, and 20 days.)

ARTICLE VI

In all criminal prosecutions, the accused shall enjoy the right to a speedy and public trial, by an impartial jury of the State and district wherein the crime shall have been committed, which district shall have been previously ascertained by law, and to be informed of the nature and cause of the accusation; to be confronted with the witnesses against him; to have compulsory process for obtaining witnesses in his favor and to have the Assistance of Counsel for his defence. (Submitted to states September 25, 1789. Ratified December 15, 1791: 2 years, 4 months, and 20 days.)

ARTICLE VII

In Suits at common law, where the value in controversy shall exceed twenty dollars, the right of trial by jury shall be preserved, and no fact tried by a jury, shall be otherwise re-examined in any Court of the United States, than according to the rules of the common law. (Submitted to states September 25, 1789. Ratified December 15, 1791: 2 years, 4 months, and 20 days.)

ARTICLE VIII

Excessive bail shall not be required, nor excessive fines imposed, nor cruel and unusual punishments inflicted. (Submitted to states September 25, 1789. Ratified December 15, 1791: 2 years, 4 months, and 20 days.)

ARTICLE IX

The enumeration in the Constitution, of certain rights, shall not be construed to deny or disparage others retained by the people. (Submitted to states September 25, 1789. Ratified December 15, 1791: 2 years, 4 months, and 20 days.)

ARTICLE X

The powers not delegated to the United States by the Constitution, nor prohibited by it to the States, are reserved to the States respectively or to the people. (Submitted to states September 25, 1789. Ratified December 15, 1791: 2 years, 4 months, and 20 days.)

ARTICLE XI

The Judicial power of the United States shall not be construed to extend to any suit in law or equity, commenced or prosecuted against one of the United States by Citizens of another State, or by Citizens or Subjects of any Foreign State. (Submitted to states March 4, 1794. Ratified February 7, 1795: 11 months and 14 days.)

ARTICLE XII

The Electors shall meet in their respective states, and vote by ballot for President and Vice-President, one of whom, at least, shall not be an inhabitant of the same state with themselves; they shall name in their ballots the person voted for as President, and in distinct ballots the persons voted for as Vice-President, and they shall make distinct lists of all persons voted for as President, and of all persons voted for as Vice-President, and of the number of votes for each, which lists they shall sign and certify, and transmit sealed to the seat of the government of the United States, directed to the President of the Senate; — The President of the Senate shall, in the presence of the Senate and House of Representatives, open all the certificates and the votes shall then be counted; — The person having the greatest number of votes for President, shall be the President, if such number be a majority of the whole number of Electors appointed; and if no person have such majority, then from the persons having the highest numbers not exceeding three on the list of those voted for as President, the House of Representatives shall choose immediately, by ballot, the President. But in choosing the President, the votes shall be taken by states, the representation from each state having one vote; a quorum for this purpose shall consist of a member or members from two-thirds of the states, and a majority of all the states shall be necessary to a choice.

And if the House of Representatives shall not choose a President whenever the right of choice shall devolve upon them, before the fourth day of March next following, then the Vice-President shall act as President, as in the case of the death or other constitutional disability of the President. The person having the greatest number of votes as Vice-President, shall be the Vice-President, if such number be a majority of the whole number of Electors appointed, and if no person have a majority, then from the two highest numbers on the list, the Senate shall choose the Vice-President; a quorum for the purpose shall consist of two-thirds of the whole number of Senators, and a majority of the whole number shall be necessary to a choice. But no person constitutionally ineligible to the office of President shall be eligible to that of Vice-President of the United States. (Submitted to states December 9, 1803. Ratified June 15, 1804: 7 months, and 7 days.)

ARTICLE XIII

Sect. 1. Neither slavery nor involuntary servitude, except as a punishment for crime whereof the party shall have been duly convicted, shall exist within the United States, or any place subject to their jurisdiction.

Sect. 2. Congress shall have power to enforce this article by appropriate legislation. (Submitted to states April 8, 1864. Ratified December 6, 1865: 1 year, 7 months, and 28 days.)

ARTICLE XIV

Sect. 1. All persons born or naturalized in the United States, and subject to the jurisdiction thereof, are citizens of the United States and of the State wherein they reside. No State shall make or enforce any law which shall abridge the privileges or immunities of citizens of the United States; nor shall any State deprive any person of life, liberty, or property, without due process of law; nor deny to any person within its jurisdiction the equal protection of the laws.

Sect. 2. Representatives shall be apportioned among the several States according to their respective numbers, counting the whole number of persons in each State, excluding Indians not taxed. But when the right to vote at any election for the choice of electors for President and Vice President of the United States, Representatives in Congress, the Executive and Judicial officers of a State, or the members of the Legislature thereof, is denied to any of the male inhabitants of such State, being twenty-one years of age, and citizens of the United States, or in any way abridged, except for participation in rebellion, or other crime, the basis of representation therein shall be reduced in the proportion which the number of such male citizens shall bear to the whole number of male citizens twenty-one years of age in such State.

Sect. 3. No person shall be a Senator or Representative in Congress, or elector of President and Vice President, or hold any office, civil or military, under the United States, or under any State, who, having previously taken an oath, as a member of Congress, or as an officer of the United States, or as a member of any State legislature, or as an executive or judicial officer of any State, to support the Constitution of the United States, shall have engaged in insurrection or rebellion against the same, or given aid or comfort to the enemies thereof. But Congress may by a vote of two-thirds of each House, remove such disability.

Sect. 4. The validity of the public debt of the United States, authorized by law, including debts incurred for payment of pensions and bounties for services in suppressing insurrection or rebellion, shall not be questioned. But neither the United States nor any State shall assume or pay any debt or obligation incurred in aid of insurrection or rebellion against the United States, or any claim for the loss or emancipation of any slave; but all such debts, obligations and claims shall be held illegal and void.

Sect. 5. The Congress shall have power to enforce, by appropriate legislation, the provisions of this article. (Submitted to states June 13, 1866. Ratified July 9, 1868: 1 year, 11 months, and 26 days.)

ARTICLE XV

Sect. 1. The right of citizens of the United States to vote shall not be denied or abridged by the United States or by any State on account of race, color, or previous condition of servitude.

Sect. 2. The Congress shall have power to enforce this article by appropriate legislation. (Submitted to states February 26, 1869. Ratified March 30, 1870: 1 year, 1 month, and 2 days.)

ARTICLE XVI

The Congress shall have power to lay and collect taxes on incomes. from whatever source derived, without apportionment among the several States, and without regard to any census or enumeration. (Submitted to states July 12, 1909. Ratified February 3, 1913: 3 years, 6 months, and 21 days.)

ARTICLE XVII

The Senate of the United States shall be composed of two Senators from each State, elected by the people thereof, for six years; and each Senator shall have one vote. The electors in each State shall have the qualifications requisite for electors of the most numerous branch of the State legislatures.

When vacancies happen in the representation of any State in the Senate, the executive authority of such State shall issue writs of election to fill such vacancies: Provided, That the legislature of any State may empower the executive thereof to make temporary appointments until the people fill the vacancies by election as the legislature may direct.

This amendment shall not be so construed as to affect the election or term of any Senator chosen before it becomes valid as part of the Constitution. (Submitted to states May 13, 1912. Ratified May 31, 1913: 1 year and 18 days.)

ARTICLE XVIII

Sect. 1. After one year from the ratification of this article the manufacture, sale, or transportation of intoxicating liquors within, the importation thereof into, or the exportation thereof from the United States and all territory subject to the jurisdiction thereof for beverage purposes is hereby prohibited.

Sect. 2. The Congress and the several States shall have concurrent power to enforce this article by appropriate legislation.

Sect. 3. This article shall be inoperative unless it shall have been ratified as an amendment to the Constitution by the legislatures of the several States, as provided in the Constitution, within seven years from the date of the submission hereof to the States by the Congress. (Submitted to states December 18, 1917. Ratified January 16, 1919: 1 year and 29 days.)

ARTICLE XIX

The right of citizens of the United States to vote shall not be denied or abridged by the United States or by any State on account of sex.

Congress shall have power to enforce this article by appropriate legislation. (Submitted to states June 4, 1919. Ratified August 18, 1920: 1 year, 2 months, and 14 days.)

ARTICLE XX

Sect. 1. The terms of the President and Vice President shall end at noon on the 20th day of January, and the terms of Senators and Representatives at noon on the 3d day of January, of the years in which such terms would have ended if this article had not been ratified; and the terms of their successors shall then begin.

Sect. 2. The Congress shall assemble at least once in every year, and such meeting shall begin at noon on the 3d day of January, unless they shall by law appoint a different day.

Sect. 3. If, at the time fixed for the beginning of the term of the President, the President elect shall have died, the Vice President elect shall become President. If a President shall not have been chosen before the time fixed for the beginning of his term, or if the President elect shall have failed to qualify, then the Vice President elect shall act as President until a President shall have qualified; and the Congress may by law provide for the case wherein neither a President elect nor a Vice President elect shall have qualified, declaring who shall then act as President, or the manner in which one who is to act shall be selected, and such person shall act accordingly until a President or Vice President shall have qualified.

Sect. 4. The Congress may by law provide for the case of the death of any of the persons from whom the House of Representatives may choose a President whenever the right of choice shall have devolved upon them, and for the case of the death of any of the persons from whom the Senate may choose a Vice President whenever the right of choice shall have devolved upon them.

Sect. 5. Sections 1 and 2 shall take effect on the 15th day of October following the ratification of this article.

Sect. 6. This article shall be inoperative unless it shall have been ratified as an amendment to the Constitution by the legislatures of three-fourths of the several States within seven years from the date of its submission. (Submitted to states March 2, 1932. Ratified January 23, 1933: 9 months and 22 days.)

ARTICLE XXI

Sect. 1. The eighteenth article of amendment to the Constitution of the United States is hereby repealed.

Sect. 2. The transportation or importation into any State, Territory, or possession of the United States for delivery or use therein of intoxicating liquors, in violation of the laws thereof, is hereby prohibited.

Sect. 3. This article shall be inoperative unless it shall have been ratified as an amendment to the Constitution by conventions in the several States, as provided in the Constitution, within seven years from the date of the submission hereof to the States by the Congress. (Submitted to states January 17, 1920. Ratified December 5, 1933: 12 years and 19 days. The only amendment to have been ratified by state conventions, and not state legislatures.)

ARTICLE XXII

Sect. 1. No person shall be elected to the office of the President more than twice, and no person who has held the office of President, or acted as President, for more than two years of a term to which some other person was elected President shall be elected to the office of the President more than once. But this Article shall not apply to any person holding the office of President when this Article was proposed by the Congress, and shall not prevent any person who may be holding the office of President, or acting as President, during the term within which this Article becomes operative from holding the office of President or acting as President during the remainder of such term.

Sect. 2. This article shall be inoperative unless it shall have been ratified as an amendment to the Constitution by the legislatures of three-fourths of the several States within seven years from the date of its submission to the States by the Congress. (Submitted to states March 21, 1947. Ratified February 27, 1951: 3 years, 11 months, and 4 days.)

ARTICLE XXIII

Sect. 1. The District constituting the seat of Government of the United States shall appoint in such manner as the Congress may direct:

A number of electors of President and Vice President equal to the whole number of Senators and Representatives in Congress to which the District would be entitled if it were a State, but in no event more than the least populous State; they shall be in addition to those appointed by the States, but they shall be considered, for the purposes of the election of President and Vice President, to be electors appointed by a State; and they shall meet in the District and perform such duties as provided by the twelfth article of amendment.

Sect. 2. The Congress shall have power to enforce this article by appropriate legislation. (Submitted to states June 16, 1960. Ratified March 29, 1961: 9 months, and 12 days.)

ARTICLE XXIV

Sect. 1. The right of citizens of the United States to vote in any primary or other election for President or Vice President, for electors for President or Vice President, or for Senator or Representative in Congress, shall not be denied or abridged by the United States or any State by reason of failure to pay any poll tax or other tax.

Sect. 2. The Congress shall have power to enforce this article by appropriate legislation. (Submitted to states August 27, 1962. Ratified January 23, 1964: 1 year, 4 months, and 29 days.)

ARTICLE XXV

Sect. 1. In case of the removal of the President from office or of his death or resignation, the Vice President shall become President.

Sect. 2. Whenever there is a vacancy in the office of the Vice President, the President shall nominate a Vice President who shall take office upon confirmation by a majority vote of both Houses of Congress.

Sect. 3. Whenever the President transmits to the President pro tempore of the Senate and the Speaker of the House of Representatives his written declaration that he is unable to discharge the powers and duties of his office, and until he transmits to them a written declaration to the contrary, such powers and duties shall be discharged by the Vice President as Acting President.

Sect. 4. Whenever the Vice President and a majority of either the principal officers of the executive departments or of such other body as Congress may by law provide, transmit to the President pro tempore of the Senate and the Speaker of the House of Representatives their written declaration that the President is unable to discharge the powers and duties of his office, the Vice President shall immediately assume the powers and duties of the office as Acting President.

Thereafter, when the President transmits to the President pro tempore of the Senate and the Speaker of the House of Representatives his written declaration that no inability exists, he shall resume the powers and duties of his office unless the Vice President and a majority of either the principal officers of the executive department or of such other body as Congress may by law provide, transmit within four days to the President pro tempore of the Senate and the Speaker of the House of Representatives their written declaration that the President is unable to discharge the powers and duties of his office. Thereupon Congress shall decide the issue, assembling within forty-eight hours for that purpose if not in session. If the Congress, within twenty-one days after receipt of the latter written declaration, or, if Congress is not in session, within twenty-one days after Congress is required to assemble, determines by two-thirds vote of both Houses that the President is unable to discharge the powers and duties of his office, the Vice President shall continue to discharge the same as Acting President; otherwise, the President shall resume the powers and duties of his office. (Submitted to states July 6, 1965. Ratified February 10, 1967: 3 months, and 18 days.)

ARTICLE XXVI

Sect. 1. The right of citizens of the United States, who are eighteen years of age or older, to vote shall not be denied or abridged by the United States or by any State on account of age.

Sect. 2. The Congress shall have power to enforce this article by appropriate legislation. (Submitted to states March 23, 1971. Ratified July 1, 1971: 3 months, and 8 days.)

ARTICLE XXVII

No law, varying the compensation for the services of the Senators and Representatives, shall take effect, until an election of Representatives shall have intervened. (Submitted to states September 25, 1789. Ratified May 7, 1992: 202 years, 7 months, and 12 days.)

Source: Charters of Freedom, National Archives.

ABOUT THE EDITOR AND CONTRIBUTORS

THE EDITOR

BRIEN HALLETT is a professor in the Matsunaga Institute for Peace at the University of Hawai'i-Manoa. His main interests are the conceptual foundations of Gandhi and Martin Luther King's work and war as a performative speech act. He has published two books on the declaring of war, *The Lost Art of Declaring War* (University of Illinois Press, 1998) and *Declaring War* (Cambridge University Press, 2012).

THE CONTRIBUTORS

CINDY GALWAY BUYS is a professor and director of international law programs at Southern Illinois University School of Law, where she focuses on international law, immigration law, and constitutional law. She has been a Fulbright scholar, NAFTA arbitrator, and lawyer in public and private practice in Washington, D.C.

ROBERT C. CHALWELL, Jr., is an assistant professor in the Social and Behavioral Sciences Department of Broward College Judson A. Samuel South Campus. His diverse political, policy, social, and development economics interests are tied together by interdisciplinary approaches to understanding observed behaviors. He has published peer-reviewed articles and presented on topics including postcolonial development, economic development, youth marginalization, race and identity politics, voter participation, tourism-driven economic development, higher education, the achievement gap, and minority male academic success.

MARY M. CHEH is the Elyce Zenoff Research Professor of Law at the George Washington University Law School. She writes and teaches primarily in the areas of constitutional law and criminal procedure. In 2014, she was elected to serve a third term on the Council of the District of Columbia.

ROBERT JEFFERSON DILLARD completed his BS in history from the United States Military Academy at West Point and both his MA and PhD in political science from Texas Tech University. His research and teaching interests include: U.S. foreign aid, international development, and Latin American politics.

JUDITH K. FITZGERALD is a professor of practice at the University of Pittsburgh School of Law. As a retired U.S. bankruptcy judge, her main interests are in creative solutions to financial and business problems and the practicalities of dealing with the bankruptcy system currently in effect in the United States. She is the co-editor of *Rutter Group National Practice Guide—Bankruptcy*.

CRAIG GOODMAN is an assistant professor in the School of Arts and Sciences at the University of Houston-Victoria. He researches and teaches in the areas of Congress and the presidency and is currently working on a book manuscript about the development of the appropriations process in Congress. His work has appeared in *Political Research Quarterly*, *Legislative Studies Quarterly*, and *American Politics Research*.

DONALD E. HEIDENREICH, Jr., is a professor of history at Lindenwood University and a retired Major from the Missouri National Guard. His studies are primarily in the areas of military and political history, particularly the early U.S. republic.

JACOB HOLT is an assistant professor at the University of Wisconsin-La Crosse. His main research interests are legislative organization and legislative elections. His work on the Canadian Parliament has been published in the *Journal of Legislative Studies*, and he has an article examining independent expenditures by interest groups in congressional elections forthcoming in *Social Science Quarterly*.

ERIK M. JENSEN is the Coleman P. Burke professor of law at Case Western Reserve University. He has taught tax law for over thirty years and has written many articles on the subject. He is the author of *The Taxing Power* (2005).

PAUL LORENZO JOHNSON is a PhD candidate at University of California, Davis. His main interests are comparative military policy, state repression and political violence, and civil-military relations. His dissertation focuses on the effect of military conscription and ethnically broad-based recruitment on military willingness to follow through on orders to violently repress mass protests.

REBECCA L. KEELER is an associate professor at East Tennessee State University in Johnson City, Tennessee. She teaches mostly law-related classes in the legal studies, political science, and public administration programs, having practiced local government law for seventeen years prior to moving to academia. Her research interests include public law, administrative ethics, and the changing institutional roles of public and private sectors in modern Western society.

RICHARD B. KIELBOWICZ, an associate professor of communication at the University of Washington-Seattle, studies the history of communication policy. Author of *News in the Mail: The Press, Post Office, and Public Information, 1700–1860s,* and articles in social science journals and law reviews, he has also prepared reports for federal agencies.

NANCY MARCUS is the founding constitutional law professor and an assistant professor of law at Indiana Tech Law School.

JESSE MERRIAM is an assistant professor of public law in the political science department at Loyola University Maryland. His main interests are constitutional theory (with a special focus on law and religion) and legal philosophy (with a special focus on the relationship between the rule of law and legal consistency).

COLIN D. MOORE is assistant professor of political science at the University of Hawai'i at Manoa. He has served as a research fellow at Yale University's Center for the Study of American Politics and as a Robert Wood Johnson Foundation Fellow in Health Policy Research at the University of California, Berkeley. His work has appeared in *Studies in American Political Development, Perspectives on Politics,* and the *American Political Science Review.* Moore recently completed a book titled *American Imperialism and the State, 1893–1921* (Cambridge University Press, forthcoming).

JOANNA MOSSER is an associate professor of political science at Drake University in Des Moines, IA. Her research explores the constitutive force of the sovereign territorial state order, with a particular emphasis on bordering, people-building, immigration, asylum-seeking, and law's codification and standardization of everyday social practices.

JEFFREY S. PEAKE is professor of political science and department chair at Clemson University, Clemson, SC. His primary research interests include presidential leadership, presidential-congressional relations, and U.S. foreign policy. He is author of numerous journal articles on these topics and co-author of two books, including *Treaty Politics and the Rise of Executive Agreements: International Commitments in a System of Shared Powers* (2009, University of Michigan Press, with Glen S. Krutz) and *Breaking Through the Noise: Presidential Leadership, the News Media, and Public Opinion* (2011, Stanford University Press, with Matthew Eshbaugh-Soha).

DAVID R. SMITH graduated from the University of Texas at Dallas with his PhD in Political Science in 2012. His dissertation was entitled *Getting Earmarks Right: Examining Both Requests and Awards to Members of the U.S. Congress.* Dr. Smith's research interests are voting behavior, Congress (House and Senate), and members of Congress voting behavior.

MITCHEL A. SOLLENBERGER is an associate professor of Political Science and associate provost for Undergraduate Programs and Integrative Learning, University of Michigan-Dearborn. He is the author of *The President Shall Nominate: How Congress Trumps Executive Power* (University Press of Kansas, 2008) and *Judicial Appointments and Democratic Controls* (Carolina Academic Press, 2011). He most recently co-authored with Mark J. Rozell *The President's Czars: Undermining Congress and the Constitution* (University Press of Kansas, 2012).

INDEX